Dynamic Negotiations

Teacher Labour Relations in Canadian Elementary and Secondary Education

Edited by
Sara Slinn and Arthur Sweetman

Queen's Policy Studies Series
School of Policy Studies, Queen's University
McGill-Queen's University Press
Montreal & Kingston • London • Ithaca

Educ.
LB
2844.57
.C3
D95
2012

SCHOOL OF
Policy Studies

Publications Unit
Robert Sutherland Hall
138 Union Street
Kingston, ON, Canada
K7L 3N6
www.queensu.ca/sps/

The preferred citation for this book is:
Slinn, S. and A. Sweetman, eds. 2012. *Dynamic Negotiations: Teacher Labour Relations in Canadian Elementary and Secondary Education.* Montreal and Kingston: Queen's Policy Studies Series, McGill-Queen's University Press.

Library and Archives Canada Cataloguing in Publication

Dynamic negotiations : teacher labour relations in Canadian elementary and secondary education / edited by Sara Slinn and Arthur Sweetman.

"Queen's Policy Studies series".
Includes bibliographical references.
Co-published by: McGill-Queen's University Press.
ISBN 978-1-55339-304-7

1. Collective bargaining—Teachers—Canada. 2. Teachers' unions—Canada. 3. Public schools—Canada. I. Slinn, Sara Jane, 1969-   II. Sweetman, Arthur III. Queen's University (Kingston, Ont.). School of Policy Studies

LB2844.57.C3D95 2012   331.89'041371100971   C2011-902454-3

CONTENTS

ACKNOWLEDGEMENTS

We believe that cross-jurisdictional comparisons are a necessary component of an evidence-based foundation for practice and policy, and we hope that this volume of research essays provides useful insight.

The chapters in this volume have benefited enormously from the work of several anonymous referees and we thank them for their time. We would also like to acknowledge the staff at the School of Policy Studies Publications Unit, Mark Howes and Valerie Jarus, for their many efforts. In addition, thanks go to copy editor Ellie Barton for her extreme diligence.

We would like to acknowledge support from the Ontario Ministry of Education. This is part of a project aimed at assisting labour relations in Ontario through training and information dissemination. All views expressed in the essays in this collected volume are solely those of the respective authors. This volume does not necessarily reflect the views of the Ontario Ministry of Education, or the Ontario Ministry of Health and Long-Term Care that funded Arthur Sweetman's research chair at McMaster University.

Sara Slinn
Associate Professor
Osgoode Hall Law School
York University

Arthur Sweetman
Professor, and
Ontario Research Chair in Health Human Resources
Department of Economics
McMaster University

Chapter 1

INTRODUCTION: LABOUR RELATIONS IN PRIMARY AND SECONDARY CANADIAN EDUCATION

Sara Slinn and Arthur Sweetman

Teacher labour relations, including collective bargaining, in public sector elementary and secondary (K–12) education are a primary concern for Canada's provincial governments. Total expenditures in the sector largely comprise employee compensation and account for a substantial portion of each province's spending, second only to health care. Public sector labour relations are extremely complex in general, and those in education are more so than the average, with negotiations ranging from protracted and acrimonious, to collegial and productivity enhancing.

Most K–12 educational instruction is publicly provided. As a result, substantial institutional and organizational gaps exist between the payers, providers, and recipients of educational services. In fact, given the nature of public financing, even the identities of, for example, the payers are not very clear. With deficit financing, costs are not entirely borne by current taxpayers, a group that only partly overlaps with voters. Further, given our federation's system of equalization payments and the Canada Social Transfer (both multi-billion dollar transfers from the federal government to the provinces) and the mix of provincial and school board tax authorities across the country, the relevant taxpayers are in many cases residents of regions and provinces other than those involved in each set of negotiations. These types of disjunctions cause informational asymmetries and

Dynamic Negotiations: Teacher Labour Relations in Canadian Elementary and Secondary Education, ed. S. Slinn and A. Sweetman. Montreal and Kingston: Queen's Policy Studies Series, McGill-Queen's University Press.

affect incentives on both sides of the table which, in turn, affect outcomes. Stakeholders having different financial interests may therefore arrive at diverse conclusions regarding the merits of alternative labour relations outcomes—and these are in addition to any differences in opinion following from substantive issues related to educational delivery, pedagogy and the like. Of course, the distribution of benefits is also diverse and complicated.

One particularly important and recurring theme is the substantial systemic stress following from the confluence of centralizing and decentralizing elements in education. For example, the negotiators—that is, the bargaining agents—are sometimes not well identified in practice even where they are identified in law. This follows from controversy regarding the appropriate location for negotiations: Should they be provincewide, at the school board level, or multi-level? Not only the parties, but the provincial governments, sometimes bypass one or more of the relevant bargaining agents. More complexity follows from the role of public sentiment in influencing negotiations. Uncertainty and even ambiguity regarding the very structure of bargaining and labour relations more generally are common. Incentives in negotiations are, therefore, far from clear and sometimes appear to encompass issues unrelated to the delivery of educational services, teacher remuneration, and related workload/employment issues.

Typically, the provision of education is also monopolistic (although there are some differences across provinces with, for example, Quebec having more choice given its de facto voucher system for funding private schools), which puts another type of gap between negotiators and the outcomes of the labour relations process on the one hand, and service recipients on the other, dampening or muting feedback to the process relative to that in situations with a greater number of service providers. Moreover, the monopolistic and public sector context increases the likelihood that teacher collective bargaining will be subject to governments' capacity to directly intervene in negotiations and legislate a settlement. Disputes and negotiated outcomes appear to be significantly constrained by the possibility of this occurrence, and even more strongly affected when it actually occurs. However, adding to this complexity are recent developments in the scope of constitutional protection for the freedom of association, which may significantly restrict governments' ability to directly intervene to resolve bargaining disputes or to restrict the scope of bargaining.

Despite the complexity and importance of labour relations in education, relatively little recent research has been undertaken looking at public sector, never mind education sector, labour relations in Canada. Since so little attention is given to the issue, the research that is undertaken tends to take the form of updates and overviews, rather than in-depth analysis.

For example, a broad interprovincial comparison of the then current state of the public sector arena is presented in the volume edited by Thompson, Rose, and Smith (2003). It provides a useful context for the current study. Another important precursor that is more directly relevant to the current set of studies in that it focuses on the public sector, but with a primary interest in the civil service, is the collection by Swimmer (2001).

Most work focusing on primary and secondary education labour relations and bargaining is more dated. One useful overview, however, is the chapter by Thomason (1995) who describes the evolution of collective bargaining from the beginning of the century to the early 1990s. He concludes that since World War II the teachers' associations cum labour unions have been extremely successful in advocating for their members and have made Canadian teachers among the highest paid in the world. He also, however, points to emerging areas of discontent such as concerns regarding school performance, high taxes, and provincial government budget deficits. More detailed analyses tend to be older; for example, Downie (1978, 1992) studies labour relations and bargaining in the education sector with a focus on the Ontario situation.

On the labour economics front, as opposed to the more strictly industrial relations side of research, there is a modest set of literature looking at relevant issues. There is an older literature that tends to be analytical and focuses on issues more tightly aligned with industrial relations. For example, Currie (1989) looks at interest arbitration among British Columbia teachers, and Currie (1991) subsequently examines employment determination as an outcome of bargaining for Ontario teachers. From a theoretical perspective, but one relevant for the current situation, Gu and Kuhn (1998) look at the relationship between (de)centralization and the probability of strikes. Podgursky (2010) conducts an international survey, but with a US focus, of the relationship between compensation and collective bargaining.

In contrast to the older labour economics literature, more recent work has sought to quantify the relationships between industrial structure and labour relations activity, and outcomes associated with the delivery of educational services. For example, Johnson (2011) explores the effect of strikes and work-to-rule campaigns on student outcomes as measured by Ontario's provincial assessment. In the same vein, Card, Dooley, and Payne (2010) study the impact of (slightly) reducing the monopoly delivery of educational services by looking for variations in outcomes associated with students in Ontario who have more, or less, choice resulting from proximity to both public and Catholic schools. In the US some researchers studying public sector labour relations, such as those included in the volume edited by Brock and Lipsky (2003), are also interested in this class of issues. While this volume does not pursue these ideas, it is relevant background for those who do so.

This volume offers an industrial relations/labour law approach and provides a comprehensive descriptive analysis and evaluation of the structure and practice of K–12 teacher collective bargaining in a representative set of Canadian provinces. It examines overarching issues regarding the features of these systems associated with success in terms of labour relations outcomes.[1]

COMPARING PROVINCIAL LEGAL FRAMEWORKS

In chapter 2, "Crosscurrents: Comparative Review of Elementary and Secondary Teacher Collective Bargaining Structures in Canada," Karen Schucher and Sara Slinn provide an overview and comparative discussion of the basic legal frameworks regulating K–12 teacher bargaining. Intended as a touchstone for readers of the province-specific studies that follow, this chapter identifies and compares legal frameworks along the following dimensions: the type and statutory regulation; the degree of centralization of bargaining; the legal regulation of bargaining agency; the scope of matters that may be negotiated; available dispute resolution procedures; and legal limits on work stoppages.

The subsequent series of nine province-specific studies offer in-depth and comparative analyses of K–12 teacher bargaining systems in six key jurisdictions: British Columbia, Alberta, Manitoba, Ontario, Quebec, and Newfoundland. Each chapter addresses a common set of core issues in relation to a particular jurisdiction as well as exploring matters important or unique to that province. The present chapter concludes by considering the themes and issues emerging from the jurisdiction-specific chapters in this volume.

British Columbia

In chapter 3, "The Great Divide: School Politics and Labour Relations in British Columbia before and after 1972," Thomas Fleming delves into the influence on teacher labour relations of the decades-long struggle for control of public education in British Columbia. This chapter identifies key developments in the pre- and post-1972 periods and their effects. Fleming contends that this strife has its roots in postwar changes to the organization and management of schools in the province, which led to a breakdown in historical structures and relationships in the K–12 education sector, especially in the post-1972 period. He concludes that the turbulence in teacher collective bargaining is a product of more than conventional labour-management differences. Rather, Fleming argues, this discord is "embedded in the mainframe of provincial school history." It involves both a lack of committed and dedicated government leadership on the one hand and, on the other, the relentless ambition of the teachers' federation to set the province's social agenda. This chapter concludes by posing several questions about the future of teacher labour relations given that the key actors are "locked in the grip of the past."

In chapter 4, "Conflict without Compromise: The Case of Public Sector Teacher Bargaining in British Columbia," Slinn traces the development of teacher bargaining structures in BC through three distinct historical periods. These include the pre-1987 period of narrow-scope, informal local negotiations operating outside the general labour relations statutory scheme; the 1987 to 1993 period of local bargaining under labour legislation; and the existing system of two-tier bargaining introduced in 1994, which allocates all significant matters to provincial-level negotiations, leaving only a few minor issues to be bargained locally. Slinn concludes that, by any measure, K–12 teacher collective bargaining in British Columbia has not been a success. Instead it is marked by conflict, protracted bargaining, legal and illegal work stoppages, failure to voluntarily settle agreements, and frequent direct government intervention.

Slinn identifies the key impediments to effective teacher bargaining in this province. First, poor implementation of the two-tier bargaining structure hampered transition to a provincial collective agreement such that significant portions of pre-1994 local collective agreements continue to exist and complicate negotiations. Second, the teachers' federation continues to reject the two-tier bargaining model and has been engaged in a continuing dispute with government and the provincial school boards' bargaining agent over whether certain matters—most notably working and learning conditions—are to be the subject of negotiation or treated as public policy matters within the government's sole discretion. These disputes have produced a tremendous amount of litigation and delays in negotiations. Effective negotiations are also impeded by the government and teachers' federation repeatedly negotiating directly with each other, disregarding the statutory employer bargaining agent and its role. A final obstacle is the lack of an effective and available dispute resolution mechanism. The government has demonstrated that it is unwilling to permit full teacher strikes yet, unlike in some other provinces, interest arbitration is not available for teachers' disputes in British Columbia. Consequently, teacher disputes in this province typically involve lengthy partial withdrawals of service that put little or no pressure on either party to reach agreement. Without an effective dispute resolution tool, it is unlikely that the parties will reach voluntary agreements given their high level of disagreement on fundamental aspects of the structure and content of negotiations. The author is not optimistic about the future prospects for constructive teacher bargaining in British Columbia. The procedural supports for teacher negotiations and other recommendations of past commissioners tasked with reviewing bargaining in this sector have not been adopted, and the legal and ideological conflicts between the teachers' federation and government continue unabated.

Alberta

Kelly Williams-Whitt in chapter 5, "Oil and Ideology: The Transformation of K–12 Bargaining in Alberta," maps the development of K–12 teacher bargaining, which has been strongly influenced by a series of provincial government social-reengineering efforts that shaped the province as a whole. The Alberta experience is distinct in several respects. Unlike most other jurisdictions, teachers' terms of employment are governed by both a collective agreement and individual employment contracts, although the individual contract terms cannot conflict with statutory requirements or the collective agreement. As grievance provisions are included in individual rather than collective contracts, discipline is contested individually by teachers, and the teachers' association has no fair representation duty to pursue discipline grievances. This jurisdiction employs local collective bargaining. However, the Alberta Teachers' Association, unlike teachers' bargaining agents in other provinces, does not support a local bargaining structure. Instead, it endorses centralized bargaining that is directly with government to align negotiations with the provincial funding structure. Some ad hoc central negotiations have already occurred. Disputes about the appropriate level of bargaining in this province emanate from school boards. Williams-Whitt concludes that the system will likely move toward a two-tiered bargaining structure.

Manitoba

Manitoba presents an interesting case, addressed in chapter 6 by Valerie Matthews Lemieux. Two distinctive features of this system contribute to Manitoba's relatively stable teacher bargaining system. First, under its "dual statutory" system, terms and conditions of teachers' work are governed by both a collective agreement and an individual contract of employment, regulated by different legislation. Individual contracts have effectively removed certain matters from collective negotiations. Second, use of interest arbitration as the long-established mechanism for settling teacher bargaining disputes has shifted the primary location of the contest for power toward the recurring question of the appropriate scope of interest arbitration and the role of the individual employment contract rather than, as in other provinces, the scope of collective bargaining. This is particularly so given that Manitoba teachers currently do not have a right to strike. Another feature of this model is that teachers have achieved significant gains in terms and conditions of employment through grievance arbitration, rather than bargaining or interest arbitration. As in other jurisdictions, the location of bargaining is contested, with the teachers' association seeking centralized, provincial-level bargaining, and the employers' association wanting local negotiations. Unlike many other jurisdictions, K–12 education in this province continues to be partially funded by local taxes.

Matthews Lemieux concludes that bargaining and arbitration outcomes have been relatively stable—with some evidence of pattern bargaining—with most negotiations settling rather than going to arbitration. Those that do go to arbitration tend to concern disputes over working conditions and equity issues. Matthews Lemieux argues that the fundamental weakness of the existing structure lies in the continued use of individual contracts of employment within a collective bargaining system. This fosters instability by encouraging use of short-term contracts, and has allowed the Ministry of Education to use these contracts to impose obligations on teachers beyond the scope of collective bargaining. The author notes that the parties' relationship significantly influences the functioning of the system and that many disputes are rooted in conflicts originating decades ago.

Ontario

Ontario is dealt with in three separate chapters. In chapter 7, "The Evolution of Teacher Bargaining in Ontario," Joseph Rose traces the evolution of teacher collective bargaining in this province from its pre-collective bargaining roots, through several distinct stages, including the 1997–2001 restructuring of the bargaining system as well as the current era in which the provincial government has taken a more conciliatory, two-tier approach to negotiations. Rose evaluates the effects of external factors on bargaining structure, process, and outcomes, and assesses the effectiveness of dispute resolution procedures. He concludes that a consistent theme throughout this history is the struggle about the issue of control over education policy and, in particular, teachers' voices in bargaining workload.

In chapter 8, "Collective Bargaining for Teachers in Ontario: Central Power, Local Responsibility," Elizabeth Shilton offers a close study of the most recent stage in the development of teacher bargaining in Ontario. She examines the structure and functioning of teacher bargaining under both the Conservative government (1997–2001) and the subsequent Liberal government, including the latter's innovative and informal introduction of centralization, and the effects of these approaches on fostering or impeding bargaining. Shilton concludes that the changes introduced in the late 1990s by the Conservative government with Bill 160 produced a "mismatch" between the formal location of bargaining, which was at the local level, and the provincial control over teachers' terms and conditions of employment. Shilton also concludes that the ad hoc system of two-tier bargaining introduced by the Liberal government, together with large funding increases, has succeeded in reducing bargaining disputes. However, she notes that this is a political rather than a legal solution, and as such is likely temporary, unenforceable, and inherently unstable. This chapter concludes with the prediction that Ontario is likely to see formalized, mandatory centralized bargaining imposed on this sector, and that it will likely be multi-tier rather than simple provincewide bargaining.

The Ontario case concludes with chapter 9, "The Centralization of Collective Bargaining in Ontario's Public Education Sector and the Need to Balance Stakeholder Interests," contributed by Brendan Sweeney, Susan McWilliams, and Robert Hickey. Employing data from interviews with education sector stakeholders, this study assesses the degree to which the more centralized bargaining structure that existed during teacher negotiations in 2005 and 2008 addressed and balanced stakeholders' interests. Among the key conclusions of this chapter are that the increasing centralization of education policy and funding in this province has relocated key decision-making from the local to the provincial level, and that this process of centralization is unstable, or at least still in process, since it is not yet matched by a similar shift toward the institutionalization of centralized bargaining structures in some of the main organizations involved in negotiations. Continuing decentralization on the employer side is particularly problematic for this lack of stability. The authors further conclude that greater centralization in Ontario K–12 education offers some benefits, but also requires the development of a new understanding of the role of local stakeholders.

Quebec

In chapter 10, "Labour Relations in the Quebec K–11 Education Sector: Labour Regulation under Centralization," Jean-Noël Grenier and Mustapha Bettache examine the case of Quebec. The authors distinguish the progressive centralization of collective bargaining as a key theme in primary and secondary teacher collective bargaining in this province. After carefully tracing the development of the current bargaining structure against the backdrop of the significant changes in the political context and broader public sector labour relations, Grenier and Bettache outline and assess the existing teacher bargaining structure and its outcomes. Unlike other jurisdictions employing a multi-level teacher bargaining structure, the Quebec system explicitly involves negotiations at three tiers: provincial cross-sector, provincial education sector, and local or regional school board. Both the issues to be addressed at each level and a negotiating timetable are specified by statute. This produces a unique degree of formality, centralization, and coordination, along with the effects of being integrated into multi-sector public sector negotiations.

The authors conclude that this highly structured bargaining framework has produced very predictable conduct from the parties and that the prohibition on local-level strikes has eliminated local union-management conflicts as a source of work stoppages. Teachers have been able to engage in meaningful bargaining over monetary issues, in part as a result of the determinative effect of cross-sector negotiations on ensuring that government compensation mandates are met. Sometimes, however, the provincial government resorts to ad hoc legislation to impose settlements. In the face of this, Grenier and Bettache predict that unions will seek to negotiate compensation outside of the formal bargaining process, as other groups of public sector workers have succeeded in doing. They also predict that, in this context, teachers and other public sector workers will resort to political means, and domestic and international alliance-building, in an attempt to achieve their goals.

Newfoundland and Labrador

Newfoundland and Labrador has a long history of provincial collective bargaining for teachers that has enjoyed remarkable stability and a lack of disputes or direct government intervention, with the structure unchanged since the early 1970s. Drawing on archival information and interviews from school board, school board association, and teacher association representatives, Travor Brown, in chapter 11, "K–12 Teacher Collective Bargaining in Newfoundland and Labrador," concludes that this centralized, full-scope bargaining system has generally succeeded in meeting the needs of the parties. Brown identifies five features of the system contributing to its success.

First, Brown identifies the high degree of centralization in negotiations as a notable strength of this system, observing that this structure helps balance the power between teachers and the key employer-side decision-maker, the Treasury Board. Limiting the teachers' association membership to teachers helps ensure a reasonable balance of power between the negotiating parties. Brown also points to the conciliation process as a constructive dispute resolution tool as it ensures that both negotiating parties and the teacher associations' membership fully understand key areas of disagreement, and allows "cooler heads to prevail," thereby tending to avoid work stoppages. The sociocultural context, including the high union density and tight-knit community, produces strong relationships among actors and is another important influence on the success of teacher bargaining in this province. Finally, parties have engaged in forms of continuous bargaining, helping ensure ongoing communication and addressing issues prior to formal bargaining.

However, Brown does identify a few weaknesses. First, the centralized bargaining may prevent certain issues from reaching the negotiating table. Second, the primary role of the Treasury Board may be contributing to pattern settlements and impeding certain important, non-monetary issues from being negotiated. Although this provincial government has not yet legislated a settlement to teacher bargaining, Brown observes that the government has increasingly turned to this tool in other disputes, and raises the concern that such government intervention would be an undesirable development.

CONCLUSION

"Follow the money" is a famous Hollywood phrase about politics and power, and it is an apt aphorism for the structure of bargaining in education. This study reveals that a common issue among jurisdictions is achieving alignment between funding and negotiations. Provinces are increasingly moving toward greater centralization in education funding, with a significant motivation being to ensure equity of education services among school districts. In provinces where funding is centralized, bargaining tends to be so as well. Those provinces that continue to employ local-level bargaining in the context of a more centralized funding structure struggle with the difficulty of ensuring local accountability for collective agreement expenditure commitments. Consequently when a jurisdiction, such as Ontario, shifts to more centralized funding, greater centralization of teacher bargaining is generally not far behind.

Establishing legislative, institutional, and organizational structures on all sides of the table that address both provincial and local issues is an ongoing challenge in many jurisdictions, and is concurrently crucial to solving the diverse range of issues involved in labour relations. A structured multi-level process, as in Quebec, seems like a useful model on this front. However, the British Columbia experience with two-tiered negotiations demonstrates the importance of properly implementing a multi-tiered structure and the long-term bargaining dysfunction that can result from an unsuccessful transition to a new bargaining structure.

The challenges of centralization are important issues on the agenda in K–12 labour relations. With increased centralization comes a need to address the scope of bargaining and the appropriate negotiating table or level in a multi-tiered structure at which each element is discussed. A key point of dispute in many provinces is the appropriate scope of bargaining. Such disagreements tend to centre on the issue of workload and associated issues such as class size and composition. While teachers generally regard these as key bargaining issues, governments often consider them to be important matters of public policy that are outside the bounds of negotiation. Some issues are predominantly local, but providing sufficient negotiating room at the local level, without financial levers or leeway, can prove difficult. Similarly, the experiences of several provinces examined in this study demonstrate that it is crucial that the bargaining agents be appropriate to the bargaining structure and reasonably matched in terms of capacity for bargaining. Instances of mismatches between poorly resourced and inexperienced local-level negotiators on one side of the table and sophisticated, well-resourced, and provincially coordinated negotiators on the other side, have led to unstable bargaining outcomes and corrosive labour relations.

Availability of an effective dispute resolution mechanism also emerges as an important issue. The provincial studies in this volume demonstrate a wide array of approaches to resolving bargaining breakdowns in this sector, ranging from mandatory interest arbitration to unfettered strikes and lockouts. A comparative review of provincial experiences suggests that it is more important that some dispute resolution process exist, and that it be allowed to operate without government interference, than the particular form the process takes. Governments are often reluctant to entrust teacher collective agreements to interest arbitration, yet also find it difficult to withstand the public's dissatisfaction with partial or full work stoppages in K–12 education. Consequently, appropriately and effectively dealing with teacher bargaining disputes is a significant challenge that few provinces have successfully addressed.

Finally, one of the more intractable and difficult to address impediments to successful negotiations in K–12 education is the tendency for education issues to become highly politicized and for long-running and destructive ideological divides to develop between government and teachers' groups. As seen in several provinces at different times in their K–12 collective bargaining history, such differences can significantly hamper constructive labour relations in this sector.

Going forward, in an era when deficit financing of public services seems to have hit its limits, and current taxpayers need to fund any new increases as well as interest payments (and perhaps the debt itself) on borrowing for previous government expenditures, the structure of labour relations will likely grow in importance since generous settlements cannot be employed to assuage differences. The future will benefit from not only descriptive analyses such as are provided in this volume's chapters, but deeper and more structured research that builds on this work and enables the continued development of effective and efficient labour relations to support and facilitate the delivery of instruction in Canada's K–12 system.

Simultaneously, much new research seems to be driven by the idea that Canada's increasingly global and knowledge-based economy requires highly skilled citizens. There is a move by some to more clearly develop our understanding of the links between labour relations practices in K–12 and educational outcomes. Calls to adapt labour relations to help improve student outcomes are being heard in some quarters. This is likely to add pressure to future negotiations. To deal with this, however, we need to understand the complex and diverse labour relations foundations in Canadian education, as laid out in this volume.

NOTE

1. Note that this study addresses provincially regulated K–12 teacher bargaining. It does not include the exceptional and limited cases of K–12 education regulated by the federal or territorial governments, nor does it include teacher bargaining in First Nations K–12 education.

REFERENCES

Brock, J. and D.B. Lipsky, eds. 2003. *Going Public: The Role of Labor-Management Relations in Delivering Quality Government Services*. Champaign, IL: Industrial Relations Research Association.

Card, D., M. Dooley, and A. Payne. 2010. "School Competition and Efficiency with Publicly-Funded Catholic Schools." *American Economic Journal: Applied Economics* 2(4).

Currie, J. 1989. "Who Uses Interest Arbitration? The Case of British Columbia's Teachers, 1947–1981." *Industrial and Labor Relations Review* 42(3): 363-79.

—. 1991. "Employment Determination in a Unionized Public Sector Labor Market: The Case of Ontario's School Teachers." *Journal of Labor Economics* 9(1): 45-66.

Downie, B.M. 1978. *Collective Bargaining and Conflict Resolution in Education: The Evolution of Public Policy in Ontario*. Kingston, ON: Industrial Relations Centre at Queen's University.

—. 1992. *Strikes, Disputes and Policymaking: Resolving Impasses in Ontario Education*. Kingston, ON: Industrial Relations Centre at Queen's University.

Gu, W. and P. Kuhn. 1998. "Centralization and Strikes." *Labour Economics* 5: 243-65.

Johnson, D.R. 2011. "Do Strikes and Work-to-Rule Campaigns Change Elementary School Assessment Results?" *Canadian Public Policy/Analyse de politiques* 37(4): 479-94.

Podgursky, M. 2010. "Teacher Compensation and Collective Bargaining." In *Handbook of the Economics of Education*, Vol. 3, edited by E.A. Hanushek, S. Machin, and L. Woessmann, 279-313. Amsterdam: Elsevier.

Swimmer, G., ed. 2001. *Public-Sector Labour Relations in an Era of Restraint and Restructuring*. Oxford: Oxford University Press.

Thomason, T. 1995. "Labour Relations in Primary and Secondary Education." In *Public Sector Collective Bargaining in Canada: Beginning of the End or End of the Beginning?* edited by G. Swimmer and M. Thompson, 273-312. Kingston, ON: IRC Press.

Thompson, M., J.J. Rose, and A.E. Smith, eds. 2003. *Beyond the National Divide: Regional Dimensions of Industrial Relations*. Montreal and Kingston: McGill-Queen's University Press.

Chapter 2

CROSSCURRENTS: COMPARATIVE REVIEW OF ELEMENTARY AND SECONDARY TEACHER COLLECTIVE BARGAINING STRUCTURES IN CANADA

Karen Schucher and Sara Slinn

In Canada, education and collective bargaining are matters within provincial legislative jurisdiction.[1] The ten provinces have different histories, different social contexts, and different economies, all of which contribute to the ways in which teacher collective bargaining regimes have evolved and currently function. From this perspective, teacher collective bargaining regimes in Canada "are as varied as the country itself" (Korbin 1993, F11). On the other hand, Canadian provinces do not exist in complete isolation from one another. Just as there are patterns in the regulation and governance of kindergarten to grade 12 (K–12) public education across Canada, there are also patterns in the structure and regulation of K–12 teacher collective bargaining regimes across Canada.

This chapter provides a comparative overview of the current statutory framework governing K–12 teacher collective bargaining regimes in public education across the ten Canadian provinces.[2] The discussion is organized around the following six key elements of teacher collective bargaining regimes:

1. Which statutes regulate teacher collective bargaining?
2. At what level does teacher collective bargaining take place: local, provincial, or multi-tiered?

Dynamic Negotiations: Teacher Labour Relations in Canadian Elementary and Secondary Education, ed. S. Slinn and A. Sweetman. Montreal and Kingston: Queen's Policy Studies Series, McGill-Queen's University Press.

3. How is bargaining agency allocated?
4. What is the scope of negotiable issues?
5. What dispute resolution procedures are available?
6. What restrictions apply to the right to strike and lockout?[3]

These elements are fundamental to collective bargaining in K–12 education, and proposals to reform teacher collective bargaining regimes have tended to focus on one or more of these dimensions.[4] Appendix A provides a summary table of the provincial K–12 collective bargaining structures outlined in this chapter.[5]

The purpose of the discussion is to provide an overview of the formal, legal structures of Canadian teacher collective bargaining regimes in their current forms. Two cautions are in order: first, this review does not examine the evolution of these statutory structures and, second, informal practices may depart from the legislative framework outlined in this chapter. These matters are taken up by the jurisdiction-specific studies in this volume.

STATUTES REGULATING TEACHER COLLECTIVE BARGAINING

Canada's teacher collective bargaining regimes reflect five different models of statutory regulation: a general labour relations statute, a general public sector labour relations statute, a special teacher collective bargaining statute, a general education governance statute, or a combination of statutes, as shown in Table 1. The following discussion briefly describes each of these different models of statutory regulation.

TABLE 1
Statutes Regulating Teacher Collective Bargaining

	Statutory Regulation Model				
	General Labour Relations Statute	General Public Sector Labour Relations Statute	Special Teacher Collective Bargaining Statute	General Education Governance Statute	Combinations of Statutes
Province	Alberta	New Brunswick	Nova Scotia Newfoundland and Labrador	Saskatchewan Prince Edward Island	British Columbia Manitoba Ontario Quebec

General Labour Relations Statute: Alberta

Alberta is the sole province in which teacher collective bargaining is regulated exclusively by the province's general labour relations statute, the *Labour Relations Code*, R.S.A. 2000, c. L-1 (*AB LRC*). The regular provisions of the *AB LRC* apply to teacher collective bargaining, and it contains no special provisions for collective bargaining in education.

Public Sector Labour Relations Statute: New Brunswick

New Brunswick is the only province regulating teacher collective bargaining exclusively through the general public sector collective bargaining statute, the *Public Service Labour Relations Act*, S.N.B. 1973, c. P-25 (*NB PSLRA*). The statute regulates all aspects of collective bargaining, and all provisions of the statute apply to all areas of the public service which it regulates. New Brunswick's school districts are designated as part of the public service governed by the *NB PSLRA*.

Special Teacher Collective Bargaining Statute: Nova Scotia, and Newfoundland and Labrador

Nova Scotia and Newfoundland are the two provinces in which teacher collective bargaining is regulated exclusively by a special teacher collective bargaining statute. This statute, which in both provinces is called the *Teachers' Collective Bargaining Act* (*Teachers' Collective Bargaining Act* R.S.N.S. 1989, c. 460 (*NS TCBA*); *Teachers' Collective Bargaining Act*, R.S.N.L. 1990, c. T-3 (*NL TCBA*)) regulates all aspects of teacher collective bargaining from representation rights to dispute resolution options and procedures.

General Education Governance Statute: Saskatchewan and Prince Edward Island

In two provinces, Saskatchewan and Prince Edward Island, teacher collective bargaining is regulated exclusively by the general education statute. In Saskatchewan, this statute is *The Education Act, 1995* S.S. 1995, c. E-0.2, ss. 234-269 (*SK EA*). Although teachers are not expressly excluded from Saskatchewan's general labour relations statute (*Trade Union Act*, R.S.S. 1978, c. T-17), the "Collective Bargaining" part of the *SK EA* comprehensively addresses all matters relating to teacher collective bargaining, from bargaining agency to bargaining assistance and dispute resolution. The statute also provides for a separate administrative regime for teacher collective bargaining, under the authority of a body called the Educational Relations Board. In Prince Edward Island, teachers are expressly excluded from the general labour relations statute (*Labour Act*, R.S.P.E.I. 1988, c. L-1,

s. 7(1)(h), definition of "employee," *PEI LA*). All aspects of teacher collective bargaining are regulated by the *School Act* and, more specifically, the *Instructional Personnel Regulations* made under this statute (*School Act*, R.S.P.E.I. 1988, c. S-2.1, *PEI SA*; *Instructional Personnel Regulations*, P.E.I. Reg. EC481/98, *PEI IPR*).

Combination of Statutes: British Columbia, Manitoba, Ontario, and Quebec

In British Columbia, Manitoba, Ontario, and Quebec, teacher collective bargaining is regulated by a combination of statutes.

In British Columbia, four pieces of legislation regulate teacher collective bargaining. A teacher collective bargaining statute, the *Public Education Labour Relations Act*, R.S.B.C. 1996, c. 382 (*BC PELRA*), establishes bargaining agency and the general structure of K–12 collective bargaining. Next, the province's general labour relations legislation, the *Labour Relations Code*, R.S.B.C. 1996, c. 244 (*BC LRC*), applies to the extent that its provisions are not in conflict with or inconsistent with the provisions of the *BC PELRA* or the *School Act*, R.S.B.C. 1996, c. 412 (*BC SA*). The *BC LRC* governs the bargaining and dispute resolution processes, including essential services designations. Third, the *Public Sector Employers Act*, R.S.B.C. 1996, c. 384 (*BC PSEA*), regulates employer bargaining agency in the public sector, including K–12 education. And, finally, the province's general education statute, *BC SA*, excludes certain issues from the scope of teacher collective bargaining.

In Manitoba and Ontario, teacher collective bargaining is regulated by a combination of the province's general education statute and the province's labour relations statute: *Public Schools Act*, C.C.S.M., c. P250, s. 98(1) (*MB PSA*); *Labour Relations Act*, C.C.S.M. c. L10 (*MB LRA*); *Education Act*, R.S.O. 1990, c. E-2, Part X.1, ss. 277.1-277.13.1 (*ON EA*); *Labour Relations Act, 1995*, S.O. 1995, c. 1, Sch. A (*ON LRA*). In both provinces, the general education statute contains provisions relating specifically to the teacher collective bargaining regime; the general labour relations statute applies to issues that are not already addressed, and only as long as its application is consistent with the provisions of the general education statute.

In Quebec, teacher collective bargaining is regulated by a combination of a general public and parapublic sector statute, *An Act Respecting the Process of Negotiation of the Collective Agreements in the Public and Parapublic Sectors*, R.S.Q. c. R-8.2 (*PQ PNCAPPS*) and the general labour relations statute, the *Labour Code*, R.S.Q. c. C-27 (*PQ LC*). The general labour relations statute applies primarily to regulate certain aspects of the collective bargaining process, including strikes and lockouts; other aspects are regulated by the general public and parapublic sector collective bargaining statute.

The different approaches to regulating teacher collective bargaining that are currently in effect in the provinces are a product of different teacher collective bargaining histories. By themselves, these different statutory approaches do not dictate particular approaches to the five aspects of teacher collective bargaining discussed in the next sections of this chapter. However, the fact that several jurisdictions regulate teacher collective bargaining fully or partially under a general education govern-ance statute may reflect a symbolic and functional distancing of teacher collective bargaining from collective bargaining in other sectors of the labour force, including other areas within the public sector.

LOCATION OF BARGAINING: LOCAL, PROVINCIAL, OR
MULTI-TIER NEGOTIATIONS

Canadian teacher collective bargaining regimes reflect three different approaches to bargaining structure: single-tiered bargaining at the local level in each school district, single-tiered bargaining at the provincial level, and multi-tiered bargaining, usually two-tiered bargaining divided between the provincial and local levels, as shown in Table 2.

TABLE 2
Location of Teacher Collective Bargaining

	Level of Bargaining		
	Local	*Provincial*	*Two-Tier*
Provinces	Alberta	New Brunswick	British Columbia
	Manitoba	Prince Edward Island	Saskatchewan
	Ontario	Newfoundland and Labrador	Quebec
			Nova Scotia

Local Bargaining: Alberta, Manitoba, and Ontario

Teacher collective bargaining takes place at the local level in Alberta, Manitoba, and Ontario (*AB LRC; MB PSA*, s. 97(1) definition of "party"; *ON EA*, s. 277.3). In local bargaining regimes, a separate collective agree-ment is bargained in each school district, covering teachers employed by that district. The parties to the collective agreement are the school board and the local teachers' bargaining agent. Thus, local bargaining means that the collective agreement is negotiated at the school board level; it does not relate to the structure of the teachers' bargaining agent, which may be either a local or a provincial organization.⁶ Similarly, local bargaining does not imply that the education system is locally funded by local tax revenues or levies. The K–12 education system in Manitoba is partially funded by the local government; however, the systems in Alberta and Ontario are funded entirely by the provincial governments.

Although local bargaining is the formal structure in these provinces, there have been some departures from this statutory structure. For instance, in Alberta in 2007, 12 school boards engaged in regional rather than local bargaining, forming a voluntary "Employer Bargaining Association" under the *Labour Relations Code*, to bargain with the Alberta Teachers' Association (BCPSEA 2007).⁷ In Ontario, in 2005, the provincial government developed a provincial bargaining framework under which teachers' unions, school boards, and the province reached a four-year framework agreement. The elementary teachers' unions formally participated in this arrangement; the secondary, Roman Catholic separate school, and Francophone teacher unions participated informally (BCPSEA 2007; Ontario Ministry of Education 2005a, 2005b).⁸

Provincial Bargaining: New Brunswick, Prince Edward Island, and Newfoundland and Labrador

New Brunswick, Prince Edward Island, and Newfoundland and Labrador are the three provinces where teacher collective bargaining is conducted at the provincial level (*NB PSLRA*, s. 1 - "employer"; *PEI IPR*, s. 24; *NL TCBA*, ss. 10, 11). In these regimes, there is one set of negotiations and one collective agreement for all teachers in the province. In the fourth Atlantic province, Nova Scotia, bargaining occurs at two levels.

Two-Tiered Bargaining: British Columbia, Saskatchewan, Quebec, and Nova Scotia

In British Columbia, Saskatchewan, Quebec, and Nova Scotia, K–12 teacher negotiations are conducted at both provincial and local or regional levels. In these two-tier systems, the general division is between major cost items, which tend to be negotiated at the provincial level, and low-cost or non-monetary items, which are generally bargained at the local or regional level. However, each system takes a different approach to defining the boundaries of provincial and local bargaining. As Table 3 demonstrates, in some cases the boundaries are defined in general terms, whereas in other cases the boundaries are more specifically defined. In the Quebec system, there are also two aspects to provincial bargaining: intersectorial bargaining, which applies to all areas of the public and parapublic service covered by the statute; and sectorial bargaining, which applies to each particular sector of the public and parapublic service.⁹

TABLE 3
Two-Tiered Bargaining Systems: Matters Negotiated at Each Level

Province	Matters Negotiated at	
	Provincial Level	Local or Regional Level
British Columbia	• Cost provisions, which are defined to include all provisions relating to salaries and benefits, time worked, and paid leave • All other matters that the bargaining agents designate as provincial • Either party may refer a dispute about a local matter to provincial bargaining if they are not able to reach agreement	• Non-cost items, including items the parties agreed to designate as local in a 1995 Letter of Understanding
Saskatchewan	• Salaries, group insurance, and sick leave for teachers • Superannuation of teachers • Allowances for principals and vice-principals • Criteria to designate non-teachers • Duration of agreement • Any other matters ancillary or incidental to these matters, or necessary for their implementation • Other matters not designated as local matters	• Educational leave, pay periods, sabbatical leave, and special allowances for teachers • Salaries for substitute teachers • Duration of a local agreement • Other matters not designated as provincial • Where a matter is in a local agreement and is subsequently covered by a provincial agreement, the local agreement prevails
Quebec	• Salaries and all matters not assigned to local bargaining	• Recognition of local parties; communication and posting of union notices; use of school board premises for union purposes; documentation; union prerogatives; union representative; deduction of union dues; mechanisms of participation; engagement (subject to employment security, employment priorities, and tenure acquisition); personal record; dismissal and non-reengagement; resignation and breach of contract; regulations concerning absences; leaves without pay (except parental leaves, leaves for participation in public affairs, and leaves for union activities); leaves for activities relating to education; professional improvement (subject to allocated amounts and provincial improvement programs); payment of salary; travel expenses; distribution of work days in the calendar year; distribution of duties and responsibilities among the teachers of a school board; distribution of working hours; assignment and transfer procedure; supervision of arrival and movement of pupils not included in teaching task; supply teaching, group meetings, and meetings with parents; hygiene and safety; civil liability; grievance and arbitration (only as to matters negotiated locally); savings fund

... continued

TABLE 3
(Continued)

	Matters Negotiated at	
Province	Provincial Level	Local or Regional Level
Nova Scotia	• Salaries of teachers, including substitute teachers • Group life insurance and medical care plans for teachers • Terms and conditions of employment that are of a general nature • Allowances for supervisory personnel • Any other matters that are ancillary or incidental to these matters, or necessary for their implementation • Any other matter that is not specified as local, or that the parties agree to negotiate provincially. The parties have agreed to include: ○ accommodation; advanced reporting credit; attendance at negotiation meetings; capital projects; class size; class composition; contracting out; deductions; educational events; employment insurance premium reduction; falsely accused employee assistance; harassment; hiring of substitutes; individual contracts; liability insurance; long-term disability insurance; marking and preparation time for teachers; professional development fund; service award/death benefit; school day for teachers; school calendar; supervisory and administrative time for principals and vice-principals; and travel allowance	• Sick leave, sabbatical leave, and educational leave for teachers • Pay periods for teachers • Other terms and conditions not negotiated provincially

Local, provincial, and two-tier collective bargaining regimes each have advantages and disadvantages. In principle, potential advantages of a local collective bargaining model are that issues can be negotiated by parties who know each other, and that local concerns and differences can be properly addressed. Some commentators argue, however, that these advantages may not always be realized in practice. One argument is that there is often an imbalance of power in favour of teachers, because local teachers are either legally represented by a provincial organization or receive significant support from a provincial organization, whereas local school boards tend not to have similar support (Thomason 1995, 286-87; Wright 2003, 4-5). Another argument is that provincial teachers' organizations pursue bargaining goals and agendas for all teachers in the province, which may override local differences and the potential benefits of local bargaining. It has also been argued that school boards can become vulnerable to whip-sawing in a local bargaining regime, and that there tend to be more labour disputes in local bargaining regimes (BCPSEA 2003, 59-60; Manitoba Education and Training 1996, 6; Wright 2003, 3-4).

Another criticism of local bargaining is that it can lead to inequities in teacher compensation, benefits, and working conditions, as well as inequities in student learning opportunities. This concern is often raised to support arguments in favour of funding and bargaining at the provincial level, since a key potential advantage of a provincial bargaining regime is that it establishes the same standards and benefits for everyone in the system. Some commentators also suggest that the process of provincial bargaining may be less costly and may involve fewer labour disputes, although it is also possible that any cost savings related to bargaining may be made up by increases in salaries and benefits (Korbin 1993, F23; Thomason 1995, 288). Again, however, a more centralized system can have its own disadvantages. In addition to reducing local autonomy, the challenges of reconciling diverse local interests may make a centralized bargaining process more difficult to manage and implement (Lawton et al. 1999, 50; Thomason 1995, 287-88). Provincial bargaining may fail not only to address local needs and differences, but also to deal with the effect of local realities on how common standards and benefits are in fact applied at the local level (Wright 2004, 21-22).

In principle, a two-tiered approach to bargaining can offer the benefits of both provincial and local bargaining, while avoiding their disadvantages. For example, the provincial tier allows for uniform standards in areas where uniformity is desirable, and the local or regional tier allows local or regional differences to be addressed. Thus, the provincial tier provides a remedy for concerns about inequities in the system on fundamental issues such as teacher salaries, and the local or regional tier avoids the one-size-fits-all disadvantage of provincial bargaining on all issues. However, as long as major cost items are negotiated at the provincial level, a two-tiered structure leaves only a minimal role for local bargaining. The effectiveness of two-tiered negotiations may also be affected by other aspects of the bargaining structure, such as how bargaining agency is allocated and sources of school funding. For instance, one commissioner charged with reviewing British Columbia's K–12 bargaining structure emphasized the importance of alignment between the bargaining structure and accountability for financing the school system to achieve a properly functioning system. Thus, the report concluded that in circumstances where the provincial government provided virtually all education funding, this necessitated that main cost items be bargained at the provincial, rather than local, level (Wright 2004, 19).

BARGAINING AGENTS

Bargaining agency in public sector negotiations can be more complicated than in the private sector because of the variety of institutions that can be regarded as the employer and the possibility for statutorily designated bargaining agents, and these complexities are seen in teacher collective bargaining as well. First, in some jurisdictions the teachers' bargaining agent is the provincial union; in others it is the provincial union's local affiliates. Second, in the private sector employers generally negotiate individually, rather than in a group with a common bargaining agent. However, in the education sector there are a variety of levels of government that could be regarded as the employer: the administration of particular schools, school boards, and the provincial government. Though school boards are most commonly regarded as the employer, the entity representing management at the teacher bargaining table may not be the school board or, in fact, school administration or the government. Particularly in jurisdictions where collective bargaining is conducted in whole or in part at the provincial level, negotiations are conducted by a bargaining agent for management, rather than by school boards. Finally, although there is often a connection between the level at which collective bargaining occurs and how bargaining agency is allocated, this is not always the case. Similarly, there is no necessary connection between the government level at which education is funded and the level at which collective bargaining occurs. Nor is it the case that union and management agency will be at the same level. For example, in some provinces with local bargaining, the local school board is the employer bargaining agent while a provincial teachers' organization is the union bargaining agent.

Teacher Bargaining Agency

Specialized teacher associations or unions are the bargaining agents for teachers in all provinces. These organizations have a long history in Canada, in most cases dating back to the early twentieth century (Lawton et al. 1999, 17-30). There is one such provincial teachers' association in British Columbia, Alberta, Saskatchewan, Manitoba, New Brunswick, Nova Scotia, Prince Edward Island, and Newfoundland and Labrador; four such associations in Ontario; and two in Quebec. Bargaining rights are legally held either by these provincial teachers' associations or by their local affiliates.

The legal framework for teacher collective bargaining agency matches the level at which negotiations occur in six jurisdictions. In Manitoba, where bargaining occurs at the local level, local affiliates of the provincial teachers' association are the bargaining agents (MB PSA, s. 97(1), definition of "party"). In Saskatchewan and Quebec, where two-tiered bargaining occurs, provincial bargaining rights are held by provincial entities and local bargaining rights are held by local entities. In Quebec, provincial bargaining rights are held by provincial associations, and local bargaining rights are held by local affiliates of the provincial associations (PQ PNCAPPS, ss. 26, 27(g)). In Saskatchewan, bargaining rights at both the provincial and local levels are held by committees of four members appointed by the provincial teachers' association (*SK EA*, ss. 234(1), 235(2)). In the three provinces with provincial bargaining structures—New Brunswick, Prince Edward Island, and Newfoundland and Labrador—the provincial teachers' association is the bargaining agent (Lawton et al. 1999, 53-54; *PEI IPR*, s. 25; *NL TCBA*, s. 9).

In the remaining four provinces, the legal framework for teacher collective bargaining agency does not match the level(s) at which collective bargaining occurs. In British Columbia and Nova Scotia, which have two-tiered bargaining structures, the provincial teachers' association is the bargaining agent for both provincial and local bargaining (*BC PELRA*, s. 6(1); *NL TCBA*, ss. 2(a)(v)). In practice, however, in British Columbia the provincial bargaining agents must establish policies and procedures to delegate authority to local boards of education and local teachers' associations to engage in local bargaining (*BC PELRA*, ss. 8(1), (2), (4)). Local matters that cannot be resolved at that level may be unilaterally referred to the provincial table (*BC PELRA*, s. 8(3)). However, local agreements are tightly controlled by the provincial bargaining agents and must be ratified by them. In Alberta and Ontario, which have local bargaining structures, the provincial teachers' associations are legally constituted as the bargaining agents. In practice, however, local teachers' associations in Alberta and Ontario are also actively involved in the collective bargaining process, with support from the provincial organizations (BCPSEA 2003, 64, 68; Lawton et al. 1999, 50; Ontario Ministry of Education 2006, 5; Reshef 2007, 681).

Teacher collective bargaining agency also has several distinctive aspects. The first relates to the way in which teacher associations acquire and maintain representation rights. Public sector unions often obtain bargaining rights by way of statutory designation, and this is the case for a number of teacher bargaining agents. As shown in Table 4, specific teacher organizations are designated as the bargaining agent by statute in six provinces: British Columbia, Saskatchewan, Ontario, Nova Scotia, Prince Edward Island, and Newfoundland and Labrador (*BC PELRA*, s. 6; *SK EA*, ss. 234(1), 235(2); *ON EA*, s. 277.3(2); *NS TCBA*, ss. 2(a),(v); *PEI IPR*, s. 25; *NL TCBA*, s. 9). In three of these provinces—Saskatchewan, Ontario, and Nova Scotia—the legislation makes no provision for changing this statutory designation of bargaining rights. In the other three provinces—British Columbia, Prince Edward Island, and Newfoundland and Labrador—the legislative frameworks allow for changes in bargaining agency; however, there have been no challenges to the bargaining rights held by these unions. In British Columbia, the designation of the British Columbia Teachers' Federation is made expressly subject to the change of bargaining agents and revocation of bargaining rights provisions of the general labour relations statute (*BC PELRA*, s. 6(2)); in Prince Edward Island, the statutory bargaining rights remain in place "so long as a majority of the instructional personnel employed in the province has authorized [the Prince Edward Island Teachers' Federation] to represent them for negotiation purposes" (*PEI IPR*, s. 25); and in Newfoundland and Labrador, the Newfoundland and Labrador Teachers' Association is recognized as the bargaining agent "unless it is replaced by a certified bargaining agent" (*NL TCBA*, s. 9).

Bargaining agency is determined by certification in the remaining four provinces: Alberta, Manitoba, Quebec, and New Brunswick. In all of these provinces, legal representation rights are held by the provincial teacher associations or their local affiliates. Legal certification processes generally came after the teacher associations were formed, and formalized existing informal arrangements (Lawton et al. 1999, 22-32; Muir 1969, 12-18; Thomason 1995, 282-83). Although these legal frameworks would allow changes in bargaining agency, bargaining rights obtained through certification have always been held by the teacher organizations and there have been no challenges to these bargaining rights.

TABLE 4
Teacher Bargaining Agency: Statutory Designation and Certification

By Statutory Designation	By Certification
British Columbia	Alberta
Saskatchewan	Manitoba
Ontario	Quebec
Nova Scotia	New Brunswick
Prince Edward Island	
Newfoundland and Labrador	

A second distinctive aspect of teacher collective bargaining agency is the way in which membership in the provincial associations is constituted. In nine provinces, membership in these provincial teachers' associations is compulsory and determined by statute: Alberta (*Teaching Profession Act*, R.S.A. 2000, c. T-2, s. 5; *BC TPA*), British Columbia (*PELRA*, ss. 1 "teacher," 4-6), Saskatchewan (*Teachers' Federation Act, 2006*, S.S. 2006, c. T-7.1, s. 17), Manitoba (*Teachers' Society Act*, C.C.S.M. c. T30, s. 5), Ontario (*Teaching Profession Act*, R.S.O. 1990, c.T-2, s. 4), New Brunswick (*Act Respecting the New Brunswick Teachers' Federation, the New Brunswick Teachers' Association and l'Association des enseignantes et des enseignants francophones de Nouveau-Brunswick*, S.N.B. 1983, c. 107), Nova Scotia (*Teaching Profession Act*, R.S.N.S. 1989, c. 462, s. 12), Prince Edward Island (*An Act to Incorporate the Prince Edward Island Teachers' Federation*, S.P.E.I. 1974, c. 61), and Newfoundland and Labrador (*Teachers' Association Act*, R.S.N.L. 1990, c. T-2, s. 6). This form of statutory membership in provincial teachers' associations has a long history in Canada, dating back to the 1930s and 1940s (Muir 1969, 9-12).

The final distinctive feature of teacher representation is that many provincial teacher associations function both as professional associations, providing professional development services for example, and as collective bargaining representatives. In nine jurisdictions, the mandate of the provincial teachers' associations includes both roles: British Columbia, Alberta, Saskatchewan, Manitoba, Ontario,[10] Quebec, Nova Scotia, Prince Edward Island, and Newfoundland and Labrador. In New Brunswick, teachers have access to professional representation services through two separate provincial organizations, the New Brunswick Teachers' Association and l'Association des enseignantes et des enseignants francophones du Nouveau-Brunswick.

In two provinces, British Columbia and Ontario, there also exists a separate regulatory body responsible for teacher credentials, discipline, and related professional matters—the BC College of Teachers (*BC TPA*), and the Ontario College of Teachers / Ordre des enseignantes et des enseignants de l'Ontario (*Ontario College of Teachers Act, 1996*, S.O. 1996, c. 12).

Employer Bargaining Agency

The legal framework for employer bargaining agency tends to reflect the level at which negotiations are held, in the sense that the structure of the entity that engages in bargaining tends to match the level at which bargaining occurs. In the provinces where bargaining occurs at the local level, the school board is the employer bargaining agent. Similarly, in the provinces with a two-tiered collective bargaining structure, a provincial entity bargains provincial matters, while school boards are responsible for local bargaining.[11]

At the provincial bargaining level, both in provinces with exclusively provincial bargaining and in provinces with two-tiered bargaining structures, the employer bargaining agent in eight jurisdictions is an entity composed of school board and provincial government representatives. In British Columbia, the employer bargaining agent is the British Columbia Public School Employers' Association (BCPSEA), an employers' association established under the *Public Sector Employers Act*. BCPSEA is governed by a board of directors composed of nine school trustee representatives, four provincial government representatives, and one non-voting representative each from the British Columbia School Superintendents' Association and the British Columbia School District Secretary-Treasurers' Association. In Saskatchewan, the employer agent for provincial bargaining is a nine-person bargaining committee designated by statute. Four members of this committee are appointed by the Saskatchewan School Boards' Association, and five members are appointed by the Lieutenant Governor in Council (*SK EA*, ss. 1, definitions of "association" and "provincial agreement"; 234(2)).

In Quebec, the employer bargaining agents for provincial bargaining are committees established for the French-language school boards, the

English-language school boards, the Crie School Board, and the Kativik School Board. These committees are composed of members appointed by the Minister of Education, Recreation and Sports and by the group of school boards (*PQ PNCAPPS*, ss. 30(1)-(2), 31, 35). By statute, these committees have delegated authority to prepare draft bargaining proposals, to obtain bargaining mandates from the Conseil du trésor, and to carry out negotiations within the scope of these mandates (*PQ PNCAPPS*, s. 33). However, in relation to salaries, it is the Conseil du trésor which has the statutory authority to negotiate, "in collaboration with the management negotiating committees." In addition, the Conseil du trésor is responsible for ensuring the "orderly progress of the negotiation" of provincial matters and, for purposes of fulfilling this responsibility, must authorize bargaining mandates and may delegate an observer to the negotiating sessions. The Conseil du trésor is also required to invite the Minister of Education, Recreation and Sports (and the Minister of Health and Social Services, where appropriate) to participate in its deliberations on matters for provincial bargaining (*PQ PNCAPPS*, ss. 42-43, 53).

In Prince Edward Island, the Education Negotiating Agency is designated by statute as the employer bargaining agent. This Agency is composed of representatives of the Minister of Education, the Treasury Board, and school boards; it cannot make an offer having financial implications without the prior approval of the Treasury Board. In Newfoundland and Labrador, a "school board committee" is designated by statute as the employer bargaining agent. This seven-member committee appointed by the Lieutenant-Governor in Council is composed of four school board representatives and three provincial government representatives. The government representatives, one of whom is the chief negotiator, are selected by the president of the Treasury Board. The Lieutenant-Governor in Council may accept nominations for school board representatives where the persons nominated have the support of least 75 percent of school boards; where school board nominations do not have the 75 percent level of support, the Minister of Education nominates school board representatives (*NL TCBA*, s. 10).

Finally, New Brunswick and Nova Scotia are the two jurisdictions where the employer collective bargaining agent does not include school board representation. In New Brunswick, where there are no longer any school boards, the provincial government is designated by statute as the employer and the party to the collective bargaining relationship. In Nova Scotia, the legislation does not designate employer bargaining agency, as such, but rather designates the Minister of Education as the employer in relation to provincial bargaining matters.

The complexities of the relationships between the level of bargaining and the level of bargaining agency on the teacher and employer sides are summarized in Table 5.

TABLE 5
Bargaining Agency in Relation to Location of Bargaining

Province	Bargaining Level	Level of Teacher Bargaining Agency	Level of Employer Bargaining Agency
British Columbia	Two-tiered	Provincial agent (British Columbia Teachers' Federation); BCTF locals have delegated authority to bargain locally.	Provincial agent (British Columbia Public School Employers' Association) bargains at provincial level. Authority for local bargaining is delegated to school boards. The provincial agent maintains significant oversight of local bargaining.
Alberta	Local	Provincial agent (Alberta Teachers' Association) holds legal bargaining rights; local affiliates actively participate in bargaining.	School board; some voluntary multi-school board arrangements.
Saskatchewan	Two-tiered	Provincial committee bargains at provincial level and local committee at local level.	Provincial committee bargains at provincial level and school boards at local level.
Manitoba	Local	Manitoba Teachers' Society local affiliates.	School board.
Ontario	Local	Provincial agents hold legal bargaining rights; local affiliates actively participate in bargaining.	School board.
Quebec	Two-tiered	Provincial agents bargain at provincial level and local affiliates at local level.	Provincial agents bargain at provincial level and school boards at local level.
New Brunswick	Provincial	Provincial agent (New Brunswick Teachers' Federation).	Provincial agent.
Nova Scotia	Two-tiered	Provincial agent (Nova Scotia Teachers Union) bargains at provincial and local levels.	Provincial agent bargains at provincial level and school boards at local level.
Prince Edward Island	Provincial	Provincial agent (PEI Teachers' Federation).	Provincial agent.
Newfoundland and Labrador	Provincial	Provincial agent (Newfoundland and Labrador Teachers' Association).	Provincial agent.

SCOPE OF COLLECTIVE BARGAINING

There is much debate over whether matters relating to public services can or should be the subject of collective bargaining, or whether public services are a matter of public policy that should be determined by government or managers, although perhaps in consultation with public sector unions. From a more conventional labour relations perspective, workload issues are about fair treatment of workers and, therefore, properly the subject of collective bargaining. In a public sector and professional context, however, workload issues also raise questions about the nature of the service, professional responsibilities in relation to delivering that service, and government's decisions about how to allocate public resources. In the K–12 education context, these issues raise questions about the responsibilities and duties of teachers, about where these questions should be addressed, and about who should address them. Teachers' unions often position themselves in relation to these issues by arguing that students' learning conditions translate directly into teachers' working conditions and, therefore, such matters are properly the subject of collective bargaining (Wright 2004, 39-41). Meanwhile, employers in education view these matters as necessary subjects of managerial discretion, as employers must meet changing educational programming and fiscal demands. This disagreement about whether all aspects of the work of public services can be the subject of collective bargaining or whether some aspects are matters of public policy that should be determined through processes other than collective bargaining is long-standing in education.

Collective bargaining in the K–12 education sector is also affected by other challenges associated with public sector bargaining, including government initiatives to rationalize and control costs of public services. These challenges typically affect public sector collective bargaining, and collective bargaining in the K–12 education sector is no exception.

When teacher associations first began negotiating informally with school boards, these negotiations tended to focus on salary issues. As these bargaining relationships became more formalized, and then legally regulated, teacher associations sought to negotiate collective agreement provisions dealing with a range of other working conditions issues such as class size limits, job security, and preparation time. Bargaining priorities are also affected by changes in the social and economic environment. In periods of declining student enrolment, for example, teacher associations might give more priority to issues of job security and might propose new approaches to addressing these issues, such as job sharing (Lawton et al. 1999, 34-35; Muir 1969, 12-14, 22-31; Thomason 1995, 295-96). Since the mid to late 1990s, workload issues have been a major focus of attention. In the K–12 education context, workload issues are often addressed through provisions relating to class size, instructional time, preparation time, and cocurricular or extracurricular activities. There has been a flurry of legislative activity around these issues in the last decade, which has included the enactment of both permanent and temporary restrictions on the scope of collective bargaining (Reshef 2007, 681-89; Rose 2002, 106-107, 113-20; Thomason 1995, 208-301).

The current scope of collective bargaining in the K–12 education sector can generally be described as broad in the sense that most jurisdictions do not impose express restrictions on the scope of collective bargaining. At the same time, however, collective bargaining in this sector takes place within a highly regulated context. In most jurisdictions, a range of statutory provisions affects terms and conditions of teachers' employment, without expressly removing these matters from the scope of collective bargaining. In addition, some provincial governments have passed temporary or ad hoc legislative measures imposing restrictions on the scope of teacher bargaining. Thus, the scope of collective bargaining in the K–12 education sector is affected by three forms of regulation: express restrictions on the scope of collective bargaining that are part of the regulatory framework; statutory provisions that affect terms and conditions of employment; and temporary statutory restrictions on the scope of collective bargaining. The discussion below reviews each of these three forms of regulation of the scope of teacher collective bargaining.

Express Restrictions on the Scope of Collective Bargaining

British Columbia and Saskatchewan are the two provinces that currently include express statutory prohibitions on the scope collective bargaining in their regulatory frameworks. In both provinces, matters expressly excluded from collective bargaining relate to various aspects of teacher working conditions. These matters are set out in Table 6.

In British Columbia, the *School Act* identifies these matters as ones that "must not be included in a teachers' collective agreement," and further states that that any collective agreement provision that conflicts or is inconsistent with this prohibition "is void to the extent of the conflict or inconsistency" (ss. 27(3), (5)).[12] In Saskatchewan, the prohibition in the *Education Act* states that collective agreements cannot contain terms dealing with the listed matters (s. 237(6)).

TABLE 6
Express Prohibitions on Scope of Bargaining

Province	Matters Expressly Excluded from Collective Bargaining
British Columbia (*School Act*, s. 27(3))[a]	• Regulating the selection of teachers, the courses of study, the program of studies or the professional methods and techniques employed by teachers • Restricting or regulating the assignment of teaching duties to principals, vice principals, or directors of instruction • Limiting a board's power to employ persons other than teachers to assist teachers in carrying out their responsibilities • Restricting or regulating a board's power to establish class size and class composition • Establishing or imposing class size limits, requirements for average class sizes, or methods for determining class size limits or average class sizes • Restricting or regulating a board's power to assign a student to a class, course, or program • Restricting or regulating a board's power to determine staffing levels or ratios, or the number of teachers or other staff employed by the board • Establishing minimum numbers of teachers or other staff • Restricting or regulating a board's power to determine the number of students assigned to a teacher • Establishing maximum or minimum caseloads, staffing loads, or teaching loads
Saskatchewan (*Education Act, 1995*, s. 237(6))	• Regulating the selection and appointment of teachers, the courses of study, the program of studies, and the professional methods and techniques employed by a teacher

[a]The British Columbia Supreme Court ruled, in April 2011, that certain exclusions from the scope of bargaining set out in the *BC SA* (ss. 27 (3)(d)-(j), (5) and (6)) are unconstitutional and invalid because the government, by removing these traditionally negotiated matters from the scope of bargaining, had violated teachers' *Charter*-protected freedom of association. The Court suspended the declaration of invalidity for one year (*British Columbia Teachers' Federation v. British Columbia*, 2011 BCSC 469).

Statutory Provisions Regulating Terms and Conditions of Employment

In all provinces, there are matters affecting terms and conditions of teacher employment that are prescribed by statute and regulation. As shown in Table 7, the particular matters prescribed vary from one province to another, and range from school holidays and vacations to class sizes and pensions.

These statutory prescriptions are not framed as express prohibitions against negotiating about these matters. However, they are part of the context in which teacher collective bargaining takes place and can affect the scope of teacher collective bargaining in several ways. In some cases, such as provisions that regulate class size, the statutory prescription effectively prohibits collective bargaining. In other cases, such as regulated

TABLE 7
Statutory Regulation of Matters Affecting Teacher Terms and Conditions of Employment

Province	Matters Prescribed or Regulated by Statute
British Columbia *School Act*, ss. 17, 76.1; B.C. Reg. 114/2002, Sch. 1 and Sch. 1 (supplement); *Public Sector Pension Plans Act*, S.B.C. 1999, c. 44	• Teachers' responsibilities • Class size (maximum, average in the aggregate) • Maximum number of instructional and non-instructional days • Holidays and vacation periods • Pensions
Alberta *School Act*, R.S.A. 2000, c. S-3, ss. 56(2), 97(2)(a)-(b), 98, 101-108; *Teachers' Pension Plans Act*, R.S.A. 2000, c. T-1	• Vacation periods to include as a minimum a period from December 24 to January 2 • Maximum of 1,100 hours of instruction per school year, and of 200 teaching days per school year • Probationary, interim, temporary, and part-time contracts • Transfer of teachers between schools • Suspension and discharge of teachers • Calculating payment of annual salary • Periods of absence due to illness • Pensions
Saskatchewan *Education Act, 1995*, ss. 163-166; *The Teachers Superannuation and Disability Benefits Act*, S.S. 1994, c. T-9.1	• 200 school days in a school year • Program of instruction from 9 a.m. to noon and 1 to 3:30 p.m., and two 15-minute recess periods • Holidays and vacation periods • Pensions
Manitoba *Public Schools Act*, ss. 78(1), 92, 92.1, 93-95, 96; Man. Reg. 468/88 R, ss. 39-40; *Teachers' Pensions Act*, C.C.S.M., c. T20	• Holidays • Sick leave • Teacher contracts • Teacher access to personnel records • Teacher duties and responsibilities • Teacher to be on duty in the school at least ten minutes before morning session begins and at least five minutes before the afternoon session begins • Pensions
Ontario *Education Act*, ss. 261, 264, 277.11(1), 277.11(5), 277.14-23, 277.28-45; O. Reg. 99/02, s. 170.1; O. Reg. 399/00, s. 2(3.1); R.R.O. Reg. 298, ss. 3 (1)-(2), 20; R.R.O. 1990, Reg. 304, ss. 2(3.1), (4); *Teachers' Pension Act*, R.S.O. 1990, c.T.1	• Probationary period not to exceed two years • Duties of teachers • Collective agreement term to be two or four years, and prohibition against renewal provision • Teacher performance appraisal, including process and consequences • Method for determining average class sizes • Minimum of 194 days in a school year • Minimum of two and maximum of four professional activity days • Holidays and vacations • Instructional program of not less than five hours per day excluding recesses or scheduled intervals between classes, beginning not earlier than 8 a.m. and ending not later than 5 p.m. • Pensions

... continued

TABLE 7
(Continued)

Province	Matters Prescribed or Regulated by Statute
Quebec *An Act Respecting the Process of Negotiation of the Collective Agreements in the Public and Parapublic Sectors,* ss. 52-56; *Education Act,* R.S.Q. c. I-13.3, s. 22; R.Q. c. I-13.3, r.3.1, ss. 19, 22-23.1; *Labour Code,* s. 111.1; *An Act Respecting the Teachers' Pension Plan,* R.S.Q. c. R-11	• Salary determination by regulation if the parties cannot reach agreement • Teacher obligations • Holidays • Suggested hours of instruction per subject • Maximum three-year term for collective agreement • Pensions
New Brunswick *Education Act,* S.N.B. c. E-1.12, s. 27; N.B. Reg. 97-150, ss. 3(2), 5, 25(1), 26(1), 27; *Teachers' Pension Act,* R.S.N.B. 1973, c. T-1	• Teacher duties and responsibilities • Hours of instruction per day • Vacations • Calculating salary payments • Teacher resignation • Pensions
Nova Scotia *Education Act,* S.N.S. 1995-96 c. 1, ss. 26, 30, 32, 33, 34; N.S. Reg. 80/97, ss. 2(1), (4)-(6), 3; *Teachers' Pension Act,* S.N.S. 1998, c. 26	• Duties of teachers • Teacher contracts • Suspension and termination • 195 school days • Holidays and vacations • Teaching hours • Pensions
Prince Edward Island *School Act,* ss. 82-85; 91, 98; P.E.I. Reg. EC481/98, s. 33(3); *Teachers' Superannuation Act,* R.S.P.E.I. 1988, c. T-1.	• Teacher contracts • Discipline of teachers • Teacher responsibilities • Teaching positions • Maximum three-year collective agreement term • Pensions • Section 7(2)(h) of the *School Act* empowers the Minister to make directives to determine the number and type of positions in each school board, and such directives have been made.
Newfoundland and Labrador *Schools Act,* 1997, S.N.L. 1997 c. S-12.2, ss. 28, 33; *Teachers' Pension Act,* S.N.L. 1991, c. 17	• Minimum hours of instruction • Responsibilities of teachers • Pensions

vacations and pension plans, the statutory provision creates a benefit that the parties may not have to negotiate. Sometimes, however, matters that are regulated outside of the collective bargaining process can also have an impact on teacher collective bargaining.

Temporary Statutory Restrictions on the Scope of Collective Bargaining

In addition to ongoing statutory regulation of the scope of collective bargaining, provincial governments in several jurisdictions have used their legislative power to temporarily remove certain matters from the scope of bargaining. This type of intervention often occurs in the aftermath of a bargaining dispute. Examples of such temporary restrictions on bargaining include the following. In 2002 the Alberta government passed the *Education Services Settlement Act*, S.A. 2002, c. E-0.5 following a strike by teachers in 22 of the province's 40 public school boards.[13] The Act prohibited inclusion of provisions relating to class sizes, hours of instruction, and pupil-teacher ratios in the collective agreements negotiated or arbitrated in that bargaining round (s. 23). In Manitoba, in 2000, the provincial government imposed a two-and-a-half year prohibition against including class size and class composition in collective agreement interest arbitrations (*The Public Schools Amendment and Consequential Amendments Act*, S.M. 2000, c. 43, ss. 4, 7).

Notably, these government interventions in the scope of bargaining occurred prior to a 2007 Supreme Court of Canada decision that reversed decades of jurisprudence, holding that the section 2(d) *Charter*-protected freedom of association includes a limited right to collective bargaining (*Health Services and Support-Facilities Subsector Bargaining Assn. v. British Columbia*, 2007 SCC 27). Recently, the British Columbia Supreme Court held that the province's 2002 legislation—which permanently removed key issues from the scope of teacher bargaining in the province, including class size, workload, and staffing ratios; prohibited any provisions allowing negotiation of these matters; and voided any such collective agreement clauses—was an unjustifiable violation of teachers' freedom of association (*Public Education Flexibility and Choice Act*, S.B.C. 2002, c. 3; *British Columbia Teachers' Federation v. British Columbia*, 2011 BCSC 469).[14] This decision also brings into question whether government action temporarily removing matters from the scope of bargaining would also breach the *Charter* freedom of association.

DISPUTE RESOLUTION

The ultimate goal of a collective bargaining process is a collective agreement negotiated by the parties. Collective bargaining can, however, be a difficult process. Therefore, Canadian labour relations regimes typically offer third-party assistance to help the parties reach their own negotiated agreements. This assistance usually takes the form of mediation and conciliation. The mediation process, as well as the process of conciliation with a single conciliation officer, tends to be in the nature of a bargaining process. Conciliation with a three-person conciliation board, on the other hand, is a process that is more in the nature of an informal hearing.

Many labour relations regimes also make the option of voluntary binding arbitration available to the parties. With voluntary binding arbitration, the parties jointly agree to submit the issues in dispute to an arbitrator or arbitration board. The arbitrator or arbitration board conducts a hearing, during which the parties may present evidence and make submissions about the issues in dispute. In some jurisdictions, the legislation prescribes statutory criteria that the arbitration board must consider in making its award.

Some provinces also include fact-finding, inquiry, and investigation options. These options lie somewhere between mediation and conciliation, and voluntary arbitration. They are generally designed to enable a third party to collect information about the parties' positions and to assess those positions.

As Table 8 demonstrates, at least some of these dispute resolution options are available in every K–12 teacher collective bargaining regime; and, in some jurisdictions, all of these options are available.

TABLE 8
Dispute Resolution Options

Mediation	Conciliation	Mediation and Conciliation	Fact-Finding, Commissions of Inquiry	Voluntary Binding Arbitration
British Columbia	Saskatchewan	Saskatchewan (but mutually exclusive)	British Columbia (fact-finding, industrial inquiry commission)	Alberta
Alberta	Manitoba			Saskatchewan
Saskatchewan	Ontario	Manitoba		Ontario
Manitoba	New Brunswick	Ontario	Manitoba (industrial inquiry commission)	Quebec
Ontario	Nova Scotia	Nova Scotia		New Brunswick
Quebec	Prince Edward Island		Ontario (industrial inquiry commission)	Nova Scotia
Nova Scotia	Newfoundland and Labrador		New Brunswick (commissioner)	Newfoundland and Labrador

The discussion below reviews in more detail how these options are structured in the different jurisdictions.

Mediation

Mediation is available in seven jurisdictions—British Columbia, Alberta, Saskatchewan, Manitoba, Ontario, Quebec, and Nova Scotia. In most jurisdictions, mediation may be requested by either one of the collective bargaining parties (*BC LRC*, s. 74(1); *AB LRC*, s. 64, informal assistance, and ss. 65(1)(a), 65(2)(a), appointment is discretionary; *MB LRA*, ss. 95(1), where joint request, appointment is mandatory, and 95(1.1), where request by one party, appointment is discretionary; *ON LRA*, s. 19; *PQ PNCAPPS*, ss. 47, 48, the Minister of Labour may appoint the mediator or the parties may agree on their own mediator). In Saskatchewan, mediation and conciliation are mutually exclusive routes; it is the teachers' bargaining agent that selects the route to be taken, but either party may request mediation once that route has been selected (*SK EA*, ss. 239, 243(1)-(3)). In British Columbia, Alberta, Saskatchewan, and Manitoba, mediation can also be initiated by a third party;[15] and in Nova Scotia, mediation can be initiated only by a third party, the Minister of Education (*NS TCBA*, s. 27).[16] The mediation officer is often required to make a report on the mediation, which is provided to the relevant government official (*BC LRC*, s. 74(4), (5); *SK EA*, ss. 103(1)(a)-(b), 243(4); *MB LRA*, s. 103(1); *ON LRA*, s. 35; *PQ LC*, s. 96; *NS TCBA*, s. 27(3)). In some jurisdictions the mediator's report may also be provided to the parties (*MB LRA*, s. 104 (a); *ON LRA*, s. 34(5); *PQ Act Respecting the Process of Negotiation (PQ ARPN*, s. 47), and in some jurisdictions the report either can or must be published (*BC LRC*, s. 74(4), (5); *MB LRA*, s. 105, the report may be published at the discretion of the Minister of Labour; *PQ ARPN*, s. 47, the report must be made public unless dispute settles). In British Columbia, where the mediator prepares a report on the collective bargaining dispute at the request of a party or at the direction of the Minister of Labour, the mediator may include recommended terms of settlement in the report (*BC LRC*, s. 74(5)). In Alberta, the mediator either must recommend terms of settlement for the parties to accept or reject within a time fixed by the mediator, or must notify the parties that he or she does not intend to make a recommendation. Where the mediator recommends terms, either party may require that a vote be conducted on the recommendation (*AB LRC*, ss. 65(6), 68). In Saskatchewan, the chair of the Educational Relations Board may also appoint a mediator at any time to assist in the resolution of a dispute (*SK EA*, s. 240). In Manitoba, the mediator's report must set out any matters on which the parties cannot agree, and must include a recommendation about whether any further proceedings might be taken to facilitate a settlement (*MB LRA*, ss. 103(1)(a)-(b)). In Quebec, any provincial issue may be the subject of mediation, with the exception of salaries (*PQ PNCAPPS*, s. 46).

Conciliation

Conciliation is available in seven jurisdictions. In three of these jurisdictions—New Brunswick, Prince Edward Island, and Newfoundland and Labrador—conciliation is the only bargaining assistance option available. In the remaining four jurisdictions—Saskatchewan, Manitoba, Ontario, and Nova Scotia—conciliation is available along with mediation although, as noted above, in Saskatchewan mediation and conciliation are mutually exclusive routes. In some jurisdictions, the statute provides for conciliation with a conciliation officer as well as conciliation by a three-person conciliation board (*ON LRA*, ss. 18, 21; *NB PSLRA*, ss. 47, 49; *NS TCBA*, ss. 23, 45; *NL TCBA*, ss. 13, 14). In Saskatchewan, the only option is conciliation with a conciliation board (*SK EA*, s. 251), and in Prince Edward

Island, the only option available is conciliation with a conciliation officer (*PEI IPR*, s. 34). Conciliation with a conciliation officer can usually be initiated at the request of a collective bargaining party (*ON LRA*, s. 18(1); *NB PSLRA*, s. 47; *NL TCBA*, s. 13), although in some provinces it may also be initiated by a third party—by the Minister of Education in Nova Scotia, if the parties do not begin bargaining at the appropriate time (*NS TCBA*, s. 23), and by the Minister of Labour in Prince Edward Island (*PEI IPR*, s. 34(b),(c)). In some provinces, a conciliation board process can be initiated at the request of either a collective bargaining party or a third party;[17] in other provinces, it can be initiated only by a third party;[18] and in Nova Scotia it can be initiated only at the request of the collective bargaining parties (*NS TCBA*, s. 25). Conciliation officers and conciliation boards are generally required to make reports on the performance of their duties (*SK EA*, s. 257(8); *MB LRA*, s. 103(1); *ON LRA*, ss. 20(1), 34(1)-(4); *NB PSLRA*, s. 57(1); *NS TCBA*, ss. 24, 48; *PEI IPR*, s. 35(2)). In Newfoundland and Labrador, only the conciliation board is required to report (*NL TCBA*, s. 14(16)). These reports are provided to the parties (*SK EA*, 260(1); *MB LRA*, s. 104; *ON LRA*, s. 34(5); *NB PSLRA*, s. 58; *NS TCBA*, s. 24; *NL TCBA*, s. 14(16)), and in some provinces the report of a conciliation board may also be made public (*MB LRA*, s. 105; *SK EA*, s. 260(1); *NB PSLRA*; *NS TCBA*, s. 68).

Fact-Finding and Commissions of Inquiry

Fact-finding is currently available only in British Columbia.[19] The fact-finder is appointed by the associate chair of the Labour Relations Board, and is required to make a report after conferring with the parties and inquiring into the dispute. The fact-finder's report is provided to the parties and may be provided to the public at the discretion of the associate chair of the Labour Relations Board (*BC LRC*, s. 77).

The legislative frameworks in British Columbia, Manitoba, Ontario, and New Brunswick also provide for the appointment of an industrial inquiry commission.[20] In British Columbia, the 2006 round of teacher collective bargaining was carried out with the assistance of an industrial inquiry commissioner.[21] In Ontario, the legislative framework also authorizes the Minister of Labour to appoint a special officer or a Disputes Advisory Committee to assist the parties during bargaining (*ON LRA*, ss. 38-39).

Voluntary Interest Arbitration

Voluntary interest arbitration is available as an alternative dispute resolution option in seven jurisdictions: Alberta, Saskatchewan, Ontario, Quebec, New Brunswick, Nova Scotia, and Newfoundland and Labrador.[22] Voluntary arbitration is initiated by agreement of both parties. None of the jurisdictions place statutory restrictions on the voluntary arbitration process (*AB LRC*, s. 93; *SK EA*, s. 260(2); *MB LRA*, s. 40 – and this agreement is "irrevocable"; *PQ LC*, s. 74; *NB PSLRA*, s. 66; *NS TCBA*, s. 26(1); *NL TCBA*, s. 21).

However, Ontario, New Brunswick, and Newfoundland and Labrador impose statutory restrictions on how the substance of the award is to be determined. In Ontario, the arbitration board must "take into consideration all factors it considers relevant, including the following criteria" (*ON EA*, s. 277.10):

1. The employer's ability to pay in light of its fiscal situation.

2. The extent to which services may have to be reduced, in light of the decision or award, if current funding and taxation levels are not increased.

3. The economic situation in Ontario and in the municipality or municipalities served by the board.

4. A comparison, as between the employees and other comparable employees in the public and private sectors, of the terms and conditions of employment and the nature of the work performed.

5. The employer's ability to attract and retain qualified employees.

In New Brunswick, the arbitration board must consider the following statutory criteria in order "to ensure that wages and benefits are fair and reasonable to the employees and to the employer" (*NB PSLRA*, s. 82):

(a) Wages and benefits in private and public, and unionized and non-unionized, employment;

(b) The continuity and stability of private and public employment including employment levels and incidence of layoffs;

(c) The fiscal policies of the Government of the Province of New Brunswick;

(d) The terms and conditions of employment in similar occupations outside the Public Service taking into account any geographic, industrial or other variations that the arbitration tribunal considers relevant;

(e) The need to maintain appropriate relationships in terms and conditions of employment between different grade levels within an occupation and between occupations in the Public Service;

(f) The need to establish terms and conditions of employment that are fair and reasonable in relation to the qualifications required, the work performed, the responsibility assumed and the nature of the services rendered; and

(g) Any other factor that the arbitration tribunal considers relevant to the matter in dispute.

In Newfoundland and Labrador, the *Teachers' Collective Bargaining Act* includes a provision that precludes an arbitration board from awarding terms that would require the enactment of legislation or the making of a regulation in order to be valid.

WORK STOPPAGE RESTRICTIONS

The labour relations system contemplates that negotiating parties will have recourse to the economic weapon of strike or lockout as an element of their bargaining power. However, work stoppages in the public sector raise a variety of different questions and problems than in the private sector. As a result, for many parts of the public sector work stoppages are prohibited by legislation or are limited by essential service requirements. In the education sector, it is often argued that the work done by teachers is, at least in part, an essential service and should not be subject to work stoppages. Under the essential service approach, the relevant legislation empowers a third party, generally the labour board, to designate those services that are "essential" and, therefore, unable to be withdrawn in a strike. In some instances the essential service designation can cover virtually all of the work and workers at issue. Finally, governments have often passed emergency legislation to end public sector strikes or lockouts that would otherwise be permitted.

Though it has been found that permitting strikes is associated with a higher strike incidence (Gunderson, Hebdon, and Hyatt 1996), removing this right does not eliminate strikes, as illegal strikes still occur in these circumstances. Furthermore, researchers have found that removing the right to strike from the public sector leads to the conflict being expressed through other means such as grievances, political activities, and job action (Hebdon and Stern 1998, 2003). Each of these three alternatives to work stoppages has advantages and disadvantages. Thus, suppressing or controlling the right to strike may reduce work stoppages but may also produce other negative consequences: illegal job action as well as increased conflict in other areas of the labour-management relationship.

In Alberta, Saskatchewan, Ontario, and Newfoundland and Labrador, strike and lockout options are available with no essential services restrictions. However, in Alberta there is legislative authority in situations where a strike is found to create an "emergency" (AB LRC, s. 112), and in Ontario the Education Relations Commission may provide advice about whether a work stoppage will jeopardize the successful completion of courses of study (ON EA, s. 57.2). In Quebec and Nova Scotia, strike and lockout options are available for provincial bargaining and without essential services restrictions, although in Quebec the strike and lockout option can be exercised in relation to salary negotiations only for salaries that are payable in the first year of the collective agreement. In British Columbia and New Brunswick, strikes and lockouts are available with essential services restrictions. There is no strike and lockout option in Manitoba or Prince Edward Island (Table 9).

TABLE 9
Regulation of Work Stoppages

Unrestricted Access	Controlled Work Stoppage	No Access to Work Stoppage
Saskatchewan	Alberta[a]	Manitoba
Nova Scotia	British Columbia	Prince Edward Island
Newfoundland and Labrador	Ontario[b]	
	Quebec	
	New Brunswick	

[a] Where a strike is found to create an "emergency" (*AB LRC*, s. 112).
[b] Where completion of the students' course of study is in jeopardy (*ON EA*, s. 57.2).

The discussion below reviews each of these three models, and concludes with a comparison of the statutory provisions relating to voluntary interest arbitration, which is available as an alternative dispute resolution option in most provinces.

Dispute Resolution with and without Options for Work Stoppages

Unrestricted access to work stoppage

Full strike and lockout options, that is, strike and lockout options that are not subject to essential services restrictions, are available in six provinces: Alberta, Saskatchewan, Ontario, Quebec, Nova Scotia, and Newfoundland and Labrador. In Alberta, Ontario, and Quebec, the strike and lockout option is regulated by the general labour relations statute. In Alberta, these provisions apply with no exceptions or modifications for teacher collective bargaining. In Ontario these provisions also generally apply, with the exception of the definition of strike. In place of the definition of strike in the general labour relations statute, the *Education Act* (*ON EA*, s. 277.2(4)(b)) defines "strike" for purposes of teacher collective bargaining to include

> ... any action or activity by teachers in combination or in concert or in accordance with a common understanding that is designed or may reasonably be expected to have the effect of curtailing, restricting, limiting or interfering with,
>
> (i)   the normal activities of a board or its employees,
>
> (ii) the operation or functioning of one or more of a board's schools or of one or more of the programs in one or more schools of a board, including but not limited to programs involving co-instructional activities, or

(iii) the performance of the duties of teachers set out in the Act or the regulations under it, including any withdrawal of services or work to rule by teachers acting in combination or in concert or in accordance with a common understanding.

In addition, the Education Relations Commission exists to advise the government when the continuation of a strike or lockout "will place in jeopardy the successful completion of courses of study by the affected pupils" (*ON EA*, s. 57.2(2)).

In Quebec and Nova Scotia, the strike and lockout option is available in relation to provincial bargaining but not in relation to local bargaining. As noted above, in Quebec the strike and lockout option in relation to salaries can be exercised only for salaries payable in the first year of the collective agreement (*PQ LC*, s. 111.14).[23] Although the K–12 education sector in Quebec is not generally subject to the essential services provisions of the *Labour Code*, the Conseil des services essentiels has the authority to make an ad hoc ruling that a "conflict is or is likely to be prejudicial to a service to which the public is entitled" and to "make an order to ensure that a service to which the public is entitled is available" (*PQ LC*, s. 111.17). In Nova Scotia, the strike and lockout option is also available only in relation to provincial bargaining and is regulated by the *NS TCBA*, s. 20(1). Principals and vice-principals, who are included in teacher bargaining units, may withdraw their services after they have provided for the safe dismissal of pupils and for the security and maintenance of the building, and have reported to the person in charge of the school system that these necessary provisions have been completed (*NS TCBA*, s. 34(5)).

In Saskatchewan, the legislation does not contain provisions that expressly regulate the strike or lockout option. As discussed above, there are two mutually exclusive collective bargaining processes: mediation and conciliation. When the mediation route is selected by the teachers' bargaining agent, arbitration is available at the request of either party. When the conciliation route is selected by the teachers' bargaining agent, arbitration is available only if jointly requested by the parties. Thus, the strike and lockout option is available only in connection with the conciliation route (*SK EA*, ss. 239(1), 241-260; BCPSEA 2003, 102).

Controlled work stoppages

Two provinces currently have strike and lockout options with formal essential services restrictions: British Columbia and New Brunswick. In British Columbia, strikes and lockouts may only occur at the provincial level, and work stoppages are subject to the *Labour Relations Code*'s essential services provisions. The chair of the Labour Relations Board may investigate whether or not a dispute poses a threat to the health, safety, or welfare of the residents of British Columbia, or to the provision of educational programs to students and eligible children under the *School Act*. This investigation may be initiated either by application of a party to the labour dispute or by the chair of the Board, and the results of the investigation are reported to the Minister of Labour. It is up to the Minister to determine whether or not a labour dispute poses these threats, and the Minister may do so either after receiving the chair's report or on his or her own initiative. If the Minister considers that the labour dispute poses a threat, the Minister may direct the Labour Relations Board to designate as essential the services necessary to prevent the threat. When the Minister makes such direction to the Board, the associate chair of the Mediation Division may appoint one or more mediators to assist the parties to reach an agreement on essential services designations (*BC LRC*, ss. 72(1)-(3)).

In New Brunswick, teacher work stoppages are subject to the essential services provisions of the *Public Service Labour Relations Act*. The employer may advise the Labour and Employment Board and the bargaining agent that they consider the services provided by the bargaining unit to be in whole or in part essential in the interest of the health, safety, or security of the public. The Board provides the employer and the bargaining agent with an opportunity to reach agreement identifying which services are essential, the level of service to be maintained, and the positions in the bargaining unit to be designated to ensure delivery of the services. If an agreement cannot be reached, the Board determines these issues after receiving evidence and representations from the parties (*NB PSLRA*, s. 43.1).

No access to work stoppage

Manitoba and Prince Edward Island are the two provinces that do not provide for lawful teacher strikes or lockouts. In these provinces, binding interest arbitration is the only dispute resolution mechanism available in the event of impasse. In Manitoba, either party may initiate interest arbitration proceedings in a first round of collective bargaining. Thereafter, the collective agreement must either include or be deemed to include provisions for the arbitration of all collective bargaining disputes. The parties may agree to have the dispute resolved by a single arbitrator, and if they do not agree, the dispute is referred to an arbitration board (*MB PSA*, ss. 100, 102-103). The governing statutes, the *MB PSA* and the *MB LRA*, do not impose any substantive restrictions on the arbitration process. In particular, they do not limit the issues or evidence that may be considered, nor do they impose criteria that must be considered.

In Prince Edward Island, an arbitration board is established at the request of either party or if the Minister of Labour is of the opinion that an arbitration board should be established. The regulation prescribes the following criteria on the basis of which the arbitration board is required to make its award (*PEI IPR*, ss. 37, 43(1)):

(a) the relationship of income and other benefits for teachers to those available to teachers in other Atlantic provinces, giving appropriate consideration to the varying provincial economic capacities, including available assistance from outside sources;

(b) the trends and inter-relationship of pay and other factors within various professional and non-professional groups in both the private and public sectors;

(c) the requirement to obtain and retain competent teachers within the school system;

(d) the relationship between pay, professional qualifications and responsibility; and

(e) such other factors as may be relevant including conditions of work and fringe benefits.

As noted above, in Quebec, Nova Scotia, and British Columbia, legal work stoppages may not occur at the local level. In Quebec, the parties have access to a mediation-arbitration process for resolving local collective bargaining disputes. The mediator-arbitrator can decide not to issue a report, in which case she or he is required to make a report on her or his recommendations to the parties and to release this report to the public as well (*PQ ARPN*, ss. 62-65). It is also open to the parties to agree to another method of resolving the dispute (ibid., s. 66). In Nova Scotia, binding arbitration is the option available to resolve disputes at the local bargaining level (*NS TCBA*, s. 19). In British Columbia, matters that cannot be resolved at local negotiations are sent to the provincial table (*BC PELRA*, s. 8(3)).

Ad hoc intervention in work stoppages

Governments in several provinces have resorted to ad hoc back-to-work legislation to bring an end to teacher disputes, in some cases within days of a partial withdrawal of services, and before a full strike or lockout has occurred. In some cases the legislation renews an expired collective agreement, in others it legislatively imposes new collective agreement terms or directs interest arbitration if the parties are unable to settle within a specified period of time. Ontario and British Columbia are the jurisdictions that have most often resorted to these forms of direct government intervention in disputes. Ontario has imposed ad hoc back-to-work legislation nine times in individual school districts since the early 1990s.[24] Three times since 1998, British Columbia has passed ad hoc legislation imposing provincial collective agreements, thereby ending bargaining disputes. In the first instance, no work stoppage had yet occurred at the time a collective agreement was statutorily imposed (*Public Education*

Collective Agreement Act, S.B.C. 1998, c. 41). In 2002, a lengthy partial withdrawal of services, in accordance with essential service restrictions, had taken place when the legislation was passed (*Education Services Collective Agreement Act*, S.B.C. 2002, c. 1). In the most recent instance, in 2005, the government introduced ad hoc legislation after three days of a controlled strike, again subject to essential service limitations (*Teachers' Collective Agreement Act*, S.B.C. 2005, c. 27).[25] As noted above, Alberta has also used this type of legislation recently (*AB ESSA*).

CONCLUSION

This chapter provides an overview of the wide range of statutory structures for teacher collective bargaining currently existing across Canada. This comparative introduction offers both context and a reference point for the jurisdiction-specific analyses that follow.

NOTES

The authors thank Konrad Pola for his able research assistance.

1. This provincial jurisdiction is established in the *Constitution Act, 1867* (U.K.), 30 & 31 Vict., c. 3, s. 93, reprinted in R.S.C. 1985, App. II, No. 5.
2. The provinces in geographical order from west to east are British Columbia, Alberta, Saskatchewan, Manitoba, Ontario, Quebec, New Brunswick, Nova Scotia, Prince Edward Island, and Newfoundland and Labrador. Although some K–12 education is regulated by the federal and territorial governments, this study does not include these exceptional instances, instead focusing on provincially regulated K–12 public schools. Nor does this study cover substitute teachers or First Nations education. Unless otherwise noted, the information in this chapter is current to 30 December 2010.
3. The decision to focus on these questions was informed by Don Wright's analysis and the questions he posed in his review of teacher collective bargaining in British Columbia (2003, 2004).
4. See, for example, Wright (2004); Alberta Commission on Learning (2003), recommendations 75 and 81; Manitoba Education and Training (1996); and Paroian (1996).
5. Appendix A also provides information about the inclusion of principals and vice-principals in teacher collective bargaining, and about the existence of separate teacher regulatory bodies.
6. In Alberta and Ontario, bargaining rights are legally held by the provincial teacher organizations, although in practice local teacher affiliates of the provincial organizations are significantly involved in collective bargaining with school boards (see BCPSEA 2007, 64, 68; Lawton et al. 1999, 50; Ontario Ministry of Education 2006, 5; Reshef 2007, 681). In Manitoba, bargaining rights are held by local teachers (see BCPSEA 2003, 66).
7. For further discussion, see Williams-Whitt (2012) in this volume.
8. See Rose (2012) and Shilton (2012) for further discussion.

9. Matters negotiated at the intersectoral provincial level are salaries, pension plans, group insurance plans, regional disparities, and parental rights. Matters negotiated at the provincial sectorial level are job security, workload, and other major working conditions (Management Negotiating Committee for English-Language School Boards 2003, 48).

10. In Ontario there is also an umbrella professional teachers' association, the Ontario Teachers' Federation, which is constituted by the four other teacher associations and which has never had any collective bargaining role or responsibilities (*Teaching Profession Act*, R.S.O. 1990, c. T.2).

11. In Saskatchewan, the school boards and the Conseil scolaire are designated by statute as the employer bargaining agent: *SK EA*, ss. 1 (definitions of "local agreement" and "conseil scolaire"), 235(1), 236(1). The Conseil scolaire Fransaskois is a corporation established to exercise governance authority in relation to francophone education. In Nova Scotia, the school boards are designated as the employer in relation to local bargaining matters: *NS TCBA*, ss. 2(h)(i),(ii).

12. Note that the British Columbia Supreme Court ruled, in April 2011, that certain exclusions from the scope of bargaining set out in the *BC SA* (ss. 27 (3)(d)-(j), (5) and (6)) are unconstitutional and invalid because the government, by removing these traditionally negotiated matters from the scope of bargaining, had violated teachers' *Charter*-protected freedom of association. The Court suspended the declaration of invalidity for one year (*British Columbia Teachers' Federation v. British Columbia*, 2011 BCSC 469).

13. For a further discussion of this legislation, see Reshef (2007).

14. For further discussion, see Slinn (2012).

15. In British Columbia, the Minister of Labour may appoint a mediation officer or a special mediator: *BC LRC*, ss. 74(3), 76; in Alberta, the Minister of Labour may require the appointment of a mediator: *AB LRC*, ss. 65(1)(b), 2(b) (the appointment is mandatory); in Saskatchewan, the chairperson of the Educational Relations Board may appoint a mediator: *SK EA*, s. 240; in Manitoba, the Minister of Labour may appoint a mediator: *MB LRA*, s. 95(2).

16. In Nova Scotia, the collective bargaining parties may request the assistance of a conciliation officer. The provisions relating to mediation also state that the report of a mediator may be deemed to be the report of a conciliation officer.

17. In Saskatchewan, a conciliation board may be established either at the request of a party or at the initiative of the Educational Relations Board; *SK EA*, ss. 251-253. In New Brunswick, a conciliation board process can be initiated either by the parties or by the Labour and Employment Board: *NB PSLRA*, s. 49. In Newfoundland and Labrador, a conciliation board may be established either at the request of a party or at the initiative of the Minister of Employment and Labour Relations: *NL TCBA*, s. 14(1).

18. In Manitoba, the government is responsible for initiating the conciliation process: *MB LRA*, s. 97. In Ontario, the minister asks the parties to recommend members for a conciliation board when conciliation with a conciliation officer fails to result in a collective agreement: *ON LRA*, s. 22(1).

19. Fact-finding used to be an important feature of Ontario's teacher collective bargaining system; see, for example, Downie (1992). The fact-finding component was eliminated when the process for teacher collective bargaining in Ontario underwent significant change in 1997. See Shilton (2012) and Rose (2012).

20. In British Columbia, the appointment of a commission is at the discretion of the Minister of Labour, acting either on his or her own initiative or in response to an application: *BC LRC*, s. 79. In New Brunswick, the Labour and Employment Board may on the request of a party appoint a commissioner instead of a conciliator, and the commissioner has the power to report on the findings and make recommendations for the resolution of the dispute: *NB PSLRA*, s. 60.1. For Manitoba see *MB LRA*, s. 113(1)-(5); for Ontario see *ON LRA*, s. 137.

21. For further discussion, see Slinn (2012).

22. In Saskatchewan, voluntary arbitration is available where the teachers' bargaining agent selects the conciliation route: *SK EA*, ss. 239(1), 244-245, 260 (2).

23. Salaries payable in the second and third years of the collective agreement are determined by government regulation if the parties cannot reach agreement: *PQ PNCAPPS*, ss. 52-56. The parties must try mediation before the strike and lockout option can be exercised, but the mediator has no jurisdiction in relation to salaries: *PQ ARPN*, s. 46; *PQ LC*, s. 111.11.

24. *Windsor Teachers Dispute Settlement Act, 1993*, S.O. 1993, c. 42; *East Parry Sound Board of Education and Teachers Dispute Settlement Act, 1993*, S.O. 1993, c. 24; *Lambton County Board of Education and Teachers Dispute Settlement Act, 1993*, S.O. 1993, c. 22; *Lennox and Addington County Board of Education and Teachers Dispute Settlement Act, 1997*, S.O. 1997, c. 1; *Back to School Act, 1998*, S.O. 1998, c. 13; *Back to School Act (Hamilton-Wentworth District School Board), 2000*, S.O. 2000, c. 23; *Back to School Act (Toronto and Windsor), 2001*, S.O. 2001, c. 1; *Back to School Act (Simcoe Muskoka Catholic District School Board, 2002)*, S.O. 2002, c. 20; *Back-to-School Act (Toronto Catholic Elementary) and Education and Provincial Schools Negotiations Amendment Act*, S.O. 2003, c. 2. See Shilton (2012) and Rose (2012) for further discussion of these events.

25. See Slinn (2012) for further discussion.

REFERENCES

Alberta Commission on Learning. 2003. *Every Child Learns, Every Child Succeeds: Report and Recommendations*. http://education.alberta.ca/media/413413/commissionreport.pdf.

British Columbia Public School Employers' Association (BCPSEA). 2003. *Teacher Collective Bargaining in BC: Exploring Alternatives, Assessing Options: Resource/Discussion Paper*. Vancouver, BC.

—. 2007. *Provincial Bargaining Structure in Canada*. Vancouver, BC. http://www.naen.org/CB%20Systems/Canadian%20Provincial%20Bargaining%20Structure%20.pdf.

Downie, B.M. 1992. *Strikes, Disputes and Policymaking: Resolving Impasses in Ontario Education*. Kingston, ON: IRC Press.

Gunderson, M., R. Hebdon, and D. Hyatt. 1996. "Collective Bargaining in the Public Sector." *American Economic Review* 86: 315-26.

Hebdon, R. and R. Stern. 1998. "Tradeoffs among Expressions of Industrial Conflict: Public Sector Strike Bans and Grievance Arbitrations." *Industrial and Labour Relations Review* 51: 204-21.

—. 2003. "Do Public Sector Strike Bans Really Prevent Conflict?" *Industrial Relations* 42: 493-512.

Korbin, J. 1993. *Commission of Inquiry into the Public Service and Public Sector: Final Report*, Vol. 2. Victoria, BC.

Lawton, S.B., G. Bedard, D. MacLellan, and X. Li. 1999. *Teachers' Unions in Canada*. Calgary, AB: Detselig Enterprises.

Management Negotiating Committee for English-Language School Boards. 2003. *Comprehensive Manual for Canadian Educational Negotiators Conference 2003*. http://www.qesba.qc.ca/documents/educationalnegotiators/Comprehensive%20material%202003.pdf.

Manitoba Education and Training. 1996. *Report of the Teacher Collective Bargaining and Compensation Review Committee*. Winnipeg: Manitoba Education and Training.

Muir, J. 1969. "Canada." In *Teachers Unions and Associations: A Comparative Study*, edited by A. Blum. Urbana: University of Illinois Press.

Ontario Ministry of Education. 2005a. "First Time Provincial Dialogue Yields Student Dividends." Accessed 1 May 2011. http://news.ontario.ca/archive/en/2005/04/14/First-time-provincial-dialogue-yields-student-dividends.html.

—. 2005b. "Government Reports Major Progress Made on Teacher Agreements." Accessed 1 May 2011. http://news.ontario.ca/archive/en/2005/06/02/Government-Reports-Major-Progress-Made-On-Teacher-Agreements.html.

—. 2006. *Labour Relations in the Elementary/Secondary Education Sector*. http://www.naen.org/CB%20Systems/Ontario%20Labour%20Relations%20Overview%20Oct%202006.pdf.

Paroian, D. 1996. *Review of the School Boards'/Teachers' Collective Negotiations Process in Ontario*. Toronto, ON. http://www.edu.gov.on.ca/eng/document/reports/collect.html.

Reshef, Y. 2007. "Government Intervention in Public Sector Industrial Relations: Lessons from the Alberta Teachers' Association." *Journal of Labor Research* 28: 677-96.

Rose, J.B. 2002. "The Assault on School Teacher Bargaining in Ontario." *Industrial Relations* 57(1): 100-126.

—. 2012 "The Evolution of Teacher Bargaining in Ontario." In *Dynamic Negotiations: Teacher Labour Relations in Canadian Elementary and Secondary Education*, edited by S. Slinn and A. Sweetman, 199-220. Montreal and Kingston: Queen's Policy Studies Series, McGill-Queen's University Press.

Shilton, E. 2012. "Collective Bargaining for Teachers in Ontario: Central Power, Local Responsibility." In *Dynamic Negotiations: Teacher Labour Relations in Canadian Elementary and Secondary Education*, edited by S. Slinn and A. Sweetman, 221-246. Montreal and Kingston: Queen's Policy Studies Series, McGill-Queen's University Press.

Slinn, S. 2012 "Conflict without Compromise: The Case of Public Sector Teacher Bargaining in British Columbia." In *Dynamic Negotiations: Teacher Labour Relations in Canadian Elementary and Secondary Education*, edited by S. Slinn and A. Sweetman, 81-123. Montreal and Kingston: Queen's Policy Studies Series, McGill-Queen's University Press.

Thomason, T. 1995. "Labour Relations in Primary and Secondary Education." In *Public Sector Collective Bargaining in Canada: Beginning of the End or End of the Beginning*, edited by G. Swimmer and M. Thompson. Kingston, ON: IRC Press.

Williams-Whitt, K. 2012. "Oil and Ideology: The Transformation of K–12 Bargaining in Alberta." In *Dynamic Negotiations: Teacher Labour Relations in Canadian Elementary and Secondary Education,* edited by S. Slinn and A. Sweetman, 125-159. Montreal and Kingston: Queen's Policy Studies Series, McGill-Queen's University Press.

Wright, D. 2003. *Towards a Better Teacher Bargaining Model in British Columbia.* Report to Honourable Graham Bruce, November 2003. Victoria, BC: Ministry of Skills Development and Labour. http://www.labour.gov.bc.ca/pubs/teacher/teachers-final-report.pdf.

—. 2004. *Voice, Accountability, and Dialogue: Recommendations for an Improved Collective Bargaining System for Teacher Contracts in British Columbia.* Report of the Commission to Review Teacher Collective Bargaining, D. Wright, Commissioner. Victoria, BC: Ministry of Skills Development and Labour. http://www.labour.gov.bc.ca/pubs/teacher/04_dec_final.pdf.

APPENDIX A

TABLE A1
Summary Table of Teacher Collective Bargaining Structures in Canada

Province	Governing Statute(s)	Bargaining Structure[a]	Teacher Bargaining Agent(s)[b]	Employer Bargaining Agent[c]	Principals and Vice-Principals in Unit[d]	Separate Regulatory College	Statutory Limits on Bargaining Scope[e]	Work Stoppage Model[f]	Dispute Resolution[g]
BC	Combination	Two-tier	British Columbia Teachers' Federation*	British Columbia Public School Employers' Association*	No	Yes	Yes	Controlled provincial	Mediation Fact-finding Industrial inquiry commission
AB	General labour relations	Local	Alberta Teachers' Association	School boards	Yes	No	No	Controlled local	Mediation Voluntary interest arbitration
SK	General education	Two-tier	Saskatchewan Teachers' Federation* Committee; affiliates	Provincial bargaining committee; school boards*	Yes	No	Yes	Unfettered	Mediation Conciliation Voluntary interest arbitration Compulsory interest arbitration
MB	Combination	Local	Manitoba Teachers' Society; affiliates	School boards*	Yes	No	No	Prohibited	Mediation Conciliation Industrial inquiry commission Compulsory interest arbitration
ON	Combination	Local	Elementary Teachers' Federation of Ontario; Ontario Secondary School Teachers' Federation; Ontario English Catholic Teachers' Association; l'Association des enseignantes et des enseignants franco-ontariens*	School boards	No	Yes	Yes	Controlled local	Conciliation Mediation Inquiry Voluntary interest arbitration

	Bargaining structure	Teachers' bargaining agent	Management bargaining agent	Inclusion of principals and vice-principals	Scope of bargaining	Work stoppage controls	Dispute resolution
QU	Combination	Quebec Provincial Association of Teachers; Fédération des syndicats de l'enseignement; Local and regional affiliates.	Provincial negotiating committee*	No	No	Controlled provincial	Mediation; Voluntary interest arbitration
NB	Provincial	New Brunswick Teachers' Federation	Board of Management*	Yes	No	Controlled provincial	Conciliation; Commissioner; Voluntary interest arbitration
NS	Two-tier	Nova Scotia Teachers' Union*	Province school boards*	No	No	Unfettered provincial	Mediation; Conciliation; Voluntary interest arbitration; Compulsory interest arbitration (local)
PEI	General education	Prince Edward Island Teachers' Federation*	Education Negotiating Agency*	Yes	No	Prohibited	Conciliation; Compulsory interest arbitration
NL	Special K–12	Newfoundland and Labrador Teachers' Association*	School board committees*	No	No	Unfettered	Conciliation; Voluntary interest arbitration

Notes:

[a] **Bargaining structure.** For BC: *Public Education Labour Relations Act*, R.S.B.C. 1996, c. 382, ss. 2(b), 7, 8 (*BC PELRA*); for AB: *Labour Relations Code*, R.S.A. 2000, c. L-1 (AB LRC); for SK: *Education Act, 1995*, S.S. 1995, c. E-0.2 (*SK EA*), ss. 2, 234(1)-(2), 235(1)-(2); for MB: *Public Schools Act*, C.C.S.M. c. P250 (*MB PSA*), s. 97(1) [definition of "party"]; for ON: *Education Act*, R.S.O. 1990, c. E-2 (ON EA), ss. 277.4(1); for QC: *An Act Respecting the Process of Negotiation of the Collective Agreements in the Public and Parapublic Sectors*, R.S.Q. c.R-8.2 (*PQ PNCAPPS*), ss. 44, 45, 70.1; for NB: *Public Service Labour Relations Act*, R.S.N.B. 1973, c. P-25, (*NB PSLRA*), s. 1 - "employer"; For NS: *Teachers' Collective Bargaining Act*, R.S.N.S. 1989, c. 460 (NS TCBA), s. 2(h); for PEI: *Instructional Personnel Regulations*, P.E.I. Reg. EC481/98 (*PEI IPR*), s. 24; for NL: *Teachers' Collective Bargaining Act*, R.S.N.L. 1990, c. T-3 (NL TCBA), ss. 10, 11.

[b] **Teachers' bargaining agent.** *Denotes that the teachers' bargaining agent is named in the statute. For BC: *BC PELRA*, s. 6; for AB: *BCPSEA* 2003, 64, 68; for SK: *SK EA*, ss. 234(1), 235(2); for MB: *MB PSA*, s. 97(1) [definition of "party"]; for ON: *ON EA*, s. 277.3(1),(2); for QC: *PQ PNCAPPS*, ss. 26, 27; for NB: www.nbtf-fenb.nb.ca; for NS: *NS TCBA*, ss. 2(a),(u),(v); for PEI: *PEI IPR*, s. 25; for NL: *NL TCBA*, s. 9.

[c] **Management bargaining agent.** *Denotes that the management bargaining agent is named in the statute. For BC: *BC PELRA*, ss. 1, 4; for SK: *SK EA*, ss. 234(2), 235(1). 236(1); for MB: *MB PSA*, s. 97(1) [definition of "party"]; for ON: *ON EA*, ss. 277.3(1); for QC: *PQ PNCAPPS*, ss. 30, 31; for NB: *NB PSLRA*, s. 61; for NS: *NS TCBA*, s. 2(h); for PEI: *PEI IPR*, s. 24; for NL: *NL TCBA*, ss. 10-11.

[d] **Inclusion of principals and vice-principals.** For AB: *Alberta Labour Relations Board*, Information Bulletin #9, 13 March 2008; for SK: *SK EA*, s. 2 [definitions of "principal" and "teacher"]; for MB: *MB PSA*, s. 98(2); for ON: *ON EA*, s. 277.1(1) [definition of "teacher"]; for NB: *Education Act*, S.N.B. 1997, c. E-1.12 (*NB EA*), s. 1 [definition of "teacher"]; for NS: *NS TCBA*, s. 2(u); for PEI: *School Act*, R.S.P.E.I. 1988, c. S-2.1, (*PEI SA*), s. 1(a).

[e] **Scope of bargaining.** For BC: *School Act*, R.S.B.C. 1996, c. 412 (*BC SA*), ss. 27(2),(3),(5),(6); for SK: *SK EA*, s. 237(6).

[f] **Work stoppage controls.** For BC: *Labour Relations Code*, R.S.B.C. 1996, c. 244 (*BC LRC*) [essential services], s. 72(2.1); for AB: *AB LRC*, ss. 112-113 [emergencies]; for ON: *ON EA*, s. 57.2; for QC: *Labour Code*, R.S.Q. c. C-27 (*PQ LC*), ss. 111.14, 111.17; for NB: *NB PSLRA*, s. 43.1 [essential services].

[g] **Dispute resolution.** For BC: *BC LRA*, ss. 74, 76, 77, 79; for AB: *AB LRC*, ss. 64-65, 94; for SK: *SK EA*, ss. 240, 243-260; for MB: *MB PSA*, s. 100 and *Labour Relations Act*, CCSM. c. L10, ss. 95-113; for ON: *ON EA*, ss. 277.2(1), *Labour Relations Act, 1995*, S.O. 1995, c. 1, Sch. A, ss. 18-21, 37, 40; for QC: *PQ PNCAPPS*, ss. 46-48, 62-64; for NB: *NB PSLRA*, ss. 47, 60.1, 66; for NS: *NS TCBA*, ss. 21, 23, 26; for PEI: *PEI IPR*, ss. 34, 37; for NL: *NL TCBA*, ss. 13, 21.

Chapter 3

THE GREAT DIVIDE: SCHOOL POLITICS AND LABOUR RELATIONS IN BRITISH COLUMBIA BEFORE AND AFTER 1972

Thomas Fleming

The troubled state of labour relations in British Columbia's public school sector is certainly not new. It has been going on for more than 40 years and is part of a deeper struggle for control of public education that can be traced back to the 1960s and to postwar changes in how schools were organized and managed. The tumult surrounding collective bargaining in schools is thus something more than a result of the traditional kinds of differences that separate parties during negotiations. Conflict in British Columbia's school sector far transcends conventional matters to do with salaries, job protection, and conditions of work. Instead, it may be traced to circumstances and events embedded in the mainframe of provincial school history, which include the post-1945 emergence of governance structures that eventually proved adversarial in nature; the collapse of the school community and the disappearance of the sociability that historically lubricated educational relationships; a vacuum in power that followed the end of government's imperial age in schools; and the raging ambitions of the British Columbia Teachers' Federation (BCTF) to shape the province's social agenda.[1]

The turbulent organizational character of provincial schools—and the forces that brought it about—can best be illustrated by comparing the two distinct historical eras that comprise the provincial system (Fleming 2003). The first period chronicles the rise of provincial education from

Dynamic Negotiations: Teacher Labour Relations in Canadian Elementary and Secondary Education, ed. S. Slinn and A. Sweetman. Montreal and Kingston: Queen's Policy Studies Series, McGill-Queen's University Press.

1872 to 1972, a time of remarkable tranquility and success when public schools basked in the warm appreciation of satisfied communities and when educational decisions were routinely weighed inside the educational civil service with little, if any, political interference or oversight. This sedate era vanished, however, as the counter-cultural revolutions of the 1960s and 1970s transformed society and its institutions, including its most conservative agency—the public school.

A new era began in 1972 that has continued to the present. It has proved to be a far different chapter in public schooling—a world characterized by schools in politics and politics in schools, the demands of educational special interest groups, and the gradual estrangement of organizations essential to the governance and management of provincial schools. Forty years of school wars since the early 1970s have taken their toll. Long-standing relationships between government and the schools have crumbled. Relationships between the Education Ministry, the BCTF, and the British Columbia School Trustees Association (BCSTA) have likewise collapsed. Decades of hostility and distrust in the educational sector have also produced immense public fatigue and skepticism with all things educational, as well as an impasse in collective bargaining. Fifteen years of government-legislated contracts underscore the ruptured condition of collective bargaining.

The following discussion attempts to examine the problematic state of educational labour relations within the recently troubled history of provincial schools, as well as the larger history of public schooling since 1872. The discussion is organized into three sections. The first and second sections sketch out key developments that defined the pre- and post-1972 school eras, the structural and other relationships that changed over time, and the impact of these changes on the provincial system. The third section examines the current challenges facing the public system, and the prospects for government, teachers, and the schools in a system marked by organizational disconnections and the school's diminishing place in the province's institutional life.

THE COMMON SCHOOL'S ASCENDANCY

The institution we know today as public schooling was born in the second half of the nineteenth century in a floodtide of civic optimism about the exhilarating possibilities of state-supported education. In the popular imagination that ignited Victorian liberalism on both sides of the Atlantic, aspirations for the common school seemed boundless. Schools could prepare children for the world of work, assimilate the poor and foreign born, civilize society in general, inculcate in pupils a sense of provincial and national identity, and prevent crime, delinquency, and idleness by keeping youngsters off the streets. In the face of untrammelled industrial and urban growth—where family, church, and community seemed to falter in providing social stability—public schooling promised to provide a state of social equilibrium by equalizing children's social and intellectual development, and by providing a level of socialization that would minimize family and individual differences (McDonald 1978, 98).

A simple but effective governance and administrative system underpinned the public school's success. Confederation in 1871 conferred complete statutory control over schools to provincial authorities. Accordingly, the province was empowered to assign school texts and set the curriculum; examine, appoint, and inspect teachers; define, appeal, alter, or amend school district boundaries; allocate funds for school support; and intervene in any matter at any time for the good of the system. All the functional levers required for directing the course of public education were in the hands of the province. The *Public Schools Act* of 1872 made it clear that the government's Education Office would govern and administer the system from on high (Fleming 2001a, 161). Local boards, comprised of elected trustees, would actually deliver school programs or services in communities around the province and, in so doing, would represent community interests and priorities. This separation of responsibilities was immensely practical. Given the province's vast size of 950,000 square kilometres, its daunting and mountainous topography, great distances between settlements, and no more than a handful of roads that pushed hesitantly into the province's interior, it was impossible for educational government to do anything but manage the new school system from afar.

Because government's statutory powers far exceeded the province's "hands-on" capacity to influence local educational events, provincial educational officials designed an uncomplicated management information system that would let them see into the state of schools—and administer them—from afar. Using the teachers' register as the system's basic instrument of record, an empire of statistical information was constructed that could provide class level, school level, district level, and provincial level portraits of pupils' attendance and progress; the number of reports sent to parents and school officials; the number of youngsters disciplined, suspended, expelled, or truant; and sundry matters—on a daily, weekly, monthly, or yearly basis as required (Fleming and Raptis 2005, 183). In effect, the entire institution of provincial schooling could be managed on paper—and was—quite successfully (Fleming 2001a). For nearly 100 years, it was a system of school governance that functioned by remote control. Nevertheless, the public was well pleased with its schools and its educators. Schools were accessible and respected, and they fulfilled expectations that appear remarkably modest by today's reckoning.

Schools before Politics

From the system's earliest beginnings, Education Office staff in the provincial headquarters and trustees scattered in small educational parishes across the province understood and appreciated the mutuality of their interests. Government knew it was dependent on trustees and local communities to achieve its educational mission. More particularly, the Education Office relied on trustees to provide educational facilities, govern local schools, hire and pay teachers, and provide the wood, water, and janitorial services that schools required. Alternatively, trustees were no less dependent on government. Trustees knew that the government's men could be counted on to help provision a local school, pay for and round up a teacher in districts where taxes would not cover a teacher's salary, push for a capital allowance to improve schools in good times, and generally keep volunteer trustees on the right side of departmental rules and regulations (Fleming 2001b, 36). Certainly, until the late 1960s—in some instances even later—relationships between government and many trustee boards were closer than they were between many trustee boards and their own provincial association (London 2005, 207).

The absence of politics—most notably partisan politics—made relationships easier. The educational world was generally unsullied by political intrigue until the 1960s and, in this regard, credit is due to the wisdom of politicians of all stripes who remained content to leave public education "out of politics" for the best part of a century. Aside from the key position of superintendent of schools (after 1931 the deputy minister's position), an office where educators traditionally served "at the pleasure of the government," the education portfolio remained free of political influence.[2] As late as 1971, senior bureaucrats claimed that the imperial age of school administration remained intact and refused to acknowledge that partisan politics were seeping into school government, or that the province's educational officers would ever witness educational decisions being shaped by the rough hands of politicians.[3]

A long tradition of civil service authority and provincial history suggested otherwise. Since the nineteenth century, British Columbians had come to accept that most teachers and educational civil servants were "small-l" liberals who were progressive minded in their views about schools and society. Little could be considered radical about the ideas of most educators, who envisioned teaching as a "helping profession" and their work as an important part of social service (Lortie 1975). In the main, however, "professional" and "union" interests remained generally well balanced in the BCTF until the late 1960s. All in all, for the best part of a century, the province's educational cohort likely reflected in microcosm British Columbia's body politic, a bell curve that straddled the ideological centre with a slight inclination to the left.

In short, from the 1870s to the 1970s, British Columbia's public school system, like the province as a whole, had remained something of "a world in itself," to borrow Margaret Ormsby's description of British Columbia's historical tendency toward self-absorption (1958, 491 and 494). For 100 years, schools had been governed and administered out of the public spotlight by a small educational bureau of government that was imperial in its authority and unobtrusive in its practices. It was a system in which governance and administration were coterminous, where information and problems flowed upward from local communities and decisions and solutions flowed downward from headquarters. Over this time, public education remained government's least visible and "quietest" portfolio. All things considered, British Columbia's first century of schooling was spectacular in its educational attainments. Educators and the public agreed: British Columbia had built a provincial school system that was admired, envied in fact, by other jurisdictions across the nation (Fleming and Conway 2001).

FROM UNITY TO DISCORD

The Department of Education's *1971–1972 Annual Report* on the schools offered little intimation that the future of public schooling would differ much from its past. But changes were already underway that were beginning to rattle the very foundations of provincial schooling and the lives of those who managed and worked in public education. One of the most important of these changes was a structural change that government itself had initiated 25 years earlier. This was the decision to consolidate school districts and schools, which provincial authorities had undertaken in 1946 following University of British Columbia professor Max Cameron's (1945) inquiry into the state of school finance.

War's end prompted new questions about how to fulfill the promise of making secondary schooling available to everyone, a promise largely deferred by the Great Depression and World War II. The Depression had illuminated as never before immense disparities in educational opportunities available to children in urban and rural schools, and had spurred government to commission Cameron's study. School governance and finance, Cameron discovered, were in a shambles in many small districts. By 1944, the province's 650 school districts were governed by 437 school boards and 213 government-appointed official trustees, usually school inspectors (Johnson 1964, 125). Making matters more complicated was the fact that 590 of these districts were rural and, although they represented about half of all provincial schools, they enrolled no more than 23,000 youngsters, or slightly less than 20 percent of the approximately 125,000 children then enrolled in provincial schools (British Columbia Department of Education 1972, 68).

Cameron's report confirmed what was already well known—namely, that many of the province's rural districts were inefficient and too small in size to provide a tax base capable of sustaining secondary schools. British Columbia's immense geography, Cameron observed, would forever preclude the elimination of all differences, but he proposed that a massive amalgamation plan to reduce the number of districts and enlarge the size of those remaining could greatly reduce many inequalities. Cameron's recommendations were fast-tracked and translated into 1946 legislation with far-reaching effects. Following a year of planning and consultation, some 650 school districts were reorganized by the province in 1947 into 89 districts and, in 1971, reduced further to 74 (Johnson 1964, 97).

In its enthusiasm for educational equity and a more effective tax regime, government failed to contemplate consolidation's other effects, most notably its impact on school boards, along with the social and political strains that amalgamation might provoke between provincial and local authorities. Instead of safeguarding budgets of hundreds of dollars, as they historically had done, postwar boards began to oversee budgets of millions of dollars for local schools scattered across broader and more diverse jurisdictions. Board autonomy was also greatly enlarged in several respects after mid-century as the province relaxed some regulations, allowing trustees greater influence in shaping parts of the educational program. Taxation powers also enabled boards to shape school districts' identities through particular capital construction projects.

Furthermore, consolidation changed the locus of school leadership. Transition to larger governance units led to board demands for their own educational officers, demands the province finally acceded to in 1980. Local employment of district superintendents changed the entire alignment of the educational universe. It separated legislative and administrative authority—two elements of governance that had been unified for more than 100 years. This separation bespoke a fundamental disconnection at the core of public education's administrative structure. From now on, the people who would make the rules—and shape government's legislative agenda—would be distinct from the people who administered school legislation and regulations in local schools. The departure of district superintendents from government likewise ensured that school management would be more adversarial in character. Locally appointed superintendents were now naturally obliged to compete with each other—and do battle with provincial authorities—for their district's share of the public school budget. District leadership, in fact, had not simply shifted from provincial to district officers within professional ranks, it had also passed from professional and provincial ranks directly into the hands of district trustees, who now enjoyed full and unprecedented authority over their own locally selected and "paid for" superintendents.

Local employment proved equally costly to educational government. After 1980, the educational civil service increasingly found itself isolated from "the real world of the schools," as practitioners put it, sadly missing the close relationships, vital information, subtle grasp of events, and common sense that government school inspectors and superintendents out there "in the field" had supplied for nearly a century.

Broader school territories, grander schools, substantial staffs, and the post-1945 move to comprehensive high school education also forced district administrations to expand their operational scope, and to develop specialized structures for the many responsibilities schools were now shouldering—in effect, to bureaucratize. This process carried its own by-products: typically, changes in size and structure formalized relations between district offices and government, between district offices and their staffs, and between school districts, schools, and the families they served. Bureaucratization meant that rules, regulations, and policies—rather than experience or interpersonal relations—now prescribed behaviour, and not just at the provincial level but also at district and school levels. By creating larger governance units and more powerful school boards, consolidation also inadvertently created larger and more powerful local bargaining units for teachers, and formalized relations between teachers' locals and district offices.

In changing the territorial scale of school governance and administration across the province, consolidation created new and larger organizational structures unanticipated in early school legislation. The practices that subsequently evolved to manage and direct provincial schools included powerful teacher bargaining units at the district level, school district bureaucracies, a more ambitious provincial trustee association, and superintendents' offices "owned and operated" by local trustees. Altogether, Cameron's plan for consolidation no doubt produced a school system more equitable in educational and, especially, fiscal terms, but it was not without costs. It had unwittingly set into motion a train of events that gave rise to adversarial governance, and administrative and labour structures that would eventually dissolve the cooperative and harmonious relations that historically characterized the educational community.

Drift and Disappearance in Educational Government

A decline in the expertise and authority of educational government was the second development that greatly transformed the state of provincial schools after 1972 and contributed to schooling's currently haunted condition (Fleming 2003). Even before the 1960s drew to a close, it was apparent the old order of school governance and administration in British Columbia was unravelling. By the late 1960s, the Education Department had become an aging unit of government that had done little to renew itself since 1945. It had, in effect, become a "closed shop" where older officers selected younger officers much like themselves—and where advancement increasingly became a matter of "waiting one's turn." With scant guidance from ministers, and little supervision from the deputy's office, the department operated for much of the time without an explicit agenda, save for "more of the same."

Other factors were also hastening the demise of the established administrative order. The NDP's election in 1972 made matters worse for an

Education Department already surrendering its influence to politicians (Persky 1979, 138). The new government's distrust of its own educational civil service was soon made apparent when Education Minister Eileen Dailly, former teacher and Burnaby school trustee, moved aside the department's senior staff in favour of outside appointments and overturned long-standing traditions that vested authority in the civil service and district superintendents.

By the mid-1970s, the Education Department also seemed overcome by a constellation of new forces swirling around government. On one side, it found itself obliged to respond to an array of equity and access issues raised by long-neglected and disenfranchised constituencies who now saw fit to challenge the fairness of schools and their responsiveness to children with disabilities or "special needs" (Fleming 2003, 214). On the other, government was besieged by demands for different kinds of accountability to improve academic performance and cut school spending. In fact, for much of the time between 1975 and 1989, educational government was preoccupied with three tasks—resourcing a school mandate that seemed out of control, restraining school costs, and reforming instructional and other practices to improve public confidence in provincial education and school-community relations (Fleming 2010).

Incessant personnel changes at political and senior civil service levels in the 1980s and 1990s intensified the ministry's confusion. By the 1980s, the deputy's office and the minister's office were becoming organizational carousels where few elected or appointed officials remained for long. Between 1989 and 1996 seven deputies supervised the agenda for educational government. Education ministers did not prove much more durable. Between 1980 and 1996, 11 ministers were in charge of the portfolio, averaging about a year and a half each. Between 1997 and 2005, another seven ministers were handed responsibility for education, again averaging little more than a year in office. Small wonder the ministry seemed in a perpetual quest for its own identity and mission after the mid-1990s, particularly when key bureaucratic positions once held by educators were restaffed with individuals who knew something about administration but virtually nothing about education. By the time the 1990s gave way to a new millennium, such developments suggested to many educators that, aside from its financial function, the schools ministry was mostly peripheral to local school operations and, therefore, irrelevant in educational terms.

A Rising Tide of Teacher Power

The third and final factor that changed the character of education in British Columbia was the inexorable growth of teacher influence and power. Nothing influenced the educational world in the decades since 1972—or the relationships between teachers and government—quite as profoundly as two developments that occurred in teachers' ranks between 1961 and 1975, namely, the impressive rise in teachers' academic credentials and the BCTF's "conversion to partisanship," as political scientist Marlene Yri (1979) termed it. As these events became intertwined, they would forever change the face of public schooling in British Columbia.

Throughout much of public education's first century, scant academic preparation had sullied teachers' reputation and retarded the profession's development and status. It was traditional for teachers—especially in rural and elementary schools—to enter teaching upon the completion of grade 10 or, sometimes, junior matriculation, followed by a brief stint at normal school that might range anywhere from a mere two months to a year.[4]

By the early 1960s, however, the culture of teaching was changing. Increasing numbers of teachers were returning to Victoria College (until 1956 the Provincial Normal School in Victoria) or the University of British Columbia to upgrade their credentials. By 1972, the Education Department could proudly boast for the first time that the "percentage of teachers (including part-time teachers) with at least one university degree has gone over 60 percent," a jump of nearly 57 percent from the previous year (British Columbia Department of Education 1971–1972, D15). Credit for the post-1960 rise in teachers' qualifications could largely be attributed to the British Columbia Teachers' Federation. After mid-century, the BCTF had encouraged its members to burnish their educational qualifications through in-service, specialist training, and university study.

Portents of the BCTF's rising professionalism were manifest in 1961 when three BCTF representatives were appointed to each of the Education Department's curriculum committees for elementary and secondary schools. Such developments were carefully noted inside educational government. By 1966, the department's curriculum chief, the scholarly John Meredith, was lamenting that curriculum control, a responsibility long zealously guarded by provincial authorities, was passing out of the government's hands and into the hands of others (British Columbia Department of Education 1965–1966, F50).

Apart from straining relations with government, teachers were also making trustees nervous by their increasing involvement in school board elections. At the 1967 BCSTA convention, delegates passed a resolution requesting government to amend the *Public Schools Act* in such a way that would preclude teachers from election as school trustees, "if education is to serve society rather than its own establishment" (London 2005, 275). In 1971, the Social Credit government deemed teachers ineligible to run in school board elections, but the incoming NDP government overturned this prohibition the following year (ibid.).

Demonstrating a new zest for professional leadership, the BCTF convened an in-house educational commission on the future of public education and issued a 1968 report, *Involvement: The Key to Better Schools*. Among its 189 recommendations, the BCTF proclaimed the importance of many "big ticket" items including aspects of education delivery and assessment, greater decision-making authority for teachers, and full partnership between government and the BCTF in curricular policies and decisions.[5]

On a deeper level, however, the report was freighted with something else—a broad statement of intent outlining the pedagogical territory the BCTF was seeking to contest. *"Involvement,"* the BCTF-chronicler William Bruneau (1978, 71) claims, armed teachers with the "confidence that they could occupy the vacuum" in policy-making that was crippling the education department as legislative priorities shifted from grades 1 to 12 to the post-secondary sector. After nearly a half century of waiting in the wings of educational decision-making, teachers were now pushing their way onto centre stage with the *Involvement* report, angling for ways to unlock the structures that historically governed how schools were run, what was taught, what was learned, and what was measured. No longer would the BCTF be a "second-order structure," traditionally subservient to the primacy of powerful local associations as it had been since consolidation (Bruneau 1978, 22). By 1968, the BCTF had arrived as the province's most important educational organization, ensuring that teachers' power was as centralized as the power in educational government. According to Bruneau, 1968 signified "a great divide in the history of B.C. education … the start of a chain of events leading to overt political action in a provincial election campaign, and to unprecedented internal politicalization on a wide range of social-educational problems" (64).

Great ambitions were matched by more truculent behaviours on the part of teachers and their organizations. Glimmers of a change away from the old strategies of quiet persuasion and negotiation could be detected as far back as the early 1960s when teachers began to press school boards more openly to extend local bargaining beyond salaries and benefits by including workload and class size considerations. These demands reflected a shift in emphasis, historian James London suggests, from teachers who firmly believed their "prime concern … should be the furtherance of public education" to those who "steadfastly considered the main goal of their organization to be the economic welfare of its members" (2005, 273).

Teachers' aspirations, however, were transcending the achievement of more than contract provisions. Summing up his year in office, BCTF president J. Harley Robertson emphasized the membership's changing attitude in 1967: "Teachers have shown that they no longer wish to be cast in a submissive role in education. The growing militancy has led teachers directly to campaign on class size, to act politically, to use publicity in their areas of interest [and] to seek support for their educational demands" (Johnson, n.d., 259). By 1969, the BCTF's new president, Tom Hutchinson, was warning: "Teacher power is only a beginning." He asserted further that the BCTF had to "become political" and, if necessary, "engage in militant action" (Ungerleider 1996, 2). Teachers were about to cross two lines never crossed before—one leading to partisan political action and one, perhaps even more dangerous, leading teachers to contest an elected government's right to determine public policy in schooling.

The rising mood of teacher militancy has been traced to the fact that the BCTF was a "predominantly young organization" comprised of teachers with "no more than six years' experience" (Kilian 1985, 37). Yri's (1979) study of the BCTF's history from 1966 to 1972 contends that at least five factors coalesced to drive teachers toward partisan politics: the social activism of the 1960s and the rising militancy of teachers elsewhere; the reduction of teachers' bargaining rights by the Social Credit government; a struggle for power between old and new factions inside the BCTF; the BCTF's growing financial clout and influence; and, finally, the Education Department's stagnation and the government's shift in provincial priorities to post-secondary education.

Teacher militancy was variously expressed. *B.C. Teacher* editorials roundly criticized the government's building program. The teachers' 1969 "apple" campaign (so named because of the BCTF's use of an apple logo to separate "teacher friendly" from other legislative candidates) greatly elevated the province's political temperature, as did public attempts by the BCTF to challenge funding levels. Aghast at rising school costs, Bennett's Social Credit government was disinclined to placate teachers or the BCTF.

The background to such developments was a postwar period of educational growth that had proved startling in size. In the quarter of a century following the end of World War II, pupil populations in British Columbia schools jumped from 125,135 to 534,523, a sharp rise of 427 percent. Teachers' ranks during this time grew even more quickly, climbing from 4,354 to 22,840, an increase of 524 percent. Student numbers were increasing in breathtaking fashion "not because of legal requirements, but because of social and parental pressure" (Conway 1971, 7), as one provincial official explained, since schooling was increasingly seen after mid-century as the principal means of economic and social advancement. Retention rates for grades 1 to 12, in fact, had climbed from 32 percent in 1932 to over 90 percent by 1970 (ibid., 8).[6]

School costs were no less impressive: between 1945 and 1972, total public expenditures on education rose more than 4,000 percent from $13.7 million to nearly $558 million annually. Over this time, the provincial government's expenditures on education skyrocketed from just over $5 million annually in 1945 to more than $383 million in 1972, a jump of more than 7,600 percent (British Columbia Department of Education 1971–1972, D190-91). By 1971, educational spending constituted about 33 percent of total provincial expenditures. Educational budgets doubled in the five-year period from 1966 to 1971 (British Columbia Department of Education 1972, 90). Altogether, from 1947 to 1971, school budgets increased 35-fold, surpassing the entire provincial budget only nine years earlier (ibid.). As the 1970s began, exploding public sector spending, along with the grave condition of public finances, prompted the Economic Council of Canada to forecast that if education and health care spending continued to rise at about 9 percent annually, these costs would absorb Canada's entire Gross National Product (GNP) by the century's end (ibid., 15).

Teachers had done well financially, in fact, since the end of the Great Depression. Between 1941 and 1971, only medical doctors surpassed teachers in terms of salary gains (Bruneau 1978, 43). Within such a context, government felt obliged to slow increases in capital and operating costs for school districts and to ignore repeated BCTF requests for substantial increases to the pensions of retired teachers (London 2005, 256). Government's refusal to address the pension issue only stiffened teachers' resolve, provoking a one-day teachers' strike on 19 March 1971—a strike supported by 96 percent of the membership who voted (ibid., 275).

Relations between government and the BCTF continued to deteriorate. Irritated by the BCTF's unprecedented intrusion into the 1969 election, Education Minister Leslie Peterson warned the BCTF to "stay out of partisan politics" (Bruneau 1978, 78). When he then introduced a legislative amendment to excuse teachers from automatic membership in the BCTF in 1971, the time for retribution was at hand. Although clearly designed to break the back of the teachers' union by reducing the organization's numbers, the legislation failed miserably. Fewer than 100 of the province's 22,000 teachers chose to revoke their membership (Ungerleider 1996, 1).

But skirmishes between government and the BCTF were far from over. The following year, the Bennett government instructed school boards to hold referenda for expenditures more than 6.5 percent above the previous year's budget, effectively "setting teachers' salaries without negotiation" (Bruneau 1978, 79). The teachers responded in kind. Prior to the summer election of 1972, a Teachers' Political-Action Committee (TPAC) was formed to raise funds to oppose the re-election of the Social Credit government, thereby circumventing the legal question about whether the BCTF's general revenues could be used to campaign against a political party. Without newspaper headlines or formal notice, both sides had quietly declared war.

The BCTF decisively won the next battle in what would turn out to be a long and bitter encounter. After 20 years in power, a Social Credit government well into its dotage was defeated in the late summer of 1972, despite Bennett's unsettling warning to the electorate that "the socialist hordes were at the gates" (CBC News 1972). Thirty-two of the 35 candidates endorsed by TPAC won seats as Dave Barrett's new NDP administration won 41 out of 57 ridings and began its gaffe-ridden "1,000 day" regime.

Emboldened by claims to a new-found professionalism, the BCTF began to target conditions of work as "a battle to be won" in the 1970s.[7]

Targets included a broad suite of items for negotiation in the decades ahead, including "firm class size limits," "preparation time expressed as hours of instruction," "full professional autonomy and professional control over educational change," definition of the "work year and the duration of the school day," and "professional control over teaching."[8] A few local associations also sought additional payment for teacher involvement in extracurricular activities. An article in a teachers' newsmagazine advised that achieving a "5.5 hour working day" required eliminating homework assignments, as well as "all coaching and refereeing" duties, school-award programs, "volunteer supervision," committee service, fundraising, and "social conscience" activities.[9]

As the BCTF's militancy intensified in the 1970s, its willingness to confront the provincial government increased. Election of the "radical Marxist" Jim MacFarlan, to use historian F. Henry Johnson's (n.d., 260) description, as BCTF president between 1973 and 1975 brought a new mood of class-consciousness to the BCTF's executive office. MacFarlan was certainly not reluctant to exercise his considerable political muscle. Following the NDP's refusal to provide assurances in the 1974 throne speech that class sizes would be reduced, the Surrey teachers voted in favour of a one-day strike and 1,000 arrived to protest at the legislative buildings in Victoria. This action coerced Education Minister Dailly to arrange an impromptu meeting between the Premier and MacFarlan where, according to MacFarlan, "the Premier and I negotiated on a completely ad hoc basis and came up with a proposal that called for the government to reduce the pupil-teacher ratio by 1.5 per year over a three-year period" (London 2005, 296).

By 1975, two things were becoming obvious: first, governments on either side of the aisle could be pushed around by the BCTF; and, second, the historically serene "schools" portfolio of government was now turbulent. In less than a decade, major public policy decisions about schools had shifted from dignified civil service offices to newspaper headlines and lead stories on regional broadcasts, rupturing a long-standing agreement among legislators in all parties, as well as by trustee and teachers' organizations, that negotiations about educational matters would remain confidential and out of public view, and that schools should be kept "out of politics."[10]

Formation of the Teachers' Viewpoint in 1977, a BCTF splinter group, ushered in a "new kind of progressive caucus" to an already activist-minded organization (Tyllinen 1988, 41). Fronted at times by Surrey teacher David Chudnovsky, the Teachers' Viewpoint aspired to achieve the same sort of labour solidarity that Rural Teachers' Federation advocates had solicited back in the 1930s and 1940s. As Chudnovsky argued, "It is essential that there be an organized group of B.C. teachers openly and consciously working to build a union with the right to strike—in other words beginning the task of uniting teachers with other workers" (ibid.).

In this new workers' union, Chudnovsky saw no place for principals or others who held "primarily management functions" (ibid., 42), a sure sign of things to come. This militant spirit quickly infected the emergent BCTF executive. Three of the BCTF's presidents from 1981 to 1987—Larry Kuehn, Pat Clarke, and Elsie McMurphy—all belonged to the Teachers' Viewpoint, as did other officers supporting the executive (ibid., 69).

No single event likely contributed to the BCTF's *sturm und drang* view of the world, or its vision of the hostile environment around it, than the public sector restraint program introduced in 1982 by W.R. "Bill" Bennett, W.A.C.'s son. A deepening recession, rising unemployment, rampant inflation, shrinking revenues, and a growing taxpayer revolt prompted Bill Bennett's Social Credit government to pass two pieces of legislation—the *Public Service Restraint Act* and the *Education Interim Finance Act*—to control soaring education and other public sector costs. Public school spending had totalled about $900 million in 1976; by 1981, with 32,000 fewer students in the system, the provincial budget for schools had mushroomed to $1.6 billion (Fleming 1985, 6-7). Between 1980 and 1981 alone, school budgets had jumped by an average of 19 percent (ibid.).

Over the next three years, Bennett's government stabilized educational spending by bringing in annual school budgets of $1.55 billion, $1.57 billion, and $1.7 billion (ibid., 9). Although the public sector restraint program did not cut educational spending drastically, it did flatten its rate of increase and, along the way, eliminated about 2,000 resource or non-structured teaching positions, thereby returning educational services to 1976 levels. As part of the larger labour protest known as Operation Solidarity, the BCTF fought loudly against the restraint program, joining a unified labour front to orchestrate a protest rally of some 50,000 people at Empire Stadium in the summer of 1983, a march of 80,000 people in October at the Social Credit Party convention, and a three-day province-wide teachers' strike in November. According to BCTF claims, the high stakes public protests of 1983 brought the BCTF to a point of "full maturity" as a political organization and showed it to be an able adversary of government (Tyllinen 1988, 28). Events of 1983, in the words of Ken Novakowski (2000), BCTF president from 1989 to 1992, represented "a transformative experience for teachers," a "political act—a protest action, taken as part of a broader labour strategy."

Doubling the size of the BCTF's membership between the 1970s and the 1990s greatly improved the BCTF's wealth and status, making it the province's largest and most influential educational organization, easily dwarfing the Ministry of Education in importance. Twice, at least by its own count, the BCTF was instrumental in bringing governments down—notably in 1972 and 1991 (Novakowski 2004, 1). Over this time, no union, public sector or otherwise—not even the redoubtable mother-ship of west coast unionism, the BC Federation of Labour—would prove to be a more capable or dangerous adversary for government.

Certainly, the BCTF proved adroit in presenting its organizational persona and popularizing its policies. One notable BCTF triumph has resided in its success in persuading parents and the public that certain educational outcomes—notably higher thinking, creativity, and love of learning—defy measurement by standardized tests and that "input measures" such as higher teachers' salaries, smaller class sizes, and other improvements in learning conditions somehow constitute more credible measures of educational quality than outcomes from mathematics and language tests. The popularity of this idea has ensured that the BCTF always seems to hold better pedagogical cards than government in public policy debates about what is important in schooling.

As a new millennium began, no reading of the provincial tea leaves was required to predict that the BCTF and the British Columbia Liberal Party would quickly find themselves at odds. Even before the 2001 election, when Gordon Campbell's free-enterprise Liberal government won 77 of 79 ridings in the largest electoral landslide in provincial history, the main narrative line in the script about government-teacher conflict had already been written. The Liberals had stumped on austerity and making education an "essential service" (BC Teachers' Federation 2011). The BCTF, in response, had paid for a campaign of negative advertising to discredit them. If such things were not sufficient in themselves to destroy relations, a tradition of unresolved contract negotiations inherited from NDP governments in the 1990s continued to fester. For one thing, the provincial bargaining model created in 1994 with the passage of the *Public Education Labour Relations Act* and the creation of an employers' association did not enjoy BCTF support. An absence of transitional provisions to reconcile the existence of 75 employers, 75 teacher locals, and 75 collective agreements with a provincial approach to bargaining forced government to become involved in bargaining in 1996 and to legislate a contract in 1998.

A historically divisive management-labour climate grew even more rancorous after 2001 when government embarked on a series of initiatives to codify rights for parents and to amend the *Labour Relations Code* to designate K–12 public education an "essential service." Government also continued limitations on public sector compensation introduced in various forms since the early 1990s. Two pieces of legislation introduced at the end of January 2002 proved particularly controversial—Bill 27, the *Education Services Collective Agreement Act,* and Bill 28, the *Public Education Flexibility and Choice Act.* Bill 27 was, for the most part, back-to-work legislation that provided terms for a return to work. Bill 28 fulfilled the government's commitment to situate school organization issues in a legislative framework, thereby removing them from collective bargaining, collective agreements, as well as the rule-making process that characterized labour relations between unions and employers. The *Public Education Flexibility and Choice Act,* in effect, shunted school organization matters from the collective agreement and collective bargaining to the realm of law and public policy.[11]

Two broad schools of thought surrounded the question about whether school organizational matters should be legislatively determined, or whether they should constitute items for bargaining. The government's position, with general support from the British Columbia Principals' and Vice-Principals' Association (BCPVPA), the British Columbia Council of Parent Advisory Councils (BCCPAC), along with some trustees and parents, was that school organizational issues were of general public importance to many others in the educational and provincial community apart from teachers—including parents, principals, school boards, and the public at large—and therefore should be addressed as a matter of public policy, not as bargaining chips within a collective agreement.[12] The BCTF strongly opposed this view. They also opposed the findings of Don Wright, who headed a one-person government commission into school bargaining structures, claiming that "Wright got it wrong" and, in so doing, "committed the next generation of teachers to a potentially career-long struggle for equality and fairness at the bargaining table" (Novakowksi 2005).

Bills 27 and 28 prompted further developments that would lead to a 2005 school strike. Infuriated with what amounted to a salary freeze and government's lack of interest in continuing to reduce class sizes, nearly 90 percent of teachers voted on 27 September 2005 to engage in job action, threatening more severe measures if negotiations failed. Enraged by what they perceived as government's high-handedness, the BCTF called a strike, albeit illegal, on 7 October 2005 that left 600,000 students and their parents stranded for the best part of two weeks. Some 25,000 support staff workers also walked off the job (Steffenhagen 2005). "Thousands of public school teachers across British Columbia are out on strike," national columnist Andrew Coyne (2005) observed, adding caustically, "What else is new?"

Looking back, the 2005 strike should be seen for exactly what it was—just another unhappy chapter in a lengthening history of unsettled labour relations in British Columbia schools. Strike action in the 1970s began the story. Three bitter years of public sector warfare from 1982 to 1985 followed the public sector restraint program. Even convening a royal commission in 1987 produced no more than a brief respite from a conflict that could already be traced back two decades. Sadly, nothing was solved, nothing was learned save, perhaps, for this: except for brief episodes of short-lived tranquility, governments of all political stripes—Social Credit, NDP, and Liberal—have found themselves in a state of almost perpetual conflict with the BCTF over control of the schools for 40 years. Even the year-to-year issues have not changed markedly—salaries, conditions of work, compulsory membership in the teachers' union, class size and composition, and the right to strike remain as contentious today as they ever were.

CURRENT DISCONNECTIONS AT THE CORE

The discussion thus far suggests that the structures at the heart of the British Columbia school system in the twenty-first century have changed little since they were designed in the mid-nineteenth century. Almost all governance, administrative, and pedagogical structures supporting the delivery of public instruction, school history suggests, are archaic in origin. Classes are grouped into schools and schools are defined by grades. Schools are organized geographically into districts that are locally governed, provincially sanctioned, and provincially funded. It is, in almost every respect, a system built in and intended for another age.

The designated agency in charge of schooling is an education ministry that is actually "a ministry without schools," an organization that neither operates schools nor delivers school programs and services, although it does nominally oversee the K–12 system. For reasons already discussed, connections between the ministry and the system's schools appear fewer and more tenuous than at any time in the province's history. The Ministry of Education, the BCSTA, and the BCTF constitute the province's three most important educational organizations and serve—intentionally or otherwise—as agencies for the prevention of change.[13] Although rarely acting in concert, these organizations exhibit certain common characteristics. They are bureaucratic in nature, anti-visionary and unimaginative in outlook, prescriptive and non-cooperative in behaviour, anti-technological in practice and, generally speaking, committed to the status quo. Even though all rhetorically embrace the idea of change, they appear reluctant to sponsor actual alterations in their own organizations, or in the public school system at large. Consequently, the institution of public schooling appears mired in the past and unable to offer a bold new vision for designing or delivering future education programs and services. As the third and final section will now show, reasons for this state of organizational malaise are complex and largely attributable to the breakdown in institutional and labour relations among the three key organizational actors around which the public education sector revolves.

Failures of Leadership

The troubled state of the schools can be traced in large part to a question of leadership—or, more accurately, to the absence of it. Since the 1970s when partisan and special interest politics wrenched apart the old mandarin-managed empire of schools, the education ministry has become a shadow of its former self. Once the principal architect and driving force for the system, as well as education's chief advocate, the Education Ministry has steadily retreated from providing either real or symbolic leadership. From the margins of the system, it now performs a handful of modest monitorial and regulatory functions in addition to its key duty as paymaster. Not surprisingly, it no longer serves as a point of reference for anyone inside the system because it has little, if any, pedagogical expertise (as measured in staff with advanced degrees in education or the social sciences).

A gradual transfer of educational decision-making from the civil service to cabinet and the premier's office over the past four decades has further eroded the capacity for leadership inside the Education Ministry. Unfortunately, leadership at the political level of government has also been in short supply. No education minister of recent decades has been able to demonstrate a comprehensive understanding of public education's great importance to the economic and intellectual life of the province, or to outline a set of educational objectives that could be operationalized across the system.

Leadership at the school district level is even more impoverished. Since school boards were granted authority to appoint their own superintendents, the once-strong tradition of effective local leadership has largely disappeared. For the most part, superintendents have become captives of the boards who employ them. The superintendents' association, the BCSSA, has also greatly declined in influence since the advent of local control over administrative appointments.

School boards themselves, now numbering 60 since the last provincial restructuring exercise in 1996, are even more problematic. Although their sense of self-importance has grown markedly since consolidation into larger governance units in the late 1940s, the tasks that boards used to perform in furnishing school buildings and taxes, negotiating salaries with teachers, representing local public interests, and establishing leadership and direction for district schools have dwindled to almost nothing. In effect, the historical criteria for their existence have mostly disappeared. Much of their time is now ineffectively spent in dealing with a welter of non-educational issues. Suffice to say, virtually all quality-directed initiatives adopted in public schooling over the past 30 years have been provincial rather than local in origin.[14]

Today, most operating and capital expenditures associated with schooling are borne by the provincial government and supported by a property tax regime directed at equalizing contributions in jurisdictions across the province. Moreover, when the province stripped boards of their commercial and residential taxation powers some 20 years ago to stem spiralling school costs, it removed much of the political accountability boards traditionally shouldered for the spending they authorized. Since then, school board budgets have been separated from the responsibilities of local property holders to pay for the district programs and services they receive. This has proven dysfunctional. "The trouble with school boards as they exist," a *Globe and Mail* editorial declared in summing things up across the country, "is that they are somewhat accountable in theory, but barely accountable in practice" ("Good-bye School Board" 1992).

Currently, the provincial government oversees and finances a system in which many decisions about spending are made beyond its reach at the local level. Government efforts to monitor and audit the financial affairs of school districts and, in so doing, to demonstrate public accountability and value for public investment are routinely contested by board members, district staff, and teachers inside the system. The political noise generated by this resistance saps time, energy, and money away from real improvements and, more often than not, leads to little more than finger-pointing exercises where government complains that school boards make poor decisions and boards complain that government has given them insufficient resources to do their work.[15] A disassociation between educational decision-making and fiscal responsibility—something provincial authorities have allowed to stand since the mid-1980s—has produced an educational passion play that has run annually for a quarter of a century. Year after year the liturgy rarely varies. Boards vigorously complain that schools are underresourced and that the province's basic education program formula to calculate funding is insufficient. Provincial authorities, in response, point to annual increases in per capita grants, various other injections of resources, and shrinking public school populations. Little is ever resolved.

The great vulnerability of school boards today is that provincial governments are no longer reliant on them to supply the local infrastructures necessary to deliver school programs and services across the province, as the boards did when British Columbia was a territory of rough trails and wagon roads. Such things can now be distributed effortlessly across an entire provincial jurisdiction through electronic and other means. And, although the presence of boards screens senior government from direct political pressure at the local level, governments across the country have increasingly found the political stance of boards and their incessant demands for resources tiresome. By their very existence, they provide a platform from which teachers' unions and various other special interest groups can mount frontal attacks on government's educational policies and levels of funding, thereby undermining any semblance of order in the public school sector. The costs of retaining boards, calculated strictly in political terms, may already far outweigh their value.

Government and the BCTF

Disconnections between provincial and local structures for school governance, and between legislative and administrative authorities in British Columbia, have been aggravated by more than 40 years of bitter conflict between provincial governments and the British Columbia Teachers'

Federation. The BCTF's story in provincial school history—and the responses of various governments to the BCTF's actions—have constituted a complicated and, mostly, rancorous tale. Fifty years of finely balancing "professional" and "union" interests, along with presenting a moderate face to government and to the educational community, were suddenly discarded in the late 1960s as the BCTF assumed a more confrontational stance toward provincial authorities and school boards.

Since the 1960s, provincial governments have proven anything but sure-handed and consistent in their responses to the BCTF's economic and political ambitions. Mandatory membership in the BCTF, for example, was legislated by government in 1947 (on the understanding that the BCTF would not exercise the right to strike), rescinded in 1971 by a Social Credit government, restored by the NDP government later in the 1970s, rescinded again by a Social Credit government in 1987, and restored by an NDP government in 1993. Similarly, the idea of designating some areas of public sector work as an "essential service" was considered by W.A.C. Bennett in 1972, and again in 1974 by Dave Barrett's NDP government (Finlayson 2009, 18-20). Legislative amendments in the mid-1970s to prevent striking, however, did not include education in the list of essential public services. Education was included in 1978 after a protracted labour dispute involving Selkirk College and four school boards in the West Kootenays (ibid., 68). Education was declared an "essential service" by William Vander Zalm and the Social Credit government, later declared non-essential by Mike Harcourt's NDP government, and still later redesignated as essential by Gordon Campbell's Liberals.

Government has been equally inconsistent in its approaches to collective bargaining with teachers. From district consolidation in 1946 until the 1987 passage of Bill 19, the *Industrial Relations Reform Act*, negotiations between school districts and local teachers' associations were excluded from the *Labour Code* and bargaining was limited to issues of salary and bonuses. Despite the fact that public education had emerged as a large sector of employment after 1945, the boards, as employers, had no duty or authority to bargain matters outside of compensation, notably the terms and conditions of teachers' employment, health and safety issues in the workplace, and disciplinary matters outside of suspension, dismissal, or probation. For reasons not altogether clear, government dragged its feet on this file for some time, no doubt preferring a status quo position to *Labour Code* changes that might prove more difficult and costly to manage.

When the *Canadian Charter of Rights and Freedoms* came into full effect in April 1985, it changed everything by affording British Columbia teachers the opportunity to challenge the constitutionality of certain sections of the *Labour Code*, specifically those that denied teachers the right to bargain collectively. Teachers filed a Writ of Summons in the Supreme Court of British Columbia, contending that certain provincial laws were unconstitutional under three sections of the *Charter*.[16] The *Charter* challenge, along with teachers' continuing demands for expanded bargaining rights, spurred William Vander Zalm's Social Credit government to introduce two pieces of legislation that would profoundly alter relationships between teachers, principals, and their employers. The *Industrial Relations Reform Act* (Bill 19) granted teachers the right to organize into unions and to engage in broad scope collective bargaining; it also awarded them a limited right to strike constrained by conditions pertaining to the classification of education as an "essential service." The *Teaching Profession Act* (Bill 20) contained consequential amendments to the *School Act*, giving teachers a choice in belonging either to a professional association or to a union.

Government's 1987 legislation proved immensely ill-conceived. Its suddenness provoked an immediate and negative response from teachers, thereby perpetuating the divisive school wars of the early 1980s. Moreover, ignoring all evidence to the contrary, government presumed that teachers would choose a model of professional association over the protection of trade union status, despite the angry protests of the restraint years and the traumatic loss of some 2,000 educational jobs. The teachers' vote was not surprising to anyone outside government: all 76 BCTF local associations selected the union model. The legislation also triggered a systemwide shutdown of schools on 28 April 1987 and, little more than a month later, prompted a general labour strike on 1 June.

Another negative outcome of the legislation was the separation of principals from teachers. Passage of Bill 20 set in motion a chain of events that finally resulted in the exclusion of principals and vice-principals from membership in the BCTF following a vote at a special general meeting. Historian James London (2005, 386) portrayed the unfolding of events as the denouement in a political power play in which both the left wing of the BCTF and the right wing of the BCPVPA triumphed in getting what they wanted—the separation of principals from the BCTF. Without the principals' presence, few checks were left on the radical views increasingly embraced by the BCTF's executive officers. Separation, in effect, exorcized what remained of the BCTF's political centre of gravity and its moderate traditions.

The 1987 legislation's hurried introduction also did nothing to prepare school boards for the rigours of broad scope collective bargaining with teachers that would soon follow. In fact, school boards were manifestly unprepared for the first round of negotiations (Finlayson 2009, 18). London's history of the BCSTA bemoaned the paucity of assistance most boards received in undertaking their first broad scope agreements and concluded that boards saw themselves "getting burned with the 'whipsaw' cleverly administered by BCTF negotiation professionals" (2005, 407-408). In the five years that followed the legislation, 50 teacher strikes were called— about 16 strikes for each round of bargaining (Finlayson 2009, 19).

Finally, by passing legislation that permitted broad scope collective bargaining, government allowed boards to negotiate class size provisions, something historically protected as a matter of public policy—and something provincial authorities traditionally determined through levels of expenditure and that was embedded in broader strategies for social, economic, and educational development. Class size, more than any other single factor, represented the largest economic driver in the public schools; far more than a condition of work as teachers described it, class size was first and foremost a condition of spending for government.

For six years (1987–1993) class size and class composition remained as bargaining items in collective agreements between school boards and local teachers' unions. Provincial bargaining replaced local bargaining in 1994 following a 1992 Commission of Inquiry into the Public Service and the Public Sector, headed by Judy Korbin. Harcourt's government embraced Korbin's notion of creating an employers' association for the K–12 sector, charging the newly formed British Columbia Public School Employers Association (BCPSEA) to bargain provincially with the BCTF, despite the fact that the commissioner had never explicitly proposed this and, also, that the BCTF opposed provincial bargaining (Finlayson 2009, 45). From 1994 to 2002, class size was bargained provincially between the BCPSEA and the BCTF, save for the April 1998 Agreement in Committee struck behind closed doors between Glen Clark's NDP government and Kit Krieger, the BCTF president. This accord, conducted without the support or knowledge of the BCPSEA and its school board members, set lower K–3 class sizes, a move that meant hiring 1,200 additional teachers and underwriting $150 million in new funding for provincial schools (ibid., 56). In 2002, class size and other matters to do with school organization were removed as collective bargaining items under Bill 28 and placed within a legislative framework by Campbell's Liberal government in the *School Act*, indicating that such matters had been returned to the realm of public policy where they resided before 1987. This issue, however, remains far from settled as the BCTF is currently contesting the legality of the government's action before the courts.

Deep divisions in the philosophical and social views of British Columbia governments—notably differences between the socially democratic and labour-friendly NDP governments of Barrett, Harcourt, Clark, Miller, and Dosanjh and, in sharp contrast, the free enterprise Social Credit and Liberal governments of W.A.C. Bennett, Bill Bennett, Vander Zalm, Johnson, and Campbell—have provided an unsteady governmental platform from which to address the vexing governance and labour relations problems that have characterized public education since the late 1960s. Nor have "on-again, off-again" intervention patterns by government been helped much by bipolar mood swings on the part of the provincial electorate.

Mistakes by the Vander Zalm government, however, produced only more mistakes—first by the Harcourt administration and, subsequently, by others. As earlier noted, anxious to restore a measure of peace and sanity to labour relations across the public sector, the Harcourt government convened a 1992 commission of inquiry into the public sector, which led to the creation of an employers' association, the BCPSEA, to bargain provincially with the BCTF despite the fact that the BCTF opposed provincial bargaining (Finlayson 2009, 45). Making matters worse, the Harcourt government imposed this new bargaining model in 1994 without any form of transitional support to ease the move from "multiple local agreements to a single province-wide agreement" (ibid.). Strong differences remained on both sides of the bargaining table. Employers were resentful they had been stampeded into agreements they could ill afford during post-1987 negotiations, and sought redress. In contrast, the BCTF refused to consider concessions of any form, describing such things as "contract stripping," and was intent on keeping what its local associations had won. Not until May 1996 was a Transitional Collective Agreement concluded between the BCPSEA and the BCTF, but only with the help of a government intermediary.

Government intervened again in 1998, as noted earlier, when Glen Clark and the BCTF signed an Agreement in Committee that excluded the BCPSEA. This intervention spoke volumes about the special relationship that existed between the NDP government and the BCTF, and government's disrespect for the BCPSEA bargaining institution it had created. True to British Columbia traditions, a political "fix" was quicker and more decisive, and therefore seemed preferable to other approaches. A behind-doors deal between the NDP and the BCTF was also important for other reasons. It damaged the fundamental labour relations notion of two parties bargaining in good faith. It granted teachers' unions unprecedented influence in determining how human resources were actually deployed in local school systems, thus greatly reducing the authority of principals and other educational administrators, not to mention that of the boards they served. And, last but not least, it promulgated the idea that legislatively imposed collective agreements could now become the new "normal" in labour relations. Since this time, NDP and Liberal governments have been obliged to legislate virtually every collective agreement into law. These actions hardly denote mature practices in modern labour relations in a post-industrial society.

The Public Relations War

Complicated governance and labour relations issues have been made even more difficult to resolve by a pattern of BCTF subterfuge. For 40 years, the BCTF's leadership has deftly waged a public relations war with government, shifting from the position of "system critic" to "system advocate" as time, circumstances, and issues changed—and as it suited the BCTF. The litany of criticism is long—the institution of public schooling is badly flawed as a result of "teacher reductions," "increased class sizes," "funding cutbacks," "leaking schools," "the glaring inadequacy of the one-size-fits-all funding formula," "the misuse of standardized tests," "regressive policies," the "unilateral decisions of government and school boards," and a host of other maladies too lengthy to recount. No organization or politician across the country has been consistently as derisive about the public system's glaring inadequacies as the BCTF, or as unmindful about how a never-ending tsunami of criticism has shaken provincial confidence in public schools and prompted the flight of many families to non-public-sector schools.

The BCTF's self-appointment as "system critic" has dressed the stage for a modern educational morality play the organization has carefully scripted and that regularly appears on the pages of the *Teacher Newsmagazine*. The story is simple and compelling: the BCTF is cast throughout as an organization with a monopoly on virtue and social conscience, while local school boards and, more recently, the provincial government are presented as forces destroying public education. Accurate or not, such a mythology no doubt assists the BCTF's executive in keeping the membership compliant, on the boil and, in line with a garrison mentality, ready to do battle at a moment's notice.

In fact, Bruneau has pointed out that the real source of historical drama or conflict in the BCTF's evolution was far more internal than external or, as he put it, "dissent and argument in the federation have always been strong" (1978, 81-83). Bruneau traced this to six "permanent disagreements," or philosophical fault-lines, that run through the organization's history fashioning its character along the way, including splits between rural and urban needs and interests; between the needs and interests of younger and older teachers; between confrontationist and non-confrontationist approaches; between teachers who favour "specialist" and "generalist" studies; and, finally, between teachers "committed to using public education to sharpen children's awareness of socio-economic injustice" and teachers who were more concerned with introducing "children to disciplined thinking in the traditional disciplines" (ibid.). The post-1969 struggle with government, measured in full historical perspective, is therefore merely one of a series of conflicts, many of them internal in origin, that have created a combative edge now emblematic of the BCTF's public persona.

During the past decade, the drama has once again been updated. The old "white hat, black hat" stereotypes of yesteryear have been supplanted by allusions to governments captured and controlled by darker and more sinister forces, notably "a new capitalism" that appears in the guises of "neo-conservatism, the corporate agenda, and, more recently, neo-liberalism" (Richardson 2010).

Through the BCTF's opaque lens, government efforts to focus system attention on student achievement become a dangerous intrusion with administrators, as one teacher put it, having "the authority to stroll into our classrooms, to look around at what our students are doing, to ask parents what they think of us, to interview us, and to direct us" ("Roaring 20s Legislation" 2007). Any notion of job supervision, or any challenge to the idea of absolute professional autonomy, it appears, is resisted by the BCTF. Again, in the BCTF's view, classroom time should be spent on "learning," not "tests." Concepts of accountability—or the government's responsibility to ensure systemwide equity in learning—appear foreign and unnecessary to the BCTF's vision of public education.

Amid a mélange of BCTF allegations and demands, several things are apparent. First and foremost, the BCTF has exclusively claimed the fiat of moral goodness, and considers its views about education superior to all others by virtue of the fact that teachers are situated closer to children and classrooms than any other actors in the system. Accordingly, the BCTF believes that it should be entitled to shape public and, therefore, fiscal policy and, in recognition of its considerable political clout, also to negotiate directly with government at the highest level. It is further entitled, the BCTF maintains, to bargain full-scope conditions of work (including class size and composition), to withdraw services and to strike, and to bargain locally as it did following Bills 19 and 20. Even if education is a vital service, the BCTF argues, in no way should it ever be deemed "essential." Such a designation would infringe on teachers' rights. Whatever rights students may enjoy to an uninterrupted educational program seem beside the point, at least as far as the BCTF is concerned.

Politics and collective bargaining forever appear intertwined in the BCTF's view. Glen Hansman, a member of the BCTF Executive Committee and president of the Greater Vancouver Elementary Teachers' Association, put the matter in context in a candid 2009 article in *Teacher Newsmagazine*: "The political context is the bargaining context, and the bargaining context is the political context. We cannot separate the two, and we have the obligation of trying to ensure the best climate for bargaining—not make improvements for our members and for our students" (3). These are remarks that teachers, parents, and, indeed, the public may wish to reflect on carefully.

Other contradictions are also evident. Although the BCTF claims to be non-partisan, it openly and unapologetically works on behalf of the NDP and has done so since the 1960s. Even before the Liberal government of the last decade was elected, it was attempting to defeat it. Such behaviours obviously do little to stabilize BCTF-government relationships. Even the NDP's historical efforts to accommodate teachers are usually abandoned when the stakes are raised beyond the government's capacity to pay, provoking a familiar stream of BCTF allegations that provincial authorities are morally indifferent to the needs of youngsters. All-encompassing concerns with "children" and the "future" (as in "the future health of public education") typically mask teacher demands for improved salaries and conditions of work. The inadequacy of "learning conditions" is likewise publicly touted as a flag of convenience to ensure that "working conditions" find their way onto the bargaining table.

And, so, government and the BCTF remain imprisoned in a Catch-22 situation, consigned to a twilight zone of acrimonious public relations marked by decades of distrust and revenge on both sides. Suffice to say, opportunities to pursue sound educational policies, or sound bargaining policies, are slight when the fundamental calculations remain political and, more often than not, vituperative on both sides. The politics of embarrassment reign supreme. Accordingly, government refrains from articulating its support or faith in public schools—and remains disinclined to shore up a great public institution now in distress—because, de facto, this might be seen to endorse what teachers do and what the BCTF does. Alternatively, teachers and the BCTF cannot really get behind the public schools—a system historically well provisioned and well respected—because this might be construed as support for government's educational policies or government itself. Consequently, government remains silent most of the time about education, never declaring expressly what it wants or what its real intentions are. Bitter experience has taught government that no educational news is good news and that media silence is, indeed, golden. Not surprisingly, government stays off the educational skyline by choice, and the resulting vacuum in leadership is evident for all to see.

In contrast, the BCTF is garrulous in expressing its criticisms, claims, and allegations: it suffers from a confusion of interests, defeating its own purposes—and those of others—by the extent of its accusations and the language of distraction it uses. Genuine BCTF interests in the institution of public education, or in correcting the inequities in the province's social condition, are lost in a landslide of criticism and complaint that typically surrounds BCTF pronouncements. And, like the government, for all its efforts the BCTF seems unable to clarify in discrete ways the exact educational, economic, political, and social objectives it has for schools. Language, in the final analysis, is just one more in a series of differences that frustrate any kind of real educational accord between the BCTF, government, and organizations that act on government's behalf.

Government, its organizational memory erased by decades of staff change and indifferent recruitment, is plagued by historical amnesia and cannot remember a time when the public schools were respected and much loved. The BCTF, with its highly selective view of educational history before 1967, seems likewise incapable of recalling an age of educational contentment when schools were recognized as the province's most important institutions and when the school year was marked by more eventful moments than running battles with government. Both sides bear the wounds of the past—government suffers from almost no historical perspective while the BCTF suffers from too much history, much of it wrong-headed. Distracted by the political reckonings that seemingly engulf every decision, neither the government nor the BCTF appears capable of reimagining a future for the public schools, or reinvigorating an institution clearly archaic in many of its practices. Locked in the grip of their own acrimonious history, government, the BCTF, and the province's other educational organizations appear to be backing into the future with nothing more than a broken rear-view mirror as a guide. Questions abound. Will the province's three major educational organizations continue to dominate schooling in years ahead, or will new technologies and providers eventually reshape the educational landscape? Will historical governance and administrative structures retain their near-monopolistic control over schools, or will new agencies and models emerge to meet the demands of an increasingly technological society? Will the complexities and frustrations that currently mark governance and labour relations persist, or will vexing bargaining and fiscal issues eventually be resolved? Or, have decades of discord so weakened public support for the organizational status quo that a new "post-public" universe of public schooling is inevitable and, with it, a new model of labour relations between public education employers and their employees?

NOTES

1. This chapter is drawn from a larger historical study, *Worlds Apart: British Columbia School Organizations, Politics, and Labour Relations before and after 1945*, published as a monograph in 2011.
2. Wilf Graham, interview by author, 11 October 1989, Chilliwack.
3. Joe Phillipson, interview by author, 28 October 1983, Victoria.
4. Working teachers could improve their certification either through six-week courses offered at the normal schools by the Education Department's "summer school of education" or, after 1920, through education courses at the University of British Columbia.
5. British Columbia Teachers' Federation (1968), pp. 16, 17, 27, 39, 48, 51, 53, 61, 71, and 72.
6. Retention rates were calculated as the percentage of "the average elementary-school cohort stream (successive grades 2 to 6)" entering grade 12.
7. *Teacher Newsmagazine* (April–May 1988), 3.
8. *Teacher Newsmagazine* 2, no. 6 (February–March 1990), 4.
9. *Teacher Newsmagazine* 3, no. 7 (June 1991), 2.
10. Former school inspectors, district superintendents, and senior government officials made this point emphatically in a series of interviews recorded in Victoria and the Lower Mainland between 1983 and 1990, including interviews with Harold Campbell, John Meredith, Stewart Graham, Les Canty, Joe Phillipson, and Bill Plenderleith.
11. For a more complete discussion of these legislative acts, see Slinn (2012).
12. During the second reading of Bill 28 on 26 January 2002, Minister of Skills Development and Labour, Graham Bruce, used the term "bargaining chip" in reference to the claim that class sizes were too important to students to be left as a bargaining chip between the BCTF and employers.

13. It is not possible to include the BCPSEA in this group. Cabinet and the premier's office have increasingly determined what would be bargained and how it would be bargained since the 1990s. Glen Clark's 1998 Agreement in Committee offered ample evidence that contracts would be determined at the "political" level of government.
14. These initiatives include the reimposition of the core curriculum, the reinstitution of grade 12 exams, early assessment requirements, introduction of an outcomes-based curriculum, improvement of the performance of special and aboriginal students, and the development of Foundations Skills Assessments (FSAs).
15. Barry Anderson, interview by author, 1 December 2009, Victoria.
16. Section 2, Freedom of association; Section 7, Everyone has the right to life, liberty and security of person, and the right not to be deprived thereof except in accordance with the principles of fundamental justice; and Section 15, Equality rights.

REFERENCES

British Columbia Department of Education. 1965–1966/1971–1972. *Annual Report of the Public Schools*.
—. 1972. *One Hundred Years: Education in British Columbia*. Victoria: Queen's Printer.
British Columbia Teachers' Federation. 1968. *Involvement — The Key to Better Schools*. Vancouver: British Columbia Teachers' Federation.
—. 2011. "Bargaining Rights: The Problem with Essential Services Legislation." Accessed 7 January. http://bctf.ca/BargainingAndContracts.aspx?id=4936.
Bruneau, W. 1978. "'Still Pleased to Teach:' A Thematic Study of the British Columbia Teachers' Federation, 1917–1978." Unpublished manuscript, University of British Columbia.
Cameron, M.A. 1945. *Report of the Commission of Inquiry into Educational Finance*. Victoria: King's Printer.
CBC News. 1972. "The 'Socialist Hordes' Break Through," 3 September. Accessed 19 December 2009. http://archives.cbc.ca/politics/provincial_territorial_politics/topics/1637-11304/.
Conway, C.B. 1971. "Pressure Points and Growing Pains in Beautiful BC: Informal Paper." Ontario Institute for Studies in Education, Toronto.
Coyne, A. 2005. "The Strike as Kitch." *Andrew Coyne.com*, 12 October. Accessed 9 November 2008.
Finlayson, H. 2009. "A History of Labour Relations in British Columbia." Unpublished manuscript, the British Columbia Public School Employers' Association (BCPSEA).
Fleming, T. 1985. "Restraint, Reform and Reallocation: A Brief Analysis of Government Policies on Public Schooling in British Columbia, 1981–1984." *Education Canada* 25(1): 6-7.
—. 2001a. "In the Imperial Age and After: Patterns of British Columbia School Leadership and the Institution of the Superintendency, 1849–1988." In *School Leadership: Essays on the British Columbia Experience, 1872–1995*, edited by T. Fleming, 161-88. Mill Bay, BC: Bendall Books.
—. 2001b. "Letters from Headquarters: Alexander Robinson and the British Columbia Education Office, 1899–1919." In *School Leadership: Essays on the British Columbia Experience, 1872–1995*, edited by T. Fleming, 19-54. Mill Bay, BC: Bendall Books.

—. 2003. "From Educational Government to the Government of Education: The Decline and Fall of the British Columbia Ministry of Education, 1972–1996." *Historical Studies in Education* 15(2): 210-36.

—. 2010. *The Principal's Office and Beyond.* Vol. 2, *Public School Leadership in British Columbia, 1961–2005.* Calgary: Detselig.

—. Forthcoming. *Worlds Apart: British Columbia School Organizations, Politics, and Labour Relations before and after 1945.* BC: Bendall Educational Publishing.

Fleming, T. and D. Conway. 2001. "Setting Standards in the West: C.B. Conway, Science, and School Reform in British Columbia, 1938–1974." In *School Leadership: Essays on the British Columbia Experience, 1872–1995,* edited by T. Fleming, 133-60. Mill Bay, BC: Bendall Books.

Fleming, T. and H. Raptis. 2005. "Government's Paper Empire: Historical Perspectives on Measuring Student Achievement in British Columbia Schools, 1872–1999." *Journal of Educational Administration and History* 37(2): 173-202.

"Good-bye School Board." 1992. *Globe and Mail,* 28 February, p. A22.

Hansman, G. 2009. "Failure to Connect?" *Teacher Newsmagazine* 21(7): 3.

Johnson, F.H. 1964. *A History of Public Education in British Columbia.* Vancouver: University of British Columbia Publications Centre.

—. n.d. "V. Revolt: The RTA in British Columbia." In *A History of Public Education in British Columbia Amended Manuscript.* University of British Columbia Special Collections.

Kilian, C. 1985. *School Wars: The Assault on B.C. Education.* Vancouver: New Star Books.

London, J.B. 2005. *Public Education Public Pride: The Centennial History of the British Columbia School Trustees Association.* Vancouver: British Columbia School Trustees Association.

Lortie, D.C. 1975. *Schoolteacher: A Sociological Study.* Chicago: University of Chicago Press.

McDonald, N. 1978. "Egerton Ryerson and the School as an Agent of Political Socialization." In *Egerton Ryerson and His Times,* edited by N. McDonald and A. Chaiton. Toronto: Macmillan.

Novakowski, K. 2000. "The Solidarity Strike of 1983." *Teacher Newsmagazine* 12(4). Accessed 9 November 2008. http://bctf.ca/publications/NewsmagArticle. aspx?id=12834.

—. 2004. "It's Who We Are." *Teacher Newsmagazine* 17(1): 1.

—. 2005. "Wright Got It Wrong." *Teacher Newsmagazine* 17(4). Accessed 8 August 2010. http://bctf.ca/publications/NewsmagArticle.aspx?id=7736.

Ormsby, M. 1958. *British Columbia: A History.* Vancouver: Macmillan.

Persky, S. 1979. *Son of Socred.* Vancouver: North Star Books.

Richardson, K. 2010. "Neoliberalism." *Teacher Newsmagazine* 22(4).

"Roaring 20s Legislation: Implications for Teachers." 2007. *Teacher Newsmagazine* 20(1). Accessed 21 November 2009. http://bctf.ca/publications/Newsmag Article.aspx?id=13530.

Slinn, S. 2012. "Conflict without Compromise: The Case of Public Sector Teacher Bargaining in British Columbia." In *Dynamic Negotiations: Teacher Labour Relations in Canadian Elementary and Secondary Education,* edited by S. Slinn and A. Sweetman, 81-123. Montreal and Kingston: Queen's Policy Studies Series, McGill-Queen's University Press.

Steffenhagen, J. 2005. "Striking BC Teachers' Union Facing Penalties." *Vancouver Sun,* 13 October. Accessed 9 November 2008. weblogs.elearning.ubc.ca/ workplace/archives/018735.php.

Tyllinen, S. 1988. "The History of the Separation of Principals from the British Columbia Teachers' Federation." Master's thesis, University of British Columbia.

Ungerleider, C.S. 1996. "Globalization, Professionalization, and Educational Politics in British Columbia." *Canadian Journal of Educational Administration and Policy*, no. 9 (15 December).

Yri, M. 1979. "The British Columbia Teachers' Federation and Its Conversion to Partisanship, 1966–1972." Master's thesis, University of British Columbia.

Chapter 4

CONFLICT WITHOUT COMPROMISE: THE CASE OF PUBLIC SECTOR TEACHER BARGAINING IN BRITISH COLUMBIA

SARA SLINN

INTRODUCTION

Commissioner Wright's 2003 report on teacher collective bargaining in British Columbia's public schools painted a dismal picture. Describing the existing labour relations as leaving an unhappy legacy, Wright reported that "no party seems to believe that the existing structure, unchanged, can lead to successful collective bargaining in the future" (Wright 2003, 7). He also noted that one experienced negotiator had told him that "nobody does it as badly as we do" (ibid.).

Bargaining in education in this province has been marked by tremendous conflict, legal and illegal work stoppages, and direct legislative and government intervention. At the same time, British Columbia has seen several substantial, thoughtful efforts to reform the bargaining structure and process to achieve more constructive and effective collective bargaining (Ready 2007; Wright 2003, 2004). For these reasons, British Columbia provides an opportunity to examine and explore a number of themes relating to the experience of collective bargaining in education. [1]

It is clear that the current experience in education negotiations is deeply affected by the history of teacher labour relations and politics in this province. Therefore, this chapter begins by reviewing the historical context and taking account of other external factors affecting the collective bargaining process in BC education. This chapter provides a chronological

Dynamic Negotiations: Teacher Labour Relations in Canadian Elementary and Secondary Education, ed. S. Slinn and A. Sweetman. Montreal and Kingston: Queen's Policy Studies Series, McGill-Queen's University Press.
© 2012 The School of Policy Studies, Queen's University at Kingston. All rights reserved.

review of three distinct periods in teacher collective bargaining in British Columbia: (a) the pre-1987 period of narrow scope, relatively informal local negotiations that took place outside the general labour relations statutory scheme; (b) the 1987 to 1993 period of local negotiations that were brought under the general labour legislation; and (c) the period of two-tier negotiations, from 1994 to the present. The first two periods are important as a backdrop explaining how the present bargaining structure came to be constructed. The third period deals with the fundamental reorganization and centralization of negotiations in education into a provincial-level bargaining structure, part of broad reform of public sector collective bargaining undertaken in 1994.

The second part of this chapter analyzes key dimensions of the existing bargaining structure in light of its historical developments and outcomes. These dimensions include the location or level of bargaining, the scope of negotiable issues, bargaining agency, and dispute resolution. The final part of the chapter offers an overall evaluation of, and prospects for, teacher collective bargaining in British Columbia.

HISTORY

There is a long history of collective bargaining by teachers in British Columbia's K–12 public education sector, reflecting several distinct eras of negotiations.[2] These include a period of informal negotiations occurring prior to 1937; the 1937 to 1987 period of formalized local negotiations with mandatory interest arbitration regulated outside mainstream collective bargaining legislation; local bargaining without interest arbitration from 1987 to 1994 under mainstream labour legislation; full-scope two-tier bargaining between 1994 and 2002; and, a period of limited-scope two-tier negotiations beginning in 2002. Finally, since 2007, the scope and process of teacher negotiations have begun to be reshaped by newly defined standards under the *Charter of Rights and Freedoms* (1982).

Pre-1937 Negotiations

Public school teachers have collectively negotiated certain terms and conditions of employment since the British Columbia Teachers' Federation (BCTF) was formed in 1916 under *An Act to Incorporate Benevolent and Other Societies* (1911). At that time, the *Public Schools Act* (1911) permitted, but did not require, school boards and local teachers' associations to negotiate within statutory limits. In 1919, following a teachers' strike in Victoria over salaries, the legislation was amended to permit school boards and teacher associations to bargain salaries and bonuses, and to resolve disputes by voluntary arbitration (*An Act to Amend the "Public Schools Act"* 1919, s. 6; Johnson 1964, 237-41). During this period of relatively informal bargaining, "two-tier" salary agreements were common. School boards would bargain minimum salaries with the teachers' association and negotiate individually with teachers for any salary above this minimum (Thompson and Cairnie 1973, 5).

Formalized Bargaining with Interest Arbitration: 1937–1987

A more formal teacher collective bargaining structure was introduced in 1937. Amendments to the *Public Schools Act* (1936) permitted either party to invoke binding arbitration of salary disputes and replaced two-tier salary negotiations with a single salary schedule negotiated between school boards and teacher associations (*Industrial Conciliation and Arbitration Act* 1937, ss. 1, 4, 5; *Public Schools Act Amendment Act, 1937*, s. 3; Johnson 1964, 242-43). Although these amendments fostered teacher collective bargaining, limited school board resources and an oversupply of teachers meant that collective bargaining and interest arbitration did not become commonplace until after the Second World War (Johnson 1964, 242-43; Thompson and Cairnie 1973, 5).

British Columbia was among the last provinces to introduce compulsory membership in the teachers' federation, and it was not until 1947 that teachers were required to be BCTF members (*Public Schools Act Amendment Act* 1947, s. 101). Previously, teachers could choose to join a local teachers' association, which was not always a member of the provincial BCTF.

In 1958 a mandatory annual bargaining schedule was introduced to the teacher bargaining framework, requiring negotiations to commence by September and conclude by December of each year, and imposing compulsory conciliation and binding arbitration where parties failed to agree by the scheduled deadline (*Public Schools Act* 1958, ss. 137-143). This system remained largely unchanged for decades. The various parties involved in public sector K–12 education enjoyed a cordial relationship until the late 1960s, when this relationship rapidly became politicized, strained, and antagonistic, setting a pattern that persists to this day (Fleming 2012).

In the 1960s, BCTF made a concerted effort to expand the scope of bargaining beyond the narrow statutory limits and, in the late 1960s, entered into the first "working and learning condition" contract with the Vancouver School District. This contract addressed workload and other workplace matters beyond the formal scope of bargaining. This strategy had limited success as only six school districts entered into these voluntary contracts.[3] Notably, although these working and learning condition contracts were not legally enforceable, no school board challenged the legitimacy of these contracts.[4] In 1971, the Social Credit government removed mandatory BCTF membership for teachers in retaliation for BCTF's public opposition to government's education policies and its efforts to reform teachers' pensions (British Columbia Hansard 1971,

680, 688).[5] However, two years later compulsory BCTF membership was reintroduced by the subsequent, NDP, government (*An Act to Amend the Public Schools Act* 1973).

During this period, and until legislative changes in 1987, teachers had no explicit statutory right to strike, and school boards contended that the existence of compulsory interest arbitration meant there was no implicit right to strike (North 1964, 80; Thompson and Cairnie 1973, 6). Nevertheless, from the earliest periods of bargaining, teachers engaged in mass resignations, strikes, work-to-rule campaigns, and "in-dispute" declarations when negotiations broke down (BCTF 2003a, 4). Between 1970 and 1987 eight work stoppages occurred, some of which were political, rather than bargaining, disputes (see Appendix A). In 1978, an amendment to the *Essential Service Disputes Act* (1977), prompted by a teachers' strike, restricted teachers' ability to strike by bringing education within essential services regulation for the first time (*West Kootenay Schools Collective Bargaining Assistance Act* 1978, c. 42, s. 11).

Full-Scope Local Bargaining: 1987–1993

In 1987, significant changes to British Columbia's labour legislation incorporated teachers into mainstream labour relations regulation; allowed BCTF to gain status as a trade union; provided a clear, though limited, right to teacher strikes and lockouts; and broadened the scope of negotiable matters (*Industrial Relations Reform Act* 1987 (Bill 19); *Teaching Profession Act* 1987 (Bill 20)). These changes had been prompted by BCTF's court challenge to the existing statutory exclusion of teachers from full collective bargaining rights as unjustifiably violating teachers' *Charter* rights of free association and to liberty and security of the person (*Charter* 1982, ss. 1, 2(d), 7, 15). The International Labour Organization's Freedom of Association Committee had also concluded that this violated Canada's commitments to international principles of freedom of association (International Labour Organization 1986). Concerned that the teachers' *Charter* challenge would succeed, the government under the new Social Credit premier Bill Vander Zalm pre-empted a court decision with this legislation.[6] Bills 19 and 20 significantly altered the structure and regulation of teacher collective bargaining and, along with replacing the *Labour Code* (1979) with the *Industrial Relations Act* (1987) (*IRA*), introduced other widespread and controversial amendments to labour relations regulation in the province. The labour movement vigorously opposed many of these changes through BCTF study sessions, protest rallies in several cities on 28 April 1987, and a provincewide general strike on 1 June 1987 (BCTF n.d., "History," 4; Novakowski 2000).

By removing the explicit exclusion of teachers from the general labour legislation, Bill 19 brought teachers within the province's mainstream labour relations legislation for the first time in their history (Bill

19, s. 2(e); *IRA* ss. 1(1)). This allowed teachers to unionize and engage in collective bargaining with their employers, the school boards, like most other employees in the province. However, directors, principals, and vice-principals were excluded from this system and, therefore, were no longer able to negotiate alongside teachers. The scope of teacher bargaining was also broadened to include salary and working conditions, although negotiation of teacher appointments, appointments of education support workers, and assignment of teaching duties to administrators were prohibited (Bill 20, ss. 69, 78; *School Act* 1979, ss. 131.2, 140). Bill 20 removed the mandatory annual bargaining schedule, and introduced conciliation and voluntary interest arbitration (Bill 20, ss. 70-74; *School Act* 1979, ss. 133-137). Teachers now had an unambiguous right to strike, though limited by essential service restrictions applicable to disputes that were a "threat to the economy of the Province or to the health, safety or welfare of its residents or to the provision of educational services in the Province" (*IRA*, s. 137.8).[7]

Bill 20 also established a College of Teachers as the certifying and professional body for teachers (*School Act* 1979, s. 140) and, in 1990, membership in the College of Teachers became mandatory (*Education Statutes Amendment Act* 1990, s. 2). Most controversial for teachers was that Bill 20 removed mandatory membership in BCTF. This effectively forced local teacher associations to choose either to become a professional association, or to certify as a trade union under the *IRA*. While the government claimed this change was responding to requests by some teachers for recognition as professionals, the BCTF viewed it as "a government attempt to split the loyalty of teachers" and a "direct attack on the Federation" (BCTF n.d., "Steps Leading to Full Bargaining Rights," 16; Novakowski 2000; Ungerleider 1996). At the time, most labour relations experts believed that the government had miscalculated and that there was no real possibility that a significant proportion of teachers would reject BCTF.[8] BCTF met this challenge with a vigorous organizing campaign and, within a few months, had successfully certified locals in every school district; about 98 percent of all teachers voluntarily joined the BCTF and its locals (BCPSEA 2006a, 12).[9] In subsequent bargaining rounds, all but a few teachers' locals also secured closed-shop provisions in their collective agreements, making BCTF membership compulsory for all teachers in the district (Lawton et al. 1999, 91).

Between 1987 and 1993, most of the province's 75 school districts held three rounds of negotiations (in 1988, 1991, and 1993). Over this period several changes affected K–12 labour relations. In 1989 the new *School Act* maintained the earlier limits on matters that could be included in a teacher collective agreement, and added a prohibition on any provision limiting a board's power to employ non-teachers as teaching assistants (*School Act* 1989, ss. 26(2), 27). K–12 funding also changed significantly. In 1990 school districts lost their taxing authority and became subject to the government's provincial education equalization funding program (*School Amendment Act* 1990). In 1991, in the midst of these changes, the NDP formed the new provincial government with a substantial majority under Premier Mike Harcourt. Finally, shortly before the third round of negotiations, the *IRA* was repealed and replaced by the *Labour Relations Code* (1992), which granted teachers full access to strikes and lockouts by removing educational services from those matters covered by the essential services provision. However, the Labour Relations Board (LRB) soon held that the amended essential services provision could still, though to a more limited degree than before, limit teacher disputes (*School District No. 54* 1993).

BCTF had set up a "war room" to set and coordinate its provincewide bargaining agenda in a system of "rolling pattern bargaining." Larry Kuehn, BCTF president from 1981 to 1984, describes this centralized, coordinated strategy as being similar to traditional pattern bargaining, but occurring simultaneously across all 75 school districts: "After every single bargaining session where somebody in some local got something, they put it on to the network which then became a bottom line for everybody ... on those issues."[10] In contrast, there was little communication among school districts and effectively no coordination.[11]

Job action in the form of "work to rule" campaigns (involving withdrawal of certain non-instructional services), strikes, and lockouts were common during this period. Over 50 local work stoppages, including three lengthy lockouts, arose in local teacher disputes, resulting in over a quarter million person days lost (Special data request, Human Resources and Skills Development Canada; see Appendix A). Essential service restrictions on strike activity were rarely sought, and appear not to have been pursued to the point of LRB designations. One labour relations expert suggests that many school boards were likely unaware that they could seek essential service restrictions on teacher work stoppages.[12] Nor was voluntary interest arbitration common. BCTF opposed arbitration during this period because it had just emerged from 40 years of a scheme of compulsory interest arbitration on narrow issues, and so to resort to arbitration under the new bargaining scheme struck BCTF as "going backwards."[13]

Also notable is that, unlike in later years, the government directly intervened in teacher bargaining only once during this era. Voluntary settlements were reached in every school district in the first two negotiating rounds, except for the 1993 bargaining round in the Vancouver School District. In the context of a declining economy and weakening support among teachers for striking, the government legislated an end to a 26-day strike after mediation failed and the parties rejected voluntary arbitration (BCTF n.d., "Steps Leading to Full Bargaining Rights, point 18, 19; *Educational Programs Continuation Act* 1993). Introduced and passed on a Sunday, the legislation directed teachers to return to work the following day, imposed binding arbitration to resolve the dispute, and contained a clear threat to intervene in other disputes. Employers reported that this did, indeed, encourage other districts to settle (BCPSEA 1993, 9).

Although this local, near full-scope bargaining structure was in place only until 1994, it continues to play a central role in today's debates over teacher bargaining. BCTF remains committed to returning to this bargaining framework, while school boards and government remain concerned about whether boards can bargain effectively or are at a structural disadvantage in local bargaining, and about the prevalence and length of work stoppages that occurred under local bargaining.

Centralization and Two-Tier Bargaining: 1994

In 1994 the structure of public sector labour relations in British Columbia was transformed when the NDP government imposed a highly centralized and coordinated two-tier bargaining structure on each segment of the public sector (*Public Education Labour Relations Act* 1994; *Public Sector Employers Act* 1993). These changes were partly motivated by concern over the past experience with local bargaining in K–12 education and the perception that local bargaining resulted in school boards being forced to accept unaffordable collective agreements (Korbin 1993, F20). An objective of this new centralized model was to ensure that the provincial government would be able to exercise greater control over public sector costs (Wright 2004, 9).

The *Public Sector Employers Act* (*PSEA*) established an umbrella Public Sector Employers' Council (PSEC) and employers' associations in all six components of the public sector, including the BC Public School Employers' Association (BCPSEA) in the K–12 education sector. PSEC was charged with setting and coordinating human resources and labour relations strategies, offering ongoing consultation between public sector employers and employee representatives on policy issues, and providing a "framework of coordination and accountability to the government" (British Columbia Hansard 1993, 9017). As Commissioner Wright later noted, "The BCTF was opposed to this centralization and remains so to this day" (2004, 9).

The *Public Education Labour Relations Act* (*PELRA*) created a single, provincewide teachers' bargaining unit, and deemed BCTF and BCPSEA the bargaining agents for all K–12 public school teachers and school boards in the province. The statute also established a two-tier bargaining model, with negotiations to occur at both provincial and local tables.[14] All cost provisions were statutorily required to be negotiated at the provincial table (*PELRA* 1994, ss. 7(3), (4)), although BCTF and BCPSEA could delegate responsibility to school boards and teachers' local unions to negotiate certain, non-cost matters at local tables. BCTF and BCPSEA were entitled to designate which bargaining issues would be provincial or local matters (ibid., s. 7(2)), with the exception of "cost provisions"—defined as all provisions relating to salaries, benefits, time worked and paid leave that affected the cost of a collective agreement—which must be bargained at the provincial level (ibid., ss. 7(3), (4)). Only for negotiation of the first provincial agreement, if the parties were unable to agree on a designation, the Minister could appoint an arbitrator to resolve the designation dispute (ibid., s. 7(5)). In April 1995 BCTF and BCPSEA reached agreement on the provincial-local split of issues, with the result that only matters of limited importance to working conditions and with no cost implications would be bargained locally (BCPSEA 2006a, 22; BCPSEA 2007, Letter of Understanding 1). One matter, evaluation of teachers' performance, was submitted to arbitration, and Arbitrator Hope decided that this matter should be negotiated at the provincial table (BCPSEA 2010a, 3).

Two-Tier Negotiations under an NDP Government

Two rounds of teacher negotiations were held under this new centralized model while the NDP government remained in power. No strikes or lockouts occurred, but nor did the parties succeed in negotiating a truly provincial agreement, and the provincial government directly intervened in both sets of negotiations. The resulting collective agreements were widely seen to favour BCTF, leaving school boards with insufficient flexibility and unmanageable costs. The consequent employer resentment coloured future bargaining.

Round one: 1994–1996

Most local teacher agreements expired 30 June 1994, coinciding with the date the new bargaining legislation came into force. Negotiations began in May 1995 and from the outset promised to be difficult. First, the new legislation provided no guidance for transforming the 75 local agreements into a single provincial collective agreement nor, unlike in the health sector for instance, did it require that this round of bargaining produce such an agreement.[15] Experts regard this omission as significantly contributing to the ongoing failure of this bargaining model.[16]

Second, BCTF and BCPSEA adopted opposing views of the starting point for negotiations. BCTF took a "no concessions" approach, adopting the earlier local collective agreements as the starting point for negotiations (BCPSEA 2006a, 23). Meanwhile, BCPSEA took a "blank slate" approach, reflecting its view that "the parties were essentially creating a first collective agreement" (ibid.). Further complicating matters, school boards, feeling they had been victims in local bargaining, regarded this first provincial round as "an opportunity … to level that playing field."[17]

By spring 1996, little progress had been made, labour disputes were brewing with nurses and college instructors, and a strike of support staff was imminent in Surrey School District. In a move seen as intended to avoid labour disruption in the lead-up to the May provincial election, in April the NDP government passed emergency legislation (*Education and Health Collective Bargaining Assistance Act* 1996 (Bill 21)). Bill 21 provided that, in the health care and education sectors, recommendations of an LRC-appointed industrial inquiry commissioner or mediator would be deemed to be the collective agreement, except for matters the parties had agreed to or later agreed to vary.

With this implicit threat of an imposed collective agreement, the NDP government then engaged in direct discussions with BCTF. These actions compelled BCTF and BCPSEA to agree to a Transitional Collective Agreement (TCA) in May 1996, which rolled over pre-existing local agreements, except for a 2 percent salary increase and certain other agreed-upon provisions. The TCA had an effective date of 17 June 1996, expired on 30 June 1998, and required negotiations to restart in March 1997 (*BCTF v. BC* 2011, para. 94; BCPSEA 2006a, 24). Both BCPSEA and BCTF urged their members to accept the TCA, regarding it as a way to avoid a destructive labour dispute and give the parties a period of stability to negotiate a new provincial agreement (Boei 1996). Although many school boards vehemently and publicly opposed the proposal, concerned about its cost implications, ultimately school boards voted by a slim majority to accept it (ibid.).

Round two: 1997–1998

As required by the TCA, negotiations resumed in March 1997. BCPSEA and BCTF continued their "blank slate" and "no concessions" standoff (BCPSEA 2006a, 25). In the meantime, effective 1 December 1996, the number of school districts in the province were reduced from 75 to 60 through reorganization and amalgamation, and addition of a separate Francophone Education Authority (*Miscellaneous Statute Amendment Act* 1996). This consolidation exacerbated the existing problem of the failure to negotiate a truly provincial agreement, as teachers in the amalgamated districts refused to give up their local provisions.[18] Consequently, amalgamated districts effectively still had the two or three local agreements of the pre-existing districts.

The teachers' contract was the first public sector agreement expiring in this round. A former employer negotiator recalls that the NDP government had wanted to use the teacher negotiations to establish a specific compensation pattern, 0-0-2 percent increase over three years, for the remaining sectors.[19] This, he believes, prompted the government to become directly involved in teacher negotiations.

In February 1998, PSEC volunteered to assist BCPSEA in bargaining. However, rather than providing bargaining assistance, the NDP government negotiated directly with BCTF, and without BCPSEA's knowledge or participation (BCPSEA 2006a, 25).[20] On 17 April 1998 the BCTF and

PSEC reached an Agreement in Committee (AIC), a three-year agreement expiring 30 June 2001 that included all provisions of the TCA except for certain salary increases, improved staffing ratios, and class size reductions (BCTF 1998a, 1998b). The parties also signed a second document, a Memorandum of Agreement in K–3 Primary Class Size, establishing class sizes for kindergarten to grade 3 and funding for reduced class sizes (BCTF 1998a).

BCTF supported the AIC, and 74 percent of BCTF members voted to approve the agreement (BCTF 1998b, 1998c; Bolan 1998). However, BCPSEA and school boards strongly objected to the AIC, concerned about its lack of certainty and regulation of costs, and 86 percent of school boards voted to reject it (BCPSEA 2006a, 26).[21] BCTF then refused to return to the bargaining table and threatened a strike (BCTF 1998c). Within a few days the government passed Bill 39 imposing the AIC terms as the provincial collective agreement in force from 1 July 1998 to 30 June 2001 (*Public Education Collective Agreement Act* 1998). The Education Minister asserted that it was necessary to impose a contract since the school year began in 76 days and the parties were far from agreement (Bolan 1998). BCPSEA and many school boards regarded the AIC and Bill 39 as tying their hands and ignoring their concerns (ibid.).

Two-Tier Bargaining under a Liberal Government

The next era of centralized bargaining began under the new Liberal government of Premier Gordon Campbell, which had won all but two seats in the May 2001 election. This government was determined to undo the favourable union settlements of the predecessor government, contain costs, and rein in labour in the province. Shortly after taking office the new government introduced significant changes to the *Labour Relations Code*, including reintroducing explicit, and expanded, essential service restrictions on teachers' work stoppages (*Skills Development and Labour Statutes Amendment Act* 2001).

Round three: 2001–2002

The third round of two-tier bargaining began in 2001 and negotiations soon ran into difficulties. BCTF characterized BCPSEA's positions as "concessionary" and "contract-stripping" (BCTF n.d., "Steps Leading to Full Bargaining Rights," point 23), and brought an unsuccessful bad faith bargaining complaint that was ultimately dismissed (*BCPSEA* 2002, B340/2002).

By mid-fall 2001 teachers had commenced a work stoppage, encouraged by an October strike vote with 91.4 percent of BCTF members in favour (BCTF 2001). On November 8, the BCTF withdrew non-essential services in the first of three planned phases of strike action, threatening to withdraw teachers from classroom instruction in the next phase (BCTF n.d., "Bargaining Rights"). In early December, BCTF announced that the first phase would be expanded in January to include withdrawal of supervision for extracurricular activities (BCTF 2002; *BCPSEA* 2001, B383/2001, B431/2001). This was the first time the LRB had issued essential service designations in a teachers' dispute.

In late November the government appointed two experienced labour relations experts, Richard Longpre as a fact-finder and, soon after, Stephen Kelleher as a facilitator, to assist the negotiations. However, these efforts failed. With negotiations stalled, on 18 January 2002 Premier Campbell publicly warned the parties that the teachers' dispute would be resolved within one week (Steffenhagen 2002). On January 22, BCTF offered a "Framework for Settlement," which BCPSEA rejected.

Once the government announced it was recalling the legislature to deal with the teachers' dispute, BCTF announced it would hold a one-day walkout. In response, on January 24, BCPSEA sought an LRB declaration that a full withdrawal of services, prior to an essential services ruling, or following a legislated collective agreement and return to work, would constitute an illegal strike.

The next day, January 25, the government introduced a series of bills addressing public sector labour relations and the teachers' dispute specifically (*Education Services Collective Agreement Act* 2002; *Public Education Flexibility and Choice Act* 2002; Bills 27 and 28). With the government's overwhelming majority in the legislature, all were passed by the end of the weekend sitting. The day these bills were passed, the LRB declared it would be an illegal strike for teachers to withdraw services (*BCPSEA* 2002, B34/2002). Bill 27 imposed a collective agreement for teachers, rolling-over the expired agreement to 30 June 2004, including all terms agreed to during negotiations, and a 7.5 percent salary increase over the three years. It also provided for a review of the teacher bargaining structure, which would give rise to the 2003 Wright Commission.

Bill 28 substantially reduced the scope of teacher bargaining in K–12 education. It explicitly provided that the right of an institution to establish such matters as class size and composition, course assignment, length of the instructional day and year, and workload and staffing ratios prevails over any collective agreement or legislative provisions. Though disputes arising from Bill 28 were to be determined by arbitration, these rights could not be restrained by an injunction, prohibition, or stay of proceedings of an arbitrator or the Board, and Bill 28 would prevail over any inconsistent provision of the *Labour Relations Code* (1996). Furthermore, any collective agreement provision inconsistent with Bill 28 would be void, as would be any provision requiring parties to negotiate any such provision. Finally, Bill 28 set out a transitional process by which an arbitrator would determine, by 11 May 2002, whether provisions in the collective agreement imposed by Bill 27 conflicted or were inconsistent with the new legislative requirements. The arbitrator was required to delete any offending provision from the collective agreement, and the arbitrator's decision was to be final and binding and not subject to review or appeal. BCTF successfully challenged the arbitration arising out of Bill 28, but the government, rather than embark on an expensive appeal of this decision, simply passed Bill 19 to enact the quashed arbitral award (*BCTF v. BCPSEA* 2004; *Education Services Collective Agreement Amendment Act* 2004). As a result, many working and learning condition issues that had historically been central to teacher negotiations were now excluded from bargaining and subject to unilateral determination by the government and employers as matters of public policy.

The education and health care bills were met with widespread and angry reactions from BCTF and other public sector unions, including a one-day illegal teachers' strike on Monday, 28 January 2002. Several unions launched *Charter* challenges against the government's labour legislation, including BCTF's challenge of Bills 27 and 28, and a series of successful complaints alleging that six BC statutes passed in January 2002 and dealing with public sector labour relations contravened ILO Conventions and freedom of association principles.[22] Even after the legislated end to bargaining, teachers in several districts continued to engage in job action, including refusing to attend extracurricular activities and parent-teacher interviews outside of instructional hours (*BCPSEA* 2002, B56/2002, para. 12). This led to BCPSEA's filing an illegal strike declaration with the labour relations board, a multi-day hearing on the issue, and interim orders prohibiting illegal strike activity (*BCPSEA* 2002, B125/2002).

BCTF challenged Bills 27, 28, and certain later legislation, claiming that these bills violated the *Charter* freedom of association and equality guarantees; BCTF also charged that the government had acted in concert with BCPSEA during the 2001–02 negotiations, causing BCPSEA to bargain in bad faith. These claims were finally decided by the BC Supreme Court in April 2011 (*BCTF v. BC*). Notably, the Court also found as fact that BCPSEA and the government had been discussing the government's legislative direction such that BCPSEA was aware that the government was likely to pass legislation removing class size, composition, and non-enrolling ratios from collective bargaining, and found as a fact that this influenced BCPSEA's bargaining strategy (ibid., paras. 170, 172, 183). The Court concluded that this likely contributed to the poor progress made in negotiations. BCPSEA's hard bargaining, however, did not amount to bad faith negotiating (ibid., para. 183).

Two reports regarding the bargaining structure in K–12 education were issued following this round of bargaining. In spring 2002, a Select Standing Committee on Education report concluded, on the basis of public hearings and consultations, that collective agreements, regulations, and other bureaucratic structures resulted in an inflexible and unresponsive education system that neglected professionalism and best practices.

Among its recommendations were to amend legislation to ensure that statutory provisions supersede collective agreement provisions, and to ensure flexibility of educational institutions to assign staff, and to organize and schedule learning opportunities (Select Standing Committee on Education 2002). Second, the Commission of Inquiry to Review Teacher Collective Bargaining, known as the Wright Commission, arose out of Bill 27, tasked with reviewing and recommending changes to the structure of collective bargaining for K–12 education in the province. Commissioner Wright consulted with and sought submissions from the BCTF, BCPSEA, and British Columbia School Trustees Association (BCSTA), and met with school boards and local teacher associations before issuing a final report in December 2004 (Wright 2004). This report made a dozen recommendations for achieving "mature" collective bargaining in this sector.

Round four: 2004–2005

The next set of negotiations, commencing in November 2004, demonstrated the limits of inflexible government control over bargaining in education, and culminated in a provincewide illegal teachers' strike of unprecedented length. Several difficulties complicated this round. First, BCTF's continued rejection of Bills 27 and 28 was reflected in its bargaining agenda which prioritized restoring working and learning condition provisions "stripped" from the collective agreement by Bill 28, restoring full-scope bargaining, and increasing salaries (BCTF 2005a). Second, PSEC had set a "net zero" compensation mandate across the public sector for the 2003–2006 period even though, unlike earlier in the decade, the provincial economy was healthy, with a substantial anticipated surplus (BCPSEA 2006a).

BCTF made several efforts to engage the government directly about working and learning conditions (BCTF 2005a, 2005b; Sims 2005), and by September 2005 BCTF was seeking parallel discussions with government about working and learning conditions, rather than seeking to return these matters to the bargaining table. Education Minister Shirley Bond would not agree to a "special negotiating track" and would not revisit the question of returning class size to the negotiations (Rud 2005a). Therefore, from the very beginning of this round, BCTF was demanding that BCPSEA negotiate outside of what it understood to be its fiscal mandate and its legal authority. BCTF's complaint that this constituted bad faith bargaining was unsuccessful (*BCTF* 2006, B136/2006).

On September 19, the Minister of Labour appointed Associate Deputy Minister of Labour, Rick Connolly, as fact-finder with a mandate to determine and report on the parties' positions and perspectives and assess the prospect of success of further negotiations. The resulting fact-finding report, delivered on September 30, identified compensation and negotiability of working and learning conditions as the two key sources of impasse, and concluded that BCTF's compensation demands were irreconcilable with PSEC's mandate. Ultimately, the report concluded that there was no prospect for a voluntary resolution due to the parties' differences on the two key issues (Connolly 2005, 4).

Meanwhile, BCTF's September 20 to 22 strike vote resulted in 88.4 percent support for a strike (BCTF 2005c). The first part of BCTF's three-phase plan for job action commenced September 28, with teachers withdrawing from specific administrative duties, subject to Labour Board essential service orders (BCPSEA 2005, B255/2005, B262/2005). Notably, this is the first time that *Labour Relations Code* essential service restrictions were sought or applied in a teacher dispute.

The Minister of Labour blamed bargaining structure for the negotiations breakdown, contending that the Connolly report "confirmed that we have a broken bargaining system and we will not see negotiated settlements until that system is fixed" (British Columbia. Ministry of Labour and Citizens' Services 2005a). A week after the fact-finding report was issued, the government introduced and passed Bill 12, renewing the expired collective agreement until 30 June 2006 (*Teachers' Collective Agreement Act* 2005). The Minister explained that this was meant to give the parties "breathing space" and time for a new bargaining procedure to be devised before bargaining resumed (British Columbia. Ministry of Labour and Citizens' Services 2005a).

The BCTF immediately responded with an October 5 membership vote, with 90.5 percent of votes cast in favour of taking "a stand in protest against Bill 12" (BCTF 2005d). BCTF then led an illegal teachers' strike beginning October 7 and continuing for ten school days, to October 23. This provincewide illegal strike was the largest work stoppage in BC's history of labour relations in education, and among the largest teachers' work stoppages in the country, resulting in 380,000 lost person days (Special data request, Human Resources and Skills Development Canada; see Appendix A). BCTF and its members defied an LRB order to return to work, and BCPSEA obtained a civil contempt order fining BCTF $500,000 (*BCPSEA v. BCTF* 2005). There was surprising public support, which grew rather than diminished over the course of the strike, for teachers' illegal action (Ipsos Reid 2005). School boards were also remarkably supportive of teachers. By October 13, 26 school boards had passed motions supporting teachers, calling on the government to negotiate with teachers, some urging the government to rescind Bill 12, and others seeking a return to local bargaining (BCTF 2005e; Menzies 2005).

The day Bill 12 was introduced, the Minister of Labour also announced that an Industrial Inquiry Commissioner would be appointed to develop a new bargaining process to be instituted for the resumption of negotiations. The terms of reference of this appointment directed the Commissioner to consider the findings and recommendations of the Wright Report, and to comply with statutory restrictions on the scope of bargaining in education (British Columbia. Ministry of Labour and Citizens' Services 2005b). Three days later Vince Ready, a respected arbitrator, was appointed Commissioner (British Columbia. Ministry of Labour and Citizens' Services 2005c). At the same time, the Minister of Education announced creation of a Learning Roundtable (LRT) as a permanent forum for discussion of class size, composition, and related issues. Representatives of the BCTF, BC Confederation of Parent Advisory Councils, BCSTA, BC School Superintendents Association, BC Principals' and Vice-Principals' Association, and other stakeholders were invited to take part. The Minister also announced that the government would hold an annual Teachers' Congress, inviting teachers and others to communicate directly with government (British Columbia. Ministry of Education 2005).

On October 17, Commissioner Ready's mandate was expanded to include facilitating teachers' return to work (Ready 2005, 2). On October 19, after meeting with the parties and the government, Ready concluded that discussions had reached impasse. Ready issued his report the following evening, with recommendations "conditional on prompt votes by the parties and an expeditious return to work by the teachers" (ibid., 2-3). Ready made non-binding recommendations about harmonizing salary grids, benefits, teachers on call, and class size and composition, with a value of approximately $100 million, plus $170 million to limit class sizes in grades 4–12 and to improve special education. Ready also recommended that the government consult with BCTF regarding potential *School Act* amendments regarding class sizes; that there be more BCTF representatives on the Learning Roundtable; and that the government and BCTF engage in an ongoing process of discussion about teaching issues. Ready noted that this dispute brought to the fore the tremendous communications gap between government and BCTF, and recommended that a procedure for ongoing communication between the two be established. The provincial government and both bargaining agents accepted Ready's recommendations, and teachers returned to work the following day.

Round five: 2006

Several unusual contextual factors shaped the 2006 round of bargaining that added pressure to the government to ensure a peaceful and quick resolution to negotiations. These included the surprising public support for the teachers' illegal strike; government's desire to ensure there would be no labour disruptions for the 2009 provincial election or 2010 Vancouver Winter Olympics; and the fact that over 150 public sector collective agreements were expiring during 2006, covering approximately 97 percent of public sector workers. This round of negotiations was also relieved of some contentious issues. Ready's October 2005 recommendations, accepted unconditionally by the government, included several costly terms that went some distance toward addressing some of BCTF's earlier bargaining demands. Also, in May 2006 Bill 33 was passed, establishing class size limits for grades 4 to 12, limits on numbers of special needs students in classrooms, accountability mechanisms, and requirements for consultation with parents and teachers on class size and composition (*Education (Learning Enhancement) Statutes Amendment Act* 2006). BCTF was reported to have said it would not settle a collective agreement in this round unless class size limits were introduced for grades 4 and above (Steffenhagen 2006).

Finally, an unexpected multi-billion dollar provincial surplus allowed PSEC to establish a new, flexible, and rich Negotiations Framework that included several financial incentives. It reserved $1 billion in signing bonuses for agreements reached before expiry of the existing contract (approximately $3,700 per employee). In the teachers' case this was 30 June 2006. Three hundred million was allocated to contracts with terms four or more years, and it provided an employee dividend fund of up to $300 million of any surplus beyond the predicted 2009–2010 surplus (British Columbia. Ministry of Finance 2005).

Negotiations were closely managed by Commissioner Ready and mediator/facilitator Irene Holden. Following Ready's earlier recommendation, government appointed a representative, Paul Straszak from the Public Service Agency, to act on its behalf to convey the government position on mandates and policy in negotiations (BCTF 2006; Ready 2006a, 3). Ready also imposed a strict timeline on negotiations and offers (Ready 2006a, 3-4). Late on June 30 and just before the signing bonus expired, the parties settled a five-year agreement (BCPSEA 2006a, 66). However, this "Framework for Settlement" did not produce final settlement on all matters and over the next year or so Holden and Ready were asked to rule on a variety of matters, including the signing bonus, seniority, sick leave, preparation time, optional 12-month pay plan, and harmonization of salary grids.

In his final report, issued in February 2007, Commissioner Ready considered whether any lessons could be drawn from this round. He concluded that the specific recommendations and guidelines made in his interim report, and which the parties agreed to implement, had helped the parties avoid breakdown and make timely progress, and that the involvement of a government representative resulted in the mandate being understood and accepted. Ready specifically concluded that it was not the format or process of negotiations, but instead the parties' commitment and the provision of support—in the form of having a mediator / facilitator and government representative involved—that were key to success in this instance. As a result, Ready stated that he was reluctant to recommend changes to the process or structure, and cautioned against treating teacher bargaining apart from other sectors (Ready 2007, 7, 8).

Aftermath

As the 2006 collective agreement approached its 30 June 2011 expiry date, government and the two negotiating parties faced a significantly changed collective bargaining environment. Key provisions of Bill 28 have been ruled invalid under the newly redefined *Charter* freedom of association; the Learning Roundtable and Bill 33, informal and statutory alternatives to negotiating working and learning conditions, have faltered; and, BCTF is demanding that the split of issues between provincial and local tables be reopened.

In mid-2007, the Supreme Court of Canada issued its *Health Services* decision addressing Bill 29, companion legislation to Bills 27 and 28 passed in 2002 that restricted collective bargaining in BC's health sector. Overturning decades of case law that unequivocally held that the *Charter* freedom of association did not protect collective bargaining, the Court redefined the *Charter* freedom of association to include protection of a right to collective bargaining. This meant that governments' power to legislatively remove matters from collective bargaining was now suddenly subject to limits arising from the newly defined *Charter* protection of a right to freedom from substantial interference with the right to collective bargaining (*Health Services* 2007).

BCTF's claim that Bills 27, 28, and certain later legislation violated the *Charter* freedom of association and equality guarantees, and allegation of bad faith bargaining were adjudicated in April 2011 (*BCTF v. BC* 2011). Relying on the *Health Services* decision, the BC Supreme Court concluded that sections of Bill 28 and Bill 19 limiting the scope of teacher collective bargaining are unjustifiable violations of the *Charter* guarantee of the freedom of association. The Court rejected the government's argument that this legislation was necessary due to exigent circumstances and "labour unrest" causing "virtual paralysis of the school system" (ibid., para. 182). The Court suspended the declaration of invalidity for 12 months to permit the government to address this decision. The Court found, however, that the challenged provision of Bill 27, which provided for merger of local collective agreement schedules following a merger of school districts, did not violate the freedom of association. The Court also dismissed the bad faith bargaining allegation (*BCTF v. BC* 2011).

In response to this decision the government has initiated a consultation process, led by the head of PSEC and similar to the Bill 29 process, to negotiate implementation of the Court decision. Its plan is to reach agreement by the end of November 2011 and implement legislation the following spring. Although the government and BCPSEA take the view that the Bill 28 process must be integrated with collective bargaining, BCTF maintains that these are separate processes (British Columbia. Ministry of Education 2011; BCPSEA 2011a, 2). BCTF shows a wholly different understanding of the Court decision. It asserts that "this judgment restores provisions stripped from our collective agreements," that these matters "are now restored for the purpose of local and provincial bargaining" (BCTF 2011), and that no discussions other than compensation are in order (BCPSEA 2011a, 2). BCTF's view of the effect of the judgment is probably overly optimistic, as the decision does not necessarily mean that these issues are to be bargained, nor that the provisions deleted by the impugned provisions of Bill 28 are simply restored to the collective agreement. It remains to be seen what the ultimate effect of this judgment will be, which introduces a tremendous amount of uncertainty into teacher bargaining in this province.

In the meantime, the Learning Roundtable, established during the post–Bill 12 dispute in October 2005 and greeted optimistically by education stakeholders as a forum to address class size, has not succeeded. By mid-2010, 13 LRT meetings have been held, the last in June 2010. However, BCTF no longer participates, having officially withdrawn from the initiative in March 2009 (BCTF 2009). Irene Lanzinger, then BCTF president, condemned the LRT as simply a government "PR exercise" (Steffenhagen 2009).

Bill 33, the 2006 class-size legislation, which stakeholders had also been optimistic about and which was to have been informed by LRT discussions, has also proven an ineffective means of governing this workload issue. It has given rise to an extraordinary amount of litigation as BCTF has challenged first the legislation, and then class sizes, in thousands of classrooms each year. BCTF filed grievances alleging violation of Bill 33 for the 2006/07 and 2007/08 school years, involving 157 schools in 18 school districts and 1,699 classes. The grievances resulted in a series of arbitrations and awards, including one requiring 54 days of hearings. While disputes for the first two school years under Bill 33 are now essentially resolved, there is much more litigation outstanding and to come. BCTF has grieved class size and composition for 14,000 classes for the 2008/09 school year, numerous classes for the 2009/10 year, and has given notice to BCPSEA that it will file local class size and composition grievances for the 2010/11 year (BCPSEA 2010b, 4).

Finally, BCTF is seeking to renegotiate the agreed-upon split of issues and has announced that it is prepared to obtain this change through legal action if BCPSEA will not agree (BCPSEA 2010a, 2). BCTF demands a two-tier negotiating structure under which all matters would be negotiated locally except for wages, benefits, hours of work, and paid leave; that is, class size and composition would be bargained locally. BCPSEA has responded that it prefers to retain the current split of issues. It did propose that a third party review issues to recommend the appropriate level for negotiations, but BCTF rejected that suggestion (BCPSEA 2011b, 2).

EVALUATION AND ASSESSMENT

By any standard, teacher collective bargaining in British Columbia has not been a success. The five bargaining rounds held since the 1994 introduction of two-tier negotiating have produced only one negotiated settlement. This was not a typical round of bargaining, and not likely indicative of a change in the parties' prospects for reaching voluntary settlement in future. Moreover, the parties have not yet actually achieved a truly provincial agreement. The provincial agreement continues to contain a significant number of local provisions as a residual from the local bargaining era. The previous local bargaining structure was no more successful, producing unsatisfactory agreements and a high level of strikes and lockouts. This part of the chapter addresses and assesses four key aspects of the teacher bargaining structure—location and scope of bargaining, bargaining agency, and dispute resolution—considering incorporating recommendations of past reviews of teacher bargaining and offering some concluding thoughts on the prospects for more successful future teacher negotiations.

Location of Bargaining

The issue of where issues are to be negotiated—at the local or provincial level—has been a subject of long-running disagreement among education stakeholders. This section first assesses the local bargaining experience of 1987 to 1993 as a backdrop to evaluating the existing two-tier structure and recent calls for revisiting the distribution of issues between local and provincial bargaining tables.

Views on the success of the former local bargaining structure differ starkly among participants. BCTF favours local bargaining and has consistently and forcefully advocated for all matters to be returned to local bargaining tables along with the right to strike locally. Under local bargaining, teachers won substantial gains in working and learning provisions and very significant salary increases (BCTF n.d., "History," 5). In contrast, employers believe that the local bargaining structure gave teachers an unfair advantage, and regarded the resulting collective agreements as insufficiently flexible and unaffordable, seriously diminishing school boards' managerial role, and producing cost increases that significantly outpaced inflation (BCPSEA 2006a, 15; Korbin 1993, F20; Wright 2003, 3). Each round of negotiations in the local bargaining era also involved many, often lengthy, work stoppages.

Some summary statistics offer a sense of the scale of work stoppage activity that occurred during this era. The three rounds of bargaining held between 1987 and 1993 produced 50 work stoppages, including three lockouts. Stoppages lasted from one to 80 days, with an average length of 20.2 days. A total of 1,010 days of work stoppage occurred, involving 242,320 teacher days (see Appendix A).

BCTF contends that this was not overly disruptive because, although frequent, strikes were generally short and did not occur in the majority of districts in any round (Wright 2003, 4). Although school boards dis-agreed about whether these disputes had negative effects, many agreed that teachers' widespread, non-strike, work-to-rule initiatives had been very disruptive (BCPSEA 1993, 9).

Some school boards regarded the widespread strikes as further evidence of the "unequal bargaining position between the local school board and the BCTF" (Wright 2003, 4). Others suggested that the local bargaining structure may have encouraged strikes since once a matter had been settled in one district, teachers' locals in other districts could credibly strike to achieve the same terms. They also contended that this led to more favourable outcomes for teachers, as mediators' and arbitra-tors' decisions were influenced by other districts' settlements (BCPSEA 2006a, 15).

Contrary to employer perceptions, it was not the bargaining structure itself that gave teachers an advantage in negotiations. Instead, it arose from the relative level of coordination and preparedness of the bargaining agents. BCTF and its locals were highly coordinated, disciplined, and prepared for negotiations, while school boards were not. In effect, lo-cal negotiations pitted a well-resourced, sophisticated, and organized central teachers' union, the provincial BCTF, against individual school boards, which had fewer resources and support, and little coordination or centralization. This mismatch between the parties at the bargaining tables gave teachers an undeniable advantage and undermined effective negotiations.[23]

The BC School Boards' Association had tried to coordinate school board negotiations, but few boards chose to participate in this voluntary organization, preferring to bargain independently (Lawton et al. 1999, 91). Many boards rejected centralized bargaining because they viewed themselves as accountable only to the community that had elected them and, therefore, were not primarily concerned with the broader effects their local agreements might have on other boards (BCPSEA 2006a, 15; Wright 2003, 3-4). Commissioner Wright questioned whether school boards could ever have been as organized and disciplined in negotiations as the BCTF because of boards' orientation toward local accountability (Wright 2003, 3-4). Another complicating factor reducing the effectiveness of lo-cal bargaining was that school boards were often politicized bodies with many members endorsed by the BCTF during their election campaigns. Moreover, many principals and vice-principals, previously included in teachers' associations and agreements, had difficulty adapting to their new role which, for some, included being on the employer's negotiating team (Geisert and Chandler 1991, 7).

Assessing two-tier bargaining

Although the mismatch between parties' approaches to local bargaining, not necessarily the bargaining structure, produced outcomes that employers and government were unhappy with, the perception that local bargaining put employers at a structural disadvantage became an important driver for the NDP government's 1994 centralization of collective bargaining in education. A second key motivation for restructuring public sector negotiations was the tension between dual governmental responsibilities as employer and service provider accountable to citizens. Overall the restructuring was intended to increase central control over public sector costs, increase coordination and accountability to government, and equalize bargaining power (*BCTF v. BC* 2011, 132; British Columbia Hansard 1993, 9017; Wright 2004, 9).

Introduction of a centralized, two-tier public sector bargaining structure was controversial and BCTF, especially, remains dissatisfied with the system. However, Commissioner Wright commended the restructuring as a non-partisan decision of a government that had strong ties with teachers but that was responding to "elements which transcend partisan politics, left-right labels, and pro-labour versus pro-management sympathies. There is something about the reality of providing public education, and what the public expects of its government, that exerts a powerful influence on how any government behaves" (2003, 5-6).

The resulting legislation established a two-tier bargaining structure consisting of "provincial" and "local" matters (*PELRA* 1994, ss. 1, 7, 8). BCTF and BCPSEA agreed on the provincial-local split of issues in April 1995, and this split has remained unchanged to date. All substantive matters, including monetary provisions, are negotiated provincially. The result is that virtually all matters are bargained at the provincial table, such that the parties commonly refer to it as a "provincial" bargaining model.[24] Notably, and unlike in the similarly restructured health-care sector, there was no legislative requirement that the parties achieve a single, integrated provincial agreement.[25]

BCPSEA and BCTF were required to establish policies and procedures for delegating authority to boards of education and BCTF locals to negotiate local matters (*PELRA* 1994, ss. 8(1), (2), (4)). Local matters that cannot be resolved at that table may be referred by either party to the provincial table (ibid., s. 8(3)). The provincial agents exercise significant oversight of local negotiations. Not only must local agreements be ratified by BCPSEA, but it requires school boards to inform BCPSEA of their and BCTF's bargaining proposals and developments in negotiations, and to follow direction from the BCPSEA Board of Directors in bargaining (BCPSEA 2007, vii-viii). BCTF exercises similar control over local teacher association negotiations. Local matters can be based on locally set objectives, following review of the provincial BCTF Bargaining Conference's advice. Provincial BCTF Field Service officers are to be fully informed of proposed agreements so they can meet with and advise the local of the "wisdom of the proposal and its impact, if any, on other locals," and locals are prohibited from entering agreements without the advice of

Field Service officers (BCTF 2010, Art. 3.F). Although not requiring central ratification of local matters, the provincial BCTF does require central ratification of local agreements on local options (ibid.).

The parties have also established a mid-contract modification process, which is broadly defined to include matters involving procedure or interpretation, rather than just changes to collective agreement language. Modification is the responsibility of the provincial parties, even if reopening the matter was initiated at the local level. Both parties exercise considerable central oversight over modifications. For local matters, BCPSEA requires school boards to obtain its advice prior to negotiating modifications to local matters, and to obtain its approval of the agreement (BCPSEA 2007, 2010b). Although BCTF locals must seek Field Service advice in advance, locals may apply their own procedures to authorize modifications (BCTF 2010, Part 3, Section H).

The primary criticism of teacher bargaining under the two-tier structure is that the parties have failed to engage in what Commissioner Ready called "meaningful" negotiations (Ready 2006b, 6). This is evidenced by the parties' dismal record at settling agreements and the frequency of government interference in negotiations and legislated solutions. As discussed later in this chapter, and with the notable exception of the lengthy illegal strike in 2005, work stoppages were not a significant feature of this bargaining regime.

BCTF contends that the two-tier structure, with the split of issues agreed on by the provincial parties in 1995, does not satisfactorily address issues specific to individual school districts, that the mid-contract modification process is "broken," and that BCPSEA engages in "incessant interference" in local matters (Polukoshko and Ehrcke 2010). To get around this, BCTF says it has "gone underground," reaching informal arrangements with certain school boards.[26] This suggests that local school boards and trustees are still tractable in their dealings with BCTF. Meanwhile, the BC School Trustees Association has suggested that the "vastness of the provincial table," under the current split of issues, is an impediment to agreement (BCSTA 2003) and sees benefit in addressing local needs at local tables (BCSTA 2004, 2-3).

Revisiting the location of bargaining

Although BCTF has been determined from early on to return to full local bargaining, this option was not supported by BCPSEA, BCSTA, or by Commissioner Wright. Both BCSTA and Wright point to the existing "cogovernance" model for K–12 education in the province as necessitating a provincial bargaining table (BCSTA 2003; Wright 2004, 19). Under this model, in place since the early 1990s, the provincial government sets the major policy direction and provides almost all the funding for this sector, while delivery sensitive to local needs is the responsibility of local school boards (Wright 2004, 19). Because almost all K–12 funding comes from the province, Wright concluded that major cost items must be negotiated at the provincial level, and that it is important to maintain what he terms "alignment" between the source of funding and the level of negotiations (2004, 19). BCSTA has expressly stated that it does not favour reintroduction of local bargaining, noting that doing so would not be practical in the absence of local taxation authority, and BCSTA does not seek to return to that funding model (BCSTA 2003). After a decade of experience with the system and after considering the views of education stakeholders, Commissioner Wright in his 2004 report on teacher bargaining ultimately recommended retaining a two-tier structure.

Revisiting the split of issues

The split of issues between local and provincial tables has remained unchanged since the parties' 1995 agreement on the matter. Recently, as noted earlier in this chapter, BCTF has demanded that BCPSEA agree to a new split of issues (BCPSEA 2010a, 1). BCSTA, BCPSEA, and BCTF hold different views about the appropriate mix of local and provincial matters. BCTF wants all matters negotiated locally except for wages, benefits, hours of work, and paid leave (BCPSEA 2011b, 1). BCPSEA prefers to retain the current split of issues, though it proposed that a third party make recommendations about the appropriate level for negotiating specific issues (BCPSEA 2011b, 2). In the past, BCSTA (2003) has supported limiting major cost items at the provincial table to salary and benefits, and bargaining other items locally, on the condition that "an adequately funded bargaining support infrastructure must be available to local school boards in order to make a level playing field possible" (BCSTA 2004, 2). BCSTA addressed the concern over inefficiency, cost, and duplication of effort with 60 local tables with substantial bargaining responsibilities by acknowledging that the initial round will require more resources, but contending that subsequent rounds will be more efficient (ibid., 2-3).

In his 2004 final report, Commissioner Wright recommended retaining the two-tier structure for negotiations, revising the split of issues between the provincial and local tables, and employing a staged approach to the modifications. Wright concluded that because the provincial government is responsible for almost all funding and for major policy direction in K–12 education, a two-tier negotiating structure was required. However, he recommended that the split of issues be reconsidered, and more issues be moved to local bargaining. To preserve alignment between negotiations and accountability, major cost items should be settled at the provincial level while non-cost and employment relationship issues such as post and fill, evaluation, leaves, and discipline should be negotiated at local tables. Wright also recommended that local tables be given real autonomy to settle matters without requiring approval of the provincial BCTF or BCPSEA, as is currently the case (Wright 2004, 19-22).

To transition to expanded local bargaining and create a sustainable bargaining model, Wright made two further recommendations. First, that provincial and local matters be bargained in different years and that the resulting agreements have staggered expiration dates. In his view, temporal separation of local and provincial bargaining would reduce the likelihood of local matters being drawn onto and mixed up with those at the provincial table. Further, local tables should use the negotiating expertise that has been developed by BCTF and BCPSEA, and this will be more available if those parties are not engaged in bargaining at the same time (Wright 2004, 53). As Wright noted, individual school boards must develop infrastructure and capacity for negotiating, which has been lost in the many years since boards negotiated, and he suggested that BCPSEA could be an important source for bargaining support. In terms of efficiency, Wright also suggested that boards cooperate regionally in negotiations, as some boards do in school staff negotiations with CUPE (ibid., 53-54).

There is merit to considering revisiting the split of issues and expanding local bargaining. However, as Commissioner Wright's suggestions recognize, it is important to ensure that local boards have sufficient support and capacity to negotiate so that the local tables do not revisit some of the problems suffered during the local era of negotiations. As Commissioners Ready and Wright both emphasized, no bargaining system will succeed unless the parties are willing to make it work. This deficit is a long-standing problem in teacher bargaining in this province, with neither the parties nor the provincial government standing blameless (Ready 2006b, 6; Wright 2004, 58).

Scope of Bargaining

There is fundamental and long-standing disagreement among education stakeholders over whether certain matters are appropriate subjects of collective bargaining that may be enshrined in enforceable collective agreements, or whether they are properly matters of public policy remaining within the government's discretion to determine or to delegate to public employers. Primary among these contentious matters are what are generally referred to as teachers' working and learning conditions. Presently the *School Act* (1996, ss. 27, 28) sets out the scope of bargaining and the content of collective agreements for teachers in the province.[27] As discussed earlier in this chapter, the most contentious of these limitations on the scope of bargaining are those introduced by Bill 28 and the subject of the April 2011 *BCTF v. BC* BC Supreme Court decision. As a result of this decision, the future limits to the scope of bargaining in this sector are in question.

A key theme throughout the history of teacher bargaining in this province has been teachers' struggle to achieve and retain full-scope collective bargaining, and especially the ability to negotiate what are generally termed "working and learning conditions," which most notably involve matters of class size and composition. BCTF maintains that it is its "right to bargain workload" and that negotiations should encompass all terms and conditions of teacher employment (Polukoshko and Ehrcke 2010). In contrast, BCPSEA and other K–12 education employer groups favour continuing to exclude class size and composition issues from bargaining. While recognizing that these are, indeed, teachers' working conditions, these stakeholders are concerned that the bargaining table is not the appropriate forum to decide such issues as they affect more than simply teachers and are fundamentally matters of education policy that the government should be accountable to the public for and that government and school boards have the electoral mandate to determine (BCSTA 2004, 7-8; Wright 2004, 40-41). Consequently, these matters are better dealt with in a non-bargaining forum or through legislation (BCPSEA 2006b; Wright 2004, 40-41).

Although Commissioner Wright identified resolving the class size, composition, and teacher ratio issues as a precondition to mature collective bargaining in this sector, he also decided against recommending that these matters be returned to the bargaining table; he worried that if he did so, then "both sides would approach negotiations from hardened positions which would significantly reduce the probability of mature collective bargaining emerging" (2004, 44-45). Instead, Wright advised the government to create a policy forum to operate outside of, but parallel to, the bargaining table. Led by the Minister of Education, the forum would involve a facilitator and representatives of school districts and teachers, none of whom should be involved in bargaining (2004, 45). The objective of this forum would be to "seek agreement on cost effective approaches to improving working and learning conditions" (ibid.).

The Learning Roundtable and Bill 33, class-size legislation to be developed through broad consultation with stakeholders through the LRT, were the two non-bargaining alternatives developed by the government to deal with the most contentious working and learning issues. In spite of initial optimism, both the LRT and Bill 33 have proven to be dismal failures, and BCTF remains determined to negotiate these matters. Even before BCTF's formal withdrawal from the LRT, it had simply become another stage for BCTF, government, and other parties to quarrel rather than a constructive forum for discussion and consultation. Meanwhile, Bill 33 has led to BCTF's bringing an enormous amount of litigation in numerous forums, costing government and school boards a tremendous amount of time and money to address. As Commissioners Wright and Ready have pointed out numerous times in their reports, no structure or initiative will succeed unless the participants want it to (Ready 2007; Wright 2004). The continuing poor relationship between BCTF and the government may be the ultimate cause of the failure of these once-promising initiatives.

The recent BC Supreme Court decision on Bills 28 and 19, concluding that portions of this legislation were unjustifiable violations of the *Charter* freedom of association, makes the question of the scope of bargaining in K–12 education in this province even more complicated and uncertain than before (*BCTF v. BC* 2011). This decision does not necessarily mean that the working and learning conditions matters removed from the bargaining table in 2002 must now be the subject of negotiation and returned to the bargaining table. Nor does it mean that the government will be unable, in future, to remove issues from bargaining. It is clear, however, that governments' ability to unilaterally and without consultation reduce the scope of bargaining is now significantly constrained.

Although in this case the Court rejected the government's argument that Bills 27 and 28 were passed in exigent circumstances, specifically "labour unrest" causing "virtual paralysis of the school system," it did accept that the government's objectives of achieving greater flexibility and better use of facilities and human resources were pressing and substantial (*BCTF v. BC* 2011, para. 182). It is important to recognize that the courts, when assessing whether government action affecting collective bargaining rights violates the *Charter*, will consider a number of factors. These include the objectives of the action, the process the government followed in taking the action, and the circumstances surrounding the action (ibid.; *Health Services* 2007). The courts have offered some guidance on what objectives and circumstances may be sufficient to permit government interference with bargaining rights, noting that reducing costs or expanding management rights are not likely to be found to be sufficiently important objectives (*BCTF v. BC* 2011, para. 333). The ultimate impact of this case and governments' consultation process to implement the decision on the scope of bargaining will likely be significant, but the full effects will take some time to determine. In the meantime, these developments add considerable uncertainty to the bargaining process.

Bargaining Agency

In British Columbia, provincial bargaining agents for public school teachers (BCTF) and school boards (BCPSEA) are statutorily designated (*PELRA* 1994, s. 6). BCPSEA is also statutorily charged with coordinating collective bargaining objectives with other public sector employer associations and is accountable to a board composed of representatives of both local school boards and the provincial government (ibid., ss. 1, 4, 6(2), 7). Employer bargaining agency in BC's K–12 education sector is a contentious issue, with disagreement arising both from the choice to create a provincial employer bargaining agent with accountability to government beyond school boards, and the tendency of the provincial government and BCTF to ignore this agent's role.

BCTF has strongly objected to BCPSEA as the designated bargaining agent for employers and is critical of its role and performance (Wright 2003, 8). Consonant with its desire for a return to full local bargaining, BCTF regards school districts and local teacher associations as the appropriate bargaining agents because teachers and trustees are the parties best positioned to decide and implement decisions sensitive to local needs. It contends that BCPSEA as bargaining agent has introduced uncertainty over authority and accountability (BCTF 2003b). Notably, although Commissioner Wright acknowledged the criticisms of BCTF and some trustees which centre on the lack of successful bargaining, fundamental disagreement with provincial-level bargaining, and lack of understanding of how BCPSEA's mandate is set and its accountability, he supported BCPSEA. He concluded that BCPSEA was not singularly responsible for failed negotiations: "Quite simply, the conditions necessary for successful bargaining have not been present, and this has more to do with the willingness, capability and determination of the teachers and provincial government to make provincial bargaining work than it has to do with the efficacy of BCPSEA as a bargaining agent" (Wright 2004, 24). Wright recommended retaining both provincial bargaining agents: BCTF, and BCPSEA as the employers' bargaining agent. He also recommended confirming and clarifying that the concerns of local school boards shape BCPSEA's mandate through trustee representatives on its Board, which is accountable to both school boards and the provincial government (2004, 25). Further, he recommended that local negotiations operate with more autonomy from the provincial agents through fuller delegation of authority (2004, 26).

A recurring theme in Wright's reports and recommendations is the crucial importance of alignment between bargaining structure and accountability for costs and funding in K–12 education, which is almost wholly provided by the provincial government. The need for a provincial employer bargaining agent stems from this need for alignment. As Commissioner Wright explains:

> [The provincial government] must have the ability to approve the employers' bargaining mandate. There will naturally be tension between the interests of the provincial government with its broader responsibilities and the more focused interests of school boards. This is inevitable given the decision to blend provincial accountability for funding with local administration of the school system. The ongoing challenge for BCPSEA is to balance the fiscal and policy objectives of the provincial government with the interests of school boards as public school employers. (2004, 25)

In addition to the challenge of reconciling the interest and concerns of school boards with the provincial government's fiscal mandate and policy directions, BCPSEA has repeatedly faced the difficulty of being bypassed by the provincial government and BCTF in negotiations. As described earlier in this chapter, in 1996 the NDP government and BCTF directly negotiated the Transitional Collective Agreement; in 1998 the NDP government reached a collective agreement without BCPSEA's knowledge or participation; and, in 2001, the Liberal government threatened BCPSEA with withdrawal of millions in school district funding unless it agreed to incorporate the class-size MOA entered into by the government and BCTF a few years earlier. The BC Supreme Court described the government's own account of this latter episode as the government "forc[ing] BCPSEA to sign an agreement against its will" (*BCTF v. BC* 2011, paras. 6, 111, 113-14). More recently, in the 2004–05 round, BCTF sought parallel discussions with the provincial government over working and learning conditions (BCTF 2005a).

What we see in British Columbia is an employer bargaining agent that is frequently given inflexible bargaining mandates by government that it must abide by due to its statutory obligation to align its bargaining with other public sectors, and this hampers settlement. Moreover, this bargaining agent has repeatedly had its bargaining authority undermined by the willingness of the provincial government—both Liberal and NDP—to bypass BCPSEA to negotiate directly with the BCTF. As a result, BCPSEA has lost the confidence of both some school board trustees and BCTF as an effective bargaining agent. This is unfortunate and short-sighted, as a central employer bargaining agent such as BCPSEA could be very effective if it was granted sufficient authority and autonomy.

Dispute Resolution

Views differ widely on what is an appropriate, desirable, or even feasible dispute resolution mechanism for K–12 teacher bargaining in British Columbia. In his 2004 final report, Commissioner Wright canvassed a variety of dispute resolution mechanism options: full strike/lockout, controlled strike/lockout as it currently exists (e.g., essential services limits), more defined essential service limitations, and interest arbitration. The *LRC* strike, lockout, and dispute resolution provisions govern teacher disputes (*School Act*, s. 29), including use of mediation, fact-finding, and commissions of inquiry, and the *LRC* essential service requirements (*LRC* 1996, s. 72).[28] Currently the primary mechanism for dispute resolution is the "controlled" work stoppage: a strike or lockout subject to the *LRC* essential service limitations.

The fundamental problem with the existing dispute resolution mechanism for teacher bargaining in this province is that access to strikes and lockouts is a "pretense" (Wright 2004, 32). Since the introduction of two-tier bargaining, the provincial government has repeatedly demonstrated that it will not permit a full strike by teachers, or even a substantial withdrawal of services within the LRB's essential service orders. Instead of allowing this mechanism to operate, the government has legislated the end to disputes. In the 2001/02 round, the first time essential service limitations were invoked in a teacher strike, government legislated an end to the dispute after less than two months of classes under phase one withdrawal of work—which affected tasks such as running assemblies, preparing report cards, and attending staff meetings—and within two weeks of job action escalating to the next phase, which was withdrawal of extracurricular supervision (BCPSEA 2002, 13-14, 17-18). Not a single day of full teaching withdrawal occurred before the government intervened.

In the next round of bargaining, in 2004/05, the government reacted even more rapidly, legislating an end to the dispute on the fourth school day of phase one job action. In that dispute, it also became apparent that BCPSEA and the government held very different understandings of essential service limits. While BCPSEA accepted withdrawal of classroom instruction as satisfying essential service requirements, the Minister of Education publicly stated the government did not share this view and would not accept students' not being in classrooms (Rud 2005b). Wright condemned this as a "pretense" that has contributed to the failure of bargaining:

> One of the reasons why collective bargaining has been so ineffective over the past ten years is that we have operated on the pretense that the strike/lockout tool was available to the parties, when in fact it was not really available. Consequently, with each round of bargaining, positions and behavior got directed more and more at positioning parties for the eventual legislated settlement because there was no alternative between strike/lockout and imposition of an agreement by the legislature. (2004, 32-33)

In Wright's view, unfettered strikes and lockouts would be the best dispute resolution tool because these tactics would foster more mature bargaining, creating a strong incentive for the parties to settle. However, he declined to recommend that option, concluding that a lengthy, full-scale strike or lockout without government intervention was not politically feasible in British Columbia at that time (2004, 31-32). He also declined to recommend a controlled work stoppage mechanism unless government was willing to accept partial withdrawal of services, as he was skeptical that government was willing to do so (ibid., 33, 37). The more recent experiences in teacher bargaining in this province suggest that it is still not a realistic option.

Two additional concerns have been raised about employing controlled work stoppages as a primary dispute resolution tool in BC's teacher bargaining. First, Wright was concerned that the LRB's essential services designation process, involving preliminary meetings, mediation, and hearings, would produce uncertainty about what will be deemed essential. This uncertainty could "distort parties' perceptions of the costs or benefits of job action" (Wright 2004, 27-28). Wright contends that this type of distortion occurred in the 2001/02 round (ibid., 8).

BCPSEA also criticizes the essential service designation approach as ill-suited to the particular features of the K–12 education sector and teachers' work (BCPSEA 2002, 3, 27-28). Essential service limitations are generally defined in the context of a complete withdrawal of services, identifying the work that will still be performed by members of the striking or locked-out bargaining unit (BCPSEA 2005, B262/2005). For example, in health care, typically positions rather than specific tasks are designated essential. As a result, non-essential workers are not working and are not paid; only essential workers remain at work and receiving pay. In contrast, the LRB's essential service designations in teachers' disputes identify particular tasks that teachers need not perform. Therefore, all teachers engage in a partial withdrawal of service, no one is off work, and all continue to receive full pay. Strikes and lockouts are designed as economic weapons, for workers and the employer to test the other's economic power and resolve. To operate effectively, there must be economic consequences to both sides. As BCPSEA points out, since no teacher is forgoing pay during a controlled strike, this partial job action "allows the union to bring disproportionate pressure to bear on the employer, with little or no pressure on the union or its members" (BCPSEA 2002, 28).

Concluding that the work stoppage mechanism—controlled or unfettered—was not a feasible option in the current BC climate, Wright proposed a different approach to fostering dispute resolution. Within a strict negotiations timeline, an independent commissioner would be appointed at the outset of bargaining, who would later adopt the role of mediator/arbitrator in final offer selection if necessary. Arbitration would be guided by two criteria: ensuring terms that would promote retention and recruitment of good teachers, and the economic situation of the province and government. This transparent process provides incentives to settlement in the form of parties' reluctance to have unreasonable positions made public by the commissioner, risk of an arbitrated settlement, and a final opportunity of a limited time period to propose an alternative, negotiated agreement after final offer selection had occurred (Wright 2004, 33-37). The transparency of the process, managed by an objective source, would increase accountability to the public, which Wright believed would encourage settlement (ibid., 7).

Commissioner Ready incorporated a timeline with a set of strict deadlines for the progress of negotiations in his management of the 2006 negotiations. Although this timeline helped the parties make timely progress, Ready concluded that it was not the format or process of bargaining that led to a voluntary collective agreement in that round. Rather, Ready attributed the settlement to the parties' commitment, support from the mediator/facilitator, and involvement of a government representative to ensure the mandate was understood and accepted (2007, 7-8). Nonetheless, Ready's limited recommendations for future negotiations focused on a timeline for the process, and support for negotiations. He advised that parties establish bargaining objectives eight months before the contract expiry; a facilitator/mediator be appointed to act throughout the process; a government representative with sufficient authority serve on the BCPSEA bargaining committee; and that the parties develop a common understanding of financial, economic, and sector data necessary for bargaining (ibid., 8-9).

A final consideration regarding dispute resolution mechanisms is that the legal landscape has changed since the government's last legislative intervention in bargaining in 2005. The 2007 *Health Services* decision, discussed earlier, imposes significant restrictions on government violation of workers' *Charter*-protected right to collective bargaining. Direct government intervention, including statutorily imposed collective agreements, is no longer as readily available to governments as it was during past rounds of negotiations. Although these limits may be less strict in circumstances of financial exigency, the precise contours of these restrictions and their exceptions are not yet clear. However, experiences in other provinces suggest that back-to-work legislation—passed after lengthy disputes involving full withdrawal of services, where significant efforts have been made to assist the parties—that directs the matter to interest arbitration rather than imposing a contract, is an available mechanism (e.g., *York University Labour Disputes Resolution Act* 2009). It is unlikely that back-to-work and collective agreement legislation such as the BC government has repeatedly resorted to will meet the new *Charter* requirements except, perhaps, in extraordinary fiscal or other circumstances.

This new and significant limitation on the government's power to intervene will likely require the government to reconsider whether to permit work stoppages to play out without government interference, or whether to end the "pretense" and introduce another dispute resolution mechanism that it finds more acceptable.

CONCLUSION: LOOKING AHEAD

Teacher collective bargaining in British Columbia's K–12 public education sector has an unenviable record. For decades negotiations have been difficult and conflict-ridden, marred by legal and illegal work stoppages, litigation, imposed collective agreements, and other legislative and government intervention in bargaining. Neither the system of local collective bargaining, in place between 1987 and 1993, nor the existing two-tier bargaining structure, employed since 1994, has produced constructive or successful negotiations or outcomes. Most recently, the five rounds of two-tier bargaining have resulted in only one voluntarily negotiated collective agreement. The highly managed nature of that round of bargaining in 2006 and the unique circumstances surrounding it suggest that this singular success does not mark a new trajectory for teacher bargaining in this province.

As we look ahead to future rounds of negotiations in this sector, it is worth considering what impediments remain and what has changed, as well as reflecting on what lessons can be learned from these experiences and where new uncertainties lie. This chapter then concludes with some thoughts on the prospects for teacher labour relations in this province.

Teacher bargaining in British Columbia suffers from several "historical hangovers"—persistent, unresolved sources of conflict that interfere with constructive negotiations. First, several long-standing structural impediments exist. These include the lack of a dispute resolution mechanism, given the effective unavailability of strikes, and the lack of a truly provincial agreement unencumbered by substantial remnants of pre-1994 local agreements. Nearly two decades later, this remains a tremendous burden on negotiations and between-rounds administrative resources. Second, for decades the BCTF and successive provincial governments spanning the political spectrum have been locked in an extraordinarily acrimonious relationship. Writing in 2004, with a Liberal government in power, Commissioner Wright emphasized the enduring and pan-political nature of this discord, and his words remain fitting today:

> It would be a mistake to think this [unhealthy relationship] is solely a function of the attitude and approach of the current administration on either side. The current state of affairs is the result of developments over more than twenty years. There have been three separate political parties in power over that period of time, all struggling with a common challenge—how to manage the expectations of the public and public sector employees over a period of disappointing economic performance. (58)

All too often, this struggle has been ended by a government that is too impatient to allow teachers' negotiations to play out to conclusion. Instead, government ends the dispute by directly intervening in bargaining, bypassing the statutory bargaining agent, or legislating a solution. Such ad hoc solutions have caused lasting damage to the parties' capacity to negotiate, angering and alienating those subjected to this blunt governmental power.

Similarly, some BCTF members, school board representatives, and government officials nurse ancient grudges that continue to taint relations and negotiations long after the original harm. For example, there is a lingering anger among employers who see themselves as having been victimized and subjected to unfairness during the 1987 to 1993 local bargaining era. Not only did this lead employers to approach early rounds of two-tier negotiations as a chance to "level the playing field" and reverse what they felt to be unfair provisions, but these resentments continue to influence today's discussions of teacher bargaining structures. Another enduring focus of conflict among parties is the negotiation of working and learning conditions, which shows little indication of being resolved without leaving one or more education stakeholders bitterly disappointed.

In addition to these deep-rooted difficulties, recent years have brought several new sources of uncertainty to the legal environment governing teacher bargaining and governments' ability to directly control public sector labour relations. A series of recent court decisions clearly signals that governments substantially interfering with collective bargaining, such as by removing terms from negotiated agreements and prohibiting future bargaining on those matters, may unjustifiably violate the *Charter* freedom of association (*BCTF v. BC* 2011; *Health Services* 2007; *Ontario v. Fraser* 2011). The contours of this new limit on government action are still unclear. This creates significant uncertainty among the parties as government is suddenly left with doubtful access to a once familiar tool of governments in this province. Moreover, the recent Court decision concluding that the Bill 28 removal of certain working and learning conditions from the agreement and future bargaining is unconstitutional has left stakeholders uncertain about procedurally how government will correct this breach, whether through bargaining, consultation, or legislation and what the substantive outcome will be (*BCTF v. BC* 2011).

In searching for a more hopeful future for teacher bargaining in British Columbia, it would be prudent to keep in mind some practical lessons learned from the past and from the thoughtful and enduring reviews of Commissioners Wright (2003, 2004) and Ready (2005, 2006a, 2006b, 2007). The key lessons of the local bargaining era are the importance of ensuring alignment between accountability and the source of funding (Wright 2004, 19) and of preventing a mismatch between bargaining parties. Failure to do so in the past generated enduring problems and resentment. More concretely, and reflecting Commissioner Wright's final recommendations (2004), this means that should the location of bargaining be revisited and local parties be given greater autonomy, as he recommended, it is crucial to ensure that this is genuine independence and genuine local bargaining. This is particularly important regarding teachers' associations given the experience in the local era of the very strong, provincial body centrally controlling negotiations. A similar dynamic could occur even voluntarily between locals and the provincial BCTF, with similar results. At the same time it is important to ensure school boards have sufficient capacity and support to negotiate on an equal footing with teacher locals. Otherwise, expanded local bargaining is inviting the same type of centralized teacher coordination and rolling-pattern bargaining that school boards believed led to unsustainable and unbalanced agreements in the past.

However, overall, there is not much cause to be optimistic about significant improvement in the teacher bargaining experience in British Columbia in the short term. New rounds of negotiations are commencing without adopting the procedural supports used and recommended by Commissioner Ready (2007) in the successful 2006 negotiations, such as the use of timelines and facilitators; and without addressing many of Commissioner Wright's (2004) recommendations such as revisiting the split of issues and authority of local agents, and improving channels of communication and data-sharing. What's more, these negotiations are taking place in the context of significant uncertainty and continuing, intense conflict between BCTF and the government.

Although the structure of collective bargaining has been identified by government and other stakeholders as the cause of the negotiating difficulties, it is worthwhile for all involved to consider that both Commissioners Ready and Wright ultimately concluded that among the most significant impediments to constructive negotiations in this province is the lack of commitment to the process by key participants. In short, it is the players rather than the structure that are most in need of reform in this case.

NOTES

1. In this chapter "education" refers to the kindergarten-grade 12 ("K-12") public education system in British Columbia, and "teacher" refers to teachers in this system.

    This research includes semi-structured interviews with several key informants, conducted between winter 2008 and spring 2011. These include past BCTF presidents Irene Lanzinger (2007–10), Jinny Sims (2004–07), and Larry Kuehn (1981–84, currently BCTF Director of Research and Technology); British Columbia Public School Employers' Association's Chief Executive Officer, Hugh Finlayson; and Kenneth Halliday, a labour relations expert who has negotiated on behalf of school boards.
2. For a detailed history of this period of the BCTF's history see Johnson (1964), Muir (1969), and Thompson and Cairnie (1973).
3. Interview with Larry Kuehn, 12 September 2010.
4. Ibid.
5. Ibid.
6. Ibid.
7. This contrasted with the earlier language of the *Essential Services Disputes Act* limiting application to "substantial disruption in the delivery of educational services" (BCPSEA 2002, 38).
8. Interview with Hugh Finlayson, 23 November 2008; and Ken Halliday, 14 November 2008.
9. Interview with Larry Kuehn, 12 September 2010.
10. Ibid.

11. Interview with Ken Halliday, 14 November 2008.
12. Interview with Hugh Finlayson, 23 February 2011.
13. Interview with Larry Kuehn, 12 September 2010.
14. This two-tier bargaining is commonly referred to as "provincial bargaining" by the parties, reflecting the fact that virtually all issues are negotiated at the provincial table.
15. Interview with Ken Halliday, 14 November 2008.
16. Ibid.; interview with Hugh Finlayson, 28 November 2008.
17. Interview with Hugh Finlayson, 28 November 2008.
18. Interview with Ken Halliday, 14 November 2008.
19. Ibid.
20. Ibid.
21. Ibid.
22. Health care unions challenged Bill 29 (*Health and Social Services Delivery Improvement Act* 2002), companion legislation to Bills 27 and 28. On 8 June 2007, the Supreme Court of Canada held that key provisions of Bill 29 violated the *Charter* guarantee of freedom of association in a manner that could not be justified in a free and democratic society but suspended declaration of invalidity of the provisions for 12 months (*Health Services* 2007).
23. Interview with Ken Halliday, 14 November 2008.
24. Interview with Irene Lanzinger, 13 April 2009.
25. Interview with Hugh Finlayson, 28 November 2008.
26. Interview with Jinny Sims, 13 April 2009.
27. See Schucher and Slinn (2012, Table 6) for a detailed list of restrictions on the scope of bargaining.
28. Note that strikes and lockouts are only lawful at the provincial level because only the provincial parties—not local teachers' associations or school boards—have the authority to authorize a work stoppage (*PELRA* 1994, s. 8).

REFERENCES

An Act to Amend the "Public Schools Act," S.B.C. 1919, c. 75.
An Act to Amend the Public Schools Act, R.S.B.C. 1971, c. C-47.
An Act to Amend the Public Schools Act, R.S.B.C. 1973, c. C-142.
An Act to Incorporate Benevolent and Other Societies, R.S.B.C. 1911, c. 19.
Boei, W. 1996. "Two Union Votes to Test Clark's Will: Health-Care, Education Pacts on the Line." *Vancouver Sun* [Final Edition], 30 May, p. B3.
Bolan, K. 1998. "Minister's Move to Impose Teachers' Deal Draws Fire: Trustees Call It the End of Local Democracy While the Teachers' Union Backs the Decision Aimed at Preventing a Labour Disruption." *Vancouver Sun* [Final Edition], 26 June, p. A3.
British Columbia. Ministry of Education. 2005. "Government Commits to New Learning Roundtable." News release, 6 October. http://www2.news.gov.bc.ca/news_releases_2005-2009/2005EDU0086-000908.htm.
—. 2011. "Consultation Begins on Bill 28 Ruling." News release, 5 May. http://www2.news.gov.bc.ca/news_releases_2005-2009/2005LCS0014-000888.htm.
British Columbia. Ministry of Finance. 2005. "Province Sets New Negotiating Framework." News release, 30 November. http://www2.news.gov.bc.ca/news_releases_2005-2009/2005FIN0023-001112.htm.

British Columbia. Ministry of Labour and Citizens' Services. 2005a. "Long-Term Solution Sought for Teacher Bargaining." News release, 3 October. http://www2.news.gov.bc.ca/news_releases_2005-2009/2005LCS0014-000888.htm.
—. 2005b. "Industrial Inquiry Commissioner Terms of Reference." Backgrounder, 6 October. http://www.bcpsea.bc.ca/access/emplgroups/teacher/bargreview_wr/ready/newsbgdrissuevr/reference-oct605.pdf.
—. 2005c. "Commission Appointed to Improve Teacher Bargaining." News release, 6 October. http://www.bcpsea.bc.ca/access/emplgroups/teacher/bargreview_wr/ready/newsbgdrissuevr/ministrynews-oct0605.pdf.
British Columbia Hansard. 1971. 1971 Legislative Session: 2nd Session, 29th Parliament (15 March).
—. 1993. 1993 Legislative Session: 2nd Session, 35th Parliament (21 July).
British Columbia Public School Employers' Association (BCPSEA). 1993. *A Report to the Minister from the Chair, Implementation Working Committee.* Vancouver, BC: K–12 Sector Employers' Association.
—. 2002. *A Case of First Instance.* Vancouver, BC: BCPSEA. http://www.bcpsea.bc.ca/documents/Publications-ResourceDiscussionDocs/00-HJF-ACaseofFirstInstance-EssentialServices.pdf.
—. 2006a. *Teacher-Public School Employer Collective Bargaining in BC: Historical Perspectives.* Vancouver, BC: BCPSEA. http://www.bcpsea.bc.ca/documents/Publications-ResourceDiscussionDocs/historicalperspective2010.pdf.
—. 2006b. *Formal Reply of the BCPSEA to the BCTF Submission on Outstanding Issues Related to Teachers on Call.* Vancouver, BC.
—. 2007. *Teacher Collective Agreement Administration Manual.* Vancouver, BC: BCPSEA. http://www.bcpsea.bc.ca/documents/Publications-TeacherCollectiveManualDocs/00-BC-LOU%2001-Desig%20Prov_Local%20Matters.pdf.
—. 2010a. *Public Policy: Teacher-Public School Employer Bargaining Process Integration 2011, Discussion Paper.* Vancouver, BC: BCPSEA.
—. 2010b. *Post-Decision: The Emerging Class Size/Composition Resolution Process – Process and Consequences.* 16 July. Vancouver, BC: BCPSEA.
—. 2011a. "Government Commences Consultation with BC Teachers' Federation regarding Bills 27 and 28." *@issue* 2011-13, 20 May. http://www.bcpsea.bc.ca/Files/No%202011-13-Discussions%20re%20Bills%2027%20and%2028.pdf.
—. 2011b. "BCPSEA Meets with BCTF to Discuss Bargaining Structure." *@issue* 2011-04, 27 January. http://www.bcpsea.bc.ca/documents/20110208_030801729_No%202011-04%20Parties%20Discuss%20Bargaining%20Structure.pdf.
British Columbia Public School Employers' Association, BCLRB Decision No. B383/2001.
British Columbia Public School Employers' Association, BCLRB Decision No. B431/2001.
British Columbia Public School Employers' Association, BCLRB Decision No. B34/2002.
British Columbia Public School Employers' Association, BCLRB Decision No. B56/2002.
British Columbia Public School Employers' Association, BCLRB Decision No. B125/2002.

British Columbia Public School Employers' Association, BCLRB Decision No. B340/2002.

British Columbia Public School Employers' Association v. British Columbia Teachers' Federation, 2005 BCSC 1490.

British Columbia Public School Employers' Association, BCLRB Decision No. B255/2005.

British Columbia Public School Employers' Association, BCLRB Decision No. B262/2005.

British Columbia School Trustees Association (BCSTA). 2003. Letter to Don Wright, 22 September. http://www.labour.gov.bc.ca/pubs/teacher/appb_bcsta.pdf.

—. 2004. *A Brief to the Commission to Review Teacher Bargaining.*

British Columbia Teachers' Federation (BCTF). 1998a. "Agreement in Committee Reached." *BCTF Bargaining Bulletin* 4(27), 20 April. http://bctf.ca/publications/BargainingBulletin.aspx?id=1746.

—. 1998b. "Executive Committee Recommends Ratification of Agreement in Committee." *BCTF Bargaining Bulletin* 4(28), 21 April. http://bctf.ca/publications/BargainingBulletin.aspx?id=1748.

—. 1998c. "News Release: BCTF Responds to Trustees' Rejection of New Teacher Agreement." *BCTF Bargaining Bulletin* 4(45), 16 June. http://bctf.ca/publications/BargainingBulletin.aspx?id=1782.

—. 2001a. "91.4%." *BCTF Bargaining Bulletin* 6(57), 18 October. http://www.bctf.ca/publications/BargainingBulletin.aspx?fid=7208.

—. 2001b. "Day 59 at the Table." *BCTF Bargaining Bulletin* 6(73), 22 November. http://bctf.ca/publications/BargainingBulletin.aspx?id=1932.

—. 2002. "Negotiations 2001 to 2002." http://bctf.ca/AboutUs.aspx?id=18888.

—. 2003a. "History of Teacher Collective Bargaining 1917–2002: Attachments for Letter Submitted to Don Wright." In *Towards a Better Teacher Bargaining Model in British Columbia: Report to Honourable Graham Bruce, November 2003.* Victoria, BC: Ministry of Skills Development and Labour. http://www.labour.gov.bc.ca/pubs/teacher/appb_bctf.pdf.

—. 2003b. *Answers to Questions Posed by Don Wright.* http://www.bctf.ca/BargainingAndContracts.aspx?id=4918.

—. 2005a. "Bargaining Bulletin." *BCTF Bargaining Bulletin* 7(15), 6 June. http://www.bctf.ca/publications/BargainingBulletin.aspx?fid=7210.

—. 2005b. "Salary Proposal to Come from BCPSEA ... but Not Today!" *BCTF Bargaining Bulletin* 7(20), 14 September. http://bctf.ca/publications/BargainingBulletin.aspx?id=2104.

—. 2005c. "Teachers' Strike Vote a Resounding 'Yes'." News release, 23 September. http://bctf.ca/NewsReleases.aspx?id=1624.

—. 2005d. "Teachers Vote to Take a Stand in Protest of Bill 12." News release, 5 October. http://bctf.ca/NewsReleases.aspx?id=1634.

—. 2005e. "Support Continues to Grow for Teachers." News release, 13 October. http://www.bctf.ca/NewsReleases.aspx?id=1636.

—. 2006. "Bargaining Opened Tuesday." *BCTF Bargaining Bulletin* 8(2), 12 April. http://www.bctf.ca/publications/BargainingBulletin.aspx?fid=7212.

—. 2009. "Teachers Vote to Leave Premier's Failed Learning Roundtable." News release, 16 March. http://www.bctf.ca/NewsReleases.aspx?id=17908.

—. 2010. "Mid-Contract Modification," *Members' Guide to the BCTF 2010-11*, Part 3, Section H, p. 32. http://bctf.ca/uploadedFiles/public/AboutUs/MembersGuide/guide.pdf.

—. 2011. "This Changes Everything." *BCTF Bargaining Bulletin* 9(4), 29 April. http://www.bctf.ca/publications/BargainingBulletin.aspx?fid=8623.

—. n.d. "Bargaining Rights: The Problems with Essential Services Legislation." http://bctf.ca/BargainingAnd Contracts.aspx?id=4936.

—. n.d. "History of the BCTF." http://bctf.ca/uploadedFiles/About_Us/HistorySummary.pdf.

—. n.d. "The Steps Leading to Full Bargaining Rights." http://bctf.ca/AboutUs.aspx?id=18892.

British Columbia Teachers' Federation v. British Columbia Public School Employers' Association, 2004 BCSC 86.

British Columbia Teachers' Federation, BCLRB Decision No. B136/2006.

British Columbia Teachers' Federation v. British Columbia, 2011 BCSC 469.

Canadian Charter of Rights and Freedoms, Part I of the Constitution Act, 1982, being Schedule B to the Canada Act, 1982, c. 11, §. 1, 2(d) (U.K.).

Connolly, R. 2005. *A Fact-Finding Report on the Current Collective Bargaining Dispute between the BC Public School Employers' Association and the BC Teachers' Federation*. Victoria, BC: Ministry of Labour and Citizens' Services. http://www.bctf.ca/uploadedFiles/About_Us/History/Bargaining/2005EducationFactfinder.pdf.

Education and Health Collective Bargaining Assistance Act, S.B.C. 1996, c. 1.

Education (Learning Enhancement) Statutes Amendment Act, 2006, S.B.C. 2006, c. 21.

Education Services Collective Agreement Act, S.B.C. 2002, c. 1.

Education Services Collective Agreement Amendment Act, 2004, S.B.C. 2004.

Education Statutes Amendment Act, 1990, S.B.C. 1990, c. 38.

Educational Programs Continuation Act, 1993, S.B.C. 1993, c. 3.

Essential Services Disputes Act, S.B.C. 1977, c. 83.

Fleming, T. 2012. "The Great Divide: School Politics and Labour Relations in British Columbia before and after 1972." In *Dynamic Negotiations: Teacher Labour Relations in Canadian Elementary and Secondary Education*, edited by S. Slinn and A. Sweetman, 51-80. Montreal and Kingston: Queen's Policy Studies Series, McGill-Queen's University Press.

Geisert, G. and C. Chandler. 1991. "Learning the ABC's the Hard Way: Teacher Unionism in the 1990's." *Government Union Review* 12(2): 1-23.

Health and Social Services Delivery Improvement Act, S.B.C. 2002, c. 2.

Health Services and Support – Facilities Subsector Bargaining Assn. v. British Columbia (Health Services) 2007 SCC 27.

Industrial Conciliation and Arbitration Act, S.B.C. 1937, c. 31.

Industrial Relations Act, S.B.C. 1987, c. 24.

Industrial Relations Reform Act, 1987, S.B.C. 1987, c. 24.

International Labour Organization. 1986. *Complaint Presented by the World Confederation of Organisations of the Teaching Profession (WCOTP) against the Government of Canada/British Columbia*. Report No. 243 (Canada). ILO Dec. 1350, UN ILOOR.

Ipsos Reid. 2005. "BC Public Continues to Side with Teachers." News Release, 18 October. http://www.ipsos-na.com/news/pressrelease.cfm?id=2829.

Johnson, H.F. 1964. *A History of Public Education in British Columbia*. Vancouver: University of British Columbia.

Korbin, J. 1993. *Commission of Inquiry into the Public Service and Public Sector: Final Report*, Vol. 2. Victoria, BC: Crown Publications.

Labour Code, R.S.B.C. 1979, c. 212.

Labour Relations Code, R.S.B.C. 1996, c. 244.

Labour Relations Code, S.B.C. 1992, c. 82.

Lawton, S.B., G. Bedard, D. MacLellan, and X. Li. 1999. *Teachers' Unions in Canada*. Calgary, AB: Detselig Enterprises Ltd.

Menzies, C. 2005. "School Boards Backing Teachers!" In Support of Public Education web blog, 13 October. http://weblogs.elearning.ubc.ca/newproposals/archives/2005_10.html.

Miscellaneous Statute Amendment Act, 1996, S.B.C. 1996, c. 13, s. 29.

Muir, J. 1969. "Canada." In *Teachers Unions and Associations: A Comparative Study*, edited by A. Blum. Urbana: University of Illinois Press.

North, R. 1964. *The British Columbia Teachers' Federation and the Compulsory Arbitration Process*. Vancouver: University of British Columbia.

Novakowski, K. 2000. "Gaining Full Bargaining Rights." *Teacher Newsmagazine* 2(6): 5. http://www.bctf.ca/publications/NewsmagArticle.aspx?id=12818.

Ontario (Attorney General) v. Fraser, 2011 SCC 20.

Polukoshko, J. and T. Ehrcke. 2010. "Bargaining 2011: Charting a New Course." *Teacher Newsmagazine* 22(7). http://bctf.ca/publications/NewsmagArticle.aspx?id=21166.

Public Education Collective Agreement Act, S.B.C. 1998, c. 41.

Public Education Flexibility and Choice Act, S.B.C. 2002, c. 3.

Public Education Labour Relations Act, S.B.C. 1994, c. 21.

Public Schools Act, R.S.B.C. 1911, c. 206.

Public Schools Act, R.S.B.C. 1936, c. 253.

Public Schools Act, S.B.C. 1958, c. 42.

Public Schools Act Amendment Act, 1937, R.S.B.C. 1937, c. 68

Public Schools Act Amendment Act, 1947, R.S.B.C. 1947, c. 79.

Public Sector Employers Act, S.B.C. 1993, c. 65.

Ready, V.L. 2005. *In the Matter of a Dispute between the Province of British Columbia and the BC Public School Employers' Association and the BC Teachers' Federation*. Victoria, BC: Ministry of Labour and Citizens' Services.

—. 2006a. *Interim Report #2 for Transitional Negotiations Submitted to the Honourable Michael de Jong, Minister of Labour and Citizens' Services, Province of British Columbia*. http://www.labour.gov.bc.ca/pubs/teacher/iic-April-06-transitional.pdf.

—. 2006b. *Interim Report to the Honourable Michael de Jong, Minister of Labour and Citizens' Services, Province of British Columbia*. http://www.labour.gov.bc.ca/pubs/teacher/06-jan-teachers-interim-report.pdf.

—. 2007. *Final Report for Collective Bargaining Options Submitted to the Honourable Olga Ilich, Minister of Labour and Citizens' Services, Province of British Columbia*. http://www.labour.gov.bc.ca/pubs/teacher/07_bargaining_options.pdf.

Rud, J. 2005a. "Teachers Soften Contract Demands." *Times Colonist* [Final Edition],"1 September, p. A1.

—. 2005b. "Province Silent about Plans If Teachers Take Job Action." *Vancouver Sun*, 13 September, p. B4.

School Act, R.S.B.C. 1979, c. 375.

School Act, S.B.C. 1989, c. 61.

School Act, R.S.B.C. 1996, c. 412.

School Amendment Act, 1990, S.B.C. 1990, c. 2.

School District No. 54 (Bulkley Valley), BCLRB Decision No. B147/93.

Schucher, K. and S. Slinn. 2012. "Crosscurrents: Comparative Review of Elementary and Secondary Teacher Collective Bargaining Structures in Canada." In *Dynamic Negotiations: Teacher Labour Relatins in Canadian Elementary and Secondary Education*, edited by S. Slinn and A. Sweetman, 13-49. Montreal and Kingston: Queen's Policy Studies Series, McGill-Queen's University Press.

Select Standing Committee on Education. 2002. "System Improvement." In *Future for Learners: A Vision for Renewal of Education in British Columbia*, 31-77. Victoria, BC: Legislative Assembly of British Columbia. http://www.leg.bc.ca/cmt/37thparl/session-3/edu/reports/Rpt-37-3-SSCEducation.pdf.

Sims, J. 2005. "Teachers Will Keep Pressing for Better Learning Conditions." *Vancouver Sun* [Final C Edition], 6 September, p. A6.

Skills Development and Labour Statutes Amendment Act, 2001, S.B.C. 2001, c. 33.

Steffenhagen, J. 2002. "Campbell to Educators: Settle by Friday; But Union Warns There'll Be No 'Business as Usual' with an Imposed Settlement." *Vancouver Sun* [Final Edition], 19 January, p. A1.

—. 2006. "B.C. Bill Would Limit Class Sizes: 30-Student Cap Cuts Chances of Strike by Teachers." *Vancouver Sun* [Final Edition], 28 April, p. A1.

—. 2009. "Teachers Quit B.C.'s Learning Roundtable." *Vancouver Sun*, 16 March. http://communities.canada.com/vancouversun/blogs/reportcard/archive/2009/03/16/teachers-quit-b-c-s-learning-roundtable.aspx.

Teachers' Collective Agreement Act, S.B.C. 2005, c. 27.

Teaching Profession Act, S.B.C. 1987, c. 19.

Thompson, M. and J.F. Cairnie. 1973. "Compulsory Arbitration: The Case of British Columbia Teachers." *Industrial & Labour Relations Review* 27: 3-17.

Ungerleider, C.S. 1996. "Globalization, Professionalization, and Educational Politics in British Columbia." *Canadian Journal of Educational Administration and Policy*, no. 9 (15 December).

West Kootenay Schools Collective Bargaining Assistance Act, S.B.C. 1978, c. 42.

Wright, D. 2003. *Towards a Better Teacher Bargaining Model in British Columbia*. Report to Honourable Graham Bruce, November. Victoria, BC: Ministry of Skills Development and Labour. http://www.labour.gov.bc.ca/pubs/teacher/teachers-final-report.pdf.

—. 2004. *Voice, Accountability, and Dialogue: Recommendations for an Improved Collective Bargaining System for Teacher Contracts in British Columbia*. Report of the Commission to Review Teacher Collective Bargaining, D. Wright, Commissioner. Victoria, BC: Ministry of Skills Development and Labour. http://www.labour.gov.bc.ca/pubs/teacher/04_dec_final.pdf.

York University Labour Disputes Resolution Act, 2009, S.O. 2009, c. 1.

APPENDIX A

TABLE A1
Work Stoppages in BC Teacher Bargaining: 1988–2010

School District	Start Date	End Date	Length (Days)	Stoppage Type	Issues	Number of Workers Involved	Teacher Days Lost
Local negotiations							
Round 1							
80 Kitimat	28-Nov-88	12-Dec-88	14	General strike	Wages	136	1,360
88 Terrace	3-Jan-89	30-Jan-89	27	General strike	Wages	310	5,890
65 Cowichan	16-Jan-89	25-Jan-89	9	General strike	Wages	410	2,870
57 Prince George	23-Jan-89	27-Jan-89	4	General strike	Wages	1,200	4,800
89 Salmon Arm	6-Feb-89	7-Feb-89	1	General strike	Wages	311	180
15 Penticton	13-Feb-89	14-Feb-89	1	General strike	Collective bargaining procedure	240	120
35 Langley	27-Feb-89	24-Mar-89	25	Rotating strike	Collective bargaining procedure	850	4,510
34 Abbotsford	6-Mar-89	20-Mar-89	14	General strike	Working conditions; other issues	675	6,080
23 Kelowna	13-Mar-89	24-Mar-89	11	General strike	Rand Formula	900	7,650
76 Agassiz	1-Mar-89	13-Mar-89	12	General strike	Rand Formula	45	360
14 South Okanagan	3-Mar-89	14-Apr-89	42	Lockout	Wages	120	1,160
13 Okanagan	7-Mar-89	13-Mar-89	6	General strike	Wages	39	160
33 Chilliwack	8-Mar-89	13-Mar-89	5	General strike	Wages	434	1,300
2 Cranbrook	3-Apr-89	18-Apr-89	15	General strike	Wages	197	2,170
92 Nass Valley	17-Apr-89	19-May-89	32	General strike	Wages	32	780
76 Mission City	3-Oct-89	18-Oct-89	15	General strike	Wages	338	3,380
					Totals	**6,237**	**42,770**
Round 2							
35 Langley	06-Mar-90	26-Mar-90	20	General strike	Sympathy	850	11,900
14 Osoyoos	04-Sep-90	03-Oct-90	29	General strike	Subcontracting	130	2,730
42 Maple Ridge	13-Nov-90	21-Nov-90	8	Rotating	Wages	700	1,050

...continued

TABLE A1
(Continued)

School District	Start Date	End Date	Length (Days)	Stoppage Type	Issues	Number of Workers Involved	Teacher Days Lost
37 Delta	22-Nov-90	29-Nov-90	7	Rotating	Wages	950	1,430
61 Victoria	31-Jan-91	18-Feb-91	18	General strike	Wages	1,700	16,000
68 Nanaimo	12-Feb-91	18-Mar-91	34	Rotating	Wages	960	11,280
44 North Vancouver	14-Feb-91	16-Feb-91	2	Rotating	Failure to negotiate	1,000	1,000
39 Vancouver	18-Feb-91	28-Feb-91	10	Rotating	Working conditions	3,606	24,050
70 Alberni	19-Feb-91	20-Feb-91	1	General strike	Not reported	350	180
85 Vancouver Island	20-Feb-91	22-Feb-91	2	General strike	Various workload issues	280	280
63 Saanich	04-Mar-91	25-Mar-91	21	General strike	Various workload issues	471	5,650
1 Fernie	06-Mar-91	25-Mar-91	19	General strike	Wages	250	2,990
49 Bella Coola	06-Mar-91	08-Apr-91	33	General strike	Various workload issues	32	560
80 Kitimat	20-Mar-91	30-Apr-91	41	Rotating	Working conditions	155	2,500
60 Fort St. John	08-May-91	28-Jun-91	51	General strike	Working conditions	300	11,100
88 Terrace	13-May-91	14-May-91	1	General strike	Interunion matters	350	350
17 Princeton	13-May-91	27-May-91	14	General strike	Collective bargaining procedure	50	450
Totals						**12,134**	**93,500**
Round 3							
36 Surrey	18-Jan-93	19-Jan-93	1	General strike	Delay in negotiations	1,900	1,900
36 Surrey	25-Jan-93	08-Mar-93	42	Rotating	Wages, other issues	2,800	5,520
1 Fernie	04-Jan-93	29-Jan-93	25	Lockout	Wages	240	4,560
28 Quesnel	08-Jan-93	04-Mar-93	55	Rotating	Delay in negotiations	310	5,170
40 New Westminster	15-Feb-93	29-Mar-93	42	Rotating	Working conditions	241	1,310
47 Powell River	15-Feb-93	06-May-93	80	Lockout/rotating	Working conditions	220	5,960
42 Maple Ridge	01-Apr-93	13-Apr-93	12	General strike	Delay in negotiations	740	4,440
84 Gold River	08-Mar-93	20-Apr-93	43	Rotating	Delay in negotiations	56	970
85 Port Hardy	08-Mar-93	14-May-93	67	Rotating	Delay in negotiations	200	5,900
39 Vancouver	05-May-93	31-May-93	26	Rotating	Wages and other issues	4,500	47,250
36 Surrey	19-May-93	03-Jun-93	15	General strike	Working conditions	2,800	16,800

Location				Type	Issue		
80 Kitimat	17-May-93	25-May-93	8	General strike	Working conditions	140	770
54 Smithers	26-Apr-93	31-May-93	35	General strike	Delay in negotiations	170	2,210
70 Port Alberni	11-May-93	20-May-93	9	General strike	Wages	500	2,000
71 Comox	12-May-93	13-May-93	1	General strike	Delay in negotiations	515	260
24 Kamloops	17-May-93	18-May-93	1	General strike	Delay in negotiations	797	400
44 North Vancouver	17-May-93	21-May-93	4	Rotating	Delay in negotiations	1,250	630
Totals						**17,379**	**106,050**
Two-tier negotiations							
Round 1 (1994–96)	–	–	–	–	–	–	–
Round 2 (1997–98)	–	–	–	–	–	–	–
Round 3 (2001–02)	–	–	–	–	–	–	–
Various locations	28-Jan-02	28-Jan-02	1		Failure to negotiate	35,000	35,000
Round 4 (2004–05)	–	–	–	–	–	–	–
Provincewide	07-Oct-05	24-Oct-05	17		Negotiated issues	38,000	380,000
Round 5 (2006)	–	–	–	–	–	–	–

Source: Special data request, Human Resources and Skills Development Canada; Various records of the British Columbia Teachers' Federation (BCTF) and British Columbia Public School Employers' Association (BCPSEA).

Chapter 5

OIL AND IDEOLOGY: THE TRANSFORMATION OF K-12 BARGAINING IN ALBERTA

KELLY WILLIAMS-WHITT

INTRODUCTION

The education system in Alberta is largely shaped by an independent, religious, and conservative cultural history. Long periods of political equilibrium and reliance on natural resource revenues mean that the fate of public institutions often rests on economic rather than political upheaval. This chapter begins by describing how this context has influenced the emergence and early evolution of K–12 bargaining in Alberta. A predominantly rural and decentralized system of public education becomes increasingly standardized and administered by the province. This is juxtaposed against legislation that relaxes constraints on the education market and opens doors to more private schooling. A pivotal legislative change in 1994 dramatically alters bargaining power and ushers in a new era in K–12 labour relations.

In the second half of the chapter, "Bargaining in the Twenty-First Century," current legislation and bargaining agents are explored in depth. The *Teaching Profession Act* (2000) and the *School Act* (2000) together establish a near closed-shop status for the Alberta Teachers' Association. This is contrasted with the steadily eroding authority and financial autonomy of Alberta school boards. Next, the K–12 bargaining revolution that occurred at the beginning of the new century is described. Economic adversity and labour unrest prompt government intervention. A long tradition of local negotiating gives way as stakeholders adjust their strategies and struggle

Dynamic Negotiations: Teacher Labour Relations in Canadian Elementary and Secondary Education, ed. S. Slinn and A. Sweetman. Montreal and Kingston: Queen's Policy Studies Series, McGill-Queen's University Press.
© 2012 The School of Policy Studies, Queen's University at Kingston. All rights reserved.

to find an effective way to move forward. The chapter concludes with a brief analysis of K–12 bargaining effectiveness in Alberta and some predictions in light of an uncertain future.

HISTORY

Origins of Education in Alberta (1875–1920)

Controversy over how to best educate children on the prairies began well before Alberta joined Confederation. Section 11 of the *North-West Territories Act* (1875) accorded responsibility for education to the government of the Territories, and adopted principles from the *Constitution Act, 1867,* when it created separate schools for Roman Catholic and Protestant students. A school would be established based upon the religious majority of ratepayers within a district. If the minority wished to establish a separate school and could financially support it, this was allowed. Schools were generally monitored and controlled by the clergy. As the Territories gained greater powers of self-governance, the wisdom of the federal government's approach to education was questioned. Some territorial founders supported non-denominational schools, believing they were imperative for nation-building and that separate schools were socially divisive. Others believed that religion and education were inseparable, and that "moral demoralization" was the "natural fruit" of a public education system (Dafoe 1931, 289).

A sparse and primarily rural population in the Territories prevented substantial progress on school governance until the mid-1880s. In 1883 a bill respecting the organization of public and separate school districts was introduced to the North-West Council. This initiated a series of Territorial Ordinances that progressively eroded the sovereignty of denominational schools by centralizing school regulation, inspection, and funding. The movement toward greater government control was precipitated in part by an increasingly non-Catholic population in the west, and the autonomy movement that sought independence from central Canadian influences (Anderson 2005).

In 1901 the North-West Assembly took a momentous stride, passing a *School Ordinance* that was later adopted by Alberta when the province was hewn from the North-West Territories in 1905. Introduced by Frederick Haultain, premier and commissioner of education for the North-West Territories, the 1901 *School Ordinance* has been called "the formal end of a period of transition in school control" (Patterson 1961, 65). The tone was distinctly non-denominational, requiring the first school in any district to be public. The religious rights of minority ratepayers were protected by section 41, which allowed for the creation of separate schools for Catholic or Protestant students, depending on the nature of any existing school in the district and providing there was sufficient ratepayer support.

However, all schools were under the control of the government and were required to teach the same program with substantially the same textbooks. Teacher qualifications were regulated by the government, and section 137 of the *Ordinance* restricted religious instruction to 30 minutes at the end of each day.

Notwithstanding a polarizing debate about diluting the denominational uniqueness of separate schools (Anderson 2005), the 1901 *Ordinance* was enshrined in section 17 of the *Alberta Act* (1905). Sections 3 and 17 of the *Alberta Act* applied the education provisions of the *Constitution Act, 1867* to the new province, with the important exception that school governance continue as established in chapters 29 and 30 of the 1901 *School Ordinance*. The result was a unique framework. All schools were part of the public system and were required to abide by the same standards and regulations. The right to tax-supported separate schools was protected constitutionally, and the power of the province with respect to education was established by connecting three separate pieces of legislation, the *Constitution Act* (1867), the *Alberta Act* (1905), and the North-West Territories *School Ordinance* (1901).

This was the complex legal structure inherited by Alberta's first premier and the only Liberal leader ever elected in the province, Alexander Cameron Rutherford. Rutherford was also the first minister of education and was widely known as the "architect of the province" (Rutherford Research, n.d.). He organized construction of the provincial legislature, created a public telephone system, expanded roads and railways, built thousands of schools, and established a teacher-training facility at the University of Alberta.

Although Rutherford was a dedicated supporter of education, the early years were difficult due to the rural and agricultural nature of the province. Because the population was unevenly distributed, the responsibility for requesting schools was largely incumbent on the general public. Residents could petition for the formation of a school district provided there were a minimum of four taxable residents and eight school-aged children within five square miles (*An Act to Further Amend the Statute Law* 1909, 167).[1] If the ratepayers voted in favour of the school, the district would be established and trustees elected to run it. The district trustees were responsible for building schoolhouses, taxing property owners to supplement provincial funding, and for hiring and firing teachers. The numbers of rural and urban schools were about equal, and attendance was the chief concern because older children were often pulled from school to work in the fields. Within ten years of Alberta's entrance to Confederation, the province had more than 2,000 school districts. The vast majority of these were public with a "handful" of separate schools (Chalmers 1967, 379).

Life for an Alberta teacher was not easy. The profession was not highly regarded, and working conditions were difficult. Wages were at the whim of school trustees (Alberta Teachers' Association, n.d., *History*), and circumstances for rural teachers were especially challenging:

> Roads were only seasonally passable, mail service was often sporadic, and radio was still a luxury... Teachers hired to staff the one-room schools spread across the prairies were immature, poorly prepared, and transient. The poorer regions on the prairies, in some cases severely depopulated during the course of the war, were unable to raise a sufficient assessment to support a school operating for a full term. As well, it seemed impossible to find enough dedicated trustees to govern the hundreds of minute rural school districts. Trustees were often lax in tax collection or irresponsible in the management of what school funds there were. (Wilson 1977, 26)

These conditions led to the creation of the Alberta Teachers' Alliance in 1917. Spearheaded by John Barnett, the Alliance was the teachers' response to substandard working and living conditions. Teachers were dissatisfied with wages that did not match high living costs and wartime inflation (Manzer 1969). The increased urbanization that came with industrialization facilitated opportunities for interaction among disgruntled teachers, thereby allowing Barnett to strengthen the teachers' movement. Better transportation and shorter travel time in urban centres made it easier for teachers to attend Alliance meetings. However, organizing in rural districts was more difficult. Barnett indicated that by 1921 the Alliance "included practically all the teachers in the cities and larger towns, but only two-thirds of the teachers in the province as a whole" (Manzer 1969, 106). Furthermore, industrialization and the concentration of taxpayers in Alberta's cities contributed to funding inequities between rural and urban teachers (Wilson 1977).

Observers of early Canadian industrial relations recognized that the Alberta Teachers' Alliance embodied some unique characteristics relative to its counterparts. First, it was for teachers only, excluding senior administrators, clergy, university professors, and citizens at large. Second, all teachers had equal rights; there were no divisions by sex, teaching level, location, or subject area. Third, the objectives of the Alliance included collective action not only to improve wages and working conditions but also to promote the value of education and teaching as a profession (Kratzmann 1964).

The United Farmers of Alberta and the Dominion Labour Party (1921–1934)

The end of World War I heralded a new era in Alberta politics. The United Farmers of Alberta (UFA), originally a non-partisan lobby group representing rural interests, surprised even themselves when they defeated the Liberals in 1921 (Heritage Community Foundation, n.d.). UFA president

Henry Wisewood declined the role of premier (Herbert Greenfield stepped in to fill the position), but his political ideology would form the foundation of Alberta's new government. Wisewood believed that elected representatives should be encouraged to vote according to the wishes of the constituents they represented, rather than along party lines (Finkel 1985). No group or social class would be forced to compromise its policies or values. This philosophical stance allowed collaboration between the UFA and the Dominion Labour Party to prevent the Liberals from regaining power (Finkel 1985, 72).

In many ways UFA leadership effected little immediate change to the education sector. However, the party did introduce legislative modifications that would, in time, have a substantial influence on the power of the Alliance as well as the nature and scope of teacher bargaining in Alberta. First, in 1922, the government revised the 1901 *School Ordinance*, which became the *School Act*. In 1926, the UFA further amended the *School Act* to establish Boards of Reference (*School Act Amendment Act* 1926). The purpose of Boards of Reference was to deal with "any dispute or disagreement" between school boards and teachers (ibid., s. 197). Boards of Reference were composed of one representative from the affected school board, one from the Alliance, and a neutral third party who acted as the chair. They had the power to compel the production of documents and the attendance of witnesses, and their decisions were legally binding. In 1935, the UFA also passed the *Teaching Profession Act*. Section 6 of the Act established the Alberta Teachers' Association (ATA)[2] as a body "corporate and politic" with the power to pass bylaws concerning "the formation, government, management and dissolution of local associations." Its purpose was to promote the cause of education, raise the status of the teaching profession, and "secure conditions which will make possible the best professional service" (*Teaching Profession Act* 1935, s. 3).

The Social Credit Party (1935–1970)

At the beginning of the 1930s, Alberta, like the rest of Canada, was caught in the undertow of the Great Depression. Devastating economic conditions and inadequate government assistance fuelled the search for alternative thinking, and for a short period of time Alberta became a Communist stronghold (Hannant 1985). Rural and religious roots, however, would quickly overtake any Marxist political leanings.

High school teacher and radio evangelist William Aberhart became enthralled with an economic theory developed by C.H. Douglas.[3] Douglas blamed banking institutions for creating debt, and believed that consumers needed more money to purchase the goods produced by industry (Hannant 1985). In his view, the answer was government-issued "social credit." Aberhart eventually became convinced that social credit was the solution to the crisis facing Alberta and began preaching the tenets of the philosophy on his program. Aberhart's approach appealed to working-class Albertans, including teachers and farmers (Hannant 1985). The newly formed party won 56 of 63 seats in the provincial election in August 1935 (Finkel 1989).

Aberhart and the ten teachers who were elected to parliament alongside him created a unique and unparalleled "access to opportunity" (Berghofer and Vladicka 1980) for Alberta educators. Elected for his social credit approach, Aberhart's popularity allowed him to push through educational reforms with little opposition. As premier and minister of education, he supported efforts by the ATA to increase their legitimacy, enabling them to become both a professional organization and a full-fledged union. This was accomplished first by a 1936 amendment to the *Teaching Profession Act* requiring that all teachers, as a condition of employment, be members of the ATA, and giving the ATA authority to discipline members (*Teaching Profession Act 1935 Amendment Act* 1936). Second, in 1941 the *Industrial Conciliation and Arbitration Act* (s. 2) was amended to include teachers as "employees" and school boards as "employers." This amendment permitted teachers to bargain collectively, use arbitration to settle disputes, and go on strike if conciliation failed. The Social Credit government also created the *Teachers' Retirement Fund Act* in 1939. Furthermore, the government organized hundreds of rural schools into larger divisions, which addressed some of the inequities in quality and access to education that existed between richer urban and poorer rural schools (Wilson 1977).

When Aberhart passed away in 1943, Ernest Manning became the premier. Holding office for 25 years (1943–1968), Manning would completely transform the Social Credit agenda, severing party ties to labour and introducing increasingly restrictive legislation that made union organizing more difficult in order to protect the burgeoning oil and gas industry (Finkel 1988). Notwithstanding some increasingly conservative policies, the Social Credit government under Manning spent 50 percent more on education than any other province (Finkel 1988, 147). The Manning government further amalgamated school districts, and appointed a Royal Commission of Education to examine Alberta's school system. The Commission's report (Cameron 1959) contained 280 recommendations for improving education in the province. Few dealt directly with collective bargaining. However, the Commission did propose that teacher salaries should approximate those of middle managers, and advocated for an adequate grant structure to support the proposed salary grid. The report also made numerous recommendations regarding teacher qualifications and ongoing performance evaluation, strongly supporting the professional mandate of the ATA in these areas. Although it is difficult to trace legislative modifications to the Cameron Report, it contains a comprehensive reservoir of ideas that continues to influence Alberta's approach to education today.

The Progressive Conservatives (1971–2000)

What led to the demise of a Social Credit party that dominated Alberta politics for more than 30 years? Most accounts of the 1971 electoral race indicate that there was little difference between the Social Credit party and the Progressive Conservatives in the substance of their campaign platforms (Bell 1993). Both had centre-right policies and had even considered a merger prior to the election (ibid.). Popular analysis suggests that "the Conservative victory was ... more an indication of provincial trends of urbanization, secularization, increasing geographical mobility and affluence" (Palmer and Palmer 1976, 124). Other political pundits advocate that the charismatic leadership of Peter Lougheed and a savvy, well-organized campaign were more important factors (Bell 1993).

Whatever the reasons for their victory, the Tories would eventually build a political dynasty. Over the course of the next 40 years they would steer public policy increasingly to the right. Fiscal conservatism, centralized decision-making, privatization, and an economy highly dependent on natural resources would mean unpredictable funding for education.

Economically influenced change began shortly after Lougheed took office in 1971. The world faced an energy embargo in 1973/74, followed by a jump in world oil prices in 1979. Alberta's royalty regime meant the province profited from the high prices. However, the inflationary impact on the rest of Canada resulted in escalating unemployment rates[4] (Human Resources and Skills Development Canada 2010) and prompted the federal Liberal government to step in. In October of 1980, the National Energy Program (NEP) was introduced in Parliament. The main purpose of the program was to provide energy security and to establish revenue sharing across the provinces (Jenkins 1986). The NEP diverted royalties from the province to the federal government. Although Alberta successfully argued to the Supreme Court that the NEP encroached on provincial resource rights (*Re: Exported Natural Gas Tax* 1982), a drop in oil prices in the mid-1980s compounded the NEP revenue losses, sending the province into a deep recession (Decore and Pannu 1989).

The economic downturn was at first managed by hold-the-line budgets, but this would later give way to a series of spending cuts. Government spending on education dropped from 30.8 percent of the provincial budget in the mid-1970s to 18.3 percent in 1986/87 (Decore and Pannu 1989, 152). Although similar cuts were made in other provinces, the proportion in Alberta was largest despite increasing K–12 enrolments (Decore and Pannu 1989). The decrease in education funding was accompanied by a corresponding escalation in strike activity throughout the 1970s and early 1980s (Appendix A).

In addition to education spending reductions, legislative changes were made that increased centralization with the hope of improving both efficiency and consistency across school divisions. When a new *School Act* was introduced in 1988, the Minister of Education became responsible for adopting goals and standards for education in the province, and teachers were required to provide instruction only as prescribed, approved, or authorized (*School Act* 1988, s. 13). Teacher contract provisions were more specifically defined, and ministerial powers were expanded to pave the way for more comprehensive regulation governing the evaluation and discipline of teachers (*School Act* 1988, ss. 77–84).

Centralization of teacher evaluation and discipline was an outgrowth of public concern regarding teacher competence. Fuelled in part by the James Keegstra case (*R. v. Keegstra* 1990),[5] a common perception existed that performance was not regularly evaluated, and that school boards were limited in their ability to discipline or discharge teachers for anything other than the most egregious behavior (Legislative Assembly of Alberta 1983). The Department of Education responded by creating the Council on Alberta Teaching Standards (COATS) in 1985 (*Ministerial Order #078/85*). COATS was primarily an advisory body charged with conducting research and making recommendations to the Minister regarding teacher qualifications and evaluation. Then when the *Practice Review of Teachers Regulation* (1987) was passed, COATS was also empowered to investigate cases of alleged teaching incompetence, a responsibility previously belonging to school boards. The legislation never encroached on ATA territory as the union retained jurisdiction over cases involving professional conduct and ethics.[6] But for school boards, the legislative changes were just the beginning of heightened ministerial scrutiny and steadily declining authority.

Following in the footsteps of premiers Peter Lougheed (1971–1985) and Donald Getty (1985–1992), Ralph Klein continued Progressive Conservative Party dominance when he was elected to office in 1992. The Klein revolution saw Alberta's Conservative government policy move further to the right. His plan was to downsize government, balance the budget, and develop a climate for private-sector job creation (Taras and Tupper 1994). This Canadianized Reagonomics has been described as "a program of social engineering … to fit a particular ideological mould that is virtually without precedent in recent Canadian history" (ibid., 61). Klein became both the most popular and most controversial of all Alberta's premiers, winning overwhelming public support through his final term in 2004.[7]

On the heels of another recession and budgetary shortfall in the early 1990s (Wallner 2008), reengineering to fit education into PC economic ideology progressed with little objection from the electorate. First, government would reduce its total education budget by 13 percent, and decrease the number of school boards from 141 to 62 (Reshef and Rastin 2003, 115). Teachers would be asked to voluntarily accept a 5 percent wage roll back (Reshef 2007, 681). Surprisingly, the ATA complied with little protest, choosing instead to fight what they saw as the much larger threat of privatization (Reshef and Rastin 2003).

Provisions for private schools have existed in Alberta legislation since 1945 (*Act to Amend the Department of Education Act* 1945). However, the use of public funds to support private schools did not begin until 1967 (*Act to Amend the School Grants Act* 1967). By the year 2000, the *School Act* distinguished three classes of private schools: (a) registered schools, (b) accredited non-funded schools, and (c) accredited-funded schools (*School Act* 2000). Registered schools do not receive government funding, cannot offer high school credit courses, and their teachers do not require Alberta Teaching Certificates. Accredited private schools must meet additional standards including minimum instructional hours, employment of certificated teachers, and compliance with provincial high school graduation requirements. Accredited-funded private schools meet all the requirements of accredited schools, but to receive funding they must also follow the Alberta programs of study (Alberta Education 2010a). Funding for accredited-funded schools has varied over time, but currently they are eligible to receive 60 to 70 percent of the per pupil grants provided to public schools (Alberta Education 2010b). They are not eligible for some other types of funding, such as student transportation grants. Private schools may charge tuition to supplement any funding they do receive. This results in substantial savings to the province. Most private schools provide early childhood education or have a religious or special needs focus; some offer complete K–12 programs.

In 1994 Alberta became the first province to allow charter schools. Charter schools differ from private schools in that they are fully funded and cannot charge tuition fees. These schools were intended to increase competition among providers, encourage innovation, and respond to the demands of the education consumer (Alberta Education 2009). Unlike private schools, charter schools were designed to operate within the public system, but allow parents greater influence over curriculum (ibid.). Division 3 of the *School Act* (2000) establishes charter school requirements. Any individual, society, or company can apply to have a charter school approved by the Minister. To receive approval and funding, the applicant must first approach a local school board requesting an alternative program that meets the philosophical or pedagogical approach desired (*School Act* 2000, s. 31). The parties then attempt to negotiate a program that is mutually acceptable. If they are successful, the alternative program is implemented under the existing school board (Alberta Education 2009). If they cannot reach agreement and the local school board refuses to create the program, a charter will be granted, providing that the Minister is of the opinion that (a) the school will have significant support from the community, (b) it has the potential to improve student learning, and (c) the program is not already offered within the school district or division (*School Act* 2000, s. 32). Charter schools are prohibited from having any religious affiliation, and must hire teachers with valid teaching certificates

(*School Act* 2000, s. 34). The *Charter Schools Regulation* limits the number of charter schools in the province to 15.

Neither private schools nor charter schools are run by a publicly elected school board as defined in the *School Act* (2000). The *Teaching Profession Act* (2000) requires compulsory membership in the ATA only for teachers hired by a board. Although certificated teachers in private or charter schools cannot be active members of the ATA, they can be associate members with voting rights and the ability to hold office (*Teaching Profession Act* 2000, s. 6). Therefore teachers in private and charter schools must go through the union certification process if they wish to collectively bargain. The fact that the *Teaching Profession Act* was not amended to include these schools suggests that parliament, while not attempting to eviscerate the ATA, did wish to limit its power by subjecting it to the same free market forces as school boards. Teachers in private and charter schools may choose to unionize (or not) following the provisions of the *Labour Code*, and they may choose any union they like to represent them. The ATA and the Alberta School Boards Association (ASBA) generally oppose charter schools and public funding of private schools. Both organizations see such schools as promoting inequality and social fragmentation, in addition to diverting funds from a public system that already provides many alternatives (Alberta School Boards Association, n.d.; Alberta Teachers' Association, n.d., *Charter Schools*).

A frame-breaking change to the funding scheme for Alberta schools would have an even more important effect on collective bargaining than opening up the education market. In 1994 the Progressive Conservatives centralized school funding when they deprived public school boards of the right to directly tax ratepayers within their districts (*School Amendment Act* 1994). Revenues were to be pooled in a single fund that would be distributed to school boards "in provincially stipulated per-student increments multiplied by the number of students enrolled within each board's jurisdiction" (*Public School Boards Association v. Alberta* 2000, para. 6). Separate schools could opt out of the scheme and would receive supplements to match the public school funding. In the event of a surplus, separate boards were required to remit excess monies to the central fund. The main purpose of the legislation was to equalize funding between districts with disparate tax bases, although it was also described as a "cost-cutting measure implemented to reduce overall funding to education" (ibid., para. 2). The public school boards challenged the legislation in a battle that would attract interveners from across Canada and eventually be heard by the Supreme Court. In 2000, the Supreme Court sided with the province, stating that the funding system did not violate the Constitution and that school boards do not enjoy reasonable autonomy from provincial control (*Public School Boards Association v. Alberta* 2000).

This single Act would entirely transform the future of K–12 bargaining in Alberta. Prior to the funding change, collective bargaining occurred primarily at the local level. Most school boards negotiated independently (although some voluntarily collaborated to bargain regionally) and adjusted tax rates to reflect bargaining outcomes. The ATA assisted locals at the bargaining table when requested, shared information, and informally coordinated among locals. Although each school district or division was technically on its own bargaining cycle, most collective agreement terms were from one to three years so that a large number of jurisdictions could be negotiating within any 12-month period. When school boards lost the ability to match revenues to negotiated agreements, they were squeezed between a powerful ATA on one side and an inflexible provincial funding scheme on the other. The inability to manoeuvre at the bargaining table translated into labour unrest. K–12 bargaining agents would be forced to reconsider their historically decentralized approach, paving the way for a new collective bargaining structure in the new century.

BARGAINING IN THE TWENTY-FIRST CENTURY

Relevant Legislation Today and How It All Works Together

In Alberta today there are three pieces of legislation that influence K–12 collective bargaining either directly or indirectly:

1.   The *School Act* (2000), which addresses teacher qualifications, certain working conditions such as maximum hours of work, as well as the authority of the board to transfer, suspend, or discharge a teacher;
2.   The *Teaching Profession Act* (2000), which establishes the ATA as the bargaining agent for teachers and gives the ATA the right to discipline its members for unprofessional conduct; and
3.   The *Alberta Labour Relations Code* (2000), which governs certification and collective bargaining processes, including the right to strike.

The School Act

The general purpose of the *School Act* is to codify the roles and responsibilities of the Minister of Education, school boards, and teachers within the province. It establishes the right of children between the ages of 6 and 19 to have access to an education program. The Act is largely devoted to describing the authority of school boards, districts, and divisions; the appropriate constitution of boards; funding and financial reporting requirements; and building and maintaining infrastructure.

However, there are elements of the Act that have a direct impact on collective bargaining. For example, part 4 obliges school boards to employ only teachers who hold a certificate of qualification issued under the Act. It also requires that every teacher have an individual contract of employment. So a teacher's terms and conditions are determined by portions of the *School Act* itself, the collective agreement (which covers salary, benefits, leaves of absence, professional development, and grievance processes), and the individual contract of employment.

Individual contract types are prescribed by the Act and may include any condition of employment not addressed by the *School Act* or the collective agreement, but cannot contradict the working conditions established by them. The purpose of the individual contract is to confirm employment and establish the nature of the position for each teacher (e.g., probationary, part-time, continuing, substitute, temporary, or interim). Individual contracts are usually one or two pages in length and may contain provisions specifying conditions such as subject matter, grade level, playground supervision, or religious expectations for separate school districts. A sample contract is included in Appendix B. A concern with individual contracts is that they sometimes contain clauses that purport to limit a teacher's right to due process as established in the *School Act* or *Teaching Profession Act,* or that conflict with other legislation (see, for example, *Alberta Teachers' Association v. Pembina Hills* 2008). In this case, the offending clauses of the contract are unenforceable. School boards have also attempted, on occasion, to require that teachers with continuing appointments sign new contracts with less favourable terms. The ATA does not receive copies or monitor individual contracts on a regular basis, but will address concerns as they arise (Thomas 2008).

The main influence of the *School Act* on collective bargaining is that the right to transfer or discipline a teacher and the mechanisms for resolving related disputes are established in the Act rather than negotiated into the collective agreement. Part 2, Division 1 lays the foundation by institutionalizing the duties and obligations of a teacher:

18(1) A teacher while providing instruction or supervision must
  (a) provide instruction competently to students;
  (b) teach the courses of study and education programs that are prescribed, approved or authorized pursuant to this Act;
  (c) promote goals and standards applicable to the provision of education adopted or approved pursuant to this Act;
  (d) encourage and foster learning in students;
  (e) regularly evaluate students and periodically report the results of the evaluation to the students, the students' parents and the board;
  (f) maintain, under the direction of the principal, order and discipline among the students while they are in the school or on the school grounds and while they are attending or participating in activities sponsored or approved by the board;
  (g) subject to any applicable collective agreement and the teacher's contract of employment, carry out those duties that are assigned to the teacher by the principal or the board.

School boards have the right to transfer a teacher to any school within their jurisdiction. If the teacher disagrees with the proposed transfer, the *School Act* (2000) provides for an opportunity to appeal to the school board. If the board is not persuaded to alter the original decision, and the teacher refuses the transfer, the only alternative in the legislation is that the teacher resigns (s. 104). School boards also have the right to suspend or terminate a teacher they believe is guilty of gross misconduct, neglect of duties established in section 18, or refusal to obey a lawful order. Suspension can occur without warning if, in the opinion of the superintendent, the welfare of students is threatened (*School Act* 2000, s. 105). While there is no "just cause" provision, the Act states that the board must have reasonable grounds for suspension, must act reasonably in any decision to terminate, and must treat the employee fairly. Rather than proceeding through the grievance and arbitration system established in a collective agreement, discharge or suspension can only be appealed to the Minister and then referred to a Board of Reference. The Board of Reference has powers similar to those of an arbitration panel, including the right to reinstate.

Two effects flow from separating transfer, suspension, and termination dispute resolution from the collective agreement. First, individual teachers may initiate appeals on their own behalf. If transfer policies or the right to discipline were included in the collective agreement, the union would retain the right to determine whether to file a grievance and pursue it through to arbitration. In other words, the transfer appeal and Board of Reference systems allow the employee to control the process, not the union. Second, excluding transfer and discipline from the collective agreement means that the ATA is not subject to the duty of fair representation (DFR) requirements that section 153 of the *Labour Relations Code* attaches to rights negotiated into a collective agreement. So while the ATA has a DFR with respect to salary, leaves, and other conditions in the collective agreement, it does not have a similar duty regarding transfer or disciplinary issues (*Pentek v. ATA* 1989). In practice, teachers who have been subject to transfer, suspension, or termination generally have the assistance and advice of the ATA available to them. The decision to provide representation and cover related costs still belongs to the Association.

There are both benefits and detriments with this approach. The union benefits by being free from any particular duty of fair representation hurdle in difficult disciplinary cases. This means resources are not drained (through futile grievances or DFR defence) where there is little chance of success. Since the teacher can control the decision to proceed and retain independent counsel, it also means the union is less likely to be the target of member frustration. Furthermore, it prevents conflict of interest where the ATA is implementing internal disciplinary measures at the same time the board is implementing suspension or discharge. This would not be a concern if there were separate union and professional bodies. But as long as the ATA has a dual role, a teacher must have access to alternative representation. On the negative side, boards see the process as cumbersome, lengthy, and outdated (Alberta Education and MacKenzie 2009). Their view may be supported by the fact that few cases proceed to a Board of Reference. However, this may also mean the parties now know the "rules," which have largely kept pace with developments in labour law (Fraser 1999). If the Board of Reference were to be replaced with a traditional arbitration process, just cause or similar provisions would need to be negotiated into existing collective agreements.

The Teaching Profession Act

The *Teaching Profession Act* (*TPA*) affects collective bargaining by legislating something very near a closed shop for the ATA. Section 5(1) states that "the employment of a teacher by a school board is conditional on the teacher being and continuing to be an active member of the association." Technically, there is no provision in the *TPA* that confers exclusive bargaining authority upon the ATA. Another union could be certified as a teacher bargaining agent (*Pembina Hills* 1997). Realistically, however, this is unlikely. The ATA has a relationship with all teachers by virtue of section 5(1); additionally, its bargaining power and knowledge of education issues are not easily replicated by any other institution. The Act also requires that school boards automatically deduct union dues for teachers in public or separate schools (s. 13). Only teachers who are not actively teaching, or those in supervisory or administrative roles, may elect to discontinue membership. The ATA and boards must therefore establish the scope of the bargaining unit, but do not negotiate union security.

Section 5(1) is contentious for those who oppose compulsory union membership. Its effect is compounded in the case of teachers because the *Teaching Profession Act* also gives the ATA authority to discipline its members for unprofessional conduct. Unprofessional conduct is any behaviour that is detrimental to the best interests of students, the public, or the teaching profession (s. 23). Complaints can be made by any member of the public. If a member is found guilty of unprofessional conduct, the ATA hearing committee may (a) recommend that the Minister of Education cancel or suspend the certificate of that teacher, (b) expel the teacher from the ATA, (c) assess fines, or (d) make any other order it deems appropriate (s. 42).

Unions normally have the right to censure members who are engaged in conduct that is detrimental to their function or purpose. In many other sectors, one can be expelled from a union and still find work in a non-union shop. But in the teaching profession, where almost every school in the province is a union shop and the province requires that teachers be certified, a teacher who loses membership and / or certification has almost no prospect of practicing. It is the spectre of a teacher being ousted from the ATA for refusing to participate in union activities that raised red flags for "right to work" proponents.

In the mid-1990s a number of bills were introduced to the legislative assembly that proposed right-to-work legislation for the province. Bill 210 specifically targeted the *Teaching Profession Act*, attempting to reverse the ATA's closed-shop status. Those in favour of Bill 210 argued that compulsory membership denies teachers the right to choose. They considered that competence should be the yardstick for employment, not membership in the union (Legislative Assembly of Alberta 1995). However, none of the right-to-work bills were passed. Assembly transcripts show there was substantial reluctance to change a system that works well for both teachers and the public. Bill 210 was cast as a blatant attempt to break the ATA (ibid., 1464). It was criticized for failing to demonstrate how voluntary membership would improve education and the ATA lauded for responsibly exercising its power: no teacher has ever lost a job for "tutoring during a strike" (ibid., 1518). It was also unclear how the ATA could be expected to apply discipline to individuals who were not members. Finally, the professional arm of the ATA was credited with the current high quality of education in the province (Legislative Assembly of Alberta 1995). Thus it seems the dual purpose of the ATA protected its closed-shop status.[8]

The Labour Relations Code

The *Alberta Labour Relations Code* is often characterized as less than labour friendly. It requires mandatory certification votes, allows employer-initiated strike votes, offers no first contract arbitration, and does not prohibit replacement workers.

Ironically, many features of the *Labour Code* that could have a numbing influence on K–12 bargaining are effectively nullified by the security provisions established in the *School Act* and the *TPA*. Since the ATA is effectively a closed shop, there are few battles associated with organizing and first contracts. Furthermore, teacher certification requirements remove replacement worker skirmishes when strikes do occur. This is because there is no ready source of teachers who are (a) certified in Alberta, (b) not already employed, and (c) who would be willing to cross a picket line set up by a union that likely has represented them in the past or may represent them in the future. Of the 24 ATA decisions issued by the Labour Board in the past 20 years, eight were bad faith bargaining complaints (not first contract), six were disputes about specific bargaining unit exclusions, four were DFR complaints, and two were related to certification of private schools.

The application of the *Labour Code* for K–12 bargaining therefore occurs most frequently during collective agreement renegotiation. When conflict erupts, the labour relations board either mediates a settlement, issues a directive to get bargaining back on track, or ensures compliance with the *Code* in the event of a strike. Alberta teachers currently enjoy a relatively unfettered right to strike. The *Code* takes a countervailing power approach that focuses on levelling the playing field to roughly equalize bargaining power. Strikes and lockouts are still the preferred dispute resolution mechanism (Adell, Grant, and Ponak 2001). But any strike, no matter how limited in scope or duration, tends to elicit inflammatory rhetoric and calls to curb the power of the ATA.

The question now is whether the comfortable position enjoyed by the Association will continue. The concern is that in a regime based on countervailing power, government may be tempted to minimize bargaining strength on the other side of the table. Furthermore, there is movement across Canada challenging the constitutionality of legislation that mandates any particular bargaining model (e.g., *Fraser v. Ontario* 2008).

In what is probably the most interesting development in Alberta labour law for some time, the Labour Relations Board relied upon the decision in *Health Services v. British Columbia* (2007) to declare that the absence of a statutory Rand formula in the *Alberta Code* is a violation of section 2(d) of the *Charter* (*Old Dutch Foods Ltd.* 2009). Section 2(d) guarantees freedom of association and, since the *Dunmore v. Ontario* (2001) and *Health Services* (2007) decisions, it has been the subject of intense scrutiny and new litigation in the labour relations context. The Rand formula is the most common union security provision in Canadian collective agreements (Gunderson and Taras 2009). It requires that all employees covered by the collective agreement pay union dues, although they may choose not to be a member of the union. It prevents "free riding" where employees opt out of contributing, but still receive the benefits and protections negotiated by the union. Most other provinces legislate Rand as the minimal security provision in all collective agreements. The *Old Dutch* decision was intended to bring Alberta's legislation in line with what exists in other provinces, but it is currently under judicial review. If the decision of the Labour Relations Board is upheld by the highest court to hear the case, the *Alberta Labour Relations Code* (2000) would likely be amended, but there would be little impact on the closed-shop arrangements that are contained in the *School Act* and the *TPA*. However, a number of affected employees are objecting to the Rand formula provisions and are expected to argue that they have a constitutional right to freedom *from* association. If the *Old Dutch* case is overturned, the long-range impact is far from clear. The constitutionality of the closed-shop arrangements contained in the *School Act* and the *TPA* may well come into question.

Should the province remove (or be required to remove) security protections from existing legislation, or if it were to more aggressively pursue private/charter schools, significant damage to the ATA is far from assured. Overcoming inertia and moving to decertify the ATA would require that a majority of teachers (a) be ideologically opposed to unions, (b) believe that being non-union would appreciably increase utilities (e.g., wages, benefits, job security), or (c) believe the union no longer provides workplace voice (Jelf and Dworkin 1997). A closer look at the form and function of the ATA, in the following section, suggests that long-standing membership ties will likely reduce ideological tensions and thus ensure a degree of organizational stability in the face of uncertainty.

The Agents

Alberta Teachers' Association

The Alberta Teachers' Association is both a professional and a collective bargaining institution. Its objectives and powers are codified in section 4 of the *Teaching Profession Act*. These include advancing and promoting the cause of education, improving the teaching profession, establishing working conditions that make it possible to provide the best level of professional service, assessing teaching competence, as well as advising, protecting, and disciplining members.

The dual purpose of the Association has been criticized as a factor contributing to a certain level of labour compliance among members. Reshef and Rastin (2003) suggest that identification with the profession makes teachers less likely to engage in traditional union activities. Furthermore, legislated duality forces the ATA to "keep its union head low in order to protect its professional head" (Reshef and Rastin 2003, 118). Although the ATA is currently the sole bargaining agent for certificated teachers in the province, if government retaliates against an overly militant union, the two functions could be split, forcing the ATA to invest heavily to maintain its membership.

The alternative view is that the strong professional culture binds members and fortifies their commitment to the ATA. Even if teachers are less likely to engage in union action over economic issues, they remain willing to fight when their professional identity is threatened. Kratzmann (1965) argues that duality also ensures that negotiated agreements bring returns to both teachers and the community. This is particularly important when a monopoly union is bargaining with a publicly funded employer. He cites the experience of American teachers and maintains that separating the functions would result in conflicting agendas, stagnation of both institutions, and increased risk of the union arm pursuing indefensible economic goals.

The evidence suggests that the combined professional/union function has been successful for the ATA. The Association has secured among the highest salaries for teachers in Canada (Alberta School Boards Association 2008) and continues to influence education policy in the province. Unlike its school board counterparts, the ATA has also avoided extensive erosion of its authority. Although public support for teachers occasionally wavers, it may be that duality gives taxpayers some level of comfort that the power the ATA wields is tempered by members' commitment to professional responsibility.

Alberta School Boards Association (ASBA)

The *Alberta School Boards Association Act* (2000) establishes the ASBA as a corporation of publicly elected school boards. The purpose of the ASBA is to improve education in the province, increase school board efficiency, provide for the expression of school board views (particularly for the enhancement of legislation), and to advise and assist members. The ASBA supports public (rather than private) education, decentralized decision-making, and restoration of school board authority to levy taxes (Alberta School Boards Association, n.d.).

The ASBA has no legislated role in collective bargaining, nor does it have authority to force members to comply with policies or strategies that might influence bargaining. Moreover, membership is not mandatory. Prior to 1994, school boards periodically exercised their statutory right to form employers' associations for the purposes of collective bargaining (McLeod 1978). The regional bargaining that occurred through these School Authorities Associations was sometimes successful, but also resulted in lengthy strikes in some cycles (see Appendix A: 1971, 1973, 1983, 1988, and 1992). School Authorities Associations were engaged in regional bargaining on two of the five occasions when the right to strike for Alberta teachers was suspended by Ministerial Order. These were the Bow Valley School Authorities Association/ATA strike in 1971 and the Southern Alberta School Authorities Association/ATA strike in 1973 (Human Resources and Skills Development Canada 2006). In 2005, a motion to create a provincial school board bargaining agent was passed at the ASBA's annual general meeting. Only 59 percent of member boards supported the proposition. This suggests that there remains substantial disagreement about the perceived roles and priorities of school boards, as well as the effectiveness of a centralized structure (MacKenzie 2008).

Those who oppose a centralized model argue that local bargaining is the main purpose of school boards and removing that responsibility could eventually lead to the dissolution of boards altogether. They believe local bargaining allows school boards to better address unique problems and can create more cooperative relationships with teachers and the community. Those in support of centralization argue that local bargaining increases turnover in trustees, creating an opportunity for the ATA to influence trustee elections and infiltrate local boards. For rural areas, local bargaining may have a particularly negative impact when the size and isolation of a community require both sides to interact outside of work. Smaller boards also tend to prefer provincial bargaining of economic issues because it reduces competitive forces that sometimes lure good teachers from their districts. Finally, it has been argued that the current model generates a significant imbalance in bargaining power as a well-coordinated ATA successfully plays school boards off against one another (MacKenzie 2008).

The philosophical divide over centralized ASBA bargaining led to the creation of two new entities: the Coalition for Choice and the School Board Employer Bargaining Authority (SBEBA). The Coalition for Choice is a group of 11 school jurisdictions that support local bargaining. The Coalition has attempted to influence provincial policy by preparing and presenting a paper to Alberta's Standing Policy Committee on Education and Employment (MacKenzie 2008). SBEBA took a much more direct approach by forming an employers' organization for the purpose of collective bargaining. The struggle of SBEBA, the ASBA, and the ATA to successfully reach agreements following the *School Amendment Act* in 1994 is chronicled below.

The Bargaining Revolution

By 2001, cuts to public sector budgets under the Progressive Conservatives had peaked and relief was on the horizon (Boessenkool 2001). Improved oil and gas revenues combined with an upcoming provincial election encouraged government generosity. Early in the year physicians negotiated a 22 percent fee increase, making them the highest-paid doctors in the country. Nurses followed shortly thereafter with a 17 percent increase, and MLAs voted to give themselves a 17.3 percent raise (Reshef 2007, 681-82).

The rich settlements in government and health care created high hopes for educators. But these would be dashed when a Teacher Salary Enhancement Fund set aside just enough money for school boards to give teachers a 6 percent increase over two years (Reshef 2007, 682). Not only did the salary adjustment fail to make up for losses incurred in the 1990s, it fell well below the high expectations of teachers who felt they had done their part in 1994. Sixty of the 62 school jurisdictions were bargaining in 2001. By January of 2002 negotiations between the ATA and school boards across the province were breaking down: 14 bargaining units had overwhelming support for job action, 9 had applied for supervised strike votes, and 28 were in mediation. Only 9 units had settled. Backed into a corner, the ATA, for the first time in its history, coordinated simultaneous strikes across the province beginning on 4 February 2002 (Reshef 2007). On February 21, after 13 days, the Klein government declared the strikes a public emergency and ordered teachers back to the classroom. The back-to-work legislation was struck down by the Court of Queen's Bench on March 1:

It must be borne in mind that the very purpose of a strike is to cause some hardship in order to raise the profile of the issues being contested, and to pressure the other side into making concessions. If a strike did not cause some degree of hardship it would be pointless. That is why the hardship suffered must be unreasonable before the Government can order teachers back to work, and that means there must be some imminence and inevitability before any hardship can be considered unreasonable. (*Alberta Teachers' Association v. Alberta* 2002, para. 10)

Teachers returned to the classroom as ordered by the Minister on February 22. As a show of good faith and to help negotiations get back on track, the ATA asked that they remain on the job even after the Queen's Bench ruling. Their good will was "rewarded" on March 11 with the passing by the legislature of the *Education Services Settlement Act* (*ESSA*). The *ESSA* applied to all 48 school jurisdictions that had not yet reached an agreement. It established an arbitration process for settling salary issues but limited the settlement to what each board could afford. It also prohibited the arbitration panel from addressing anything to do with class size, student-teacher ratios, or instructional time, and stopped teachers from striking for the duration of the Act, which would be repealed in August of 2003. Every collective agreement settled under the *ESSA* also had to expire on 31 August 2003. The ATA, shocked by the extraordinary restrictions placed on traditional collective bargaining and interest arbitration, engaged in a work-to-rule campaign and threatened legal action.

Disputes about the content of the *ESSA* delayed any further progress until the end of April 2002. After lengthy backroom negotiations, the government, the ATA, and the ASBA signed an addendum to the *ESSA*. The agreement was announced in a joint news conference on April 19. In exchange for the ATA's discontinuing its legal challenge and ending work-to-rule directives, the arbitration tribunal would be allowed greater flexibility and the government would pay the teachers' portion of their unfunded pension liability for the next 12 months. The parties also established that classroom conditions could be discussed during the arbitration process, and the parties could reach settlement on those issues. However, some specific classroom conditions (i.e., class size, student-teacher ratios, and instructional time) could not form part of the collective agreements (Alberta Teachers' Association 2002). This departure from traditional labour relations created an interesting problem regarding the legality, operation, and enforcement of these ancillary agreements. To get around the unusual requirement, working conditions clauses that existed prior to the *ESSA* were replaced with, or restricted to, clauses requiring school boards to consult with the union in some capacity prior to making any changes. Finally, in July, the arbitration panel submitted the first of its awards, which would eventually be replicated in the remaining bargaining units. Teachers were delighted when they received

14.09 percent over two years (Reshef 2007, 687). However, when the province refused to top up the 6 percent promised in the original Salary Enhancement Fund, a number of boards announced layoffs and increased class sizes (Veenbaas 2003).

In the wake of the dispute in 2002 and to follow through on commitments made in the *ESSA*, the government appointed Alberta's Commission on Learning to conduct a comprehensive and consultative review of K–12 education. The Commission's report was issued in 2003 and made 95 recommendations addressing curriculum, class size, hours of instruction, and the funding model, among other concerns. The Commission took a distinctly pro-board stance when it suggested tinkering with collective bargaining. The report advised

- amending the *Labour Relations Code* to establish an employer bargaining association with mandatory membership;
- limiting what could be bargained for collectively, specifically excluding class sizes and instructional time;
- expanding teachers' professional responsibilities to include currently voluntary services such as curriculum development, marking provincial exams, and supervising student teachers; and
- replacing the Board of Reference with an arbitration process consistent with models in place for most other employees under the *Labour Relations Code* (Alberta Education 2003).

Eighty-four of the Commission's recommendations were supported by the provincial legislature, nine were delayed pending further study, and two were voted down. Among those requiring further study were the recommendations that dealt with revising the existing bargaining model. Minister of Learning Lyle Oberg indicated that changes in this arena would have a substantial impact on stakeholders, and therefore the government preferred to take a more cautious approach. The recommendations that school boards regain their taxing authority, and that school infrastructure be consolidated within the Department of Learning, were turned down. Strong public opposition, inefficiency, and a lack of benefit for learners were cited as the rationale for the denial (Government of Alberta 2003).

In spite of Minister Oberg's suggestion to the contrary, some of the report's recommendations did prompt legislative change that would affect bargaining. When the *School Act* (2000) was amended in 2004, section 18(2) was added, expanding teacher obligations as recommended by the Commission:

(2)   At any time during the period of time that a teacher is under obligation to the board to provide instruction or supervision or to carry out duties

assigned to the teacher by a principal or the board, a teacher must, at the request of the board,

(a) participate in the curriculum development and field testing of new curriculum;

(b) develop, field test and mark provincial achievement tests and diploma examinations;

(c) supervise student teachers.

Furthermore, principals or other teachers engaged in administration or supervision would be allowed to opt out of ATA membership. If they chose to do so, they would also be excluded from the bargaining unit (*School Act* 2000; *Teacher Membership Status Election Regulation* 2004; *Teaching Profession Act* 2000). In an effort to address concerns expressed to the Commission regarding discipline, the 2004 amendment to the *School Act* detailed new procedures for Boards of Reference and outlined matters that they must consider before rendering a decision. The *TPA* was also revised in 2004. Most significantly, the powers of the ATA were expanded to include assessing professional competence and developing a Professional Practice Review process for members (*Teaching Profession Act* 2000, s. 4vii). COATS, the ministerial body previously charged with this responsibility, was now limited to assessing professional competence for teachers not covered by the *TPA* (e.g., teachers in private or charter schools).

In 2007, 52 of the ATA's bargaining units had contracts expiring at the end of August. Ed Stelmach won the Progressive Conservative Party leadership race following the resignation of Premier Klein. With an upcoming provincial election and strong oil and gas revenues, the government was again juggling the budget in an attempt to secure the support of the electorate. Settlements for nurses and the Alberta Union of Provincial Employees resulted in salary increases of between 15 percent and 23 percent over three years. But the province wanted to hold the line on education spending, offering only a 3 percent grant increase to school boards for 2007 (Svidal 2007). Both the ATA and school boards expressed concern that the budgeted increase would not keep pace with inflation, stating that job action could be expected if funding was not increased (Edmonton Journal 2007; Svidal 2007).

As predicted, bargaining was off to a rocky start with negotiations overshadowed by the outstanding $2.1 billion unfunded pension liability and a month-long strike involving 674 teachers (*Parkland School Division v. ATA* 2007). The pension problem had increasingly become an irritant for teachers who bore the burden of paying for actuarial miscalculations that had occurred before 1992 (Alberta Education 2007). The ATA had been pressuring the government to get the pension issue resolved, and in 2007 indicated it was ready to engage in negotiations with the province to settle it. The ATA further proposed that although the province had intended to create funding equity when it began collecting school taxes in 1994, in the process the government had also "undermined the role of school boards," making it much more difficult to bargain effectively (Alberta Teachers' Association 2007). The union made it very clear that local bargaining was no longer working, and teachers wanted the "direct participation" of the provincial government (ibid.).

In April of 2007 the province announced that it would strike a task force to study the pension issue, with the expectation that a report would be ready by the end of October (Government of Alberta 2007a). The official position of the province was that regular bargaining and the unfunded liability were separate issues and should be kept that way. Premier Stelmach had previously stated that he would "never use such an emotional matter as a bargaining chip in the heat of a labour dispute" (Legislative Assembly of Alberta 2007, 689). However, in an address to the ATA, Education Minister Ron Liepert (appointed only a few months earlier in December of 2006) indicated that work on the unfunded liability might be suspended in the event of a labour dispute (Bruseker 2007b). The ATA declined the invitation to participate on the task force. It was the union's position that negotiations should commence immediately and that under the current system of local bargaining, it could not guarantee that teachers in any particular local would not need to resort to some type of labour action (ibid.).

The ATA took an opportunity to further press its case in August, when SBEBA attempted to force the union to engage in multi-unit bargaining. The ATA refused to entertain negotiations with what it called the SBEBA "cartel" (Alberta Teachers' Association 2007). Citing the difficulty of ne-gotiating divergent interests and previously ineffective attempts at joint bargaining as the rationale for its refusal, the ATA pointed to the strikes in 1973 (Southern Alberta, 18 boards), 1985 (Elk Island, 6 boards), 1988 (North Central East SAA, 17 boards), and 1992 (Battle River, 10 boards). In response, SBEBA filed a bad faith bargaining complaint with the Labour Relations Board. SBEBA asked the board to determine whether collective bargaining should be conducted at one table (SBEBA's position) or many (the ATA's position). Although the Board upheld the bad faith bargaining complaint, the members also concluded they had no authority to order the multi-unit bargaining (*School Boards Employer Bargaining Authority v. ATA* 2007).

Persistent pressure from the ATA to get Education Minister Ron Liepert directly involved in negotiations was eventually successful. Premier Stelmach directed that negotiations begin at the end of the sum-mer (Government of Alberta 2007b). As co-sponsors of the pension plan, only the province and the ATA were involved in the negotiations. Both parties agreed to a communications blackout for the duration of the dis-cussions (Alberta Education 2007).

On November 15, a tentative agreement was reached between the province and the ATA that traded pension relief for labour peace. In the *Memorandum of Agreement* (*MOA*), the province agreed to pay the unfunded liability, but also established rates of pay for all 62 bargaining units for the next five years. Local bargaining of all other issues had to be completed by the end of January 2008, without strike or lockout, and all collective agreements were to expire in August of 2012. The government promised it would provide school boards with the support necessary to meet the salary increases provided all 62 bargaining units ratified the *MOA* (*Memorandum of Agreement* 2007).

The *MOA* not only represented a radical break from the tradition of local bargaining, it also highlighted the power of the ATA and placed demands on school boards who were not parties to the agreement. All provisions of the *MOA*, including school board funding, were conditional on the school boards and the ATA signing local collective agreements. Although school boards complied with the pressure to conclude agreements within the timeframe required by the *MOA*, their acquiescence was not without discomfort. School boards felt excluded and were under significant pressure from the government to conform. Some suggested they were threatened with dissolution if they failed to sign agreements on time (MacKenzie 2008, 6). While appreciating the five years of labour peace and provincewide indexing of salaries, boards also felt that the time limits and provincial pressure forced them to accept provisions they would not have agreed to otherwise. In their view, the ATA "gave up very little in exchange for a very costly ($2.1 billion) assumption of the unfunded pension liability" (ibid.).

Finally, the fact that the province was not a party to the collective agreements containing *MOA* provisions created a new legal conundrum. A dispute over 2009 salary adjustments prompted the ATA to file a number of policy grievances.[9] Although the terms of the *MOA* were enshrined in ATA/school board contracts, the ASBA regarded the salary grievances as a provincial responsibility. To resolve the issue, the Education Minister proposed that the dispute be referred to a single arbitrator, under the terms of the original *MOA* (Theobald 2009). This meant the parties in arbitration were the province and the ATA. School boards were excluded from the discussion again, and it was once more unclear how they could be required to comply with the arbitrator's decision. The ATA agreed to the process provided the government used its "best efforts" to convince boards to implement any resulting decision, and provided grievance arbitration would remain available to them if any school board refused. Arbitrator Andrew Sims heard arguments in January of 2010 and decided in favour of the ATA. School boards have since complied with the arbitration order.

Until the twenty-first century, the story of K–12 bargaining in Alberta was one of evolution rather than revolution. But the transformations occurring over the last decade beg the questions: What actually works and where do we go from here?

Did Local Bargaining in Alberta Work?

To evaluate how well a particular bargaining structure functions, it is helpful to consider three factors:

1. Whether the structure promotes labour peace
2. Whether it is procedurally fair
3. Whether the outcomes are equitable

The best available measure of labour peace is strike activity. In the first 30 years of the ATA's existence (from 1941–1969), there were a total of eight strikes in the province involving 976 teachers with fewer than 100 school days lost. In the post-Conservative era the number of strikes grew to more than 50, involving over 55,000 teachers and more than 600 lost school days (Appendix A). What amplified the unrest? It is possible that as the ATA gained strength and as teacher autonomy was threatened by increasingly centralized policies affecting curriculum and pedagogy, the union became more militant. However, a look at strike activity shows clusters of unrest that roughly correlate with PC policies of fiscal restraint (mid-1980s and early 1990s), or periods of relative prosperity without corresponding increases to education spending (early 1970s and early 2000s). This suggests that the more fundamental irritant in collective bargaining is provincial funding. Prior to 1994, boards could mitigate the impact of inadequate grants to some degree through taxation. Local bargaining was functional, albeit imperfect. After 1994, the effects of the funding restrictions became unmanageable and local bargaining eventually failed completely.

The courts have determined that fairness in collective bargaining means accessibility, limited third-party intervention, and a relatively level playing field (*Health Services v. British Columbia* 2007). In Alberta, fairness concerns arose because the playing field was precariously balanced prior to 1994, and completely unbalanced after school boards' taxation authority was removed. Alberta statutes already gave the ATA something of an advantage. Its dual union/professional role and closed-shop status helped create a powerful institution that the ASBA had difficulty replicating. ATA expertise, strategic coordination, and financial security meant the pressure for small boards to conform to bargaining demands was high even before they lost the authority to levy taxes. Although the legislation has always allowed the ASBA to form an employers' organization, ideological divisions among boards have prevented a sustained, coordinated approach. When the last leg of bargaining power for boards was pulled from under them, local bargaining failed and third-party intervention became the norm. It began with a back-to-work order and ended with the province negotiating the financial terms and conditions of collective agreements and pressuring locally elected boards to accept them. So in spite of some legislative attempts to ensure a level field and restrict government interference (e.g., *Alberta Labour Relations Code 2000*, s. 112), the temptation for powerful actors to override those protections is strong with the current funding and bargaining structure.

Thoroughly assessing the equity of bargaining outcomes is beyond the scope of this chapter. However, two indicators that might provide a useful snapshot are relative wage rates and education performance. Most sources suggest that Alberta's teachers are currently at or near the top of the salary range relative to their counterparts from other provinces (Alberta Education, n.d., *Facts and Statistics*; Alberta School Boards Association 2008; Education Canada Network, n.d.). Although satisfied with the 2007 agreement (Bruseker 2007a), the ATA also points out that interprovincial wage parity is difficult to assess and may not be the best yardstick. The union's analyses rely on comparisons with other public sector employees in Alberta rather than teachers in other provinces. When measured against wage increases for nurses, provincial employees, and MLAs, the ATA argues that teachers have not historically fared as well. The union suggests that between 1990 and 2002 the real (adjusted for inflation) wage of an Alberta teacher actually decreased by 3.4 percent (Alberta Teachers' Association 2001). The report card for education quality is also somewhat mixed. Alberta students outperform their Canadian peers in mathematics, reading, writing, and science. However, Alberta also has higher student-teacher ratios, a lower graduation rate, and proportionally lower spending on education than any other province (Statistics Canada 2005). On the whole, it appears that the local bargaining structure, limited forays into privatization, and the ATA's dual professional and union role have not been detrimental. Teachers' salaries are generally comparable to (if not always better than) those of other provincial employees and colleagues in other provinces, and education outcomes for Alberta students are satisfactory.

Where Do We Go from Here?

The shift away from local bargaining in Alberta appears to have been largely unintended. It began when school boards lost the ability to control revenues with the *School Amendment Act* in 1994. The *Education Services Settlement Act* in 2002 provided a short-term solution to the resulting labour unrest, but did nothing to effect long-term structural change that would resolve the power imbalance between school boards and the ATA. The need to resolve the pension issue and a desire for labour peace then opened the door to direct negotiations with the province on other collective agreement terms and conditions.

In June of 2010, Minister of Education Dave Hancock approached the ATA and the ASBA to develop a collective bargaining process that would "extend labour peace and ensure workforce stability beyond

2012" (Theobald 2010). At this point it is unclear what the outcome of these discussions will be. On the surface, the joint discussions appear to be an attempt to involve all three stakeholders (ATA, ASBA, and Alberta Education) in the negotiation of a successor agreement to the *MOA* of 2007. The broad mandate for the discussions and having all three parties at the table will doubtlessly complicate negotiations. However, if the parties are successful, it may lead to legislative change, cementing a new bargaining structure within the *School Act* revisions that are planned for 2011 (Alberta Education, n.d., *School Act* Review).

Given the development of K–12 bargaining in Alberta and an unlikely return to a decentralized funding model, there is some reason to speculate that the final structure will have two tiers. A two-tier system would see economic issues negotiated centrally (between the government and a provincial executive committee of the ATA) and non-economic issues negotiated at the local level (between individual school boards and ATA locals). There are some clear benefits to developing such a structure. For the ATA, two-tier bargaining mostly retains the preferred relationship between individual locals and the corporate head. Centralized negotiation of economic issues allows the ATA to use its muscle to meet the utility expectations of the membership. At the same time, local bargaining of non-economic issues accommodates workplace voice by providing opportunity for direct influence on individual collective agreements. For the ASBA, the five-year agreements typical of two-tiered bargaining will secure longer periods of labour peace and decrease economic uncertainty (as long as the province follows through on funding promises). A two-tier system also makes room for divergent opinions, allowing local boards to manage local issues. The ASBA bargaining power problem is substantially mitigated because the province is at the table. The difficult question is how the structure will be integrated into the legislation. The ad hoc tools used to centralize bargaining in 2002 and 2007 do not provide the predictability the parties need to avoid labour strife.

Recent upheaval in collective bargaining law across Canada and the consultative approach being taken by the Government of Alberta as it seeks to rebalance K–12 bargaining also suggest that legislative revisions will be undertaken very cautiously. It will be important to establish the standing of the province in collective agreements, and to develop a mechanism that ensures appropriate funding of negotiated salary increases. The closed-shop status of the ATA may also come under close scrutiny. But the playing field will not be level if the ATA is weakened when it is required to negotiate directly with the government. Finally, when boards held taxing authority, the link between monies collected and service provided was very transparent to the taxpayer. Centralized bargaining will elevate expectations for provincial accountability, and the consequences of public disapproval will be felt at the polls. Prickly negotiations could entice intervention or limitations on the right to strike to avoid political fallout. In the move from local bargaining to a new structure, it is clear the courts will remain important arbiters of equity in the highly politicized arena of K–12 bargaining in Alberta.

NOTES

1. The Minister of Education could also order the formation of school districts and appoint trustees where there were ten taxable residents and 20 children (*School Ordinance* 1901).
2. The name Alberta Teachers' Alliance was changed by the Act to Alberta Teachers' Association.
3. C.H. Douglas was a Scottish-born engineer, educated at Cambridge University. He authored a number of works on monetary systems and presented his ideas to the Canadian House of Commons Standing Committee on Banking and Industry in 1923.
4. The unemployment rate in Canada peaked at 12 percent in 1983 (Human Resources and Skills Development Canada 2010).
5. Jim Keegstra was a teacher in Eckville, Alberta, who was discharged and had his certificate withdrawn for teaching anti-Semitism in his classroom. The case pitted freedom of expression against promoting hate. Keegstra lost the battle when the Supreme Court ruled that his infringement on the rights of others was not justifiable under section 1 of the *Charter*.
6. Eventually the ATA would be given authority over practice competence as well (*Teaching Profession Amendment Act* 2004).
7. In 1993, Klein won 51 out of 83 seats in the legislature; in 1997, he won 63. By 2001 he had 74 seats, but in his last election in 2004 his popularity declined to 62 seats.
8. The constitutionality of union security clauses (particularly mandatory dues payment) had already been addressed by the Supreme Court in *Lavigne v. Ontario Public Service Employees Union* [1991] *S.C.J. No. 52*. However there was nothing in the decision that would prohibit the right-to-work legislation being proposed by Bill 210.
9. The *MOA* tied salary increases to the Alberta Average Weekly Earnings (AAWE) Index produced by Statistics Canada. But when Statistics Canada changed the method of calculating the AAWE, it affected the interpretation of the salary clauses. The Minister of Education had budgeted for a 4.82 percent increase (which was implemented by school boards). The ATA believed the increase should have been 5.99 percent.

REFERENCES

Act to Amend the Department of Education Act, S.A. 1945, c. 21.
Act to Amend the School Grants Act, S.A. 1967, c. 74.
Adell, B., M. Grant, and A. Ponak. 2001. *Strikes in Essential Services.* Kingston, ON: IRC Press, Queen's University.
Alberta Act, 1905, 4-5 Edw. VII, c. 42.
Alberta Education. 2003. *Report and Recommendations – Alberta's Commission on Learning.* Edmonton: Government of Alberta.

—. 2007. "Teachers' Unfunded Pension Liability: Frequently Asked Questions." http://education.alberta.ca/media/658265/faqs.pdf.

—. 2009. *Charter Schools Handbook*. Edmonton: Government of Alberta. http://education.alberta.ca/media/434258/charter_hndbk.pdf.

—. 2010a. "Private Schools." http://education.alberta.ca/parents/choice/private.aspx.

—. 2010b. "Funding Allocations for Accredited Funded Private Schools." http://education.alberta.ca/media/826607/grantratestableshortversion.pdf.

—. n.d. *Facts and Statistics on Education Funding and Teaching in Alberta: How Teachers Are Paid*. Edmonton: Government of Alberta.

—. n.d. "School Act Review: Discussion Paper for Legislative Review." http://education.alberta.ca/media/1165978/consultationdiscussionpaper.pdf.

Alberta Education and P. MacKenzie. 2009. *Fifth Anniversary Retrospective: Alberta's Commission on Learning Report*. Edmonton: Government of Alberta.

Alberta Labour Relations Code, R.S.A. 2000, c. L-1.

Alberta School Boards Association. 2008. *2007/2008 Average Provincial Salary Grid Comparison*. http://www.asba.ab.ca/files/pdf/canada_salaries08.pdf.

—. n.d. *Alberta's School Act: Creating Our Future*. School Act submission. http://www.asba.ab.ca/files/pdf/school_act_submission.pdf.

Alberta School Boards Association Act, R.S.A. 2000, c. A-32.

Alberta Teachers' Association. 2001. "What's Fair?" *ATA News* 36(8).

—. 2002. "Agreement Reached: ATA, Government and ASBA Agree to Address Education Crisis." *ATA News* 36(18).

—. 2005. "Strikes by Alberta Teachers Since 1942." Table prepared by Parkland Teachers' Local 10. http://local10.teachers.ab.ca/SiteCollectionDocuments/Local10.teachers.ab.ca/PDF%20files/STRIKES.PDF.

—. 2007. "School Boards Form Bargaining Cartel: Is Provincial Bargaining Next?" *ATA News* 41(14).

—. n.d. *Charter Schools, Private School and Vouchers*. http://www.teachers.ab.ca/News%20Room/IssuesandCampaigns/Ongoing%20Issues/Pages/Charter%20Schools%20Private%20Schools%20and%20Vouchers.aspx.

—. n.d. *History of Public Education*. http://www.teachers.ab.ca/Teaching%20in%20Alberta/History%20of%20Public%20Education/Pages/Index.aspx.

Alberta Teachers' Association v. Alberta, [2002] A.J. No. 268 ABQB 240.

Alberta Teachers' Association v. Pembina Hills Regional Division No. 7, [2008] A.J. No. 121 ABQB 87.

An Act to Further Amend the Statute Law, S.A. 1909, c. 5.

Anderson, S.M. 2005. "Venerable Rights: Constitutionalizing Alberta's Schools 1869–1905." In *Forging Alberta's Constitutional Framework*, edited by R. Connors and J.M. Law. Edmonton: University of Alberta Press.

Bell, E. 1993. "The Rise of the Lougheed Conservatives and the Demise of Social Credit in Alberta: A Reconsideration." *Canadian Journal of Political Science/Revue canadienne de science politiques* 26(3): 455-75.

Berghofer, D. and A. Vladicka. 1980. *Access to Opportunity 1905–80: The Development of Post-Secondary Education in Alberta*. Edmonton: Alberta Advanced Education and Manpower.

Boessenkool, K.J. 2001. *Keeping Alberta on the Path of Fiscal Happiness*. Toronto: C.D. Howe Institute.

Bruseker, F. 2007a. "A Letter to Members from ATA President Frank Bruseker." *ATA News* 42(SI 1).

—. 2007b. Letter to the Honourable Ron Liepert, Minister of Education, 22 May. http://www.teachers.ab.ca/SiteCollectionDocuments/ATA/Features/2006-07/May%2022%20Letter%20from%20Bruseker%20to%20Liepert. PDF.

Cameron, D. 1959. *Report of the Royal Commission on Education in Alberta.* Edmonton: Province of Alberta.

Chalmers, J.W. 1967. *Schools of the Foothills Province: The Story of Public Education in Alberta.* Toronto: University of Toronto Press.

Charter Schools Regulation, A.R. 212/2002.

Constitution Act, 1867 (U.K.), 30 & 31 Victoria, c. 3.

Dafoe, J. 1931. *Clifford Sifton in Relation to His Times.* Toronto: MacMillan.

Decore, A. and R. Pannu. 1989. "Alberta Political Economy in Crisis: Whither Education?" *Canadian Journal of Education/Revue canadienne de l'education* 14(2): 150-69.

Dunmore v. Ontario (Attorney General), 2001 SCC 94, [2001] S.C.R. 1016.

Edmonton Journal. 2007. "Alberta Unions Think Big." *Canada.com,* 24 February. http://www.canada.com/edmontonjournal/news/story.html?id=18900f9b-0acd-48ba-987c-dcc4925a6a7c.

Education Canada Network. n.d. "Salaries." http://resource.educationcanada.com/salaries.html/.

Education Services Settlement Act, S.A. 2002, c. E-0.5.

Finkel, A. 1985. "The Rise and Fall of the Labour Party in Alberta, 1917–42," *Labour / Le Travail* 16: 61-96.

—. 1988. "The Cold War, Alberta Labour and the Social Credit Regime." *Labour/Le Travail* 21: 123-52.

—. 1989. *The Social Credit Phenomenon in Alberta.* Toronto: University of Toronto Press.

Fraser, C. 1999. "What Is the Board of Reference?" *ATA News* 33(Special Issue No.2).

Fraser v. Ontario (Attorney General), [2008] O.J. No. 4543, ONCA 760.

Government of Alberta. Department of Education. 2003. *Government Supports 84 Commission Recommendations.* Edmonton, Alberta.

—. 2007a. "Government Takes Initial Step to Address Teachers' Portion of Unfunded Pension Liability." News release, 19 April. http://education.alberta.ca/department/newsroom/news/2007/april/20070419-2.aspx.

—. 2007b. "Teachers, Students, School Boards and Taxpayers Benefit from Solution to Unfunded Pension Liability." News release, 15 November. http://education.alberta.ca/department/newsroom/news/2007/november/20071115.aspx.

Government of Alberta. Employment and Immigration. 2010. "Legal Work Stoppages." Edmonton, Alberta.

Gunderson, M. and D. Taras. 2009. *Canadian Labour and Employment Relations.* 6th ed. Toronto: Pearson Education Canada.

Hannant, L. 1985. "The Calgary Working Class and the Social Credit Movement in Alberta, 1932–35." *Labour/Le Travail* 16: 97-116.

Health Services and Support – Facilities Subsector Bargaining Assn. v. British Columbia [2007] S.J.C. No 27; [2007] A.C.S. no. 27; 2 S.C.R. 391.

Heritage Community Foundation. n.d. "Alberta's Political Parties." In *Alberta Online Encyclopedia.* http://www.abheritage.ca/abpolitics/events/party_intro.html.

Human Resources and Skills Development Canada. 2006. "Orders Suspending the Right to Strike or to Lock Out." http://www.hrsdc.gc.ca/eng/lp/spila/clli/irlc/EMER-ORD-E.PDF.

—. 2010. "Indicators of Well-Being in Canada: Unemployment Rate." http://www4.hrsdc.gc.ca/.3ndic.1t.4r@-eng.jsp?iid=16.

Industrial Conciliation and Arbitration Act Amendment Act 1941, SA 1941, c. 20.

Jelf, G.S. and J.B. Dworkin. 1997. "Union Decertification Research: Review and Theoretical Integration." *International Journal of Conflict Management* 8(4): 306-37.

Jenkins, B. 1986. "Obsolescing Bargain: A Study of Canada's National Energy Program." *International Organization* 40(1): 139-65.

Kratzmann, A. 1964. "The Alberta Teachers' Association: A Vision Vindicated." *The Phi Delta Kappan* 45(6): 288-92.

—. 1965. "The Alberta Teachers' Association and Collective Bargaining." *Theory into Practice* 4(2): 75-78.

Legislative Assembly of Alberta. 1983. *Alberta Hansard,* 18 April. Edmonton: Government of Alberta.

—. 1995. *Alberta Hansard,* 2 May. Edmonton: Government of Alberta.

—. 2007. *Alberta Hansard,* 30 April. Edmonton: Government of Alberta.

MacKenzie, P. 2008. *Fair Bargaining for a Better Future: Report on the 2007–2008 Collective Bargaining Process.* Edmonton: Alberta School Boards Association.

Manzer, R. 1969. "Selective Inducements and the Development of Pressure Groups: The Case of Canadian Teachers' Associations." *Canadian Journal of Political Science/Revue canadienne de science politiques* 2(3): 103-17.

McLeod, G. 1978. "Collective Bargaining between School Boards and Teachers: A Social-Dramaturgical Interpretation." *Canadian Journal of Education/Revue canadienne de l'education* 3(1): 19-38.

Memorandum of Agreement between the Province of Alberta and the Alberta Teachers' Association. 2007. Edmonton, Alberta.

North-West Territories Act, S.C., 1875, c. 49.

Old Dutch Foods Ltd. (Re), [2009] A.L.R.B.D. No. 56; 171 C.L.R.B.R. (2d) 1; 188 L.A.C. (4th) 289.

Palmer, H. and T. Palmer. 1976. "The 1971 Election and the Fall of Social Credit in Alberta." *Prairie Forum* 1: 123-24.

Parkland School Division v. ATA, 2007, [2007] A.L.R.B.D. No. 19; [2007] Alta. L.R.B.R. LD-016; 147 C.L.R.B.R. (2d) 135.

Patterson, R.S. 1961. *F.W.G. Haultain and Education in the Early West.* Master's of Education thesis, University of Alberta.

Pembina Hills Regional Division No. 7 (Re), [1997] Alta. L.R.B.R. 329; [1997] A.L.R.B.D. No. 30.

Pentek v. Alberta Teachers' Association, [1989] Alta. L.R.B.R. 303.

Practice Review of Teachers Regulation, AR 153/87, Repealed.

Public School Boards Association of Alberta v. Alberta Attorney General, [2000] S.C.J. No. 45; [2000] S.C.C. 45; 2 S.C.R. 409.

R. v. Keegstra, [1990] 3 S.C.R. 697.

Re: Exported Natural Gas Tax, [1982] S.C.J. No. 52; [1982] A.C.S. no 52; [1982] 1 S.C.R. 1004.

Reshef, Y. 2007. "Government Intervention in Public Sector Industrial Relations: Lessons from the Alberta Teachers' Association." *Journal of Labor Relations* 28: 677-96.

Reshef, Y. and S. Rastin. 2003. *Unions in the Time of Revolutions: Government Restructuring in Alberta and Ontario.* Toronto: University of Toronto Press.

Rutherford Research. n.d. *Alexander Cameron Rutherford History.* RRX Rutherford Research. http://www.rutherford-research.ca/rrx/corporate/alexanderCameron RutherfordDetails.php.

School Act, R.S.A. 1922, c. 51.

School Act, S.A. 1988, c. S-3.1.

School Act, S.A. 2000, c. S-3.

School Act Amendment Act, S.A. 1926, c. 57, s.197.

School Amendment Act, S.A. 1994, c. S-29.

School Boards Employer Bargaining Authority v. Alberta Teachers' Association, [2007] Alta. L.R.B.R. 240; [2007] A.L.R.B.D. No. 108; 146 C.L.R.B.R. (2d) 117.

School Ordinance, C.O. 1901, c. 75.

Statistics Canada. 2005. *Education Indicators in Canada.* Ottawa: Statistics Canada.

Svidal, S. 2007. "ATA President Looks Ahead to Pension Resolution." *ATA News* 42(3).

Taras, D. and A. Tupper. 1994. "Politics and Deficits: Alberta's Challenge to the Canadian Political Agenda." In *Canada: The State of the Federation,* edited by D. Brown and J. Hiebert. Kingston, ON: Institute of Intergovernmental Relations, Queen's University.

Teacher Membership Status Election Regulation, Alta. Reg 260/2004.

Teachers' Retirement Fund Act, S.A. 1939, c. 21.

Teaching Profession Act 1935, S.A. 1935, c. 81.

Teaching Profession Act 1935 Amendment Act 1936, S.A. 1935, c. 88.

Teaching Profession Act, R.S.A. 2000, c. T-2.

Teaching Profession Amendment Act, S.A. 2004, c. 27, s. 2.

Theobald, D. 2009. "Provincial Arbitration (Maybe)." *ATA News* 44(4).

—. 2010. "Partners to Discuss the Future of Education." *ATA News* 45(2).

Thomas, G. 2008. "Contract Appears to Limit Rights – Is That Legal?" *ATA News* 42(2).

Veenbaas, J. 2003. "Teacher Layoffs Spark Debate." *AlbertaVenture.com,* 1 December. http://albertaventure.com/2003/12/teacher-layoffs-spark-debate/.

Wallner, J. 2008. "Legitimacy and Public Policy: Seeing beyond Effectiveness, Efficiency, and Performance." *The Policy Studies Journal* 36(6): 421-43.

Wilson, L. 1977. "Perren Baker and Alberta's School District Reorganization." *Canadian Journal of Education/Revue canadienne de l'éducation* 2(3): 25-36.

APPENDIX A
Teacher Strikes in Alberta 1942–2006

Year	School Jurisdiction	Start Date	End Date	Teachers Affected	Days Lost	Premier and Party
1942	Vegreville	n/a	n/a	75	33	Aberhart, SC
1953	West Jasper Place	01/04	01/08	78	5	Manning, SC
1954	Newell	n/a	n/a	65	n/a	Manning, SC
1955	Clover Bar	n/a	n/a	80	9	Manning, SC
1957	Normandy	n/a	n/a	25	19	Manning, SC
1960	Leduc	n/a	n/a	170	9	Manning, SC
1963	Strathcona	n/a	n/a	245	7	Manning, SC
1969	Three Hills	03/10	03/13	112	4	Strom, SC
1969	Minburn	07/04	09/17	126	13	Strom, SC
1971	Calgary Public	04/21	04/24	4113	3	Strom, SC
	North Central West (8 boards)	10/08	10/25	852	10	Lougheed, PC
	Bow Valley (7 boards)	11/29	12/20	652	15	Lougheed, PC
1973	Southern AB (18 boards)	03/12	04/03	1357	15	Lougheed, PC
1975	Devon District	10/06	10/20	43	9	Lougheed, PC
	Acadia	10/20	11/06	55	13	Lougheed, PC
1978	Edmonton Public	09/07	09/20	3900	10	Lougheed, PC
1979	County of Vermillion River	06/05	09/05	127	21	Lougheed, PC
1980	Calgary Public	05/27	09/25	4644	43	Lougheed, PC
1983	North Central East (8 boards)	09/20	09/29	626	7	Lougheed, PC
	County Lac Ste Anne	10/24	11/17	151	25	Lougheed, PC
1985	Fairview	01/07	01/08	90	3	Lougheed, PC
	St. Albert	01/14	01/16	308	4	Lougheed, PC
	Leduc	01/21	02/01	257	11	Lougheed, PC
	Elk Island (6 boards)	02/19	03/18	621	21	Lougheed, PC
1987	Grande Prairie County	12/03	12/11	195	8	Getty, PC
1988	North Central East (7 boards)	03/01	04/05	440	26	Getty, PC
	Athabasca	03/01	03/07	118	4	Getty, PC
1990	Sherwood Park Separate	04/19	04/20	176	2	Getty, PC
1991	Leduc	04/11	05/06	49	18	Getty, PC
	Calgary Separate	08/19	09/02	1744	2	Getty, PC
1992	Calgary Public	01/13	01/17	6618	5	Getty, PC
	Grande Prairie Public	03/18	03/30	285	8	Getty, PC
	Battle River (10 boards)	04/06	05/13	1382	28	Getty, PC
	Southern AB (13 boards)	04/27	05/08	791	10	Getty, PC
2002	22 Jurisdictions*	02/04	02/21	21146	2-13	Klein, PC
2004	Medicine Hat Separate	12/13	1/10	165	11	Klein, PC
2006	Parkland School Division	2/16	3/20	674	22	Klein, PC

Note: *Battle River, Calgary RCSSD, Calgary SD, Canadian Rockies RD, Chinook's Edge #73, Edmonton SD, Elk Island PSRD 14, Foothills #38, Fort McMurray RCSSD 32, Fort McMurray SD 2833, Grande Prairie RCSSD 28, Grande Prairie SD 2357, Grande Yellowhead RD 35, Greater St. Albert CRD 29, Holy Spirit CSRD 4, Lethbridge SD 51, Livingstone Range Division 68, Northern Gateway RD 10, Palliser RD 26, Peace Wapiti RD 33, Rocky View Division 41, Wolf Creek Division 72.

Source: Compiled by the author by combining data from Government of Alberta (2010), Reshef (2007), and Alberta Teachers' Association (2005).

APPENDIX B

This sample contract is replicated in whole with permission from Appendix A-4 of the Almadina School Society Collective Agreement, signed 9 January 2007, in force and effect until 31 August 2011.

CONTINUING FULL-TIME TEACHING CONTRACT

(SECTION 99 – *SCHOOL ACT*)

<<NAME>>

<<ADDRESS>>

<<CITY>>

1.   You have been appointed to the teaching staff of _____ School pursuant to Section 99 of the *School Act* on a continuing full-time teaching contract.

2.   This offer of employment and your acceptance hereof, is subject to ratification by the Board. Failure to ratify will nullify this appointment.

3.   Your employment is subject to the provisions of all applicable statutes of the Province of Alberta and regulations passed thereunder, such rules as may be made from time to time by the Board for the administration, management and operation of schools and school buildings under its jurisdiction and the applicable provisions of the Board's collective agreement with the Alberta Teachers' Association.

4.   Specific assignment to a school and to a grade(s) level shall be made by the Board and its duly authorized Officers from time to time.

5.   This contract contains the entire Agreement between the parties hereto and there are no representations, warranties or collateral agreements other than those as are expressed herein.

6.   30 days notice of contract termination by either party must be stated in writing as per Section 108 of the *School Act*.

7.   The Teacher attests that s/he is in good health.

8.   OVERPAYMENT: The Teacher agrees that if at any time the Board has paid wages to the Teacher in excess of the amount due to the Teacher at the time of payment, the Board may deduct an amount equal to the overpayment from any money owing to the Teacher by the Board

and the Teacher hereby irrevocably authorizes the Board to deduct such amounts.

9. NO UNTRUTHS: The Teacher expressly promises that the Teacher's application form is truthful in all respects and the Teacher has not intentionally failed to provide the Board with any information pertinent to the Board's decision to make this offer of employment.

10. CRIMINAL RECORDS: The Teacher expressly promises that the Teacher has never been convicted under the *Criminal Code of Canada*, or similar legislation of any jurisdiction, of an offence relating to sexual misconduct, fraud, theft or physical violence.

11. DUTY OF FIDELITY: The Teacher agrees that by accepting employment with the Board, the Teacher assumes a responsibility to at all times display conduct that is appropriate to the role of a teacher, that does not harm in any way the reputation of the Board and that serves as an appropriate role model for students.

12. EFFECT OF NONCOMPLIANCE: This offer of Employment is conditional. If the Teacher does not strictly comply with all terms and conditions, this offer is null and void and the Teacher's acceptance is of no force or effect. Failure to respond by _____(date), will nullify this offer.

DATED at the City of Calgary,

In the Province of Alberta,

this _____ (date), Accepted this _____ day of

_____ , 20 _____

_____

Superintendent Appointee

_____

Witness

Chapter 6

TEACHER COLLECTIVE BARGAINING IN MANITOBA

VALERIE J. MATTHEWS LEMIEUX

This chapter examines teacher collective bargaining in Manitoba. It begins by examining the cultural backdrop that helped shape the structure of education and teacher collective bargaining in the province, then traces the development of a teachers' association into a bargaining agent over the first half of the twentieth century. The chapter explains the unique dual statutory model regulating teacher employment in Manitoba and key junctures in the development of this model, and the organization of the education system in a highly politicized context. Teacher collective bargaining in Manitoba is entwined with the historical and political dynamic within the province, and many of the issues that continue to divide teachers and their employers today have their roots in the socio-political history of the province. This chapter traces this history and its impacts on teacher collective bargaining as evidenced by the actions taken by its key players. It concludes by offering some observations on the effectiveness of the collective bargaining structure for kindergarten to grade 12 public school teachers in Manitoba as well as possible impacts on future bargaining.

CULTURAL BACKDROP: LANGUAGE AND RELIGIOUS DISPUTES

Dating from Manitoba's entry into Confederation, disputes over French language and religious education helped to shape this province's education system. The *Manitoba Act* passed in 1870 guaranteed denominational schools and that all Manitoba laws would be enacted in French and English (*Manitoba Act, 1870*, 33 Vic., c. 3 (Canada), ss. 22 and 23 or

Dynamic Negotiations: Teacher Labour Relations in Canadian Elementary and Secondary Education, ed. S. Slinn and A. Sweetman. Montreal and Kingston: Queen's Policy Studies Series, McGill-Queen's University Press.

Manitoba Act, 1870, R.S.C. 1970). A provincial Board of Education was appointed to oversee education in the province. Twenty-four school districts were established on religious lines: 12 Protestant English-speaking districts, and 12 Catholic French-speaking districts. The provincial Board of Education gave each group responsibility for their respective school systems, which included selecting the academic materials to be used and the type of religious education to be provided, and the examination and licensing of teachers. After the Red River Rebellion ended and Manitoba joined Confederation on 15 July 1870, there was a significant influx of mainly Protestant immigrants from Ontario. Protestant schools soon eclipsed Catholic schools, and the French-speaking population dropped from 50 percent to less than 10 percent within two decades. This led to the Manitoba Legislature's abolishing the separate French and English school systems in 1890 and replacing them with a "single, tax-supported public school system" where teaching was allowed to take place only in English (*The Public Schools Act* 1980, 53 Vic., c. 38; Chafe 1969, 11-13).

French Catholics were outraged and spent years in court fighting what was seen as a fundamental betrayal of their constitutional rights. They ultimately lost when the Privy Council overruled a Supreme Court of Canada decision that had upheld the original *Manitoba Act* (*Reference Re Manitoba Statutes Relation to Education* 1894, 22 S.C.R. 577). This decision led to the "Manitoba Schools" question becoming the central issue in the 1896 federal election campaign. After almost a decade of protest, Manitoba's *Schools Act* was finally amended to allow instruction in the French language if there were at least ten students in a school who spoke French.

However, by the early twentieth century, with thousands of immigrants from Eastern Europe pouring into Manitoba, this victory did not last long. By 1916 the Act was amended again so that only English could be taught in Manitoba's public school system. These amendments were sought by the predominantly British immigrants from Ontario to prevent Manitoba's growing Eastern European immigrant population from attaining linguistic and cultural rights within the public school system (Cousins 1998, 50). Mandatory school attendance was also introduced at the same time, thus creating a secular, unilingual, universal Manitoba school system (Osborne 1998/99).

Although francophones objected strongly to the abolishment of French-language education in the public school system, they were unable to reverse this law until 1985 when the Supreme Court of Canada decided all of Manitoba's laws had to be enacted in French and English as guaranteed in the original *Manitoba Act* (*Reference Re Manitoba Language Rights* 1985, 1 S.C.R. 721). This decision eventually led to the establishment of a provincewide francophone school division that continues to exist today. French schools in various parts of the province were transferred into the new division, bringing with them differing terms and conditions of employment (*The Public Schools Amendment Act*, S.M. 1993, c. 33 and the *Francophone Schools Governance Regulation*, M.R. 202/93). A major challenge in establishing this new provincewide division was the negotiation of one teacher collective agreement with the new francophone school board to replace ten existing collective agreements. For a number of years, teachers in this division had different terms and conditions of employment as the existing agreements remained in effect until the new collective agreement was bargained. This division is currently the only one in Manitoba funded entirely from provincial revenues, but like other school divisions there is a board of school trustees and local control over bargaining.

THE ROCKY ROAD FROM PROFESSIONAL ORGANIZATION TO BARGAINING AGENT: 1918–1948

Manitoba teachers were unrepresented until the fall and winter of 1918/19, when they formed a provincewide professional organization to advance their interests. At that time, their terms and conditions of work were essentially dictated by hundreds of small school districts operating across the province. The movement to organize a federation was spurred on by the rapidly changing political milieu. By 1918, inflationary pressures, the Bolshevik revolution, and unemployment among soldiers returning from World War I resulted in workers uniting to demand a living wage. At the same time, a new political movement was forming among suffragettes, socialists, and church leaders preaching the social gospel (Osborne 1998/99, paras. 82-84). Teachers spent the fall and winter drafting a constitution to establish a provincewide teachers' federation and appealing to teachers to unite by joining the new federation. This was a difficult task as Manitoba, like the rest of the world, was in the grip of the Spanish influenza and schools were shut down for weeks at a time. But through the perseverance of a handful of people, the Manitoba Teachers' Federation was established at a general meeting held in Winnipeg just two weeks before the May 1919 Winnipeg General Strike, arguably the most influential strike in Canadian history (Chafe 1969).

The fledgling Federation faced further setbacks as it sought recognition by school districts and the establishment of a salary grid just as a major recession hit. It struggled for years to expand its membership base, especially in rural areas. In response to the economic climate, school boards began terminating teachers and hiring replacements at lower salaries. In Brandon, Manitoba's second-largest city, the school board demanded that teachers accept a 25 percent decrease in wages. They refused and were fired. This led to all 80 teachers in the district "resigning." The Federation actively supported them, and teachers throughout the province came to their financial aid, resulting in what some refer to as the Federation's "first great test of solidarity" (Chafe 1969, 44-46). Some other boards adopted a similar approach, which led to considerable hostility for many years. These heavy-handed events continue to be referred to in collective bargaining today.

The Manitoba School Boards Association (formerly known as the Manitoba Association of School Trustees or "MAST") was then established to provide support to Manitoba's public school boards. The current dual nature of Manitoba's teacher employment system, under which teachers' terms and conditions of work are regulated both by a statutory individual contract of employment with a board and by a school division–wide collective agreement, is rooted in a 1927 agreement reached between MAST and the Federation. At that time, they agreed to the first form of contract to be signed by individual teachers and the school district employing them. This written agreement provided for a set term of employment, a probationary period, remuneration that encouraged annual increases, notice upon termination, and the right to have the termination reviewed by an independent board.

However, even though the Federation and MAST reached agreement on this form of contract, most school districts refused to bargain collectively with the Federation to establish terms and conditions of employment beyond those set out in the agreed upon individual contract. As a result, the Federation continued to face recognition problems for many years. The Depression added to its woes as serious financial constraints made it even harder for the organization to garner support. A lack of support became a vicious circle as it was also harder to negotiate uniform salary schedules throughout the province as school boards and provincial politicians did not believe the Federation had the support of Manitoba teachers (Chafe 1969).

The employment contract negotiated between the Federation and MAST was given statutory recognition in 1935 (Chafe 1969, 86). It was virtually identical to the earlier negotiated individual contract of employment and has remained essentially the same since that time (*The Public Schools Act*, R.S.M., c. P250, s. 92 and Form of Agreement [School Boards and Teachers] Regulation, M.R. 218/204). As is discussed later in this chapter, this arrangement—sought by the Federation in its infancy—has been the subject of much bargaining and litigation over the past two decades, particularly in relation to teacher tenure, which the Federation thought it had resolved in 1935 by preventing "the automatic lapsing of contracts" (Chafe 1969, 86).

The Federation continued to press for wage improvements, higher standards in teacher training, and for larger school districts as it had to seek recognition in thousands of small school districts. During the war years, new graduates could make more money working in industry than in the classroom. This, combined with the large number of school districts throughout the province, some of which had less than a dozen students, led to a teacher shortage and the introduction of a permit system, where persons without teaching certificates were allowed to teach.

These arrangements became part of the overall teachers' classification and compensation model that continues to exist by regulation and is still referenced in all teacher collective agreements today (*Teaching Certificates and Qualifications Regulation,* M.R. 515/88, as amended, *The Education Administration Act,* R.S.M. 1987, c. E10).

The Federation then pursued legislation to require mandatory membership in its organization. In the 1930s the government had indicated it would not grant this request until the Federation could prove 65 percent of the teachers in the province wanted to join the organization (Chafe 1969, 90, 122-23). The Federation's initial goal was to obtain recognition as a professional organization rather than as a union. In March 1942, the foundation was laid for mandatory membership when the Federation became the newly named Manitoba Teachers' Society. Under this model teachers could opt out of the organization, but if they did not, then they were considered members. This remains the current model in the Society's constitution (*The Teachers' Society Act,* C.C.S.M., c. T30), although the mandatory membership requirements added to Act as part of the 1956 Deal referred to later in this chapter were repealed. The Society's current constitution permits teachers to opt out, but teachers opting out must still pay membership dues in accordance with the Rand formula (*The Labour Relations Act,* R.S.M. 1987, c. L10, s. 76).

Teachers' salaries had not improved much by 1945. In addition, the provincial government granted hundreds of unqualified people permits to teach. These permit teachers were not trained as teachers, but were permitted to teach once they obtained a permit. This compounded the problem as it was difficult to convince school boards to pay qualified teachers more when there were so many unqualified people ready to work for lower wages. The Society sought numerous changes to salaries, tenure, academic qualifications, and educational finance among other matters, which were generally opposed by the trustees (Chafe 1969, 145-57). By this time, the Co-Operative Commonwealth Federation (CCF), the forerunner to the New Democratic Party, in the hopes of forming the next provincial government promised to enact progressive labour legislation, including changes sought by the Society that would allow it to bargain collectively and control its own membership (Chafe 1969, 157). Such promises have become part of the politics of teacher collective bargaining and have been repeated many times since. With the war years over, Manitoba, like other jurisdictions, enacted provincial labour relations legislation in 1948 to replace the *Wartime Labour Relations Regulation* Order in Council P.C. 1003 (1944).

MANITOBA'S DUAL STATUTORY MODEL

Manitoba's first general labour legislation applied to teachers, although they were also required to enter into individual contracts of employment pursuant to *The Public Schools Act*. It was at this time that Manitoba's dual model for teacher collective bargaining was firmly established with the general labour relations statute regulating teacher collective bargaining and education legislation regulating individual contracts of employment. Collective bargaining took place at the local level, and individual contracts of employment were entered into between teachers and school districts. Teachers, like other Manitoba workers, also gained full access to the right to strike under the Act. Under this model, teachers finally started to achieve modest salary improvements, particularly in rural areas. The importance of this legislation to teacher collective bargaining has been described as "a major breakthrough, the answer to one of the Society's most fervent prayers" because it provided teachers with "the necessary legal machinery, both for orderly collective negotiation if requested by either teachers or trustees in regard to salaries, pensions and work conditions, and for conciliation of disputes" (Chafe 1969, 157). But by 1952 the gains came to a grinding halt with the creation of the Manitoba Urban Trustees Association (MUTA), whose primary goal was to eliminate teacher collective bargaining rights. In the small rural school district of Elphinstone, a member of MUTA, the local teachers' association went to conciliation over a salary dispute. The conciliation board found in favour of the teachers, but the Elphinstone Board refused to implement the decision, arguing the provisions of *The Public Schools Act* took precedence over *The Labour Relations Act* so the trustees did not have to bargain collectively with teachers. MUTA sought an amendment to the legislation to give effect to its view of the legislation, which was rejected by the conciliation board. If successful, teachers would no longer have any statutorily guaranteed bargaining rights and they would lose their right to strike—a right enjoyed by other unionized Manitoba workers (Chafe 1969, 188-90).

THE 1956 HISTORIC DEAL

With the coalition Liberal government of Douglas Campbell firmly on the side of MUTA, the Society met with the Manitoba Association of School Trustees to determine if a solution could be found. On 6 June 1955, they made a joint submission to the government requesting legislative amendments to "transfer" teacher collective bargaining to *The Public Schools Act*, with binding interest arbitration to replace the right to strike. In addition, teacher tenure would be achieved after two years of service with the same school board and teachers would have the right to have any dismissal investigated by an independent body. School boards would remit dues to the Society if a teacher who was a member of the Society provided the board with a written request to do so (MAST and MTS 1955).

The legislation was to be administered by a separate administrative tribunal, the Collective Agreement Board, instead of the Manitoba Labour

Board. There would be teacher and trustee representatives on the new board, which would be chaired by a government representative. The duty of the new Board would be to administer the operation of those clauses of the Act that referred to collective bargaining. A broad definition of "dispute" was to be included in the legislation. At that time, the parties agreed a dispute meant

> any dispute or difference between a bargaining agent and a school district, as to matters or things affecting or relating to terms or conditions of employment or work to be done or as to privileges, rights and duties of the School District or its teachers, but [did] not include a dispute arising out of the termination or threatened termination of the teacher's contract, where the grounds of termination [are] alleged to be on moral grounds for conduct unbecoming a teacher. (MAST and MTS 1955, 8)

This definition, which provided interest arbitrators with broad jurisdiction, was one of the most important points in the submission given subsequent decades of litigation over the scope of bargaining and what was intended to be dealt with by third-party arbitration. The joint submission concluded by saying:

> This proposed legislation is the result of good understanding and earnest co-operation between the executive of The Manitoba School Trustees' Association and The Manitoba Teachers' Society. *Each group believes that its best interests are being protected and promoted,* and that the other group is, by this legislation, enabled to attain its legitimate ends with greater facility. Stated bluntly, this legislation will ensure greater peace and harmony between teachers and trustees. In the final analysis, the children of Manitoba will benefit, for the education they receive will be the better for the co-operation that will exist between School Boards and teachers. This is the best reason why the Government of Manitoba should enact the legislation here requested. (ibid., 6; emphasis added)

This historic deal became law in 1956 and remained the model for teacher collective bargaining in Manitoba for over 40 years. It also became the reference point for the legislative and litigation battles of the past four decades, which since 1995 have become increasingly tense as the ideological divide between the Society and MAST on the one hand, and the major political parties on the other, widened.

CONSOLIDATING AND REVAMPING MANITOBA'S EDUCATION SYSTEM

Manitoba's public school system was in disarray in the late 1950s when Duff Roblin's Progressive Conservatives were elected after years of fiscally conservative coalition governments. Much controversy ensued while the government attempted to consolidate over 1,500 school divisions and school districts into fewer than 50, where elementary and secondary schools would be administered by one board of trustees in each area designated by the Minister (Cousins 1998, 21). Most of the Society's local bargaining certificates under this new regime were issued by the Collective Agreement Board between 1958 and 1960.

The Society and MAST once again joined forces and approached the government to hold a provincewide referendum on the issue of school district consolidation. The Roblin government concurred and several referenda were held before consolidation took place across the province after 1959 (Cousins 1998, 45). A new funding formula was proposed so that Roblin's Progressive Conservatives could obtain support for consolidation in rural areas, their political base. By the time the NDP was first elected in 1969, the province was responsible for 65 percent of education costs, with the remainder being paid for through local tax levies.

In the 1960s, MAST sought significant changes to the historic deal, indicating that "the present legislation has never been altogether satisfactory in the opinion of most trustees" even though the joint submission clearly said the opposite. In particular, they sought a limitation on the scope of bargaining on the basis that the language of the existing scope of bargaining clause, "terms and conditions of employment," was "open to the widest of interpretations" and would "lead to further and more acrimonious disputes between teachers and trustees" (MAST 1968a, 4). In their view, as certain administrative matters had to be delegated to superintendents and principals, everything could not be negotiable or the effectiveness of these personnel would be severely limited. MAST argued that bargaining needed to be contained within reasonable limits "or there will be no end to disputes, and teacher-trustee relations will become a shambles" (1968b, 13). These same arguments were to be repeated over and over again during the course of the next three decades.

Although MAST and the Society both sought larger bargaining units within these consolidated school divisions, MAST also wanted additional salary payments to be made on the basis of teacher merit rather than qualifications, exclusion of school administrators from teacher bargaining units, and a prohibition on the Society's ability to blacklist a school division during negotiations. Not surprisingly, the Society opposed the changes being sought by MAST.

The road to consolidation confirmed that rural Manitobans did not want to give up local control over education even though larger urban centres supported consolidation as a means of exerting considerable control over the public school system (Cousins 1998). The outcome of this much-needed modernization of Manitoba's public school system was that local control over education is still firmly entrenched today. Almost annually MAST reaffirms its support for local bargaining, even though the Society's policy has shifted over the past decade in support of provincewide bargaining.

The system of local teacher collective bargaining has been in effect since 1948 (almost 63 years), and while the Society believes this system has generally served teachers well, it has produced uneven results in the 39 existing collective agreements bargained by the Society's associations. In 2002, shortly after Manitoba's labour legislation was amended to regulate most teacher collective bargaining issues, the Society's Provincial Council passed a resolution to seek provincewide bargaining so that all public school teachers would be governed by the same terms and conditions of employment. The trustees continue to oppose provincial bargaining on the basis that a provincewide collective agreement would not be sufficiently sensitive to local issues, particularly educational finance issues, given Manitoba's system is financed in part through local tax levies.

STABILITY OF THE COLLECTIVE BARGAINING MODEL

Although Manitoba's general labour laws were modernized several times in the 1970s and 1980s, the model for teacher collective bargaining has remained fairly static. However, the scope of collective bargaining and the definition of "dispute" were challenged a number of times during interest arbitrations. The Society began seeking improvements to working conditions in addition to wage improvements. It also attempted several times to negotiate on behalf of substitute teachers. The Society's position was that the 1956 Deal gave them open scope bargaining, while MAST argued the legislation established limitations on collective bargaining to protect trustees' ability to manage public schools.

The pattern of bargaining since at least the 1980s has been for the Society to seek improvements in working conditions during tough economic times and to seek financial improvements, particularly to salaries and allowances, when the economy strengthened.

At the height of the recession in the early 1980s, the Society sought legislative changes to address delays in the dispute resolution process. It sometimes took years to conclude a collective agreement. The Minister of Education asked MAST and the Society to try to reach a consensus on how to resolve the timeliness issues plaguing the interest arbitration system. Their joint report to the Minister in March 1981 indicated that they had reached consensus on the use of the conciliation process and on certain procedural aspects of the arbitration process (MTS and MAST 1983, 3).

In addition, they also agreed to go to court to determine whether sick leave was negotiable, after which the legislation was amended to confirm that negotiations beyond the minimum rights were negotiable (*The Public Schools Act*, C.C.S.M., c. P250, ss. 93-95). However, they were unable to reach consensus on replacing three-person representational boards with single arbitrators, mediation-arbitration, final offer selection, the establishment of a panel of arbitrators, or the role of arbitration boards in dispute resolution. All of these matters were addressed in Manitoba's modernized labour relations legislation in 1985 (*The Labour Relations Act*, C.C.S.M., c. L10, Part VII, although final offer selection was subsequently repealed). But the parties could not reach consensus on their application to teachers, and so education legislation was never amended to make similar improvements part of the teacher collective bargaining model.

It was acknowledged by both parties that the probable effect of continued confrontations on the scope of bargaining and the jurisdiction of arbitrators would be "detrimental to both the public interest and the educational enterprise in the long run"; however, they could not reach agreement (MTS and MAST 1983, 9). These same issues became the focus of their heightened warfare in the 1990s.

In 1981, the Progressive Conservatives led by Sterling Lyon lost power after only four years in office. Shortly after the NDP was elected again, the Society sought legislative changes to address their ongoing concerns with the interest arbitration process. MAST (1983) opposed any changes, particularly changes that would affect the scope of bargaining. MAST took the same position it had historically, arguing that Manitoba's education legislation implicitly included certain limits on the scope of bargaining and, since those matters fell within the rights of management, they were not negotiable or arbitrable. It also continued to oppose the extension of collective bargaining rights to substitute teachers.

The Society continued to assert that the 1956 Deal was intended to ensure teachers had the same bargaining rights as all other Manitoba workers, other than the right to strike, which they had given up for interest arbitration. In the Society's view, the collective bargaining model applicable to teachers had not kept pace with the changes made to *The Labour Relations Act* in the 1970s, let alone the changes the government had enacted in 1985. The 1985 changes were described as "innovative" and "extensive" (Adams 2010, 2-47), yet teacher collective bargaining remained unchanged.

MAST characterized resolutions passed by the Society at its 1986 annual general meeting as an attempt to ignore the 1956 Deal and the additional benefits teachers had under *The Public Schools Act*—such as legislated sick leave and individual contracts of employment—and have only the most beneficial aspects of *The Labour Relations Act* apply to teachers (1986, 2-3). While legislated sick leave was a benefit other Manitoba workers did not have, the Society no longer saw individual contracts of employment as a benefit to teachers. Even though the Society, and previously the Federation, had fought for individual contracts decades earlier, they were now viewed as a major impediment to teacher tenure. By contrast, when first enacted in 1935, these contracts were seen as resolving teacher tenure issues. As will be seen, MAST's refrain was to be repeated each time the Society sought legislative changes.

MAST again adamantly opposed the extension of bargaining rights to substitute teachers, arguing it was "a willful decision for obvious reasons" to deny them access to bargaining as they were casual, short-term employees who had no community of interest with regular teachers (1986, 7). The trustees' association also asserted that the Society—one of the largest and most politically powerful labour organizations in the province—was requesting these changes not to advance the rights of teachers but to protect and improve its ability to control its members (ibid., 2). MAST's views paralleled those of the Winnipeg and Manitoba Chambers of Commerce, which also adamantly opposed the NDP's changes to labour legislation, going so far as to take out full-page ads in Manitoba daily newspapers alleging that the changes were "a black cloud over Manitoba" (*Winnipeg Free Press*, 26 June 1984).[1]

The majority NDP government of Howard Pawley fell unexpectedly in 1988 when a disenchanted member of the government voted in favour of the Opposition's amendment to the budget. The government's defeat was surprising as it was just two years into its second term. Before being defeated, the Pawley government had agreed to establish a form of contract for term teachers, although it failed to pass legislation regulating its use. With its early defeat, none of the changes requested by the Society to make the teacher collective bargaining model more consistent with *The Labour Relations Act* model were considered further at that time. The status quo remained in place until the mid-1990s, although teachers continued to seek improvements to working conditions through arbitration, particularly interest arbitration. The 1990s saw a return of recessionary conditions to Manitoba, along with heightened warfare on the labour relations front.

ASSAULT ON TEACHER COLLECTIVE BARGAINING

From 1988 to 1990 while Gary Filmon's Progressive Conservatives had a minority government, no changes were made to Manitoba's labour legislation. But shortly after winning a majority, the Filmon government began introducing what would become major changes to Manitoba's labour legislation by the time they were defeated in 1999. The initial changes were primarily in relation to certification procedures with certification votes replacing automatic certification on the basis of membership cards, which did not affect teachers. After winning a second majority government, the Conservatives began an all-out assault on labour starting in 1996 with the detailed regulation of union dues. The Society, along with all other Manitoba unions, was required to disclose financial information about the receipt of union dues, including the salaries and benefits paid to its staff.

However, the most acrimonious debates relating to teacher collective bargaining arose when the Filmon government issued a position paper entitled "Enhancing Accountability, Ensuring Quality." The government's position was that the teacher collective bargaining model established under the 1956 Deal "served the system well during times of buoyant provincial and national economies, and so long as the public tolerated increasing levels of taxation and government borrowing … but that fiscal circumstances and public attitudes are different [now] and demand a re-examination of the [model]" (Manitoba Education and Training 1996, 3). The government announced that two of its Members of the Legislative Assembly and the Deputy Minister of Education would hold hearings throughout the province on this position paper. Teachers and trustees mobilized hundreds of people across the province to appear before the Dyck/Render/Carlyle Committee.

The Society's detailed presentation stated the government's proposals would "effectively turn back the clock several decades to a time when public school teachers in Manitoba did not have any bargaining rights" (1996a, 7-8). The Society argued the Filmon government had betrayed and devalued teachers, attacked their professionalism, and held them up for public scorn (ibid., 8).

MAST supported the government's position because school trustees had long recognized the need for changes to the collective bargaining process. The association reasserted its position from several decades earlier that the scope of matters referable to interest arbitration needed to be narrowed to recognize the management rights of trustees. In an April 1996 brief to the Minister of Education and Training, MAST listed nine fundamental areas over which an arbitrator should not have jurisdiction (1996c, 4):

1. The selection, appointment, assignment and transfer of teachers

2. Subject to the Act, the duties a teacher is to perform

3. Teacher evaluation

4. Teacher termination

5. Opening and closing time of schools, contact time and preparation time

6. The number, kind, grade and description of schools

7. Courses and programs of study

8. Class size, teacher/pupil ratio, and number of classes

9. Any matter which may be ancillary or incidental to any of the foregoing

MAST again took the position that the interest arbitration model in *The Public Schools Act* should be changed from a three-person board to a single arbitrator who would be required to consider the school division's ability to pay. Alternatively, MAST asserted that if the government was not prepared to limit the scope of bargaining or require consideration of the ability to pay, the strike/lockout model should become the default dispute resolution mechanism, on the basis that parties could still voluntarily agree to interest arbitration (MAST 1996a, 6-10; 1996b, 1996c).

Linda McIntosh, Minister of Education in the Filmon government (a former president of MAST and aunt to Hugh McFayden, one of Filmon's key advisors at the time and the current Conservative Opposition leader), introduced Bill 72 and essentially acknowledged that these changes were primarily being made to address MAST's concerns (Manitoba. Legislative Assembly 1996). Not surprisingly, this legislation incorporated MAST's submissions regarding limiting the jurisdiction of interest arbitrators and required them to consider the ability of school divisions to pay. The parties could negotiate items that could no longer be referred to interest arbitration, but as teachers did not have the right to strike and no dispute resolution mechanism was available in the event the parties could not reach agreement, the teachers had no way to effectively negotiate these issues. The legislation imposed a statutory obligation on school boards to act fairly and reasonably in administering policies and practices with respect to the items that would be negotiable but not arbitrable; however, given the jurisprudence, this legislative change simply codified existing arbitral decisions. In an attempt to present Bill 72 as balanced, the legislation also required school divisions to provide certain financial information to the Society's local associations during the bargaining process. In subsequent battles over Bill 72, these provisions were characterized by the government as steps they had taken to ensure teachers were treated fairly, in that the obligation imposed by section 80 of *The Labour Relations Act* on other Manitoba employers to administer a collective agreement fairly and reasonably had been extended to school division policies for matters not covered by the collective agreement (McIntosh 1996).

The interest arbitration model was also changed by Bill 72. A single mediator-arbitrator replaced conciliators appointed by the Minister of Labour and three-person arbitration boards. Under this model the state was no longer responsible for the costs of mediation, which became a shared cost of the parties. Although interest arbitration jurisprudence has generally rejected the application of "ability to pay" criteria in the public sector, Bill 72 directed the mediator-arbitrator to "base his or her decision primarily on the school division or school district's ability to pay" (s. 129 (3)). Under this new model, the interest arbitrator was further constrained by other factors mandated by legislation, including the economic situation in Manitoba, a comparison of private and public sector wages with primary consideration being given to comparability with particular regions of the province, and the services that would have to be reduced as a result of the award if revenues were not increased (Bill 72, s. 129 (4)).

The term of all teacher collective agreements became standardized based on the school year.

Bill 72 mobilized teachers like never before with one of the largest rallies in the history of the Manitoba legislature taking place over this legislation (MTS 1996e). Shortly after the raucous legislative session ended in early June 1996, the Minister of Education wrote an open letter to Manitoba teachers arguing that Bill 72 was fair and urging them to support it (and basically not listen to their union; McIntosh 1996). In response, the Society stepped up its campaign against Bill 72, which was to be dealt with by the legislature when it reconvened in the fall (MTS 1996b, 1996d).

At its annual collective bargaining seminar in August 1996, the Society outlined its negotiating strategy to respond to Bill 72, telling bargainers:

> Regardless of the Education Minister's assertions to the contrary, we believe that Bill 72 is designed to deprive teachers of fairness and equity. Its purpose is to control the outcomes of collective bargaining and to keep them within parameters set by the provincial government and school boards. Even with some amendments in our favour it would still remain a mechanism to destroy teacher collective bargaining power, and, as a corollary, weaken the usefulness and credibility of the Society. It is part of a broader design to transfer power from labour, to weaken or destroy collective bargaining and stifle the voice of employees. (1996c, 4)

Ongoing political action supported by legal action was a core component of the Society's strategy. As outlined in more detail later in this chapter, the legislation was challenged before interest arbitrators and in court.

In addition to its concerns about Bill 72, the Society was concerned the government would proceed with major revisions to the teacher compensation system, which was addressed in Part II of the Dyck, Render, and Carlyle (1996) report. The Filmon government took the position that the salary model negotiated by the Society and MAST over decades of negotiation was outmoded. Under this model, teachers were classified in accordance with their number of years of university education. Their salary was then based on their education and years of teaching experience. The government was responsible for classifying teachers and determining their years of experience in accordance with regulations enacted under *The Education Administration Act* (C.C.S.M. c. E10). The Filmon government argued that this salary model had achieved its purpose by motivating teachers to become well educated and to remain in the teaching profession, which now had no shortage of well-educated teachers. Therefore, teachers should no longer be able to obtain salary increases simply by obtaining more education. Instead, the Filmon government wanted to replace the existing model, which formed the basis for all collective agreement salary clauses, with a management framework where experience increments would not be automatic and annual evaluations conducted by school administrators would be the basis for pay increments. Increased qualifications would result in additional pay only if it could be established that such qualifications improved a teacher's demonstrated value to the school division.

The Society was particularly concerned with the government's underlying premise that there were too many teachers working in the public school system and that salary increases were not required to attract people to the profession and retain them. The Society also believed the Conservatives' proposals would further seriously undermine collective bargaining if teachers were allowed, in effect, to negotiate salaries on an individual basis by demonstrating the value to the school division of their additional education.

Another area of concern was the length of time a teacher had to work before being granted tenure which, by the 1990s, had been reduced to one year—although, as is discussed later in this chapter, the legislation was being circumvented (*The Public Schools Act*, R.S.M., c. P250, s. 92). It is noteworthy that these issues had their roots in the historical evolution of teacher collective bargaining prior to the 1956 Deal.

Faced with mounting public pressure over its health and education policies generally, the Filmon government appointed John Scurfield, a Winnipeg lawyer later appointed to Manitoba's Queen's Bench, to work with representatives of the Society and MAST to examine Manitoba's model of teacher compensation. Scurfield's report fuelled the fire by endorsing a predominantly management-oriented approach to teachers' compensation. He rejected the public criticisms, insisting that once his report was analyzed objectively, his evolutionary new compensation model would be seen as "more logical and equitable than the model it is designed to replace" (Scurfield 1998, 8). His key recommendations (pp. 2-6) were as follows:

1. Develop a comprehensive job description for teachers to replace the current system in which the duties of teachers and principals are described in various education acts.
2. Give principals the authority to ensure an equitable division of workload among staff (the current system allows principals to assign duties, subject to collective agreement clauses on the voluntariness of extracurricular activities and duty-free lunch hour).
3. Provide a provincially standardized compensation model with experiential increments for the first ten years of a teacher's career (the current system has experiential increments for various years depending on local bargaining).
4. Replace the existing salary grid system with a three-category system (the current system established by regulation has seven classification levels based on education). Category I would be the normative

(or usual) classification level for most teachers. Category II would be for teachers who had at least five years of experience and additional university education, and who assumed professional duties or extracurricular activities beyond the share undertaken by Category I teachers. Category III would include those teachers who had been a Category II teacher for at least two years and who have demonstrated their ability to act as leaders or mentors and their commitment to excellence in teaching; who have a master's degree or equivalent advanced study relevant to the teacher's function; and who have assumed significant, additional professional responsibilities.

5. Replace local bargaining with provincial bargaining on monetary issues.

Scurfield's views were soundly rejected by the Manitoba Teachers' Society. Implementing his new compensation model would result in almost completely rewriting all teacher collective agreements, including clauses on salary and classification, student contact, preparation time, extracurricular time, educational leave, and administrative and other allowances. The Society continued to mount a political campaign opposing the government's actions, which also simultaneously included cutting funds to public schools, increasing funding to private schools, requiring days off be taken without pay in certain circumstances ("Filmon Fridays"), implementing standardized testing, and overhauling curricula. According to the Filmon government, more public accountability and drastic changes to the system were needed because unions, such as the Society, had too much power. The combined effect of these actions created "a climate of distrust" between the Society and the Filmon government (Halliwell 2006, 6).

The Filmon government made no attempts in the two years leading up to the 1999 election to calm the situation, but instead inflamed matters by appointing Scurfield as the first interest arbitrator under Bill 72. The Society was outraged as Scurfield was seen as being biased in favour of the government and MAST given his report on teacher compensation. In an arbitration decision in a dispute between a Brandon school division and teachers' association, Scurfield commented that Bill 72 was clearly intended to change arbitral jurisdiction, although he asserted "arbitrators should be loath to abandon jurisdiction within a labour environment where the right to strike has been replaced by compulsory arbitration."[2] He then concluded his jurisdiction had been limited by the legislation and his role was not to indicate whether he agreed or disagreed with the legislation, but was simply to apply it.

In concluding that the scope of interest arbitration had been limited by Bill 72, Scurfield characterized the legislation as "a trade-off" in which the rights that teachers' associations previously had had were eliminated in exchange for the right to grieve about certain matters that had been excluded from the scope of interest arbitration. These rights consisted of teacher evaluations, transfer and assignment, hiring and appointment, and class size and composition. Accordingly, he refused to impose a clause on mainstreaming because he viewed it as an issue involving educational policy not working conditions and, in his view, teachers were not entitled to influence education policies through collective bargaining. He also refused to award a clause granting hiring preferences to part-time teachers employed by the division or clauses involving the assignment of teachers to particular grades and schools, as the legislation specifically precluded him from making such a ruling.[3]

The Society continued to propose numerous working condition clauses and, unsuccessfully, to litigate the scope of Bill 72 before interest arbitrators and in the courts. Part of its strategy was to use these negative decisions in its political campaign against the legislation. These decisions also proved to be of assistance in continuing to mobilize members to protest the assault on teacher collective bargaining.

Subsequent interest arbitrators also held that the Bill 72 amendments were intended to remove certain items from arbitration and to impose mandatory considerations in relation to financial matters in dispute.[4] Accordingly, clauses related to teacher working conditions such as the mainstreaming of special needs children, the behaviour of disruptive students, due process for principals and vice-principals, transfers between schools, and class size were held to be beyond the scope of an interest arbitrator.

Although divisions argued an arbitrator could not award other clauses such as meal periods and early retirement incentive allowances, arbitrators held that meal periods could be awarded as long as the arbitrator did not determine the time during which such breaks could be scheduled.[5] As a result, teachers were slowly able to obtain clauses allowing them duty-free lunch periods.

Manitoba courts also concluded the collective bargaining regime had changed as a result of Bill 72 amendments, characterizing the amendments as "a response to the concerns of school boards that new articles were being imposed upon them by arbitrators which were resulting in increased costs" (*Flin Flon Teachers' Association and Flin Flon School Division*, [2000] M.J. No. 393 (C.A.), pp. 2, 4, and 6). Contrary to the approach taken by Arbitrator Fox-Decent in *Fort Garry Teachers Association and Fort Garry School Division No. 5* that the exclusions to jurisdiction in Bill 72 should be narrowly construed, the Manitoba Court of Appeal directed arbitrators to interpret the amendments broadly so as not to defeat the clear purpose of the legislation.

The recession in the 1990s, followed by stringent balanced budget legislation and Bill 72, left very few areas in which teachers could make gains at interest arbitration. Nevertheless, they managed to obtain a duty-free meal period and to move their equity agenda forward. Maternity, adoptive, and parental leave top-ups were also granted by interest arbitrators in this era.[6] But MAST took issue with these decisions by specifically referencing them to oppose the NDP government's subsequent repeal of Bill 72, even though these matters did not fall within the areas excluded from interest arbitration under Bill 72.

A decision of the Manitoba Court of Appeal in 1995 in relation to term teacher contracts led the Society to also put some emphasis in the Bill 72 era on negotiating clauses to regulate the use of such contracts (*Gadient et al. v. Fort Garry School Division et al.*, [1995] M.J. No. 236). The Society alleged school divisions were using term contracts to circumvent the tenure provisions in *The Public Schools Act* (C.C.S.M, c. P 250, s. 92(4)); the Society had fought for these tenure provisions decades earlier. A number of local associations were able to negotiate clauses guaranteeing that if a teacher was employed on two successive term contracts, the teacher would be entitled to a permanent contract in the third successive year of employment. The Society also sought changes to the legislation suggested by the Court of Appeal,[7] but was unsuccessful in convincing the Filmon government that the changes were needed.

RESTORING BALANCE TO MANITOBA'S COLLECTIVE
BARGAINING SYSTEM

The election of an NDP government in 1999 resulted in a significant shift in ideology toward unions and teacher collective bargaining. The Society's relationship with government began to improve as Gary Doer's NDP government took steps to implement its election promise to repeal Bill 72 (MTS 2000a, 2000c, 2000d, 2000e). MAST on the other hand chastised the new NDP government for hastily proceeding to change the collective bargaining process (McGiffin 2000, 1). To delay the changes, MAST argued there should be an open process for thoughtful discussion of possible changes to the collective bargaining model. In MAST's view, the Society was advocating a secretive, hasty backroom deal, although MAST did acknowledge that part of the NDP's election platform was the repeal of Bill 72 (2000c; 2000d, 3).

MAST organized a political action campaign to try to prevent or at least minimize the legislative changes introduced by the Doer government. School divisions began lobbying local government officials, chambers of commerce, and other community organizations, warning that school boards were concerned about the "potential impact these legislative changes may have on the local taxpayer and the community as a whole" (Russell 2000, 2).

The Manitoba Teachers' Society also stepped up its lobbying efforts in response to the actions undertaken by the trustees. Its strategy was to use its annual general meeting that year to put pressure on the newly elected government to follow through with its election promises. The Society was adamant that while it was prepared to consult with MAST to try to reach a consensus, it would not, under any circumstances, agree to limitations on the scope of teacher collective bargaining (MTS 2000b, 1). Furthermore, it advised the government it wanted teacher collective bargaining to be regulated by *The Labour Relations Act*, R.S.M. 1987, c. L10. The Society's president summarized its position in a letter to the Premier as follows:

> We believe the best way to provide teachers the benefit of the principles of the LRA is to repeal Bill 72 and most of Parts VII and VIII of the PSA and amend the LRA to include teachers with an appropriate dispute resolution model....
>
> Teacher bargaining rights lagged behind those of other organized workers long before the Conservatives came to power. Bill 72 served to make the PSA not only outmoded but unfair as well.
>
> Our members deserve better. They expect better. They are determined to achieve better. (Speelman 2000, 2)

One of the most contentious issues related to the repeal of Bill 72 was the provision that prevented an arbitrator from imposing clauses related to class size and composition. The Society wanted all of Bill 72 repealed. MAST was particularly concerned about allowing a third party to impose such clauses given the experiences of other jurisdictions. The government sidestepped the issue, at least for its first couple of years in office. In June 2000, it notified the parties that legislation would be introduced to repeal Bill 72 and to move most teacher collective bargaining matters to *The Labour Relations Act*, R.S.M. 1987, c. L10, while maintaining interest arbitration as the dispute resolution model for teacher collective bargaining. It also advised it would establish a provincial commission to make recommendations on class size and composition (Caldwell 2000, 1-2).

When introducing Bill 42, *The Public Schools Amendment and Consequential Amendments Act*, the Minister of Education, Drew Caldwell, began by saying:

> I have been urged by all parties to ensure that any collective bargaining process is fair and sustainable. I believe the proposed legislation does just that. It is clear that the previous arrangements for collective bargaining between teachers and school boards under the former Bill 72 were designed to disadvantage teachers. The new legislation corrects this imbalance.... The former Bill 72, passed in 1996, did more than attempt to limit teachers' salaries and the scope of bargaining. The former Bill 72 attempted to single out teachers' salaries as a cause of local property tax increases. It introduced acrimony into teachers' collective bargaining and interrelations between teachers and local school divisions to the extent that there are still divisions without collective agreements settled under the Bill. This sort of approach is not helpful, nor is it productive.

> The Government of Manitoba will not achieve our goals in education by attacking teachers. (Province of Manitoba 2000)

MAST was outraged and condemned the legislation before the Law Amendments Committee in July 2000. It argued the amendments would have "a major—and overwhelmingly negative—impact on Manitoba's public school system." In support of its position that arbitrators "should not have the authority to impose decisions upon elected school boards that undermine the boards' authority to manage their community schools," MAST referred to clauses on retroactive pay, duty-free lunch hour, and maternity leave top-up, all of which were imposed by arbitrators while Bill 72 was in effect. In essence, it appeared the trustees wanted to limit the scope of bargaining even further and essentially leave virtually no issues to interest arbitration (MAST 2000a, 3).

MAST also sought changes to the definition of teacher to exclude substitute teachers and principals from teacher bargaining units. It was opposed to the government's response on class size and composition, recognizing that once the commission's report was tabled, this last remaining part of Bill 72 would be repealed. MAST concluded,

> Bill 42 proposes a bargaining process, which increases power for the teachers' union, and strips school boards of their authority to manage resources effectively, while encouraging arbitration awards that Manitoba taxpayers cannot afford. This bill will thereby accelerate the rise in education costs and will drive up property taxes significantly for years to come.... For the sake of our students, our public schools, and our communities, do not pass Bill 42. (2000b, 7-8)

The Society applauded the government's action by reviewing its outrage with the former government for passing Bill 72. It noted that teachers could not understand why they were under attack by the Filmon government when the 1956 Deal had provided over 40 years of labour relations peace between Manitoba teachers and school divisions. The Society (2000f) also noted that prior to Bill 72 being enacted, all teachers throughout the province had accepted two years of wage freezes, but property taxes had still risen.

The Society called the arguments of MAST and others "scare tactics" that "demonstrate just how outlandish and unreasonable employers can be" (2000g, 4). The Society argued the educational financing system originally introduced by the Roblin government to obtain support among its most rural constituency was flawed, which was why property taxes continued to rise when teachers' salaries were frozen.

Even though the Society achieved its primary goal of having teacher collective bargaining governed at least in part by *The Labour Relations Act*, R.S.M. 1987, c. L10, clause 4 (3)(f), it was not pleased that teacher terminations continued to be governed by *The Public Schools Act*, R.S.M. 1987, c. 250, s. 92(4); see also *The Labour Relations Act*, R.S.M. 1987, c. L10, s. 79(4). It believed Bill 42 created a disciplinary model for teachers that was unnecessarily complex and unfair. The Society was concerned that the initial disciplinary stages would be dealt with in accordance with the "just cause" standard in *The Labour Relations Act* R.S.M. 1987, c. L10, s. 79, but that termination, the ultimate sanction, would be subject to the "cause" standard under *The Public Schools Act*. The Manitoba Court of Appeal had decided years earlier that if a school division could establish it had cause to terminate, an arbitrator could not overturn the decision by substituting a lesser penalty (*Greenaway v. Seven Oaks School Division*, [1990] M.J. No. 625).

The Society's major concern was that Bill 42 still did not permit it to negotiate class size and composition, which it characterized as two critical areas that affect the ability of teachers to do their jobs and the ability of students to learn (2000f, 7). It asserted, with some justification based on various studies, that improving teachers' working conditions also improved students' learning conditions.

Not all trustees supported MAST's opposition to Bill 42. A presentation by the trustees of the Seven Oaks School Division, an urban school division in Winnipeg, supported the Society's views that Bill 72 should be repealed. These trustees argued that Bill 72 was part of a "heavy-handed attempt to 'bully' the entire education system" and that it was "conceived in an environment of fear, mistrust and disrespect for education, boards and teachers" (Seven Oaks School Division 2000, 3). It urged the government to "bring the public debate on the matter of teacher collective bargaining to a close as soon as possible so as to reduce the potential for dysfunctional public exchanges which have marked the last few years' rhetoric on this matter" (ibid., 12). However, this school board also wanted the government to leave teacher collective bargaining under *The Public Schools Act*.

Winnipeg School Division, Manitoba's largest division, raised concerns about the proposed definition of teacher, which it argued would include anyone with a teaching certificate in a bargaining unit. It wanted the government to maintain the status quo prior to Bill 72, where only those teachers who were employed pursuant to a statutory contract would have access to interest arbitration. It was specifically concerned about the inclusion of substitute teachers, principals, and vice-principals in the bargaining unit. Ultimately, the government amended the definition of teacher, but expressly included principals and vice-principals in the bargaining unit, even if they performed primarily managerial functions that under the usual *Labour Relations Act* rules would have resulted in the exclusion of such positions from a regular teacher bargaining unit (*Manitoba Labour Board Rules of Procedure*, M.R. 184/87, s. 28). This change in committee led to the further protracted litigation between teachers and school divisions over the inclusion of substitute teachers in teacher bargaining units, described later in this chapter.

The Conservatives forced the new NDP government to stay in the legislature almost the whole summer of 2000 to deal with contentious labour relations legislation. In addition to Bill 42, the government introduced Bill 44, *The Labour Relations Amendment Act*, to repeal most of the Filmon government's most specious attacks on Manitoba unions. MAST again joined with various employer organizations and chambers of commerce to oppose these changes. Once again rhetoric was the order of the day as these organizations alleged Manitoba's labour legislation would drive business out of Manitoba.

In particular, MAST wanted teachers to be required to vote on an employer's last offer. It also wanted to limit the types of grievances that could be dealt with by expedited arbitration, although very few matters involving other workers employed by Manitoba school divisions had been dealt with through those provisions in the decade between 1985 when they originally came into effect and 1996 when the Conservatives narrowed the scope of bargaining (MAST 2000b, 2-3).

The Society supported the changes on the basis that they were needed to restore the balance of power between employees and employers, and to undo the generally regressive labour legislation passed by the Conservatives (2000g, 3-4). Bills 42 and 44 were passed and, after almost 50 years, most teacher collective bargaining matters would be dealt with under *The Labour Relations Act*, although the right to strike was not granted to teachers (*The Public Schools Act*, R.S.M. 1987, c. P250, s. 110). The Commission on Class Size and Composition reported in 2001, recommending that a provincial multiyear plan be developed to implement class sizes for kindergarten to grade 4 (Nicholls Commission 2002, 59). The last remnants of Bill 72 were then repealed so that by the time the NDP government sought a renewed mandate in 2003, it had fulfilled its earlier promises related to the repeal of the Tory government's most draconian labour legislation.

With the end of Bill 72, the Society's focus shifted to other issues. In 2000 the government announced a policy to encourage the voluntary amalgamation of school divisions. However, by late 2001 it was clear that very few voluntary amalgamations were going to take place. Thus in 2002 the government enacted legislation to reduce the number of school divisions by one-third (from 54 to 38). MAST and the Society then spent significant time negotiating new collective agreements for the amalgamated school divisions. The Society's goal was to bring all teachers to the highest common denominator rather than to the lowest, both in terms of salary and working conditions. MAST's strategy was to prevent cherry picking of the best provisions in each collective agreement.

As a result of this amalgamation, the Manitoba Labour Board also issued new bargaining certificates to almost half of the Society's local associations. In preparation for the move to *The Labour Relations Act*, the Society conducted a review of all of its local association constitutions. Various amendments were adopted by each local and subsequently approved by the Society's provincial executive to bring the constitutions into compliance with the requirements under *The Labour Relations Act* (for example, clauses related to membership, dues, and ratification votes were all affected).

Around the same time, the Society also decided to pursue the elimination of individual contracts of employment, which continued to be governed by *The Public Schools Act*, R.S.M. 1987, c. P250, s. 92(1.1). The Society viewed these contracts as ongoing impediments to teacher tenure. In Manitoba, teachers are granted due process rights under the legislative scheme only after they have been employed on a statutory contract for more than one school year. Divisions employed teachers on term contracts for less than a school year, thus ensuring teachers had no recourse to arbitration. The effect was that in many school divisions, teachers placed on successive term contracts were on probation for many more years than the one year mandated by legislation.

MAST opposed any restrictions on school divisions' ability to hire teachers on successive term contracts, arguing the status quo should be maintained even though the Society was prepared to negotiate probationary periods into their collective agreements. Instead, in 2004 the government enacted a regulation to permit the Minister of Education to enact various forms of statutory contracts, including term contracts (*Form of Agreement – School Boards and Teachers Regulation*, M.R. 218/2004).

This dual model, actively supported by the Society decades ago to address the problems of a different era, continues to create instability and is especially unfair to new teachers who are often not granted tenure for years. Under this model, term teachers are also reluctant to enforce other provisions of the collective agreement, such as a duty-free lunch hour, voluntary extracurricular activities, and prep time clauses for fear their term contracts will not be renewed and tenure will forever be beyond their reach if they complain. However, with the enactment of the new regulation, the parties' focus shifted to other issues (*Form of Agreement – School Boards and Teachers Regulation*, M.R. 218/2004, amended by M.R. 109/2005). No empirical research has been undertaken to assess the effectiveness of the regulatory changes, and so the extent to which school divisions are hiring term teachers after the beginning of a new school year to prevent term teachers from meeting the regulatory preconditions for obtaining tenure is unknown. While there is some anecdotal evidence that indicates this is being done, to date the matter has not been litigated.

IMPACTS OF THE CURRENT BARGAINING MODEL

In 2001, the Manitoba Labour Board decided to issue new bargaining certificates to replace the old certificates issued by the Collective Agreement

Board. This process was complicated by the government's decision to require school divisions to amalgamate and by the ongoing dispute between the Society and MAST over the inclusion of substitute teachers in regular teacher bargaining units.

The Society asked the Manitoba Labour Board to rule that substitute teachers employed by school divisions were included in the existing bargaining units represented by its local associations. The divisions took the position that substitute teachers were not teachers under Part VIII of *The Public Schools Act* as they were not employed on statutory contracts. Therefore, MAST's position was that only teachers on individual employment contracts were included in the certificates of local associations issued under the old Collective Agreement Board. This meant that substitute teachers who were not employed pursuant to a statutory contract were denied bargaining rights. MAST also argued that local associations had never been voluntarily recognized as the bargaining agents for substitute teachers even though they had bargained rates of pay and in some cases other benefits for substitute teachers. On 14 January 2003, the Board agreed with the school divisions but left open the issue of whether substitute teachers were employees under the Act for purposes of a certification application (*Re Manitoba Teachers' Society*, [2003] M.L.B.D. No. 13).

For the first time in decades, the Society had to organize teachers. Between 22 December 2003 and 11 March 2004, four certification applications were filed requesting that the Board certify the regular local associations as the bargaining agents for substitute teachers.[8] School divisions, with the support of MAST, argued the rules of the Manitoba Labour Board precluded the inclusion of casuals in a bargaining unit. They also took the position that a unit of casual substitute teachers was not an appropriate unit for collective bargaining.

This time the Board found in favour of the teachers, ruling on 6 December 2004 that

(a) the proposed units were appropriate for collective bargaining;

(b) the Board would apply a modified rule for determining membership support, i.e. any teacher whose name appears on the division's list of substitutes on the date of application and who had worked at any time during the 12 weeks prior to the date of application, but excluding the Christmas break from the 12-week period would be counted.[9]

This was the modified rule proposed by the Society.

The Society met the threshold for automatic certification in Pine Creek School Division (a small rural division), but membership votes were required in the other three units. The Society was able to obtain the necessary support in all units. These disputes over recognition were almost déjà vu, with both parties committing significant resources to this modern day union-recognition fight.

The Society, having concluded negotiations for a separate substitute teachers' collective agreement in Pine Creek School Division, was becoming quite concerned about the possibility of having to organize and then negotiate 38 additional collective agreements. It thus began to try to obtain voluntary recognition from the various school divisions.

In its 2003 decision, the Manitoba Labour Board seemed to suggest that the problem would be solved if substitute teachers were hired on a form of agreement similar to that used for regular and term teachers. Following this decision MAST and the Society attempted to resolve the matter, but their discussions were unsuccessful, causing the Society to again seek government intervention on the basis that the existing legislative scheme was causing ongoing disputes over this issue. If the definition of teacher had not been amended at committee when the amendments to *The Labour Relations Act* were considered in 2000, it is unlikely this dispute would have occurred. Unfortunately, the government's short-term political solution led to ongoing acrimony and expensive litigation.

In 2005 the government, using its new statutory contract regulation, enacted a form of agreement for substitute teachers that was similar to the forms of contract for other teachers, but which recognized the irregular nature of their employment (*Form of Agreement – School Boards and Teachers*, M.R. 109/2005). As with term teachers, no guidance was provided regarding the use of the contract nor did the government clarify whether substitute teachers were to be included automatically in regular teacher bargaining units. The definition of teacher was not amended. The government still refused to eliminate the statutory contract. As a result, the government's regulation did not end litigation in relation to this matter.

Instead, the trustees challenged the new substitute's contract in Brandon School Division where several jurisdictional arguments were raised at interest arbitration. The trustees argued the substitutes' statutory contract was not a valid contract and that an interest arbitrator did not have jurisdiction to impose terms and conditions of employment in relation to substitute teachers as they were not included in the regular teachers' bargaining certificate. The interest arbitration board decided the contract was valid but determined that the bargaining certificate needed to be amended to expressly refer to substitute teachers. It retained jurisdiction for one year to give the local time to obtain an amendment to the bargaining certificate.[10]

As the Manitoba Labour Board will not amend a bargaining certificate without clear evidence of membership support, it was necessary for the Brandon Teachers' Association to organize the substitutes. Also, the Brandon collective agreement was the only one in the province that did not have a salary schedule for substitute teachers in the local's regular teacher collective agreement. All other teacher collective agreements in the province included a wage rate for substitute teachers and in some instances additional benefits, such as sick leave. However, the Society wanted to find a solution to the ongoing dispute that would not result in its having to negotiate 38 additional collective agreements.

The goal was, therefore, to simply amend the existing bargaining certificates rather than to issue separate certificates. While the Society pursued this approach, it requested the Board suspend its other applications for certification of separate bargaining units for substitute teachers. Finally, on 2 August 2007, the Board decided that it would amend teacher bargaining certificates to include substitute teachers if evidence of membership support and a new collective agreement were filed with the Board demonstrating the parties had bargained terms and conditions of employment for substitute teachers.

This became the new test for local associations to obtain bargaining rights for substitute teachers. By the conclusion of that round of bargaining, all collective agreements contained clauses for substitute teachers. However, the Society has continued to have difficulty obtaining amendments to its bargaining certificates, which may cause problems if a future government decides to amend the legislation again. A constitutional argument that such action would be contrary to section 2(d) of the *Canadian Charter of Rights and Freedoms* would arguably be stronger if the Board amended each bargaining certificate on the basis of demonstrated membership support.

The Society's focus then shifted back to the equity gains it had made just before Bill 72 was repealed. In particular, it launched a series of grievances relating to improving parental leave top-up, which its locals were having considerable difficulty negotiating even though this benefit had been granted during interest arbitration along with maternity and adoptive leave top-ups.[11] This strategy led to over 125 grievances being filed. Ultimately, parental leave top-up clauses were negotiated in 36 out of 38 school divisions. Consistent with its previous approach to teacher collective bargaining, Brandon School Division again refused to follow the pattern that had been set throughout the rest of the province. In 2010 a grievance arbitrator concluded that Brandon's failure to pay biological mothers parental leave top-up on the same basis as other parents was contrary to Manitoba's human rights legislation.[12] With this decision all teacher collective agreements in Manitoba now provide for ten weeks of parental leave top-up in addition to 17 weeks of maternity leave.

Concurrently, the Society sought legislative changes to teacher pensions. For years public sector pensions in Manitoba had been an unfunded liability. The NDP government started to fund the pensions and made provision for a partial cost-of-living adjustment. However, many former Society activists, now retired teachers, balked at this solution and sought a fully indexed pension. While this issue is not directly related to collective bargaining, the Society has expended substantial political capital on it, which may partially explain why the government has been reluctant to implement some of the Society's other requests, including adopting provincial bargaining and eliminating the statutory contract.

REFLECTIONS ON THE MANITOBA MODEL

The Manitoba model, in its present form, involves bargaining between school divisions and local teachers' associations affiliated with the Manitoba Teachers' Society. As a result of provincially directed amalgamations, there are now 38 school divisions or districts that bargain with Society local associations. An analysis of the number of teachers employed in Manitoba's public school system over the past two decades provides additional insight into the impacts of Conservative and NDP policies on education. After winning their first majority government in 1990, the Filmon Conservatives pursued fiscal restraint measures that have been described as being "far more restrictive than other fiscal control measures introduced in other Canadian provinces during this period" (Brown 2008, 17). Manitoba's public school system lost 514 full-time equivalent (FTE) teaching positions between 1990 and 1999 while the Conservatives sought to balance the provincial budget. Since the Conservatives' defeat in 1999, the number of FTEs in Manitoba has grown steadily so that by the time the NDP sought its third term in 2007, the number of teaching positions in Manitoba had been restored to pre-Filmon levels (see Figure 1).

The pattern of wage settlements over the past two decades mirrors the trends in teacher employment. During the decade of fiscal restraint under the Conservatives, wage settlements steadily trended downward and then were frozen for several years, while under the NDP wage settlements increased and stabilized at around 3 percent annually for the past decade (see Table 1).

The prevalence of settled agreements is an important indicator of the success of a particular collective bargaining model as the goal of collective bargaining is to reach a collective agreement. While public school teachers fall under *The Labour Relations Act* (except for discipline, which is regulated by *The Public Schools Act*), they have no access to the strike mechanism. Instead, conciliation and interest arbitration are the only dispute resolution mechanisms available. While the scope of teacher bargaining is not statutorily limited, the simultaneous use of individual teacher contracts of employment effectively removes matters such as teacher tenure, terminations, and duties from collective bargaining and the scope of interest arbitration. Therefore, the frequency with which interest arbitration is used and its outcomes are important considerations. The majority of Manitoba's teacher collective agreements were settled without resort to interest arbitration regardless of the legislative framework (see Table 2). It is not surprising that teachers did not resort to interest arbitration to improve working conditions given that during the Conservatives' era, they had to worry about job security.

FIGURE 1
Number of PTE Teachers in Manitoba Public Schools
(Decline in Number of Teachers during Conservative Era and Recovery over NDP Decade)

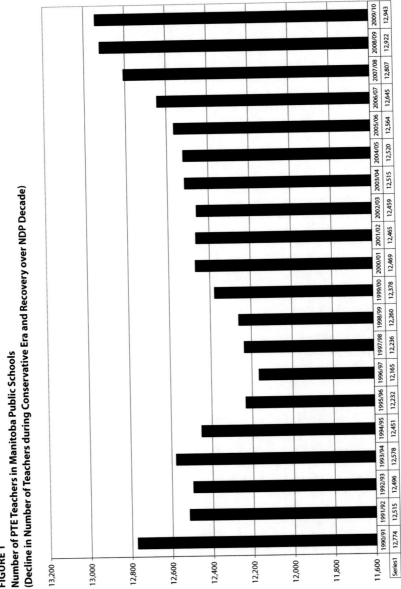

Source: Data supplied by Manitoba Teachers' Society analysts.

TABLE 1
Pattern of Wage Settlements, 1990–2010

	1990	1991	1992	1993	1994	1995	1996	1997	1998* Jan–Jun	98/99	99/00	00/01	01/02	02/03	03/04	04/05	05/06	06/07	07/08	08/09	09/10
Mean	5.03	4.73	2.08	1.98	2.24	0.00	0.10	1.44	0.52	2.00	2.05	3.00	3.00	3.09	3.12	3.09	3.04	3.04	3.13	3.27	3.50
Median	5.10	4.60	2.00	2.00	2.30	0.00	0.00	1.50	0.50	2.00	2.00	3.00	3.00	3.00	3.00	3.00	3.00	3.00	3.00	3.39	3.46
Range-high	5.50	7.30	5.10	2.10	2.80	0.00	1.50	2.00	1.50	2.00	4.00	3.00	3.00	3.61	4.80	4.89	3.67	3.82	3.90	3.66	4.82
Range-low	2.00	4.57	2.00	1.50	1.75	0.00	0.00	0.50	0.00	1.50	1.50	3.00	3.00	3.00	3.00	3.00	3.00	3.00	3.00	3.00	3.00

Note: *Data are shown as the average annual percentage wage increases for each 12-month period, with the exception of January to June 1998 when legislation changes resulted in the term of collective agreements changing from a calendar year (1 January to 31 December) to a school year (1 July to 30 June).

Source: Data supplied by Manitoba Teachers' Society, Economic Analyst Mike Bell.

TABLE 2
Pattern of Settlements for Manitoba Public School Teachers, 1998/99–2010/11 (as of 16 March 2010)

	98/99	99/00	00/01	01/02	02/03	03/04	04/05	05/06	06/07	07/08	08/09	09/10	10/11
Status of bargaining	All have contracts (n = 55)				All have contracts (n = 39)			All have contracts (n = 38)					37 w/o contract (n = 38)
% of contracts determined	100%	100%	100%	100%	100%	100%	100%	100%	100%	100%	100%	100%	2.5%
Number of end rates determined by interest arbitration awards	0	0	0	0	1	2	2	2	2	0	0	0	0
Provincial salary pattern end rate	**2.0%**	**2.0%**	**3.0%**	**3.0%**	**3.0%**	**3.0%**	**3.0%**	**3.0%**	**3.0%**	**+3.0%**	**+3.0%**	**+3.0%**	**3.0%**
% contracts with pattern end rate or higher (n = # of agreements)	97% (n = 55)	93% (n = 55)	100% (n = 55)	100% (n = 55)	100% (n = 39)	100% (n = 39)	100% (38 of 38)	100% (38 of 38)	100% (38 of 38)	100% (38 of 38)	100% (38 of 38)	100% (38 of 38)	
# of contracts with salary increases > 3%	0	0	0	0	1	4	3	3	3	10	23	35	0

Notes: This chart shows the pattern of wage settlements after the enactment of Bill 72 and following its subsequent repeal. In 02/03, school division amalgamation reduced the number of divisions/associations from 55 to 39. In 05/06, Pine Falls amalgamated with Sunrise School Division leaving 38 school divisions.

Source: Data and analysis provided by Manitoba Teachers' Society analysts.

As the change in legislation appears to have had little impact on the frequency of arbitrations, the types of teacher bargaining disputes that ended in interest arbitration were assessed by comparing the awards issued in the Bill 72 era (1990–1999) with those issued in the post–Bill 72 (2000–2010) era. This review indicated that the issues considered by interest arbitrators were similar under both regimes, and predominantly involved disputes over working conditions and equity issues.

A broad range of issues were considered by interest arbitrators during the Bill 72 era including workload/contact time, extracurricular activities, transfers between schools, sick leave, layoffs, duty-free lunch hours, early retirement incentives, mainstreaming/accommodating exceptional students, due process for school administrators, successive term contracts, hiring preferences for part-time teachers, family medical leave, sabbatical leave, executive leave, discipline, inclement weather, harassment, and freedom from violence. These matters were considered in addition to the usual compensation issues such as salary increases, allowances for various positions, and interest on retroactive pay increases.

A review of these cases suggests that while Bill 72 limited arbitrators' jurisdiction in certain areas, teachers achieved major breakthroughs in relation to maternity leave top-up, duty-free lunch hours, due process in relation to transfers, and recognition that extracurricular activities were either voluntary or deserving of some compensation. It is unlikely that the Filmon government anticipated this would be the outcome of legislation designed to limit collective bargaining gains for teachers.

In the post–Bill 72 era, no discernable patterns arise from the interest arbitration awards. It appears that proceeding to interest arbitration in those instances may have more to do with local relationship issues than with teachers' attempts to achieve provincewide improvements through pattern bargaining.[13]

Although past Conservative governments sought to limit gains teachers made through interest arbitration awards, it appears their efforts were ineffective. However, the Conservatives were unwilling to change the dispute resolution model by giving teachers the right to strike, even though collective bargaining disputes involving other Manitoba school division employees are governed by the strike/lockout model. As a result, teachers began using the expanded scope of grievance arbitration as a means for achieving gains, particularly in relation to equity issues. Therefore, in some measure, with support from Supreme Court of Canada decisions over the past decade, grievance arbitration has substituted for negotiations.[14]

Overall, it appears Manitoba's teacher collective bargaining system has worked well when measured by the number of agreements concluded through negotiations. Even though bargaining is local in Manitoba, the Society has been able to use patterning bargaining with some success regardless of attempts to restrict the scope of bargaining through legislative means. This may be seen as a weakness in the current model from MAST's perspective as its constituents want local control and no pattern bargaining. However, provincial bargaining may be the only way to achieve uniform working conditions for Manitoba public school teachers, as a primary problem with the current structure of bargaining is that teachers performing the same job function do not have the same terms and conditions of employment throughout the province. While there are a set of core clauses in place in all collective agreements, not all teachers have the same rights when it comes to other core working conditions such as preparation time, transfer and assignment, participation in extracurricular activities, evaluation, and related issues. Uniform working conditions have been difficult to achieve through collective bargaining, and these issues have been subject to litigation. Working conditions in particular vary across the province due to the local nature of bargaining. It appears to be much easier to achieve pattern bargaining for wage increases and equity issues than for other working conditions.

A second problem is that the scope of bargaining has always been limited by the legislative framework. The fundamental weakness of the current legislative structure arises from the continued use of individual contracts of employment within a collective bargaining system. These individual contracts of employment established by regulation expressly indicate teachers will carry out not only their teaching assignments but also other duties assigned "by the school board in accordance with the Acts and regulations of Manitoba."[15] Successive Ministers of Education, regardless of political stripe, have used these provisions to impose various obligations on teachers, which generally means the issues are then beyond the scope of collective bargaining.

Although it is not clear why, the number of grievance arbitrations has fallen under the current model. In the Bill 72 era between 1990 and 1999, there were 36 arbitrations, but only 28 have taken place in the post–Bill 72 period (2000–2010). However, since 2001 litigation has also taken place before the Manitoba Labour Board as teachers and school divisions now have access to the unfair labour practice provisions under *The Labour Relations Act*, RSM 1987, c. L10. In addition, as noted earlier there was lengthy litigation involving substitute teachers under both legislative regimes.

The main parties involved in teacher collective bargaining, the Manitoba Teachers' Society and the Manitoba Association of School Trustees, continue to seek changes to the negotiating structure. The Society seeks provincial bargaining to establish uniform terms and conditions of employment across the province. MAST is determined to retain local bargaining to minimize, to the extent possible, the impact on its local tax base. The Society also continues to seek the elimination of individual teacher contracts of employment to resolve ongoing issues related to teacher tenure. Given the Conservatives are again championing fiscal restraint measures, it can be expected that any future Conservative government will once again try to limit the positive gains made through interest and grievance arbitrations. As the Supreme Court of Canada reversed its previous jurisprudence and extended constitutional protection to collective bargaining[16] since the Conservatives were last in power, it remains to be seen whether attempts to reintroduce legislation similar to Bill 72 would survive a constitutional challenge.

CONCLUSION

The Manitoba model has produced a relatively stable system of teacher collective bargaining in the province, with few disputes over negotiations; however, with the Supreme Court of Canada expanding the scope of arbitral jurisdiction, disputes under this model appear to have been relocated to other forums such as grievance arbitration and complaints before the Manitoba Labour Board. Persistent lobbying for legislative change is a hallmark of Manitoba's teacher collective bargaining system.

Many of the bargaining and litigation battles of the past two decades have their roots in various disputes fought decades earlier. What can be said with certainty is that the relationship between the provincial teachers' and trustees' organizations at any particular time in their history has had a major impact on teacher collective bargaining in Manitoba. When these organizations have cooperated, they have obtained legislation and a bargaining structure that both could live with. However, when MAST pushed its agenda with the Conservative government in the 1990s and the balance shifted, the Society sought retaliation in 1999 when the NDP was re-elected.

Regardless, Bill 72 was in effect for only one or two rounds of bargaining, and so the number of agreements concluded in this time period alone cannot be used to predict the negative consequences of limiting the scope of bargaining. What is interesting is that although the Society spent considerable time, effort, and political capital on the issue of class size and composition during the Bill 72 era and after the Doer government was first elected, it made no gains through open scope bargaining on these issues. However, since the repeal of Bill 72, the government has enacted legislation that compels Manitoba school divisions to provide appropriate educational programming for all students in the public school system. Given this change and the resulting increase in workload expectations imposed on teachers, it can be anticipated that the focus of collective bargaining may again shift toward the issue of class size (MTS 2010, 36).

Another provincial election is now around the corner. It is unclear whether MAST will push for changes if the Conservatives are elected in 2011 or if they will be content to leave well enough alone after a decade under the new model. If the government changes again, recent experience in Saskatchewan and British Columbia under Conservative governments suggests a McFayden Conservative government will pursue drastic changes to the collective bargaining model, which will lead to heightened labour warfare again. In the area of teacher collective bargaining, much depends on what MAST decides to do and whether the Society can convince its members in this pre-election period to recall the lessons learned in the 1990s. On the other hand, if the NDP is re-elected for an historic fourth term, it is possible that provincial bargaining on certain core issues may finally see the light of day.

NOTES

Valerie Matthews Lemieux wishes to thank her family for their ongoing support while she completed this chapter, as well as Ken Pearce, general secretary for the Manitoba Teachers' Society; Craig Wallis, director of labour relations for the Manitoba Association of School Trustees; and Mike Bell, economic analyst for the Manitoba Teachers' Society, for access to the documents, reports, and data referenced in this chapter.

1. Black (1985) discusses the impact of this ad in some detail, and notes that "some of the most reactionary of the employer proposals were submitted by organizations representing public sector employers, specifically, the Manitoba Association of School Trustees" (144, footnote 10).

2. *Brandon School Division No. 40 and Brandon Teachers' Association No. 40 of the Manitoba Teachers' Society*, [2000] M.G.A.D. No.1; *Brandon School Division No. 40 and Brandon Teachers' Association No. 40 of the Manitoba Teachers' Society*, [2000] M.G.A.D. No. 2 (Scurfield).

3. Ibid., Decision No. 1.

4. *Fort Garry Teachers' Association of the Manitoba Teachers' Society and the Fort Garry School Division No. 5*, 30 June 2000 (Fox-Decent); *Turtle Mountain School Division No. 44 and the Turtle Mountain Teachers' Association No. 44 of the Manitoba Teachers' Society*, 10 November 2000 (MacLean); *St. Vital Teachers' Association No. 6 of the Manitoba Teachers' Society and the St. Vital School Division No. 6*, 12 February 2001 (Peltz).

5. *Flin Flon School Division No. 46 and Flin Flon Teachers' Association of the Manitoba Teachers' Society*, June 1998 (Chapman); and the Fox-Decent and Peltz decisions in endnote 4.

6. *Fort Garry Teachers' Association*, 4-5; *St. Vital Teachers' Association*, 28-33; *Transcona-Springfield Teachers' Association No. 12 of the Manitoba Teachers' Society and the Transcona-Springfield School Division No. 12*, 14 May 2001, 35-40 (Suche).

7. *Gadient et al. v. Fort Garry School Division et al.*, [1995] M.J. No. 236, p. 4.

8. Under Manitoba's labour relations legislation, a union will be certified to represent a bargaining unit if the union can demonstrate the unit is appropriate for collective bargaining and that on the date of application for certification at least 65 percent of the employees in the unit wish to be represented by the union. If the union has less than 65 percent but more than 40 percent, the Manitoba Labour Board will hold a representation vote. Employee wishes are determined on the basis of membership cards filed by the union in support of the application. The Board rules also preclude any employee taken on as a

substitute for an employee on a leave of absence from being included when determining employee wishes.

9. *Manitoba Teachers' Society (Re)*, [2004] M.L.B.D. No. 15 (Peltz).

10. *Brandon Teachers' Association and the Brandon School Division*, 16 June 2006, Interest Arbitration Award, 13-20 (Fox-Decent et al.).

11. *Transcona-Springfield Teachers' Association No. 12 of the Manitoba Teachers' Society and the Transcona-Springfield School Division No. 12*, 14 May 2001 (Suche).

12. *Brandon Teachers' Association v. Brandon School Division* (2010). Unreported grievance arbitration award (Adkins).

13. *Brandon Teachers' Association and the Brandon School Division*, 16 June 2006, Interest Arbitration Award (Fox-Decent et al.); *Prairie Rose School Division and Prairie Rose Teachers' Association of the Manitoba Teachers' Society*, 20 June 2005 (Chapman et al.).

14. See, for example, *Weber v. Ontario Hydro*, [1995] 2 S.C.R. 929 and *Parry Sound (District) Social Services Administration Board v. OPSEU, Local 324*, [2003] 2 S.C.R. 157.

15. Form of Agreement (School Boards and Teachers), M.R., 218/2004 as amended 109/2005.

16. *Health Services and Support Facilities Subsector Bargaining Association v. British Columbia*, [2007] 2 S.C.R. 391.

REFERENCES

Adams, G.W. 2010. *Canadian Labour Law*. 2nd ed., Vol. 1. Aurora, ON: Canada Law Book.

Bill 42. 2000. *The Public Schools Amendment and Consequential Amendments Act*. Manitoba: 1st Session, 37th Legislature, Manitoba, 49 Elizabeth II.

Bill 44. 2000. *The Labour Relations Amendment and Consequential Amendments Act*. Manitoba: 1st Session, 37th Legislature, Manitoba, 49 Elizabeth II.

Bill 45. 2000. *The Labour Relations Amendment Act (2)*. Manitoba: 1st Session, 37th Legislature, Manitoba, 49 Elizabeth II.

Bill 72. 1996. *The Public Schools Amendment Act (2)*. Manitoba: 2nd Session, 36th Legislature, Manitoba, 45 Elizabeth II.

Black, E. 1985. "The Process of Labour Law Reform in Manitoba, 1984." *Industrial Relations* 40(1): 140-60.

Brown, C. 2008. "Pathbreakers and Pragmatists: Manitoba and the New Public Management." Unpublished manuscript, University of Manitoba, 20 March.

Caldwell, D. 2000. Letter to Rey Toews and Jan Speelman from the Minister of Education and Training, Government of the Province of Manitoba, 22 June.

Chafe, J.W. 1969. *Chalk, Sweat, and Cheers: A History of the Manitoba Teachers' Society Commemorating Its Fiftieth Anniversary 1919–1969*. Winnipeg: Hunter Rose Company.

Cousins, M.E. 1998. "The Education Policy of the Dufferin Roblin Administration, 1958–1967." Master's thesis, University of Manitoba, Winnipeg.

Dyck, P.G., S. Render, and J.D. Carlyle. 1996. *Report of the Teacher Collective Bargaining and Compensation Review Committee*. Manitoba Education and Training, May.

Halliwell, G.M. 2006. "The Management of Accountability Expectations in Manitoba Schools: A Study of Eight Elementary School Principals." Master's thesis, University of Manitoba, Winnipeg.

Manitoba. Legislative Assembly. 1996. *Debates and Proceedings (Hansard)*. 36th Legislature, 2nd Session. Vol. 46a (5 June).

Manitoba Association of School Trustees (MAST). 1968a. "Proposed Changes in Legislation concerning Collective Bargaining in the *Public Schools Act*." 22 July.

—. 1968b. "Submission to the Government of the Province of Manitoba by the Manitoba Association of School Trustees: Proposed Changes in Legislation concerning the Negotiating of Teachers' Salaries under Part XVIII of the *Public Schools Act*." August.

—. 1983. "Position Paper: Advocating Section 97 and 113 of the Manitoba *Public Schools Act* Not Be Changed." February.

—. 1986. "Responses to Manitoba Teachers' Society 1986 A.G.M. Teacher Welfare Resolutions by the Manitoba Association of School Trustees."

—. 1996a. "Brief to the Collective Bargaining and Teacher Compensation Review Committee." 21 March.

—. 1996b. "MAST Representatives Response to Discussions of April 19, 1996, Regarding Change to the Collective Bargaining Process for Teachers." 3 May.

—. 1996c. "1996 MAST Resolutions." A Brief to the Minister of Education and Training, the Honourable Linda McIntosh, April.

—. 2000a. "A Brief by the Manitoba Association of School Trustees (MAST) to the Law Amendments Review Committee on Bill 42, *The Public School Amendment and Consequential Act*." July.

—. 2000b. "A Brief by the Manitoba Association of School Trustees (MAST) to the Law Amendments Review Committee on Bill 44, *The Labour Relations Amendment Act (2)*." August.

—. 2000c. Collective Bargaining Submission, 27 March.

—. 2000d. MAST Presentation on Teacher Collective Bargaining, 10 March.

Manitoba Association of School Trustees (MAST) and Manitoba Teachers' Society (MTS). 1955. "Brief of the Manitoba School Trustees' Association and the Manitoba Teachers' Society." Presented to the Premier of Manitoba and a Committee of Council, 6 June.

Manitoba Education and Training. 1996. "Enhancing Accountability, Ensuring Quality." Winnipeg, January.

Manitoba Teachers' Society (MTS). 1996a. "Accountability, Quality and Equity: Time for Dialogue." A Presentation to the Teacher Collective Bargaining and Compensation Review Committee by the Manitoba Teachers' Society, Winnipeg, 21 March.

—. 1996b. "Bill 72 (*The Public Schools Amendment Act*) – and You." A Brief Summary and Analysis of Bill 72.

—. 1996c. "Collective Bargaining Strategy 1995+: Responding to Bill 72." August.

—. 1996d. "Compensation Issues." Manitoba Public School Teacher Compensation Staff Team report. Draft 3, October.

—. 1996e. "Submission to the Discussion between the Government of Manitoba, the Manitoba Teachers' Society and the Manitoba Association of School Trustees regarding Collective Bargaining between Teachers and School Boards." 3 May.

—. 2000a. "Comparison of the *Public Schools Act* and *The Labour Relations Act*."

—. 2000b. Fax transmission to Provincial Executive, 25 January.

—. 2000c. Letter to the Honourable Gary Doer, Premier of the Province of Manitoba, 17 May.

—. 2000d. Meeting Minutes from *LRA* Meeting, 16 May.

—. 2000e. "New Legislation Affects Teachers." September.

—. 2000f. Presentation to the Legislative Committee on Bill 42, *The Public Schools Amendment and Consequential Amendments Act*, 26 July.

—. 2000g. Presentation to the Legislative Committee on Bill 44, *The Labour Relations Amendment Act* (2), 14 August.

—. 2010. *Teacher Workload.* Final Report of the MTS Force on Teachers' Workload. http://www.mbteach.org/library/Archives/Issues/Workload/Workload_Report.pdf.

Manitoba Teachers' Society (MTS) and Manitoba Association of School Trustees (MAST). 1983. *Report to the Honourable Minister of Education: The Collective Bargaining Process.* 4 June.

McGiffin, D. 2000. Letter to the Honourable Drew Caldwell, Minister of Education and Training, 19 January. Manitoba Association of School Trustees.

McIntosh, L. 1996. An Open Letter to Manitoba Teachers from the Minister of Education and Training. Government of Manitoba, 12 June.

Nicholls Commission. 2000. *Class Size and Composition.* Winnipeg: Commission on Class Size and Composition.

Osborne, K. 1998/99. "One Hundred Years of History Teaching in Manitoba Schools: Part 1, 1897–1927." *Manitoba History: Journal of the Manitoba Historical Society* (Autumn/Winter 1998/99): 26-36.

Province of Manitoba. 2000. Bill 42 – *The Public Schools Amendment and Consequential Amendments Act.* Meeting of the House Minutes, 29 June.

Russell, C.W. 2000. Letter to Mayor, Reeve and Council for the Rural Municipalities of Albert, Archie, Ellice, Pipestone, Sifton, Wallace, Whitehead, Woodworth, Village of Elkhorn, Town of Oak Lake, Town of Virden, Canupawakpa Dakota First Nation Presidents, Elkhorn Chamber of Commerce, Virden & District Chamber of Commerce, Virden Wallace Economic Development Board, Reston Merchants Association, Oak Lake Economies Development Board, Chairpersons of ACSL's of Elkhorn, Kola, McAuley, Oak Lake Community School, Reston Collegiate, Reston Elementary, Virden Collegiate, Goulter, Virden Junior High, and Mary Montgomery School concerning Teacher Collective Bargaining Review, Fort la Bosse School Division No. 41, 9 May.

Scurfield, J.M. 1998. "The Teacher Compensation Process." February.

Seven Oaks School Division No.10 Board of Trustees. 2000. "A Submission to the Government of Manitoba regarding Collective Bargaining with Teachers," June.

Spelman, J. 2000. Letter to the Honourable Gary Doer, Premier of the Province of Manitoba, 17 May.

Chapter 7

THE EVOLUTION OF TEACHER BARGAINING IN ONTARIO

Joseph B. Rose

This chapter examines teacher bargaining in Ontario. It traces the evolution of teacher bargaining from the pre-collective bargaining stage to the emergence of legal status collective bargaining and the development of a mature bargaining system. In doing so, the study provides an evaluation of the collective bargaining system. More specifically, it examines the influence of the external environment (e.g., political, social, and legal factors) on bargaining structure, the bargaining process, and bargaining outcomes. As well, it evaluates the effectiveness of disputes procedures for the prevention and settlement of collective bargaining impasses. The analysis of teacher bargaining is based on bargaining data compiled by the Office of Collective Bargaining Information at the Ministry of Labour.

There have been four stages in the development of teacher bargaining. The earliest stage (pre-1975) reflects the period preceding legal status collective bargaining and was based on the association-consultation model of employee representation. The second stage (1975–1997) corresponds to the period when teacher bargaining was conducted pursuant to the *School Boards and Teachers Collective Negotiations Act*. The third stage (1997–2002) featured the Harris government's assault on teachers, including major changes to the system of collective bargaining. In the final (and current) stage of bargaining, the McGuinty government has adopted a conciliatory approach to teachers and initiated a system of two-tier bargaining.

The theme running through all these stages is the centrality of negotiating teacher workloads and how much voice teachers would have with respect to these issues. Workload encompasses a broad range of issues,

Dynamic Negotiations: Teacher Labour Relations in Canadian Elementary and Secondary Education, ed. S. Slinn and A. Sweetman. Montreal and Kingston: Queen's Policy Studies Series, McGill-Queen's University Press. © 2012 The School of Policy Studies, Queen's University at Kingston. All rights reserved.

including assigned time (instructional time and number of classes), un-assigned time (e.g., supervision), and time free from teaching (preparation time). The saliency of these issues to the parties cannot be overstated. For teachers, workload issues are seen as integral to the quality of education and should be a shared decision-making responsibility. For school boards, management should have the discretion to decide education policy issues, because these issues can have a significant impact on staffing levels and education costs (Downie 1992). As documented in this chapter, differences over the appropriate workload standards and how they should be established has been a persistent and thorny issue throughout the history of teacher bargaining.

THE FIRST STAGE: ASSOCIATION-CONSULTATION (PRE-1975)

Prior to the enactment of legal status collective bargaining, the employee representation model in parts of the public sector, including education, was known as association-consultation. Under this model, teacher associations and school boards consulted on matters of mutual interest. The consultative process was narrow in scope, being confined to salaries and protection against arbitrary dismissal. As a result, school boards had the unfettered right to determine matters such as staffing and class size. Additionally, school boards could walk away from negotiations and unilaterally change working conditions.

A number of factors contributed to the downfall of association-consultation for public employees generally and teachers in particular. For one thing, there was disillusionment with the model. In addition to being narrow in scope, it was informal, advisory, and lacked an effective mechanism for resolving differences between the parties as the employer retained final decision-making authority on employment conditions. Further, the 1960s was a period of political and social upheaval and change. These changes included the Quiet Revolution in Quebec and other social movements, such as the Civil Rights movement, anti-Vietnam War protests, and campus unrest (Ponak and Thompson 1995). The removal of legal barriers to public sector bargaining resulted in a smooth and rapid transition from association-consultation to collective bargaining in most parts of the public sector (Rose 1984). Following the extension of bargaining rights for hospital workers and Crown employees in Ontario, teachers acquired the legal right to bargain collectively in 1975.

It is instructive that the limits of association-consultation contributed to a rise in disputes between teachers' associations and school boards beginning in the late 1960s and eventually laid the groundwork for collective bargaining. The rise in conflict was manifested in teacher sanctions against school boards. For example, there was an increase in pink listings, letters from teachers' associations advising members that "while it would not be considered unprofessional to accept a position with the school board 'in dispute,' any teacher who did so would not receive support from the affiliate in future disputes with the board" (Downie 1992, 13). This sanction was sometimes accompanied by threats of mass resignations by teachers.

The escalation of conflict has been attributed to a power struggle in which the teachers' organizations sought "to become partners in school board decision making and remove the vestiges of trustee paternalism and unilateral decision making" (Downie 1992, 17). The focal point of these disputes was teachers' attempts to extend negotiations to include other working conditions, most notably pupil-teacher ratios. The confluence of these and other factors—a rapidly changing education system, rising teacher militancy, and the structural changes to school boards—prompted the government to appoint the Reville Commission in November 1970 to examine negotiation procedures for teachers (Downie 1992). It is noteworthy that prior to the issuance of the Reville (1972) report, conflict escalated as teachers engaged in work-to-rule campaigns and other tactics following the introduction of government spending ceilings for school boards. By the end of 1972, there were many uncertainties surrounding the informal and underdeveloped nature of negotiating procedures, not the least of which were the scope of negotiable issues and the legality of teacher sanctions.

The early 1970s witnessed a continued deterioration of teacher–school board negotiations. While the parties wanted a bargaining law tailored to education, they did not subscribe to the Reville report recommendations, which categorically rejected the right to strike in favour of compulsory arbitration. Indeed, the Reville report never grasped "the accumulated bargaining experience of both trustees and teachers since the end of the Second World War " (Gidney 1999, 119) and, as a result, was ignored by the government (Downie 1992). Subsequent legislative proposals embracing a system of compulsory arbitration to resolve teacher–school board disputes failed to gain traction. Indeed, both school board trustees and teachers' associations eventually were united in their opposition to compulsory arbitration. In response to lobbying tactics and mass rallies by teachers, the government changed course and granted them the right to strike. There appears to have been a political motive for doing so. It has been suggested the government acted because it was concerned about "entering an election with an anti-union reputation" (Roberts 1994, 161).

THE SECOND STAGE: BILL 100 (1975–1997)

The second stage of teacher bargaining began with the adoption of the *School Boards and Teachers Collective Negotiations Act* (Bill 100) in 1975. The legislation formalized the local and fragmented negotiations that had been practised for decades. The balkanized nature of bargaining structures reflected the province's school system in that bargaining took place at the local level and was divided among public and Catholic, and English- and

French-speaking school boards and the five teacher federations. Teacher bargaining agents were statutorily recognized, and teacher bargaining units included principals and vice-principals (Rose 2002).

Unlike other major public sector bargaining laws in the province, which adopted compulsory arbitration, teachers were granted the right to strike.[1] Bill 100 established procedures for the prevention and settlement of disputes, including fact-finding and mediation. Except when the parties reached a voluntary agreement or voluntarily agreed to refer outstanding issues to arbitration, fact-finding was compulsory and a prerequisite for a legal work stoppage.

By Ontario standards, the teacher bargaining law can be described as liberal or progressive. In addition to permitting strikes, the scope of negotiable issues was broad and included class size and pupil-teacher ratios. An independent administrative agency, the Education Relations Commission (ERC), was created to administer the law, to train and appoint third-party neutrals such as fact-finders and mediators, and to oversee and monitor bargaining. In effect, the ERC had discretion to employ the "arsenal-of-weapons" approach, that is, to adopt a flexible and ad hoc approach to dispute resolution (Swimmer and Bartkiw 2003). The ERC had broad responsibilities with regard to the prevention and settlement of disputes, for example, conducting last-offer and strike votes, and recommending voluntary arbitration. As well, it was responsible for advising the government whether a work stoppage placed students' education in jeopardy. Where there was no prospect for a negotiated settlement, such advisements were generally regarded as a precondition for back-to-work legislation. This was designed to insulate collective bargaining from political interference. The ERC also maintained a comprehensive data bank on collective agreements for use by the parties and third-party neutrals (Downie 1992).

Assessing the Efficacy of Bill 100

Downie (1992) offers a systematic assessment of the performance of collective bargaining under Bill 100, up to 1990. His findings can be summarized as follows. First, teacher salaries improved significantly and were among the highest or were the highest nationally. Second, there were major improvements in workload-related issues such as class size and pupil-teacher ratios, especially during the early rounds of bargaining. This is not particularly surprising given the historical struggles over these issues and the broad legal scope of collective bargaining. Bill 100 effectively facilitated the transformation from management determination of these issues to joint decision-making responsibility. Matters related to workload have been and continue to be "militant" issues, as Downie (1992, 163) predicted nearly 20 years ago:

PTR [pupil-teacher ratio], class size and workload will continue to be major issues throughout the province in future negotiations. There is always potential for a continuing battle with respect to each of these. For both sides "principle" is involved. From the teachers' viewpoint, the first step was to obtain a provision in the collective agreement, the next was to lower the pupil-teacher ratio, the maximum class size, and so on. And there will always be numerous permutations on each issue. At the same time, school boards will always be reluctant to change because of the cost and control implications.

Third, on salary and other issues, secondary teachers often led the way and elementary and Catholic teachers followed. Fourth, the dispute settlement and strike prevention procedures under Bill 100 were effective in preventing strikes and resolving conflict between the parties. It should be noted, however, that high inflation, government wage restraints, and the emergence of collective bargaining contributed to several major disputes in the 1970s.

A second study (Rose 2002) examined several dimensions of collective bargaining, including bargaining outcomes and settlement behaviour. It began by comparing negotiated increases in base wage rates for teachers with rates for the private sector, the public sector, and education excluding teachers from 1982 to 1997.[2] In addition, the analysis compared average teacher salaries at the minimum and maximum end-rates grid salaries for Ontario and 14 jurisdictions across Canada from 1975 to 1997. Two findings are noteworthy. First, although public sector wages outpaced private sector wages, the wage index (1981 = 100) for teachers (179.1) was lower than the overall public sector index (179.5) and well below the index for education excluding teachers (191.7). Second, using a salary index (1974 = 100) for four Ontario salary grids, the Ontario salary indices in 1997 were the highest at the minimum end-rate and among the highest at the maximum end-rate, ranking from first to seventh (Canadian Teachers' Federation 1989, 1998a). The relative improvement in Ontario teacher salaries was initially associated with large increases following the introduction of collective bargaining and subsequently with robust economic growth in the late 1980s.

Firm conclusions about teacher workloads are harder to verify owing to the absence of historical and comparable data and the complexity of the issue. Workload issues have become more prevalent in Ontario and elsewhere, and reflect a bundle of collective agreement provisions, including pupil-teacher ratios, class size, instructional time, and preparation time (Canadian Teachers' Federation 1998b; Thomason 1995). Unfortunately, factors such as the interrelated nature of these provisions, variations in collective agreement coverage, and measurement issues have combined to make it difficult to directly compare workload outcomes across provinces. Further, research findings have not conclusively determined

204 JOSEPH B. ROSE

whether collective bargaining has had an independent effect on work-loads (Downie 1992).

Finally, the study (Rose 2002) considered the stages at which collective bargaining settlements are reached. As discussed below, a government-commissioned review of Bill 100 (Paroian 1996) was sharply critical of fact-finding and the right to strike, and dismissed the relevance of settlement data. Nevertheless, these data are helpful in evaluating collective bargaining performance. For example, the direct bargaining stage represents the parties' self-reliance, that is, the proportion of voluntary and mutually acceptable settlements without third-party intervention. The strike rate represents the proportion of all settlements that were the result of a work stoppage, and the dispute rate is the proportion of settlements associated with arbitration and work stoppages. Table 1 compares the settlement behaviour of teachers with that of the private and public sectors, and education excluding teachers. Two findings are particularly noteworthy. First, settlements at the direct bargaining stage were more prevalent for teachers (59.6 percent) than other groups, where settlement rates ranged from 32.8 percent to 44.6 percent. Second, the strike rate and dispute rate for teachers were 2.2 percent and 2.6 percent, respectively. Both measures were substantially lower than those for other groups. The lower strike and dispute rates are broadly consistent with earlier studies and reflect the role of the ERC in monitoring negotiations, appointing third-party neutrals, and maintaining a bargaining data bank (Downie 1984; Swimmer 1985).[3]

TABLE 1
Collective Bargaining Settlements and Settlement Rates by Settlement Stage, 1982–1997

Settlement Stage	Private Sector (n = 3,247)	Public Sector (n = 4,801)	School Teachers (n = 1,460)	Other Education (n = 778)
Direct bargaining	32.8%	39.8%	59.6%	44.6%
Non-binding procedures[a]	56.3%	28.9%	26.2%	37.1%
Arbitration	0.1%	13.9%	0.4%	0.5%
Strike	10.7%	3.4%	2.2%	4.1%
Legislation and other[b]	0.1%	14.0%	11.6%	13.6%

Notes: Settlements refer to collective agreements covering 200 or more employees.
[a] This category combines settlements at the conciliation, post-conciliation, mediation, post-mediation, fact-finding, and post-fact-finding stages.
[b] Includes wage restraint laws, back-to-work legislation, and extension of collective agreements achieved under legislative provisions and through negotiations.

Source: Calculations based on a special data request from the author to the Office of Collective Bargaining Information, Ontario Ministry of Labour.

These findings reflect positively on the performance of teacher bargaining under Bill 100. Increases in teachers' salaries were below increases in the public sector generally and substantially below other education workers. While average Ontario teacher salaries compare favourably to the national average, salary gains were influenced by buoyant economic conditions. Further, despite legitimate concerns about the effect of teacher strikes, the teacher strike and dispute rates were low in absolute and relative terms, indicating that Bill 100 contributed to stable labour relations.

The Need for Education Reform

Despite the relative stability of collective bargaining under Bill 100, of particular concern to the provincial government was the high cost of public education and the failure to achieve quality outcomes. Quality concerns were reflected in various performance indicators, for example, low graduation rates and deficiencies in literacy and numeracy skills. Interprovincial and international comparisons persuaded policy-makers that Ontario had a "high-cost, low performance" education system. In order to meet the challenge of international competition and the demand for a highly educated and skilled workforce, the province would have to reform its education system.

It can be observed that flagging public confidence in education and the need for reform was recognized long before Harris took office. Further, and in various ways, successive governments going back to the early 1980s had considered exerting greater central control over governance, curriculum, and education funding (Gidney 1999). For its part, the Rae government created a testing body, the Education Quality and Accountability Office (EQAO), to oversee mandatory provincewide assessments of student achievement. It was also considering a proposal to establish a College of Teachers to regulate the teaching profession. In many respects, there was a general disenchantment among the major political parties about the state of the education system and the need for improvement (Gidney 1999, 277-78):

> There was nothing new, or distinctively Tory, about the notion that to be competitive in a global economy, education needed to be more rigorous, relevant, or better at preparing young people for the job market. The 1995 election platforms of all three political parties promised provincial standards, a core curriculum, and more testing—in the case of the NDP far more testing than the Tories actually introduced; and both the Liberals and the NDP proposed to reduce the number of trustees, and address a series of related issues including financial disparity among the boards.

In 1996, the Harris government commissioned two studies, one to investigate the cost of education and the other to evaluate Bill 100.

The Education Cost Study

The impetus for educational change was largely based on achieving reductions in education expenditures. A study prepared for the Ministry of Education compared education costs in Ontario with other provinces for 1981/82 and 1995/96. The analysis, which was based on Statistics Canada data, concluded there had been a significant rise in education costs in the province. Whereas the estimated education cost per student in Ontario was below the weighted average of the other provinces in 1981/82, it exceeded the weighted average of other provinces in 1995/96 (Lawton, Ryall, and Menzies 1996). The increased costs were attributed to pupil-teacher ratios and teacher salaries. Not only did the pupil-teacher ratio in Ontario decline from 16.37 in 1981/82 to 15.06 in 1995/96, but the ratio went from being higher than to lower than the weighted average of the other provinces. Teacher salaries were also higher in Ontario. In 1993/94, "Ontario teacher salary grids were 15.2 percent higher than comparable grids of the nine other provinces" (Lawton, Ryall, and Menzies 1996, 3). Further, and in contrast to other provinces, Ontario teacher salaries had increased in real terms.

Notwithstanding limitations of the methodology used to make interprovincial comparisons, there is no doubt that Ontario education costs rose in absolute and relative terms. Given education is the second-largest provincial expenditure following health care, and teacher salaries represent a significant component of education budgets, it is not surprising that any serious attempt by government to rein in expenditures would concentrate on teacher salaries and staffing levels.

The Government's Review of Bill 100

The Minister of Education also appointed Leo Paroian, a lawyer, to conduct a review of Bill 100 (Paroian 1996). The review process lasted two months, and the final report was brief (only 17 pages).[4] Rather than providing a comprehensive review aimed at seeking a consensus on labour relations issues, this cursory report sought to advance the government's agenda of reducing education expenditures and exercising greater control over education. Despite the perfunctory analysis, this report proved to be more influential than that of the Reville Commission.

The report called for the repeal of Bill 100 and placement of teacher bargaining under the *Labour Relations Act*. It portrayed fact-finding as ineffective and maintained that the conciliation and mediation procedures under the *Labour Relations Act* would be more effective in resolving bargaining impasses.[5] It is noteworthy the report did not justify why conciliation and mediation were superior to fact-finding. Despite statistical evidence demonstrating the infrequency of teacher strikes, the report also recommended removing the right to strike, describing teacher strikes as "hostage taking" requiring a "ransom to be paid" (Paroian 1996, 13). As an alternative, it recommended arbitration as a substitute for strikes, despite research evidence that arbitration lowers dispute costs but increases wage costs (Currie and McConnel 1991). Because both school board and teacher representatives rejected compulsory arbitration, "the report, albeit reluctantly, made an alternative recommendation that teachers would be subject to the strike definition in the *Labour Relations Act* and would not be entitled to pay when they engaged in work-to-rule campaigns" (Rose 2002, 105).

Finally, the report considered professionalism and collective bargaining to be incompatible and recommended restoring management's unfettered right to determine matters such as staffing and class size. It criticized the open-ended scope of bargaining under Bill 100 for having an adverse impact on education and argued that restoring management rights was necessary to safeguard the "public interest in a quality education" system (Paroian 1996, 11). Accordingly, management rights and responsibilities for school boards should be enshrined in statute as non-negotiable issues. While the report recognized that a more restrictive approach would generate cost savings and give school boards control over educational programs, it failed to consider the potential labour relations costs or consequences.

As described in greater detail below, these reports contributed to sweeping reforms of the education system and collective bargaining. In 1996 the provincial government slashed funding for public education by more than $1 billion and announced plans to overhaul and improve the education system (Reshef and Rastin 2003; Rose 2002). While the primary focus of this chapter is on collective bargaining developments, it is instructive to view these changes as part of the Harris government's Common Sense Revolution, which included education reform, restructuring, and cost containment. The package of reforms recognized the shortcomings of the existing education system and the need for change.

THE THIRD STAGE: THE ASSAULT ON AND DEFENCE OF TEACHER BARGAINING (1997–2002)

The third stage of teacher bargaining was highly politicized and featured efforts by the Harris government to impose higher workloads on secondary school teachers, limit their right to strike, and constrain interest arbitration. It was characterized by numerous legal restrictions on collective bargaining and by intensified conflict as the government implemented reforms and secondary school teachers defended their working conditions and right to bargain collectively. This took place at a time of increasingly hostile relations between the Harris government and organized labour, as evidenced by the first strike ever by Crown employees in 1996 and protests against the Common Sense Revolution by unions and community groups (through "Days of Action") from late 1995 to 1998 (Rose 2001).

Legislative Changes

On the legislative front, the *Fewer School Boards Act, 1997* (Bill 104) sought to reduce education costs by amalgamating school boards effective 1 January 1998, and established the Education Improvement Commission (EIC) to oversee educational governance in the transitional period for consolidating school boards. The most significant and controversial reforms were contained in the *Education Quality Improvement Act, 1997* (Bill 160) which was introduced in September 1997. One major change was the repeal of Bill 100, and placement of teachers under the *Labour Relations Act*. The Education Relations Commission was retained, ostensibly to advise the government of the need for back-to-work legislation.

A second reform restricted the scope of negotiable subjects by making issues such as class size and instructional time statutory terms of employment. Of note, it would increase the instructional time of secondary school teachers by 125 minutes per day (to 1,250 minutes per week) by reducing their preparation time by the same amount. This change was based on the government's desire to have teachers spend more time in the classroom and its belief that secondary teachers in Ontario had more preparation time than teachers in other provinces.[6] Bill 160 also gave the provincial government greater control over education reform and funding. Under a new funding model, the government would determine both the level of provincial funding and the amount of the local property levy. Prior to 1997, school boards could raise their own revenues to support local education initiatives from local property taxes (Gidney 1999). As well, the new funding model was expected to increase money for classroom instruction since increases in instructional time and caps on class size would increase teacher workloads.

The proposed law prompted the province's five teachers' unions, representing 126,000 teachers, to walk out for two weeks in November 1997, thereby idling 2.1 million students.[7] This dispute was not simply concerned with teachers' economic interests, but reflected "the need to protect their capacities to regulate the teaching profession and process and the quality of education through collective bargaining" (Reshef and Rastin 2003, 126). While the protest did not significantly alter the legislation, it did disclose the government's true agenda, which was to cut education expenditures and eliminate teacher positions. Although the government initially denied this, Premier Harris subsequently admitted that his government's target was to cut an additional $600 million in "waste" out of the education system (Mackie and Lewington 1997).

Bill 160 (and Bill 104) represented the initial phase in restructuring the education system. In 1997 and 1998, the general thrust was "the reorganization of local governance, the centralization of control over educational spending, and the introduction of a new funding model" (Gidney 1999, 231). Further, by gaining control over class size, preparation time, and other issues, the provincial government's aim was to lower expenditures and increase teacher productivity—that is, attain a bigger bang for the education dollar. In subsequent years, the emphasis was on regulating the teaching profession, including the establishment of the Ontario College of Teachers to oversee matters such as teacher recertification and a system of mandatory teacher performance appraisals.

Without question, Bill 160 was a watershed event in that it signalled a paradigm shift in the framework of teacher bargaining. It increased the powers of the Minister of Education to regulate the education system, thereby reducing the role of school boards, and restricted "the unions' capacity to regulate the teaching process using collective bargaining" (Reshef and Rastin 2003, 94). In a nutshell, bargaining pursuant to Bill 100 came to a close and a period of constrained bargaining was about to begin.

Bargaining Disputes and Escalating Hostilities

Negotiations to reach two-year renewal agreements in the 1998 and 2000 bargaining rounds were stymied by the workload issue. Specifically, the principal issue was how to increase instructional time given the funding and other constraints of Bill 160. School boards believed this could be achieved by increasing the normal teaching load (from 6 to 6.67 classes annually), and the teachers staunchly opposed this. The unilateral imposition of higher workloads by several school boards at the start of the 1998/99 school year led to labour disputes (strikes, lockouts, and work-to-rule campaigns), even though several secondary school agreements had maintained a teaching load of six classes. Although there was no advisement from the ERC, the government passed back-to-work legislation and referred disputes at eight school boards to mediation-arbitration. The next day it enacted Bill 63, the *Instructional Time: Minimum Standards Act, 1998*, which defined instructional time as time in the classroom with students.[8] The imposed arbitration scheme was highly constrained (Rose 2000). For example, awards had to consider the definition of instructional time and could not result in a budget deficit and, in some cases, retired judges were appointed as arbitrators.[9]

Although all of the arbitration awards resulted in higher teacher workloads, board-teacher relations deteriorated as teachers refused to volunteer for extracurricular activities.[10] An important function of arbitration is whether it effectively regulates interest-group conflict, that is, results in compliance with or acceptance of the process and awards (Feuille 1979). In this instance, arbitration did not result in a final and binding resolution of all outstanding issues, and hostilities escalated between the parties. The withdrawal of extracurricular activities led to protests from parents.

Facing increased pressure from parents, the school boards proposed restoring the six-class teaching load for the 1999/2000 school year. Lower teaching loads were eventually restored except in the Durham public and Catholic boards, where board-teacher relations had deteriorated to the point that teachers rejected the board offers. It was never made clear how these school boards could "accommodate a six-class teaching load a few months after informing arbitrators that they could not afford to do so without creating a budget deficit" (Rose 2002, 116).

The tumultuous nature of bargaining is captured by settlement stage data. In 1998 and 1999, only 40.2 percent of teacher settlements were reached at the direct bargaining stage (compared to 59.6 percent under Bill 100) and the strike rate was 23.8 percent (compared to 2.2 percent under Bill 100). The dramatic change was not associated with an upturn in labour conflict in the province, but was unique to teacher bargaining. Indeed, there was no appreciable change in settlement patterns for the public and private sectors, and for education employees other than teachers, in the 1982–1997 and 1998–1999 periods. With a provincial election expected in 1999, the government postponed any attempt to establish a uniform and higher standard of instructional time.

Prior to commencement of the 2000 bargaining round, the government passed Bill 74, the *Education Accountability Act 2000*. Bill 74 tightened the definition of instructional time and essentially increased it to 6.67 classes per school year.[11] Principals could also override collective agreement provisions on instructional workload and staffing. The most controversial feature of Bill 74 related to extracurricular activities. In addition to making voluntary extracurricular activities mandatory, principals were given broad authority to assign these duties, bargaining over extracurricular activities was prohibited, and the failure to perform them would be deemed a strike. Although this section of the law was not proclaimed, the government made it clear it would do so if teachers refused to perform these activities as a bargaining tactic.

Like the preceding bargaining round, the focus of the 2000 negotiations was secondary school teachers. For the most part, teachers' unions chose to comply with the law rather than confront the government.[12] The Ontario Secondary School Teachers' Federation (OSSTF) reached renewal agreements containing the higher instructional time standard. It added that higher workloads likely meant individual teachers would have less time available to voluntarily participate in extracurricular activities.

Despite a sharp drop off in extracurricular activities in the 2000/01 school year, the government never proclaimed the section of the law covering extracurricular activities. Initially it denied there was a problem. In all likelihood, the government wanted to avoid another major confrontation with teachers, "particularly since the schools were open and it might be difficult to persuade the public of the logic of making 'voluntary' extracurricular activities mandatory" (Rose 2002, 119). Subsequently, it appointed an advisory group to investigate how to restore extracurricular activities. The group's recommendations, which included a call to repeal the unproclaimed sections of Bill 74, adopt a more flexible approach to workloads, and increase funding, conflicted with the government's hard-line stance and were rejected (Ontario. Advisory Group 2001).

In May 2001, the government capitulated when it broadened the definition of instructional time to include remedial assistance and on-calls (i.e., filling in for sick colleagues). As well, the government indicated it would provide school boards with $50 million in additional funding (Josey and Mallan 2001). As a result, teachers' workload would consist of six classes (Urquhart 2001).[13] Several factors appear to have contributed to the government's decision to abandon the quest to impose higher teacher workloads, including public disenchantment with the state of the province's education system, declining approval of the Harris government in public opinion polls, and an emerging consensus among a broad cross-section of groups—parents, students, trustees, newspaper columnists and editorialists, and the government's advisory committee—that supported a compromise (Mackie 2001). In one survey, over 80 percent of the respondents believed government hostility toward teachers should be ended (Brennan 2001).

Another important issue in this round of bargaining was pay increases. The economic downturn in the early 1990s and the compensation restraints imposed by the *Social Contract Act* had limited teacher pay increases throughout most of the decade. Given robust economic growth, teachers were seeking catch-up even though the government had announced it would not fund broader public sector employers if they agreed to settlements exceeding 2 percent (Brennan 2000). Teacher settlements in this bargaining round exceeded the government's wage guideline (Rose 2002).

The early years of the twenty-first century were marked by political changes. Following the resignation of Harris in 2001, Eves became premier for a brief period before McGuinty won the 2003 provincial election. Based on the premise that longer-term collective agreements would contribute to labour relations stability, the government passed the *Stability and Excellence in Education Act, 2001*. It fixed the term of teacher collective agreements at three years, with an expiry date of 31 August 2004 (Ibbitson 2001). Further, as part of improving student learning and achievement and restoring public confidence in the education system, the government responded favourably and expeditiously to a task force recommendation to allocate funds for this round of collective bargaining (Rozanski 2002). Negotiated pay increases for teachers in this round were marginally higher than the increases for other public sector employees (about 1 percent), and the teacher strike rate (3.5 percent) was lower than that of other groups. The relative calm was a brief interlude between a period of politicized bargaining and the emergence of a new approach to teacher bargaining.

THE FOURTH STAGE: THE EMERGENCE OF TWO-TIER BARGAINING (2003–PRESENT)

The fourth stage of teacher bargaining coincides with the initiatives of the McGuinty government. Although a number of the Harris-era reforms would remain in place in one form or another under the McGuinty government, the Liberals were proposing a transformational change away from fragmented bargaining structures and intense and confrontational government-teacher relations to an approach based on consensus and cooperation. Building on their close ties with teacher unions, the Liberals wanted to forge a new relationship with education partners. This was considered a precondition for promoting labour peace and stability. It was also seen as an opportunity for McGuinty to restore public confidence in education and establish himself as the education premier.

Part of the new direction was outlined in *An Act to Amend the Education Act, 2005*, which provided for collective agreements of either two- or four-year terms. The goal was to establish four-year collective agreements, the first covering 1 September 2004 to 31 August 2008. The government would also provide guaranteed funding on a multiyear basis and establish a provincial dialogue with teachers' federations and school boards' associations. The dialogue would lead to provincial framework agreements aimed at providing financial certainty, salary guidelines, and adjustments on workload issues.

This represented a significant step toward aligning the centralized funding model with decentralized bargaining structures. It will be recalled that the Harris government had eliminated the ability of local school boards to generate revenue through local property taxes and had assumed responsibility for funding public education. The provincial dialogue effectively created a two-tier bargaining system in which systemwide issues (e.g., percentage increase in salaries) were agreed to by the Ministry of Education and provincial bodies representing teachers and school boards, thereby establishing the basis for negotiations over local issues at the school board level. To qualify for the terms of the provincial framework agreement, local negotiations had to be completed by a deadline (or, if necessary, an extended deadline) approved by the Ministry of Education. The failure to do so could result in the withdrawal of funding under the terms of the provincial framework agreement.

Education Minister Kennedy was extensively involved in the initial bargaining round. Although the Ministry of Education did not have a legal mandate to bargain, it informally facilitated discussions across provincial groups. The first provincial framework agreement (2004–2008) was reached in April 2005 with the Elementary Teachers' Federation of Ontario (ETFO), which represented public elementary school teachers. The agreement resulted in the cessation of work-to-rule campaigns underway at various school boards. It contained funding assurances for four years, annual pay increases of 2 percent in the first two years followed by increases of 2.5 percent and 3 percent, class-size caps, and the creation of a Provincial Stability Commission to resolve any systemwide issues arising during the four-year agreement. As well, it restored 1,300 specialist teacher positions and the preparation time (to 200 minutes a week by 2008) that had been lost as a result of funding cuts imposed by the Harris government. Most local negotiations were concluded by the 1 June 2005 deadline. Although some local boards required extensions, and in a few cases the provincial agreement was suspended in response to work-to-rule campaigns, by early July settlements covering all the school boards and teachers' unions were completed (British Columbia Public School Employers' Association 2007; Ontario Ministry of Education 2005).

The Ministry of Education adopted a more open and formal approach to achieve a second provincial framework agreement (2008–2012). It convened pre-provincial talks to iron out bargaining guidelines and identify central issues. In this round, the Ministry of Education representatives actively facilitated and mediated negotiations at the local level. The second provincial framework agreement provided pay increases of 3 percent annually (or 12.55 percent over 4 years) subject to negotiations being concluded by the deadline of 30 November 2008.[14] Negotiations commenced in January 2008 and all but one teacher federation settled by the deadline. Talks between the ETFO and the Ontario Public School Boards' Association (OPSBA) broke down in May over union efforts to reduce the gap in per student funding between secondary and elementary schools, based primarily on demands to increase preparation time. Whereas the provincial framework agreement contained increases in preparation time (from 200 to 240 minutes per week), the ETFO was seeking improvements equivalent to secondary teachers (375 minutes per week). From the OPSBA's perspective, this would necessitate additional funding to cover higher staffing levels.

The stalemate led to the ETFO assuming control over local negotiations with school boards. As a result, the ETFO was pursuing two-year agreements with local school boards providing pay increases of 10 percent and improvements in preparation time, even though such issues are determined provincially. The inability to reach a provincial agreement by the deadline meant that ETFO members would lose the proposed 12.55 percent pay increase over four years and receive instead 2 percent annually over two years. It would also affect other improvements contained in the provincial framework agreement (Faulkner 2008; Rushowy 2008).

Despite deadline extensions, a settlement remained elusive. In February 2009, the Minister of Education made an offer to frame local contract negotiations and set a deadline of two days for acceptance. The ETFO grudgingly accepted the new offer, which provided for a 10.4 percent pay increase over four years, 40 minutes in additional preparation time, 500 new positions, and other improvements (Rushowy 2009). For teachers earning $60,000, the less generous pay settlement meant their salaries would be $1,000 less at the end of the four-year agreement than had they accepted the 12.55 percent offer.

Table 2 compares wage outcomes and settlement behaviour for teachers and other sectors for the period 2004–2009. Three findings are noteworthy. Using a wage index (2003 = 100), it can be seen that public sector settlements exceeded those in the private sector, and teacher pay increases were above the public sector average and below education excluding teachers. Second, teachers were far more likely to settle at the direct bargaining stage. Over three-quarters of all teacher settlements were reached at this stage (the range in other sectors was from 38.6 percent to 58.8 percent). Third, the strike rate was significantly lower for teachers (0.5 percent) than other groups (ranging from 2.8 percent to 7.8 percent). Note, as well, the percentage of direct bargaining settlements and the strike rate for teachers were superior to those reported in Table 1 under Bill 100.

TABLE 2
Cumulative Percentage Wage Increases and Settlement Rates by Settlement Stage, 2004–2009

Settlement Stage	Private Sector (n = 1,426)	Public Sector (n = 1,664)	School Teachers (n = 600)	Other Education (n = 543)
Cumulative % wage increase (2003 = 100)	113.7	118.7	120.3	121.5
Direct bargaining	38.6%	44.3%	76.8%	58.8%
Non-binding procedures[a]	51.9%	39.2%	22.2%	37.0%
Arbitration	1.8%	13.6%	0.5%	0.0%
Strike	7.8%	2.8%	0.5%	4.2%

Note: Settlements refer to collective agreements covering 200 or more employees.
[a]This category combines settlements at the conciliation, post-conciliation, mediation, post-mediation, fact-finding, and post-fact-finding stages.

Source: Calculations based on a special data request from the author to the Office of Collective Bargaining Information, Ontario Ministry of Labour.

On the surface, these figures suggest two-tier bargaining was a success. Without question, the Liberals' close ties with teacher unions, Education Minister Kennedy's active involvement, generally favourable economic conditions, and the government's funding commitments contributed to labour peace. Nevertheless, one might ask what the cost of stability was. In the first round, the modest pay settlements were sufficient as the agreement restored employment conditions lost during the Harris years. Early in the second round, the proposed 3 percent annual pay increases were meant to induce the unions to participate in talks. The looming economic crisis and fast-approaching November 30th deadline transformed the proposed pay increases into a very attractive settlement. By 2012, the differential between teacher settlements and those for other public sector employees will widen as a result of government austerity measures.

DISCUSSION AND CONCLUSIONS

A common theme is present in the evolution of teacher bargaining. From the pre-collective bargaining stage through to the emergence of two-tier bargaining, the central issue has been the struggle over decision-making control of education policy and workload within education funding constraints. The difficulties of accommodating the interests of teachers and school boards in these areas led to the passage of Bill 100, were the focal point of the politically charged environment during the Harris years, and became a central feature of provincial framework agreements.

Whereas Bill 100 provided an extended period of labour relations stability, its repeal and other legislative initiatives of the Harris government produced turbulence. Collective bargaining by teachers was seen as an impediment to the government's goals of education reform and cost containment. That said, the government's motives went beyond instituting reforms and at times were ideological, opportunistic, and vindictive (Ibbitson 1997; Urquhart 2000). The government also failed to recognize (or chose to ignore) three important aspects of public sector bargaining. First, attempts to legally restrict the scope of bargaining are often shortsighted and detrimental to labour-management relations (Swan 1983). There is ample research evidence that restricting the scope of bargaining does not always suppress negotiations over excluded issues (Rose 2002; Swimmer and Bach 2001). Second, by centralizing control over funding, bargaining subjects, and education policy and, at the same time, retaining local bargaining structures, the government put school boards in a difficult and vulnerable position. Simply put, they were left to negotiate with teachers' unions staunchly opposed to the government's agenda. Third, the Harris government's blunt approach to strikes and its attack on interest arbitration were misguided and failed to quell teacher unrest.

The interventionist approach was at odds with the historical record. It is also noteworthy that the Harris government passed back-to-work legislation in 1998 without a jeopardy advisement from the ERC (Rose 2002).

Whereas the Harris government never hesitated to seize greater control over education policy and costs, it was not prepared to embrace provincewide bargaining. Research indicates that more centralized bargaining structures involve trade-offs. On the one hand, the potential benefits may include the professionalization of negotiations, a reduction in union whipsawing, and a decline in strike frequency. On the other hand, the potential costs may include lengthier negotiations, greater difficulty dealing with local issues, and an increase in the size and duration of strikes (Anderson 1989).

In the public sector, provincewide bargaining also poses political risks. The reluctance of the Harris government to alter bargaining structure reflected its waning popularity and concerns that centralized bargaining might spark another major confrontation with teachers' unions (Rose 2002). The adoption of provincewide bargaining would also involve greater visibility and accountability. In a sense, the government wanted to have its cake and eat it too. It shunned centralized bargaining, preferring instead to retain control over education policy and expenditures and avoid direct participation in bargaining for fear of public exposure and criticism. Accordingly, responsibility for bargaining was left to local school boards. The irony is this strategy was flawed. The government's interventionist approach and increased control over the education system actually undermined local school board control over collective bargaining. It also forced teachers' unions to directly interact with the government (Reshef and Rastin 2003). Hence rather than reducing its exposure to political risks, the visibility and political accountability of the Harris government was front and centre during the 1998 and 2000 bargaining rounds. In marked contrast, local bargaining structures under Bill 100 were associated with stable labour relations and involved minimal political interference since the ERC acted as an intermediary between the government and the collective bargaining process.

The McGuinty government chose a different path. Although it stopped short of endorsing full-blown provincial bargaining, the introduction of provincial framework agreements provided an opportunity to reconcile the centralized funding model and local bargaining structures. There was an expectation that two-tier bargaining could contribute to harmonious labour relations by addressing central issues—funding, salaries, and workload—and securing four-year agreements. This approach produced a measure of stability. Funding assurances provided the critical underpinning for monetary settlements and improvements in workload issues. The vast majority of settlements were achieved at the direct bargaining stage, and the strike rate was quite low.

By the same token, two-tier bargaining remains a work in progress. This is hardly surprising. While there was nothing comparable to the turmoil experienced during the Harris years, negotiations with the ETFO were problematic. For one thing, the provincial framework agreements reached with all other groups did not induce the ETFO to settle. Further, the improvements sought by the ETFO in last bargaining round were not resolved to its satisfaction and will likely surface again. As well, other potential challenges can be expected, including competition across teacher groups for improvements in working conditions and accommodation of local issues within this new framework.

It might be difficult to satisfactorily address these issues and perhaps others in the next bargaining round as the province seeks to rein in spending and reduce its budget deficit. Two-tier bargaining has benefited from favourable economic conditions and funding assurances. How sustainable it will be in leaner economic times is uncertain. Another uncertainty is whether austerity measures will include wage restraint legislation and how that might impact on teacher agreements that expire in 2012. If, for example, a wage freeze was introduced, there would be little incentive for teachers' unions to participate in two-tier bargaining, and shorter collective agreements could become the norm. The continuation of two-tier bargaining may hang in the balance if settlements cannot be reached without work stoppages. Indeed, if bargaining reverts to the local school board level, pressure will mount for negotiated pay increases and pattern bargaining.

The future of two-tier bargaining could also be influenced by the outcome of the 2011 provincial election. At present, there appears to be broad support for continuing this approach in some form. The public benefited from labour peace and stability, teachers made gains in bargaining outcomes, and school boards received sufficient funding and were insulated from the negative consequences of local bargaining. Nevertheless, the question remains whether informal two-tier bargaining in its present form is sustainable or needs to be codified. The present system could prove unstable and volatile in a period of depleted financial resources. In all likelihood, the political issue will focus on designing a statutory two-tier bargaining model rather than on whether a formal approach should be undertaken. Accordingly, codification can be expected to address such issues as granting school board associations central bargaining authority, specifying the role of the government, demarcating central and local issues, and defining the status of provincial framework agreements. Achieving a consensus on these and related matters will require the participation and cooperation of education partners.

NOTES

1. Police, firefighters, Crown employees, and hospital employees were subject to compulsory arbitration. Crown employees were granted the right to strike in 1994.
2. Base wage data cover collective agreements with 200 or more employees and were available only for this period. The calculations were based on a special data request from the author to the Office of Collective Bargaining Information, Ontario Ministry of Labour.
3. There is anecdotal evidence that fact-finding contributed significantly to settling bargaining disputes (Downie 1992).
4. In contrast, the Mathews Commission was established in 1979 to conduct a comprehensive review of Bill 100. It reported teachers' and trustees' groups favoured bargaining under a specialized bargaining law and rejected placing teacher bargaining under the *Labour Relations Act* (Downie 1992).
5. It was also felt that the Ontario Labour Relations Board was better equipped to consolidate the number of school boards in the province.
6. Instructional time for elementary teachers was not changed.
7. At that time, the 1.26 million person-days lost represented Ontario's fifth-largest labour dispute in the post–WWII period. In response to the protest, the final version of Bill 160 removed principals and vice-principals from teacher bargaining units.
8. Freely bargained agreements that did not to conform to this definition of instructional time were grandfathered. The failure to establish a watertight definition of instructional time and the tacit acceptance of previously negotiated contracts led to other settlements with six-class teaching loads and effectively negated the government's goal of achieving higher workloads across all school boards in this bargaining round.
9. This was a controversial issue in health care as well, and unions successfully challenged the appointment of retired judges at the Supreme Court of Canada.
10. Arbitration was avoided at one school board following a voluntary settlement that maintained the six-class teaching load.
11. Instructional time comprised 6.5 classes and 0.17 student guidance. It was suggested this might minimize the prospect of conflict since teacher unions could "claim at least a partial victory in limiting the increased workload" (Ibbitson 2000, A8).
12. The Office of Collective Bargaining figures indicate there was a significant decline in teacher work stoppages in 2000 and 2001—four strikes, resulting in a strike rate of 2.4 percent. The most notable strike involved elementary school teachers. In that dispute, the government enacted back-to-work legislation following an advisement from the ERC. It established a mediation-arbitration procedure broadly similar to the one used in the 1998 bargaining round.
13. There was a flexible guideline for an average of 6.25 classes per year for the entire system, but most school boards reverted to six classes.
14. Provincial negotiations were extended to unions representing other educational employees in 2008.

REFERENCES

Anderson, J.C. 1989. "The Structure of Collective Bargaining in Canada." In *Union-Management Relations in Canada*. 2nd ed. Edited by J. Anderson, M. Gunderson, and A. Ponak, 209-34. Don Mills: Addison-Wesley.

Brennan, R. 2000. "2% Wage Hike Enough: Harris." *Toronto Star*, 22 February, p. A7.

—. 2001. "Tories Admit School System Troubled." *Toronto Star*, 1 October. www.star.com.

British Columbia Public School Employers' Association. 2007. "2007 Provincial Bargaining Structures in Canada." http://www.naen.org/CB%20Systems/Canadian%20Provincial%20Bargaining%20Structure%20.pdf.

Canadian Teachers' Federation. 1989. "Summary of Major Teacher Salary Scales in Canada, 1970–71 to 1989–90." *Economic Service Bulletin*, no. 5 (May).

—. 1998a. "Teacher Salary Scales – Volume 2." *Economic Service Bulletin*, no. 3 (May).

—. 1998b. "Class Size and Teacher Workload." *Economic Service Bulletin*, no. 4 (June): 19-21.

Currie, J. and S. McConnel. 1991. "Collective Bargaining in the Public Sector: The Effect of Legal Structures on Dispute Costs and Wages." *American Economic Review* 81(4): 693-718.

Downie, B.M. 1984. "Collective Bargaining Under an Essential Services Disputes Commission." In *Conflict or Compromise: The Future of Public Sector Labour Relations*, edited by M. Thompson and G. Swimmer, 373-401. Montreal: The Institute for Research on Public Policy.

—. 1992. *Strikes, Disputes and Policymaking*. Kingston, ON: IRC Press.

Faulkner, R. 2008. "Teachers' Contract Talks Halted." *Hamilton Spectator*, 21 June, p. A4.

Feuille, P. 1979. "Selected Benefits and Costs of Compulsory Arbitration." *Industrial and Labor Relations Review* 33(1): 64-76.

Gidney, R.D. 1999. *From Hope to Harris: The Reshaping of Ontario's Schools*. Toronto: University of Toronto Press.

Ibbitson, J. 1997. *Promised Land: Inside the Mike Harris Revolution*. Scarborough, ON: Prentice Hall.

—. 2000. "Lo, Is That a Loophole on the Horizon?" *Globe and Mail*, 14 March, p. A8.

—. 2001. "Tories Act to Legislate Labour Calm in the Schools." *Globe and Mail*, 12 June, pp. A1, A5.

Josey, S. and C. Mallan. 2001. "Tories Cave In on School Fight." *Toronto Star*, 8 May. www.thestar.com.

Lawton, S., M. Ryall, and T. Menzies. 1996. *A Study of Costs: Ontario Public Elementary/Secondary Costs as Compared to Other Provinces*. Toronto: Ministry of Education and Training.

Mackie, R. 2001. "Poll Adds to Troubles of Harris." *Globe and Mail*, 28 June, p. A9.

Mackie, R. and J. Lewington. 1997. "3 Unions to Teach Monday." *Globe and Mail*, 7 November, pp. A1, A11.

Ontario. Advisory Group on the Provision of Co-Instructional Activities. 2001. *Report of the Minister's Advisory Group on the Provision of Co-Instructional Activities*. www.edu.gov.on.ca.

Ontario Ministry of Education. 2005. "Government Reports Major Progress Made on Teacher Agreements." News release, 2 June. http://news.ontario.ca/archive/en/2005/06/02/Government-Reports-Major-Progress-Made-On-Teacher-Agreements.html.

Paroian, L. 1996. *Review of the School Boards'/Teachers' Collective Negotiations Process in Ontario*. Toronto: Ministry of Education.

Ponak, A. and M. Thompson. 1995. "Public Sector Collective Bargaining." In *Union-Management Relations in Canada*. 3rd ed. Edited by M. Gunderson and A. Ponak, 415-54. Toronto: Addison-Wesley Publishers.

Reshef, Y. and S. Rastin. 2003. *Unions in the Time of Revolution: Government Restructuring in Alberta and Ontario*. Toronto: University of Toronto Press.

Reville, R.W. 1972. *Professional Consultation and the Determination of Compensation for Ontario Teachers*. Report of the Inquiry into Negotiation Procedures Concerning Elementary and Secondary Schools in Ontario. Toronto: Queen's Printer.

Roberts, W. 1994. *Don't Call Me Servant*. Toronto: Ontario Public Service Employees Union.

Rose, J.B. 1984. "Growth Patterns of Public Sector Unions." In *Conflict or Compromise: The Future of Public Sector Industrial Relations*, edited by M. Thompson and G. Swimmer, 83-119. Montreal: Institute for Research on Public Policy.

—. 2000. "The Ghost of Interest Arbitration." *Canadian Labour and Employment Law Journal* 8(2): 253-89.

—. 2001. "From Softball to Hardball: The Transition in Labour-Management Relations in the Ontario Public Service." In *Public-Sector Labour Relations in an Era of Restraint and Restructuring*, edited by Gene Swimmer, 66-95. Don Mills, ON: Oxford University Press.

—. 2002. "The Assault on School Teacher Bargaining in Ontario." *Relations Industrielles* 57(1): 100-26.

Rozanski, M. 2002. *Investing in Public Education: Advancing the Goal of Continuous Improvement in Student Learning and Achievement*. Report of the Education Equality Task Force. Toronto: Ministry of Education.

Rushowy, K. 2008. "Time Running Out on Offer to Teachers." *Toronto Star*, 24 November. www.thestar.com.

—. 2009. "Teachers Accept Offer." *Toronto Star*, 12 February. www.thestar.com.

Swan, K.P. 1983. "Safety Belt or Straitjacket? Restrictions on the Scope of Public Sector Bargaining." In *Essays in Collective Bargaining and Industrial Democracy*, edited by G. England, 21-41. Toronto: CCH Canada.

Swimmer, G. 1985. "Dispute Resolution in the Ontario Public Sector: What's So Wrong about the Right to Strike?" In *Public Sector Compensation*, edited by D. Conklin, T.C. Courchene, and W.A. Jones, 154-78. Toronto: Ontario Economic Council.

Swimmer, G. and S. Bach. 2001. "Restructuring Federal Public-Sector Human Resources." In *Public-Sector Labour Relations in an Era of Restraint and Restructuring*, edited by G. Swimmer, 178-211. Toronto: Oxford University Press.

Swimmer, G. and T. Bartkiw. 2003. "The Future of Public Sector Collective Bargaining in Canada." *Journal of Labor Research* 24(4): 579-95.

Thomason, T. 1995. "Labour Relations in Primary and Secondary Education." In *Public Sector Bargaining in Canada*, edited by G. Swimmer and M. Thompson, 272-312. Kingston, ON: IRC Press.

Urquhart, I. 2000. "Why Teachers? And Why Now?" *Toronto Star*, 13 May, pp. A1, A31.

—. 2001. "Education Solution May Be a Problem." *Toronto Star*, 23 July. www.thestar.com.

Chapter 8

COLLECTIVE BARGAINING FOR TEACHERS IN ONTARIO: CENTRAL POWER, LOCAL RESPONSIBILITY

ELIZABETH SHILTON

INTRODUCTION

The year 1997 was a watershed for teacher labour relations in Ontario. In that year, the Conservative government of Mike Harris enacted the *Education Quality Improvement Act* (S.O. 1997, c. 31, "Bill 160"). The new statute replaced the existing collective bargaining framework for teachers, one that had worked reasonably well for two decades (Rose 2002, 101), with a new framework. Ontario's teachers responded with ferocity, organizing an unprecedented two-week mass withdrawal of services and igniting a firestorm of litigation that saw a series of constitutional challenges to the government's policies reach the Ontario Court of Appeal and the Supreme Court of Canada.[1] History tells us that the government largely won the day; the new legislation came into effect on schedule on 1 January 1998.

In retrospect, it is clear that the real quarrel was not about the new collective bargaining framework per se. It was about a shift in power within the school system from the local to the provincial level. One of the ironies of the Harris reforms is that they did *not* radically change the formal organization of teacher collective bargaining in Ontario. What they *did* change was the extent to which familiar bargaining processes could be used effectively to give teachers a meaningful voice in establishing

Dynamic Negotiations: Teacher Labour Relations in Canadian Elementary and Secondary Education, ed. S. Slinn and A. Sweetman. Montreal and Kingston: Queen's Policy Studies Series, McGill-Queen's University Press.

their terms and conditions of employment locally. Key ingredients of the Bill 160 reforms—including loss of local power over taxation for purposes of education finance, imposition of a rigid provincewide education funding formula, and unprecedented assertion of centralized regulatory control over employment conditions—had significant consequences for teacher collective bargaining. The new structure gave the government an effective veto over meaningful local bargaining on crucial monetary and non-monetary issues and took other major issues off the bargaining table altogether.

In this chapter, I first examine the legal architecture of the new Bill 160 collective bargaining regime in the context of its history, exploring where and how it differs from its predecessor. I then explore the scope of bargaining for teachers, and the extent to which the substantive content of many of the Conservative government's centralizing reforms impeded collective bargaining. I subsequently discuss the approach to centralization taken by the McGuinty Liberal government, successor to the Conservatives, with a particular focus on the innovative approach to central bargaining which the Liberal government initiated shortly after its election in 2003. I argue that the Bill 160 regime has created a troublesome and potentially destabilizing mismatch between the formal locus of collective bargaining at the local level and the real locus of power over terms and conditions of employment for teachers at the provincial level. I conclude by discussing some continuing challenges faced by school boards and teachers' unions in making effective use of collective bargaining to address the critical issues they currently confront.

THE LEGAL FRAMEWORK FOR TEACHER COLLECTIVE BARGAINING IN ONTARIO

General Structure

Since 1 January 1998, collective bargaining for teachers in Ontario has been governed by Part X.1 of the *Education Act*. While Part X.1 establishes the framework for a special collective bargaining regime for teachers, it also provides that the Ontario *Labour Relations Act, 1995* (S.O. 1995, c. 1, Sched. A.) "applies with necessary modifications with respect to boards, designated bargaining agents and Part X.1 teachers, except where otherwise provided or required by this Part" (s. 277.2(1)).[2] The result is that the *Labour Relations Act*, the general statute governing labour relations in Ontario, is the "default" statute filling in any procedural or substantive gaps not covered by Part X.1. The Act now governs important aspects of the teacher collective bargaining regime, including unfair labour practices, bargaining procedures, both "interest" and "rights" dispute resolution processes, and the duty of fair representation. For teachers, as for other employees in Ontario, this statutory regime is largely administered by the Ontario Labour Relations Board (OLRB).

Prior to the introduction of Part X.1, regular teachers (then known as "contract" teachers) bargained exclusively under the provisions of a special statute, the *School Boards and Teachers Collective Negotiations Act* (known as Bill 100).[3] Occasional (substitute) teachers, by contrast, were not subject to this specialized regime; their labour relations were governed entirely by general provincial labour legislation. Part X.1 effected two important changes: it homogenized the regimes covering regular and occasional teachers, and gave regular teachers access to rights that they had previously been denied, such as the right to file unfair labour practice and duty of fair representation complaints.

An additional change of some significance is the removal of principals and vice-principals from teacher bargaining units. While these in-school administrators never had the right to strike under Bill 100, they had always been members of the teachers' unions, and their terms and conditions of employment had been subject to collective bargaining. Bill 160 not only took principals and vice-principals out of teacher bargaining units, but also explicitly exempted them from the *Labour Relations Act*. Now, like other managerial and confidential employees in Ontario, they have no access to a statutory bargaining framework of any kind.[4]

Ontario is unique in Canada in that it divides its public education system into four subsystems, each made up of individual school boards known as "district school boards": an English-language public system (31 boards), a French-language public system (4 boards), an English-language Catholic system (29 boards), and a French-language Catholic system (8 boards).[5] In addition to district school boards, there are a few (currently 11) much smaller educational entities known as school authorities, located in hospitals and children's treatment centres, and in geographically isolated locations. Overall, Ontario has approximately 83 "employers" of teachers functioning under this system (data supplied by the Ministry of Education).[6]

Bargaining unit boundaries are established by statute. Within each district school board, there are four separate bargaining units, divided first between elementary and secondary levels, and then further subdivided between occasional teachers and regular teachers.[7] Bargaining rights are distributed by statute among four different teachers' unions, as follows:

- The Elementary Teachers' Federation of Ontario (ETFO) bargains for all elementary teachers employed by district school boards in the English-language public system;
- The Ontario Secondary School Teachers' Federation (OSSTF) bargains for all secondary teachers employed by district school boards in the English-language public system;
- The Ontario English Catholic Teachers Association (OECTA) bargains for all elementary and secondary teachers employed in the English-language separate system; and

- The Association des enseignantes et des enseignants franco-ontariens (AEFO) bargains for all teachers at both the elementary and secondary levels in both public and separate French-language systems.

Similar statutory assignments of bargaining rights are made for school authorities.[8] There are no certification or decertification procedures, and no room for trade unions other than the designated bargaining agents to play any role. To ensure there is no misunderstanding on this point, Part X.1 "deems" the designated bargaining agents to be certified (s. 277.8(1)), "deems" the statutory bargaining units to be appropriate units (s. 277.8(1)), and explicitly provides that "no trade union is entitled to apply for certification as the bargaining agent for a teachers' bargaining unit" (s. 277.8(3)).

This allocation of bargaining rights tracks the allocation of bargaining rights under Bill 100 with one important exception: it assigns local bargaining rights to the *provincial* unions, rather than to their locals.[9] Bill 100's assignment of bargaining rights, in turn, was a unique Ontario construct reflecting historical patterns of teacher self-organization dating back to the end of World War I, when Ontario teachers first began to associate for the dual purpose of enhancing their burgeoning professionalism and protecting their interests in the workplace.[10] By the mid-1940s, the teachers had organized themselves into five separate groupings reflecting the structure of public education in the province, as well as distinct gender interests at the public elementary level. In 1944, the government passed the *Teaching Profession Act* (now R.S.O. 1990, c. T.2) recognizing a single professional organization—the Ontario Teachers' Federation (OTF)—as an umbrella for the five organizations, which then became known as OTF "affiliates." That Act made all persons teaching in public education statutory members of OTF; OTF in turn passed a bylaw (Bylaw 1) "sorting" its statutory membership among the five affiliates. Bill 100 assigned bargaining rights to "locals" of the affiliates, known as "branch affiliates."[11] While OTF itself played no formal role in collective bargaining, Bylaw 1 continued to be the mechanism for the assignment of bargaining rights. As the school system evolved and cross-panel hybrid structures such as junior high schools were created by some boards, Bylaw 1 was adapted to deal with "jurisdictional" disputes over membership assignments. While the system introduced by Bill 160 takes away the role formerly played by Bylaw 1 in assigning teachers to bargaining units, the bylaw continues to make detailed provision for membership assignment.[12] The *Teaching Profession Act* has now been amended, however, to make it clear that OTF membership assignments cannot conflict with the assignment of bargaining rights under Part X.1 (s. 13(1)).

In general, the Ontario Labour Relations Board now deals with jurisdictional disputes. In *OSSTF and Kawartha Pine Ridge District School Board v. ETFO*, the OLRB, despite reservations about whether the matter before it was really a "representation dispute" rather than a typical juris-dictional dispute, heard an application to determine whether teachers in the board's Learning and Life Skills program should be elementary or secondary teachers. Although the program did not clearly fall within either the elementary or the secondary panel, the OLRB ultimately as-signed bargaining rights to OSSTF (i.e., the secondary panel) based on criteria that included both the nature of the academic program at issue and the school within which the program was located.[13]

Occasional Teachers

Occasional teachers were not covered by the previous Bill 100 regime. In the 1980s, they began to organize under the *Labour Relations Act*, many of them represented by affiliates of the OTF stepping into new roles as "trade unions" representing educational workers. By 1998 when Part X.1 came into effect, a significant number of occasional teachers in Ontario were already unionized. Part X.1 moved these teachers into the special-ized collective bargaining regime for regular teachers and assigned their bargaining rights to the OTF affiliates.[14] This resulted in a significant influx of new members into the affiliates, requiring affiliates to adapt their internal structures to accommodate their new duties as statutory bargaining agents for occasional as well as regular teachers.

There exists at least the potential for conflict between the interests of occasional and regular teacher groups, since they perform similar func-tions, have the same qualifications, and may well be competing for the same work. Having made the policy choice to assimilate the bargaining regimes of regular and occasional teachers and assign their bargaining rights to the same unions, it is not clear why the government chose to place them in separate bargaining units, a decision that arguably makes it more difficult to reconcile conflicts of interests. The conflict problem came to a head relatively early in the Toronto District School Board secondary panel, where the occasional teacher unit had a pre-Bill 160 history of representation by a non-teacher union. The catalyst for the conflict was a proposal by OSSTF to bargain a provision in the regular teachers' col-lective agreement allowing regular teachers to fill in for absent teachers. Prior to Bill 160, regular teachers would have preferred to avoid "substi-tute" assignments. However, the new and rigid central funding formula introduced under Bill 160 had the effect both of limiting the amount of money available to local school boards, and of sharply curtailing how it could be spent, creating financial incentives for regular teachers to keep substitute work within their own bargaining unit. Furthermore, making substitute assignments available to regular teachers permitted them to "top up" their legislated workload quotas with less onerous substitute assignments, avoiding some of the planning and marking responsibilities associated with regular course loads. The occasional teachers' unit filed a duty of fair representation complaint, alleging that OSSTF, as their common bargaining agent, owed them a duty not to threaten their work opportunities. In *Re Toronto District School Board and OSSTF, District 12*, [1998] OLRB Rep. 1033, the Ontario Labour Relations Board rejected the complaint. The Board held that a union has no duty of fair representation to a group of employees except when it is acting on their behalf; when it bargains for a different group, it is free to focus on the interests of that group, even when those interests are in direct conflict with the interests of other workers the union represents. In subsequent decisions, *Toronto District School Board*, [2003] OLRD No. 804 and *Toronto Occasional Teachers' Bargaining Unit*, [2004] OLRD No. 16, the Board held that the internal battle between the occasional teachers' local and the provincial OSSTF over control of the unit fell outside labour board jurisdiction.

The integration of occasional teachers as a new interest group continues to challenge the teachers' unions. In the absence of access to the OLRB, however, it is not clear that there is any public recourse for the resolution of conflicts between occasional teacher and regular teacher groups. It is likely that disputes over conflicting perspectives, including jurisdictional disputes, will have to be dealt with under each union's own constitution.

Joint Bargaining under Part X.1

Since each school board and school authority has four separate statutory teacher bargaining units, there are well over 300 local teacher bargaining units in Ontario. In at least some cases, the interests of both the parties and the public might be best served by combining units and conducting collective bargaining on a joint basis. Part X.1 contemplates a number of different scenarios for joint bargaining:

- Two or more teacher bargaining units represented by the same affiliate may be combined with the consent of the school board (s. 277.2 (1)). *Example*: ETFO could combine regular and occasional teacher units at a single board.
- Two or more boards and/or two or more bargaining agents could bargain jointly, if all parties agree (s. 277.9(1)). *Example*: All French-language public boards could combine to bargain jointly with AEFO, with the consent of all parties.
- Two affiliates at a single board could bargain jointly (s. 277.9(3)). *Example*: ETFO and OSSTF could bargain jointly with any English-speaking public board. This type of joint bargaining does not appear to require the consent of the board.

For the first type of joint bargaining, which results in actual *combination* of the units, mutual consent is required to unravel the joint bargaining structure (s. 277.7(3)). For other kinds of joint bargaining, it would appear that any party could insist on a reversion to the former structure once the collective agreement has expired, without requiring the consent of the other party or parties.[15] There has not been a great deal of formal joint bargaining under these provisions, although in some boards the parties have bargained joint or "master" agreements applicable to both regular and occasional teachers.

One joint bargaining scenario that Part X.1 does *not* contemplate is provincewide bargaining. It is not particularly surprising that the Harris government did not build this scenario into the statute; its overall education strategy required local school boards to "take the heat" for the deterioration of teacher terms and conditions of employment in the new and more restrictive funding environment. The absence of any statutory structure for central bargaining has created some challenges for the successor McGuinty Liberal government, which has encouraged the negotiation of provincial frameworks on key financial issues (see discussion in the section "Change in Government" below).

The Bargaining Process and Dispute Resolution Mechanisms

Part X.1 does not establish any special mechanisms governing the bargaining process for teachers, which means that the timetable for serving notice to bargain, the obligation to bargain in good faith and make every reasonable effort to enter into a collective agreement, and the rules governing the timeliness of strikes and lockouts are the same for teachers as they are for any other unionized employee in Ontario not governed by a specialized regime.[16] If bargaining is unsuccessful, teachers in Ontario have the right to strike; this has been the case since the days of Bill 100. There were never any "essential services" restrictions on strikes in the education sector, although principals and vice-principals, who were at that time members of teacher bargaining units, were not permitted to strike.[17]

In order to minimize disruption in an important public service, however, the earlier statute included a variety of innovative strategies designed to make strikes less likely (Downie 1978, 91ff). Mechanisms such as mandatory fact-finding were designed to put public pressure on the parties to reach an agreement before getting into strike position. Voluntary dispute resolution procedures such as final-offer selection were offered as an alternative to a strike. In addition, in the case of an ongoing strike, Bill 100 required the Education Relations Commission (ERC), the special agency that administered the statute, to make a determination and advise the government as to whether or not a work stoppage had placed the school year of the students in jeopardy: a process that became known as a "jeopardy advisement." While there was no statutory guideline for making jeopardy advisements, the ERC developed a practice of allowing strikes to continue for at least one month before intervening.[18] While the

ERC itself had no power to order an end to a strike, a jeopardy advisement put significant pressure on the parties (or more accurately, on the teachers) to settle their dispute quickly, since the government frequently responded to such a determination with immediate back-to-work legislation and usually imposed compulsory ad hoc interest arbitration to resolve the dispute.

The new Part X.1 regime dispenses with such mechanisms as fact-finding and places teachers under the ordinary regulatory procedures governing strikes and lockouts in Ontario. Since principals and vice-principals are no longer members of the bargaining unit or members of the affiliates, there is no longer any issue about their participation in teacher strikes. The old jeopardy procedure has been formally retained; while the ERC's administration has been otherwise disbanded, it continues to have a life under the umbrella of the Ontario Labour Relations Board for the sole purpose of jeopardy advisements (s. 57.2(2)).[19]

While teachers are now subject to the ordinary mechanics of the *Labour Relations Act* strike-lockout regime, they are governed by their own unique definition of "strike," found in section 277.2(3)(b) of Part X.1:

> "[S]trike" includes any action or activity by teachers in combination or in concert or in accordance with a common understanding that is designed or may reasonably be expected to have the effect of curtailing, restricting, limiting or interfering with,
>
> (i) the normal activities of a board or its employees,
>
> (ii) the operation or functioning of one or more of a board's schools or of one or more of the programs in one or more schools of a board, or
>
> (iii) the performance of the duties of teachers set out in the Act or the regulations under it, including any withdrawal of services or work to rule by teachers acting in combination or in concert or in accordance with a common understanding.

This definition has undergone considerable reconstruction since the days of Bill 100. That earlier statute contained a definition of strike tailored to the education sector, in that it explicitly encompassed such historic teacher bargaining tactics as work-to-rule and mass resignation.[20] When Bill 100 was repealed, no special definition of strike was substituted in Part X.1, resulting in the application of the generic definition in the *Labour Relations Act*.[21] In the course of the struggles between the teachers and the government over workload and extracurricular activities (described in detail in the subsection "The Harris Government and the Era of Regulatory Micromanagement" below), the government introduced a definition of strike into Part X.1 which, like the old Bill 100 definition, made it clear that work-to-rule strategies were strikes. It also went one step further by explicitly including "co-instructional activities" (its controversial term for extracurricular activities) within the scope of the strike definition.

While the successor Liberal government repealed the reference to co-instructional activities in the strike definition, it has not repealed the new definition of strike entirely, leaving intact the explicit references to disruption of school programs and work-to-rule tactics.[22]

The shift from the Bill 100 regime to the *Labour Relations Act* regime has broadened the right of school boards to impose lockouts. Under the old regime, school boards could not use the lockout weapon pre-emptively; they could lock out teachers only after a strike had already commenced (Shilton 1996, 5-40). This meant that a lockout would be useful only in situations where a teachers' strike took the form of a partial withdrawal of services. In practice, lockouts were rarely used. Under the *Labour Relations Act*, school boards, like all employers, have a lockout right that parallels the employees' right to strike. Lockouts are rare in Ontario in any sector, and because of the public pressures to keep schools open, school boards can be expected to make only sparing use of their expanded lockout powers.

One unique feature of the teacher strike-lockout regime under the current legislation is the right of any individual "supporter" of a board (i.e., supporting taxpayer) to apply for a cease and desist order in the event of an unlawful strike (although not a lockout: s. 277.2(5)). Under the general *Labour Relations Act* regime, only parties to the labour dispute can make such an application (s. 100). This provision, introduced by the Harris government in 2000 (S.O. 2000, c. 11, s. 20), presumably reflects a distrust of the capacity of school boards to safeguard the public interest in continuity of service. It has not been repealed by the successor government.

Mechanisms for Contract Maintenance

There are no special mechanisms built into Part X.1 for the handling of contract maintenance issues; this matter is governed by the *Labour Relations Act*. Collective agreements take effect at the local level, where they are also administered. Since the provincial affiliates are the bargaining agents, however, they maintain legal control over access to grievance and arbitration procedures, subject to whatever internal constitutional arrangements have been made between provincial and local organizational units within each union. Furthermore, as bargaining agents the provincial organizations hold the purse strings. This means that even in the absence of a central arbitration mechanism, there is considerable practical scope for the strategic management of grievance and arbitration procedures to promote provincial policies, subject always to the duty of fair representation.

Despite the fact that key monetary issues have been bargained centrally for the last two rounds of negotiations through provincial framework agreements (see discussion in the section "Change in

Government" below), there is no central mechanism for the enforcement of these agreements. Where framework terms become part of local collective agreements, they are enforceable through local grievance and arbitration procedures. The provincial government has made informal mediation available to local parties to assist with resolving disputes involving framework issues, although not all teachers' unions make use of this resource.

THE SCOPE OF COLLECTIVE BARGAINING

Full-Scope Bargaining within a Statutory Framework

Teachers in Ontario have always had relatively few formal fetters on the scope of their collective bargaining. Bill 100 provided that "negotiations shall be carried out in respect of any term or condition of employment put forward by either party" (s. 8). Under the new regime, the scope of bargaining for teachers in Ontario is governed by the *Labour Relations Act*, which also mandates bargaining over all terms and conditions of employment brought to the table by either party.[23] The only specific restriction on bargaining found in Part X.1 itself relates to the term of the agreement. When Part X.1 first came into effect, it provided that start and end dates of collective agreements must coincide with the school year, and required that all first agreements have a two-year minimum term, beginning on 1 September 1998. In the midst of turbulent collective bargaining, the Harris government imposed a requirement that all agreements entered into after 1 July 2001 would expire on 31 August 2004 (S.O. 2001, c. 14, s. 9). Amended again by the Liberals, the Act now requires that all agreements be for either two years or four years (s. 277.22(a)).[24] Part X.1 does not permit gaps between collective agreements; a new agreement is always retroactive to the September 1 immediately following the expiry date of the predecessor agreement (s. 277.11(1)(b)).

Despite full-scope bargaining, however, there have always been significant limitations on teacher bargaining simply because teaching is a regulated profession. Statutory provisions regulate a minimum length for the instructional day, a minimum length for the school year, school holidays, and vacation periods. Likewise, detailed statutory lists of the duties of teachers (s. 264 and Regulation 298, s. 20) and of the duties and powers of school boards (ss. 170, 171) impose their own implicit limitations. Provisions establishing minimum and maximum standards for retirement gratuity systems (s. 180) and establishing standards for sick pay (s. 260, now repealed) shaped collectively bargained benefit plans. Prior to the 1997 reforms, all regular teachers were employed under a statutory form of contract giving them a right to specific periods of notice on termination; non-probationary teachers had a right to challenge their terminations through a statutory process known as a board of reference (Shilton 1996).[25]

Another historic fetter on the scope of bargaining arose indirectly from the special constitutional status of both separate and French-language education systems in Ontario. Since 1867, separate school boards have been protected under section 93(1) of the *Constitution Act* from attempts by provincial legislatures to restrict the rights and privileges they held at the time of Confederation relating to the denominational aspects of education.[26] Since 1983, French-language school boards have had similar protection under section 23 of the Charter for "those aspects of education which pertain to or have an effect on their language and culture" (*Mahe v. Alberta*, [1990] 1 S.C.R. 343). Neither of these constitutional provisions expressly mentions teacher terms and conditions of employment. As interpreted over the years, however, section 93 allows separate school boards a measure of autonomy in managing the denominational aspects of their employment relationships with teachers, including the hiring, firing, and promotion of teachers on denominational grounds;[27] presumably French-language boards have the same scope under section 23 of the Charter. The Constitution does not, of course, shelter boards from a general requirement to bargain collectively, but it may have some implications for the content of collective agreements. A 1977 Ontario Court of Appeal decision ruled that separate school boards could not be required to submit to statutory boards of reference for teachers terminated for denominational cause.[28] In a subsequent decision, the same court nevertheless held that a separate school board was bound by its own consent, reflected in its collective agreement, to submit teacher dismissals to grievance arbitration, even when the dismissal was for denominational cause.[29] The court observed, however, that the statute could not compel the board to bargain over denominational issues. The question of whether (and if so, how broadly) denominational (and by extension French-language) constitutional rights encroach on the scope of teacher collective bargaining has not yet been tested under Part X.1.

Although pensions are not formally excluded from the scope of bargaining, teachers' pensions have historically been dealt with outside conventional collective bargaining. Since 1917, Ontario teachers have been covered by a provincewide plan, the Ontario Teachers' Pension Plan (formerly the Teachers' Superannuation Plan), a contributory defined benefit plan. Individual school boards play no role in this plan. For many years, it was controlled solely by the government, although there was consultation with the Ontario Teachers' Federation. Under the provisions of the *Teachers' Pension Act*, R.S.O. 1990, c. T.1, the plan was converted effective 1 January 1992 to a jointly sponsored plan, co-governed by the province and the Ontario Teachers' Federation on behalf of teachers. The parties have negotiated a partnership agreement giving them the right to amend the terms of the plan, including contribution and benefit levels, subject to an arbitration mechanism built into the agreement for the resolution of disputes (Faraday, Réaume, and Turkington, n.d., 13.10.10). Currently, individual teachers contribute between 10.4 and 12 percent of their salary, and the government makes a matching contribution.[30] While the plan is widely recognized as an excellent one, it has recently, like most Canadian pension plans, faced serious funding pressures. The plan's joint sponsorship structure makes the teachers and the government equally responsible for ensuring that the plan's assets are sufficient to fund its liabilities. In 2008 the teachers voted to address a large deficit by replacing guaranteed inflation protection with a form of conditional inflation protection, which will reduce costs but also make pensions less valuable.

Under Bill 100, the density of the regulation surrounding the teacher employment relationship caused little conflict at the bargaining table. There were very few formal disputes over the scope of bargaining per se. Issues of conflict between the statutory framework and the content of collective agreements typically arose, if they arose at all, in the context of rights arbitrations in which school boards relied on regulatory restrictions to avoid unfavourable interpretations of collective agreement provisions. Very occasionally, boards also sought nullification of specific provisions of collective agreements on the grounds that they conflicted with regulatory provisions. Although arbitrators sought to harmonize the interpretation of collective agreements with the overall statutory framework, they did not generally look with favour on efforts to avoid negotiated obligations, taking the view that since boards have both the statutory power and the duty to bargain collectively, the resulting agreements should generally be binding. For example, where boards had agreed to provide dependent life insurance and sick leave gratuities in excess of statutory standards, those agreements were enforced.[31]

The Harris Government and the Era of Regulatory Micromanagement

Against this background, teachers and school boards in Ontario were well accustomed to bargaining under the shadow (and/or the shelter) of the statutory regime. The Bill 160 package, however, introduced an entirely new level of centralized regulatory control over teacher terms and conditions of employment. In one important area, Bill 160 was deregulatory; it repealed the old statutory form of contract, and with it the board of reference system for addressing teacher terminations, leaving issues of teacher tenure to be dealt with through collective bargaining.[32] In most other respects, however, its thrust was in the opposite direction. Beginning with the Bill itself and continuing throughout the period that Harris remained in power, the government used its legislative and regulatory authority to circumvent the collective bargaining process, deliberately constraining the flexibility of local parties to negotiate local solutions to the challenges created by the new funding formula. It was an approach calculated to alienate all parties to local bargaining, since it clearly reflected the government's view that school boards were captive to the teachers' unions, incapable of asserting the strong management control needed to keep both teachers and tax levels in line (Bedard and Lawton 1998).

The most notorious of Bill 160's micromanagement strategies was the introduction of very specific standards for the assignment of instructional time. The government made no secret of the fact that a particular object of these new legislative standards was to reduce the amount of preparation time secondary teachers had been successful in negotiating over the years and to compel them to take on heavier workloads. Bill 160 was explicit that these new teaching time standards were to apply notwithstanding the provisions of any collective agreement. The detailed story of teacher resistance to those standards and the Harris government's response to that resistance has been told elsewhere and need not be retold here (Rose 2000, 2002; Sitch 2005). What must be emphasized, however, is the extent to which the government's "command and control" regime undermined the institution of collective bargaining.

When the first round of bargaining under the new regime led to an unprecedented number of strikes in secondary bargaining units, draconian back-to-work legislation placed additional fetters on the scope of bargaining, including the imposition of restrictions on the authority of interest arbitrators to make awards that did not reflect the government's views (Rose 2000, 275-76). Initial teacher resistance to government initiatives to increase workload led to further and even more detailed regulation. When the teachers threatened to withdraw voluntary services, the government responded by throwing additional fuel on the workload fire, enacting the *Education Accountability Act, 2000*, S.O. 2000, c. 11 to make "co-instructional" (extracurricular) activities mandatory notwithstanding any provision in any collective agreement.[33] While many of the provisions of the 2000 statute were never proclaimed, the message was clear; the government would not allow the process of free collective bargaining to impede its objective—getting higher "productivity" out of teachers without increasing salary costs. One provision that *was* proclaimed was a new definition of strike which made it clear that work-to-rule strategies involving "co-instructional activities" were strikes, and therefore unlawful unless timely (see the subsection "The Bargaining Process and Dispute Resolution Mechanisms" above).

In addition to these high-profile efforts to increase teacher workload, Bill 160 introduced an era of unprecedented centralized supervision of teachers' professional functions. New centralized policies and procedures for promoting increased "quality," "accountability," and "excellence" in the teaching profession were constantly being introduced.[34] In 2001, the government passed two pieces of legislation introducing new pro-fessional requirements. The first, introduced in June as the *Stability and Excellence in Education Act, 2001*, S.O. 2001, c. 14, imposed a program of mandatory recertification every five years for already certified teachers, to be conducted under the supervision of the College of Teachers, the professional regulatory body with general statutory responsibility for the supervison of the professional standards of teachers in the province. The June statute was followed in December by the *Quality in the Classroom Act, 2001*, S.O. 2001, c. 24, imposing a mandatory qualifying test for new teachers; a mandatory teacher evaluation program, in which local school boards were conscripted to administer performance appraisals every two years in accordance with detailed guidelines; and a requirement that all teachers prepare and adhere to individual Annual Learning Plans to be worked out in consultation with their principals (Shilton and Schucher 2004).[35] These new professional requirements directly affected employ-ment relations and increased teacher workload, encroaching on areas that had traditionally been matters for collective bargaining.

Not surprisingly, this sustained legislative campaign to transfer con-trol from the local parties and place it in the hands of the government generated extremely difficult conditions for local collective bargaining. Joseph Rose's (2012) chapter in this volume details the chaotic outcomes of the rounds of teacher collective bargaining that followed Bill 160, pro-ducing numerous strikes, some lockouts, several back-to-work statutes, and a great deal of ill will on all sides.

CHANGE IN GOVERNMENT: CHANGE IN STRATEGY

A change in government in October of 2003 brought an end to overt hos-tilities between the government and the teachers. An important plank in the campaign platform of the newly elected Liberal government was an education peace treaty.[36] The new government rolled back some of the Harris-era legislation. There are now very few provisions still on the education statute books operating "despite any provision in a collective agreement."[37] Nevertheless, the era of centralized micromanagement of issues that might otherwise have been dealt with at the collective bargaining table is by no means over. Although mandatory qualifying tests and teacher recertification tests are now gone, there continues to be a mandatory "New Teacher Induction Program," backstopping a statu-tory two-year probationary period for all "new teachers," including experienced teachers who have transferred from other school boards (a new Part X.0.1 in the *Education Act*, enacted by S.O. 2006, c. 10, s. 38). Likewise, a highly regulated mandatory performance appraisal every two years has been replaced with a somewhat less highly regulated but still mandatory performance appraisal every five years (S.O. 2006, s. 42-50). Although a regulatory limit of four teacher professional activity days has been replaced with a limit of six (the limit prior to the Harris reforms was nine), the close regulation of the activities that can be scheduled on those days remains in place (O.Reg. 360/06). More fundamentally, the McGuinty Liberals have shown no interest in repealing the keystone of the Harris-era centralizing reforms: central control of education funding, reflected in the provincial education funding formula. There has been no move to restore taxing power to local school boards, or even to give them much flexibility in the deployment of their local budgets. The fundamental tension between local responsibility and central control therefore remains embedded in the legal framework for collective bargaining.

Rather than altering the legal framework, what the McGuinty government has done to address this tension is to adopt strategies that operate outside of, or at best parallel to, that framework. In particular, the government has implemented a central bargaining mechanism, dubbed the Provincial Discussion Table (PDT), in which the government brings representatives of school boards and teachers' unions to a provincial bargaining table to bargain over certain key cost items, taking the results back to local tables to be incorporated into local collective agreements.[38] The government first experimented with the PDT process in the 2004 round of bargaining. Fearing a repeat of the labour unrest in the education sector that typified the Harris years, Education Minister Gerard Kennedy persuaded each of the provincial teachers' unions to sit down with the umbrella organization representing the school board with which it bargained, to attempt to resolve key issues on a central basis.[39] The "bait" for both school boards and teachers was a more attractive funding package with which to pay for teacher collective agreements, in the form both of a longer-term funding commitment from the government, and of "enhancements" to the basic funding package, earmarked to pay for specific collective agreement improvements. In order to promote speedy consensus, the government imposed deadlines by which agreement had to be reached in order to obtain access to the superior funding package. The first and fairly informal experiment with central bargaining produced a full set of four-year agreements (2004–2008) without any serious labour disputes; while there were a series of work-to-rule campaigns before the provincial tables were convened in that round, there were no full strikes and all local agreements were arrived at without the need for interest arbitration.

The second bargaining round was both more formal and more contentious, although it too ultimately produced a complete package of four-year agreements without any strikes, lockouts, or arbitrated settlements. As noted above, framework bargaining was "facilitated" by deadlines imposed by government. Three out of four teachers' unions reached agreement within the stipulated time frames. However, the Elementary Teachers' Federation of Ontario—the largest of the four unions and the first to have reached agreement in the first round of framework bargaining—did not. The major sticking point for ETFO was preparation time, an issue over which it had long sought parity with secondary teachers. ETFO's position would have required a costly increase in elementary prep time, for which the government was not prepared to pay. The government's advice to ETFO was to pursue its quest for "prep time" parity at local tables, a course of action all parties knew would be futile; unless the point was conceded and funded at the central table, local boards would simply not have the money to pay. The government agreed to a modest extension of the original central deadline, but still no agreement was reached. Ultimately, under serious pressure from within the system but also from a worldwide recession, ETFO conceded and signed a framework agreement, but not soon enough to prevent the government from showing the iron fist that had been concealed in the velvet glove all along. Since ETFO had missed the government-imposed deadlines, teachers represented by ETFO received lower wage increases in the first two years of the agreement than those represented by the three unions that had played by the government's rules.[40]

In both rounds, central bargaining produced a series of documents called Provincial Discussion Table (PDT) Agreements.[41] The commitments contained in these PDT Agreements are of various kinds. Some of them are cost-free and simply reflect government policy. For example, the "Preamble" to the OECTA/OCSTA agreement states that "the Parties will include in the preamble to their Collective Agreements a statement: 'The XX School board and the YY [Union] Bargaining Units are committed to improve student achievement, reduce gaps in student outcomes and increase confidence in publicly funded education.'" Others, reflecting both teacher and school board bargaining priorities, are more substantive. For example, the 2008–2012 agreement between the Ontario English Catholic Teachers Association and the Ontario Catholic School Trustees' Association contains very specific commitments with respect to elementary preparation time and class sizes (OECTA/OCSTA PDT Agreement, ¶¶ 7 and 8). All agreements contain a commitment that the parties—the provincial unions and the umbrella school board associations—agree to "actively promote the adoption and implementation" of the terms of the PDT Agreement into local collective agreements.

The PDT ground rules contemplated not only that central frameworks would be signed within specified time lines, but also that all local agreements subject to those frameworks would be negotiated and ratified by specified dates. Initially, the government had set its own fixed date for the signing of all local agreements; ultimately, it agreed to be more flexible and allow a deadline for the signing of local agreements to be negotiated and fixed by the parties in the PDT Agreements. In most cases, local agreements came prior to the deadline. An exception was the OSSTF unit for regular teachers at the Toronto District School Board (TDSB). The OSSTF provincial office had signed a PDT Agreement with the Ontario Public

School Boards' Association containing provisions on teacher supervision duties that would require changes to the provisions of the local OSSTF-TDSB agreement. Local teachers resisted these changes and filed a bad faith bargaining complaint at the Ontario Labour Relations Board, which brought a halt to local negotiations. The complaint was never heard, and the dispute was finally resolved in August of 2009 on terms consistent with the PDT Agreement. The TDSB was able to retain the enhanced funding provided by that Agreement only because the government agreed to grant an extension of the deadline to accommodate the union's bargaining complaint.

REFLECTIONS ON THE FUTURE

While the Harris government gets most of the credit (or the blame) for centralizing control of the education system, centripetal forces were operating in the system long before Harris was elected premier. The Harris reforms gave further impetus to the shift toward centralization. While the current government has backed away from some of the most obvious incursions on local bargaining introduced by the Harris government, important features of the Bill 160 package remain firmly in place, key among them the centralized control of education funding. While the Liberal government's version of central funding may be marginally more flexible than the Conservative version, local school boards nevertheless remain wholly dependent on their provincial paymasters. The tension between central control and local responsibility continues to be a major pressure on the current education collective bargaining framework in Ontario.

The ad hoc PDT system of two-tier bargaining has been remarkably successful at staving off disruptive labour unrest for several years—no small accomplishment in the education sector in Ontario, although undoubtedly a very expensive one. Nevertheless, it is obvious that there will be instabilities in a system that places power at the centre, but assigns responsibility at the local level. There are clearly both legal and political instabilities in the PDT system. The lynchpin of central bargaining, the PDT Agreement, has no legal anchor in existing legislation, and is of doubtful enforceability, for two reasons. First, it is signed on behalf of employers by school board umbrella organizations that have no formal status within the education collective bargaining system, and no statutory mandate as bargaining agents. Second, although the government funding underpinning the agreements is essential to permit the school boards to meet the commitments they undertake at the provincial table and subsequently in local collective agreements, the government is not itself a signatory to the agreements. The agreements themselves provide no formal enforcement mechanism; although the government does provide "facilitation" to resolve implementation disputes (OECTA/OCSTA PDT Agreement, ¶2), it is clear from the language that the government does not see itself as a party to those disputes. The government's commitments appear to be purely political rather than legal.[42]

Politically, a PDT process engrafted upon a legal framework that contemplates local bargaining places government in a position in which it is very powerful but legally unaccountable. Because it controls the contents of any funding "enhancement" package used to facilitate the PDT process, it can exert direct and very specific control over the contents of collective agreements. As the ETFO experience discussed above demonstrates, government support is key to the ability of a teachers' union to push its own provincial agenda at the bargaining table; without the government's financial support, prep-time parity is simply not attainable. Within the PDT process, however, the hand of the government is designed to be an invisible one; the teachers' unions and the local school boards remain answerable to the larger community for bargaining outcomes, even though their ability to influence them is diminished under the PDT process.

The PDT Agreements must be implemented through local bargaining. There are at least two problems for local bargaining created by the current "extra-legal" structure. First, because two-tier bargaining is not formalized, there is no clear line of demarcation between central and local topics. This gives the government more leverage than it might otherwise have to use financial incentives to pressure for central bargaining on issues that are fundamentally local. As we have seen in the TDSB situation, this can result in stripping agreements of historical bargaining gains made at the local level over the years. Lack of clarity on central versus local issues also sets up the potential for friction between provincial teachers' unions and their local units, since there may well be internal disagreement about the appropriate locus for addressing specific issues. Second, because the PDT Agreements lack independent legal status, the government has used the establishment of tight time frames for local bargaining as its most powerful lever for implementing the central agreement. This may put local parties under unnecessary pressure and leave little time for serious bargaining on local issues.

It could certainly be argued that the Bill 160 regime has never had a fair chance to prove itself under "normal" conditions of collective bargaining. For the first six years, the system was at war with the Harris government, and bargaining was highly politicized. Since the Conservative government was defeated late in 2003, its Liberal successor has managed essential aspects of collective bargaining outside the formal framework mandated by statute. It is very unlikely, however, that local bargaining—Bill 160's key operating mechanism—can ever be made to work effectively in a system that is centrally funded under tight provincial control, at least for bargaining key monetary issues. In the education sector there are few terms and conditions of employment for teachers that do not sport a hefty price tag. Maintaining the principal locus of bargaining at the local level appears to be a recipe for futile conflict. The willingness of all parties to participate in PDT bargaining to date is at least tacit acknowledgement that under the current education funding arrangements, meaningful bargaining over many teacher terms and conditions of employment can take place only at the provincial level.

Nevertheless, it is also clear that collective bargaining at the provincial level poses unique challenges for a province whose public education system has four distinct subsystems, three of which can claim constitutional protection for at least some aspects of their distinctiveness.[43] The four subsystems do not always have common interests even on funding issues.[44] The separate school system has historically had something of a siege mentality; despite its constitutional foundation, the legitimacy of funding religious-based education is an issue that never really goes away in Ontario. That issue threatened to dominate the 2007 provincial election campaign when the Conservatives under John Tory proposed "equalizing" the rights of Catholics and other religious groups by providing public funding for faith-based schools in general, a proposal that may have cost the party the election and almost certainly cost their leader a seat in the legislature and ultimately his leadership. Tory's fate will no doubt give pause to any politician seeking to poke the separate school funding hornet's nest again any time soon, but the perception that these four systems are competitors for scarce public education dollars makes it more difficult for them to make common cause around funding issues.

Further stress within the system comes from the fact that the teachers are represented by four separate unions who, despite the fact that they exist under a common OTF umbrella, have spent much of the past 25 years in litigation against each other over issues that have been fundamentally about the distribution of power within the system.[45] Inter-union hostilities, which appeared to abate somewhat within the last few years, have been revived by recent rivalry over representation rights for a new group of educational workers, Early Childhood Educators, who will be hired to teach in Ontario's new all-day kindergarten program.[46] Ontario's four teachers' unions have very different political philosophies. Their conflicting views about their role and about the management of relations among teachers, government, and school boards have been reflected in their often-conflicting strategies in dealing with the Harris reforms, and with the post-Harris efforts on the part of government to circumvent impediments within the existing bargaining framework.

After the disruptive experiences of the past decade and a half, it is not surprising that key actors within the education collective bargaining system in Ontario are in no hurry to open the Pandora's box that comes with significant change, preferring ad hoc measures. The current PDT process, however, is not a permanent answer; while creative, it is inherently unstable and will ultimately be unsustainable. Despite the challenges

Ontario's complex education system poses for centralized labour relations, it is predictable that some form of mandatory central bargaining, probably of a multi-tier variety, will be coming soon to Ontario.

NOTES

1. The litigation war began with a preliminary constitutional challenge to certain provisions of the Harris government's first piece of legislation reorganizing local school boards, the *Fewer School Boards Act, 1997* S.O. 1997, c. 3. This challenge was almost wholly unsuccessful (see *Ontario Public School Boards' Assn. v. Ontario (Attorney General)*, [1997] O.J. No. 3184), although the challengers won a small residual victory ([1999] O.J. No. 2473, leave to appeal denied [1999] S.C.C.A. No. 425) when the Ontario Court of Appeal held that provisions in Bill 160 prohibiting spouses of school board employees from running for trustee positions violated section 15 of the Charter. Once Bill 160 was passed, teachers from both public and separate systems banded together with public school board trustees for a wholesale attack on the constitutionality of changes to the structure and funding of public education in Ontario. The primary sword-carrier for denominational rights in that litigation was the Catholic teachers' union, opposed by the Catholic school boards who sided with the government: see *Ontario English Catholic Teachers Assn. v Ontario (Attorney General)*, [2001] 1 S.C.R. 470. This challenge, too, was unsuccessful. In addition, the teachers took on the government's decision to amend Bill 160 prior to third reading to remove principals and vice-principals from teacher bargaining units, arguing that this action was retaliation for the participation in the two-week mass teacher walkout, and accordingly violated Charter-protected freedom of association and freedom of expression. The courts disagreed: see *Ontario Teachers' Federation et al. v. Attorney General of Ontario* (2000), 49 O.R. (3d) 257 (C.A.), leave to appeal denied [2000] S.C.C.A No. 457. The teachers did win one moral victory, when the Attorney General's application for an injunction to end the teacher walkout was dismissed; see *Attorney General for Ontario v. Ontario Teachers' Federation et al.* (1997), 36 O.R. (3d) 367. Although constitutional arguments were made in that case, the application was dismissed solely on the basis that it was premature.
2. Section numbers refer to sections in the *Education Act*, R.S.O. 1990, c. E.2 as amended, unless otherwise specified.
3. A useful discussion of the background and unique structure of Bill 100 can be found in Downie (1978).
4. Terms and conditions of employment for in-school administrators are heavily regulated; see Faraday, Réaume, and Turkington (n.d.), Chapter 10.
5. From the time of Confederation until Bill 160 came into effect, Ontario had two education subsystems: one "public" (i.e., non-denominational) and one "separate" (i.e., denominational or Roman Catholic). Bill 160 added two French-language subsystems, one public and one separate. There is one Protestant separate school board in Ontario, in Penetanguishene, classified as a "school authority."
6. An 84th employer is the Provincial Schools Authority (PSA), which employs teachers in schools operated directly by the Ministry of Correctional Services,

the Ministry of Education, and the Ministry of Health and Long-Term Care. Collective bargaining within the PSA is governed by the *Provincial Schools Negotiations Act*, R.S.O. 1990, c. P.35, which provides generally for the application of the *Labour Relations Act, 1995*, but makes specific provision for a statutory bargaining unit and statutory bargaining agent. The PSA system is not discussed in this chapter.

7. Part X.1 divides "Part X.1 teachers" (defined as teachers "employed by a board to teach" but excluding supervisory officers, principals, vice-principals, and instructors in a teacher training institution; s. 277.1(1)) into two categories: (a) "occasional" teachers, and (b) those teachers who are not occasional teachers (called "regular" teachers for purposes of this chapter). Occasional teachers are substitute teachers, although their period of substitution can be as long as two school years (s. 1.1).

8. School authorities known as section 68 boards (i.e., those established on tax-exempt land) have four separate bargaining units, divided along regular/occasional and elementary/secondary lines. Other school authorities also have four separate units, but divided along regular/occasional and French/English lines, with no distinction between elementary and secondary teachers. Many school authorities have been amalgamated with district school boards over the last few years; most of those still remaining are in hospitals.

9. There is one additional difference between the unions holding bargaining rights under Bill 100 and those with bargaining rights under Part X.1 that did not result directly from Bill 160. Under the prior regime, bargaining rights for elementary teachers were divided between two organizations, the Federation of Women Teachers' Associations of Ontario (FWTAO) and the Ontario Public School Teachers' Federation (OPSTF; formerly the Ontario Public School Men Teachers' Federation). The formation of a single organization to represent all elementary public school teachers came about after many years of Charter and human rights litigation challenging the assignment of women teachers to FWTAO (see note 45 below). The two organizations ultimately formed ETFO, which took over the role previously played by FWTAO and OPSTF some months after the new Part X.1 bargaining regime came into effect.

10. This history is discussed in some detail in the large body of decisions resulting from the Charter and human rights challenges to the OTF membership rules on the basis of sex and religion referred to in note 45.

11. In practice, branch affiliates of FWTAO and OPSTF invariably bargained jointly. Typically, AEFO also bargained jointly with other affiliates in either the public or the separate system.

12. The current text of Bylaw 1 can be found in the OTF publication, *We the Teachers of Ontario*, at http://www.otffeo.on.ca/english/docs/WTT_TPA_policies bylawsetc.pdf.

13. The Ontario Labour Relations Board addressed the issue in a series of decisions, reported as [2002] OLRD no. 176; [2002] OLRD no. 976; [2003] OLRB Rep. 819, application for judicial review dismissed [2005] O.J. No. 284 (Div Ct.); [2005] OLRD No. 5069.

14. Simultaneous amendments to the *Teaching Profession Act* brought occasional teachers into OTF.

15. Under similar provisions in Bill 100, the Education Relations Commission upheld the right of the affiliates involved to terminate the joint bargaining

relationship without the school board's consent. This decision is discussed in Faraday, Réaume, and Turkington (n.d., 3-9).

16. In practice, the centralized mechanisms for provincial bargaining that have evolved recently make a very significant difference to how bargaining is actually conducted.

17. Downie explains that restricting the right of principals and vice-principals to strike was seen as compromising an ongoing debate about the hybrid role of these in-school administrators as managers with special obligations to the board and to the community, and also as educational leaders with a community of interest with their fellow OTF members (1978, 67-69).

18. In *Attorney General for Ontario v. Ontario Teachers' Federation et al.* (1997), 36 O.R. (3d) 367, the decision refusing an interim injunction against the teachers' two-week withdrawal of services in 1997, the court noted the following:

Since 1975 the [ERC] has issued a student jeopardy advisement on 13 occasions. Most of these have been issued in the context of a full withdrawal of services by teachers. The earliest at which such an advisement has been issued is after 27 school days; the latest after 73 school days. In the present case the Attorney General has sought an injunction after two days.

19. By repealing Bill 100, Bill 160 eliminated the ERC. It was revived in 2001 by S.O. 2001, c. 14, in the midst of the battles with the secondary teachers about workload, for the sole purpose of making jeopardy advisements, and continues to play that role.

20. Work-to-rule was a popular strike strategy for teachers under Bill 100, for one very good reason: Bill 100 required that teachers continue to be paid while on work-to-rule campaigns (Shilton 1996). With the repeal of Bill 100, teachers lost the statutory guarantee of salary during work-to-rule campaigns. Their right to income continuance while on limited forms of strike is now determined under the same principles that govern that question for other employees under the Ontario *Labour Relations Act*, which means that whether school boards may respond to work-to-rule strategies by withholding pay is determined on a case-by-case basis. The interpretation of the strike definition under Bill 100 is discussed by Shilton (1996, 5.34–5.40).

21. The *Labour Relations Act* defines a strike in section 1(1) as follows:

"strike" includes a cessation of work, a refusal to work or to continue to work by employees in combination or in concert or in accordance with a common understanding, or a slow-down or other concerted activity on the part of employees designed to restrict or limit output.

22. It is not clear that any of these amendments were necessary in light of the OLRB's historically comprehensive approach to interpreting its generic strike definition to include such tactics as collective refusals to work voluntary overtime.

23. The scope of bargaining under the *Labour Relations Act* is governed by the combination of section 17, the general duty to bargain, and the definition of "collective agreement" (s. 1(1)) as a document that contains "provisions respecting terms or conditions of employment or the rights, privileges or duties of the employer, the employers organization, the trade union or the employees ..." The Act does, of course, include some restrictions of general application on the scope of bargaining, largely through such devices as "deemed" provisions of collective agreements. Those provisions will not be discussed here.

24. The Liberals amended the Act to provide for two- or four-year terms in 2005 (S.O. 2005, c. 4). The prohibition on three-year agreements may have been related to the government's proposed legislation scheduling fixed election dates. Amendments to the *Election Act* enacted in late 2005 scheduled a provincial election for 4 October 2007 (S.O. 2005, c. 35). Since all prior agreements had expired on 31 August 2004, three-year agreements might have led to a series of teacher strikes during the election campaign.

25. In practice, the board of reference process had fallen into disuse in Ontario, replaced by just cause clauses in collective agreements enforced through grievance arbitration. Rights under the statutory form of contract continued to be important, however; Bill 100 specifically provided that where a collective agreement clashed with the terms of the statutory form of contract, the contract would prevail (s. 54(2)). In the early days of arbitration under Bill 100, employers attempted to argue that "just cause" clauses in collective agreements conflicted with the rights of school boards under the statutory form of contract to dismiss teachers with notice. Arbitrators and courts refused to accept this reasoning: see *Re Board of Education for the City of Scarborough and OSSTF District 16* (1980), 26 LAC (2d) 160 (M. Picher), aff'd 37 OR (2d) 348 (Div. Ct.).

26. The nature and scope of these rights is well summarized in *Ontario English Catholic Teachers Assn. v. Ontario (Attorney General)*, [2001] 1 S.C.R. 470.

27. The *Human Rights Code* R.S.O. 1990, c. H.19 also explicitly protects the denominational rights of separate school boards: s. 19(1).

28. *Essex (County) Roman Catholic Separate School Board v. Porter* (1977) 89 D.L.R. (3d) 445 (Ont. C.A.). The two teachers involved had been fired for entering into civil marriages. The court emphasized that they still had the right to sue in the civil courts for damages for wrongful dismissal.

29. *Re Essex County Roman Catholic Separate School Board and Tremblay-Webster* 5 D.L.R. (4th) 665.

30. The lower contribution rate is levied on the portion of salary that is also pensionable under the Canada Pension Plan. The plan's website, http://www.otpp.com, contains considerable information about the plan's history, contribution, and benefit rates.

31. See, for example, *Re Renfrew County Board of Education and OSSTF*, unreported, 4 April 1984 (Brent); *Re Kapuskasing Roman Catholic Separate School Board and AEFO*, unreported, 21 January 1980 (Duchesneau-McLachlin).

32. One vestige of the old termination regime remains. Section 263 of the *Education Act* had always provided school boards with a right to terminate a teacher on a summary basis with pay in lieu of notice and with the consent of the Minister of Education, in exceptional circumstances that threatened "the welfare of the school in which the teacher [was] employed." Section 263 was not repealed and continues to operate "despite any provision in a collective agreement." Since collective agreements typically do not prohibit summary termination (albeit subject to the grievance and arbitration procedure), it is doubtful that this provision has any remaining application now that the statutory form of contract with its requirement of notice is gone.

33. The legislation provided that "[i]t is the exclusive function of the employer to determine how co-instructional activities will be provided by ... teachers ... and no matter relating to the provision of co-instructional activities ...

shall be the subject of collective bargaining nor come within the jurisdiction of an arbitrator or arbitration board" (ss. 170(2.3, 2.4)). The legislation also included detailed instruction to school boards about how to implement the new mandatory regime.

34. The government's agenda was reflected in its provocative style of naming statutes. For example, the Act making extracurricular activities mandatory was called "An Act to Amend the Education Act to increase educational quality, to improve the accountability of school boards to students, parents and taxpayers and to enhance the students' school experience" (S.O. 2000, c. 11).

35. Sitch (2005) argues that from the perspective of the classroom teacher, two additional contemporaneous phenomena that do not, strictly speaking, belong on this list were perceived as part of an increasing burden of centralized supervision and loss of local and individual autonomy: the creation in 1996 of a regulatory college, the College of Teachers, with its disciplinary reach beyond the boundaries of local school boards, and the introduction of provincewide standardized student testing, which put pressure on teachers to "teach to the test."

36. The new government was also anxious to placate local school boards. The *Education Statute Law Amendment Act (Student Performance), 2006*, S.O. 2006, c. 10, the Liberals' omnibus repeal of many of the Harris education reforms, also introduced mandatory consultation procedures with school board organizations (s. 4) and reduced the level of regulation regarding class size, teaching time, trustees' honoraria, and provincial authority to put local boards under trusteeship.

37. Exceptions are section 287.1(1), which provides that principals and vice-principals may perform teaching duties "despite any provision in a collective agreement," and section 263, discussed in note 32 above.

38. This framework bargaining strategy is not exclusive to teachers; it has been applied broadly across the education sector of Ontario. With respect to framework bargaining, I have supplemented information obtained from public sources through discussions with participants in the process from the Ministry of Education, teachers' unions, and umbrella school board associations. The interpretation of the process offered here is, of course, my own. Further information on the Ministry perspective can be obtained from Margot Trevelyan, Director of Labour Relations, Ministry of Education. Further information from the English public school board perspective can be obtained from Geoff Williams, Director of Labour Relations, Ontario Public School Boards' Association. Information about the views of the various teachers' unions is readily available from publications on their websites.

39. These umbrella organizations are the Ontario Public School Boards' Association (OPSBA), the Ontario Catholic School Trustees' Association (OCSTA), the Association franco-ontarienne des conseils scolaires catholiques (AFOCSC), and the Association des conseillères et conseillers des écoles publiques de l'Ontario (ACÉPO). School authorities are members of OPSBA. As noted below, none of these associations have statutory authority to represent school boards in collective bargaining.

40. ETFO members got 2 percent in each of the first two years of the agreement, and 3 percent in each of the last two years. Members of the other three unions got 3 percent in all four years (see individual framework agreements).

41. All framework agreements reached in the second round of bargaining are currently posted on the Ministry website at http://www.edu.gov.on.ca/eng/document/nr/08.07/framework.html.

42. The PDT Agreements use language like: "The Parties note the government's intention, conditional upon approval by the Lieutenant Governor in Council, to introduce an allocation in the GSN [Grants for Student Needs] to enhance professional learning opportunities for teachers." (See PDT Agreement between OECTA and the Ontario Catholic School Trustees' Association, ¶5.)

43. In *Ontario English Catholic Teachers Assn. v. Ontario (Attorney General)*, [2001] 1 S.C.R. 470, the Supreme Court rejected the argument of the English public school boards that they were entitled to "mirror equality" with boards holding denomination rights, leaving that subsystem, the largest, alone without any constitutional protection against legislation encroaching upon its historic powers.

44. In the litigation challenging Bill 160 (see note 1), English-language public school boards made common cause with the teachers, while the English-language separate school boards intervened to support the government, as did both public and separate French-language boards.

45. Between 1986 and 1989, the teachers' unions were engaged in litigation challenging the OTF membership rules on the grounds that they violated Charter guarantees of equality on the basis of sex and religion. When the Ontario Court of Appeal ruled that the OTF bylaw was not subject to the Charter (*Tomen v. FWTAO* (1989), 70 O.R. (2d) 48, leave to appeal denied, [1989] S.C.C.A. No. 376), the battle over sex equality within OTF continued under the *Human Rights Code*, ending only in 1997 when the Ontario Court of Appeal dismissed FWTAO's appeal against an adverse finding by a human rights board of inquiry on the grounds that the decision of FWTAO and OPSTF to co-found a new mixed-sex union made the issue moot: *Tomen v. Ontario (Human Rights Commission)*, [1997] O.J. No. 4446, leave to appeal abandoned, [1998] S.C.C.A. No. 39. For more recent inter-union difficulties, see *Ontario Teachers' Federation v. Ontario Secondary School Teachers' Federation*, [2002] O.J. No. 2419, in which the Court of Appeal dealt with a dispute over the division of membership fees between OSSTF and OTF. The roots of the dispute lay in the change to the dues collection mechanisms brought about by Bill 160. Under the previous regime, OTF had collected the dues and remitted a share to the affiliates determined under the OTF bylaws. The Bill 160 regime reversed the power relations here, placing dues collection in the hands of the affiliates. The results in court were mixed; OSSTF was ordered to pay the dues demanded by OTF, but OTF's suspension of OSSTF for failure to remit the dues was declared null and void.

46. Both OSSTF (see http://ecechoice.ca/) and ETFO (see http://youreceunion.ca/) are conducting organizing campaigns for Early Childhood Education (ECE) workers. In June of 2010, the government signed a framework agreement for ECE workers that excluded ETFO. ETFO has filed an unfair labour practice complaint challenging this agreement. The complaint has not yet been disposed of by the OLRB; see Hemsworth (2010).

REFERENCES

Bedard, G.J. and S.B. Lawton. 1998. "The Battle over Ontario's Bill 160 and the Shape of Teacher Collective Bargaining." *Policy Options* (July-Aug.): 49-54.

Downie, B.M. 1978. *Collective Bargaining and Conflict Resolution in Education: The Evolution of Public Policy in Ontario.* Kingston, ON: Industrial Relations Centre, Queen's University.

Faraday, F., V. Réaume, and S. Turkington. n.d. *Education Labour and Employment Law for Teachers.* 2nd ed. Loose-leaf with updates. Original authors E.J. Shilton and K. Schucher. Aurora, ON: Canada Law Book.

Hemsworth, W. 2010. "Teachers' Unions Tussle over ECE Recruitment: Fall's Launch of All-Day Kindergarten Sparks War of Words." *Hamilton Spectator,* 24 July.

Ontario Teachers' Federation. n.d. *We the Teachers of Ontario* (current edition). http://www.otffeo.on.ca/english/docs/WTT_TPA_policiesbylawsetc.pdf.

Rose, J.B. 2000. "The Ghost of Interest Arbitration." *Canadian Labour and Employment Law Journal* 8(2): 253-98.

—. 2002. "The Assault on School Teacher Bargaining in Ontario." *Relations Industrielles/Industrial Relations* 57(1): 100-128.

—. 2012. "The Evolution of Teacher Bargaining in Ontario." In *Dynamic Negotiations: Teacher Labour Relations in Canadian Elementary and Secondary Education,* edited by S. Slinn and A. Sweetman, 199-220. Montreal and Kingston: Queen's Policy Studies Series, McGill-Queen's University Press.

Shilton, E. 1996. *Education Labour and Employment Law in Ontario.* Aurora, ON: Canada Law Book.

Shilton, E. and K. Schucher. 2004. "Ontario's Teacher Testing and Recertification Programme: Can Legal Rules Enforce a Commitment to Life-Long Learning?" In *In Support of Lifelong Learning,* Proceedings of the 13th Annual Conference of the Canadian Association for the Practical Study of Law in Education, edited by R.C. Flynn, 301-17. Informco.

Sitch, G. 2005. "Professionalism and Autonomy: Unbalanced Agents of Change in the Ontario Education System." *Education Law Journal* 15(2): 139-56.

Chapter 9

THE CENTRALIZATION OF COLLECTIVE BARGAINING IN ONTARIO'S PUBLIC EDUCATION SECTOR AND THE NEED TO BALANCE STAKEHOLDER INTERESTS

BRENDAN SWEENEY, SUSAN MCWILLIAMS, AND ROBERT HICKEY

This chapter examines the centralization of collective bargaining in Ontario's public education sector since 2005. More specifically, it draws upon qualitative data collected by both Sweeney and McWilliams to examine the motivations for and distinct perspectives of three parties involved in education sector bargaining: teachers' and support workers' unions,[1] school boards, and the provincial government.[2] The case of Ontario's public education sector provides important insights into the implications of increasing centralization for labour relations and collective bargaining in the public sector. It also contributes to broader employment relations and collective bargaining research considering that this case runs counter to trends toward decentralized bargaining in the private sectors of Anglo-American political economies. In a number of important industries, such as forest products (Brunelle 1990; Eaton and Kriesky 1998; Sweeney and Holmes, forthcoming; Widenor 1995), automotive manufacturing (Holmes 2004), and transportation services (Herod 1997), employers—often assisted by the state—take advantage of their relative power to shift bargaining away from the industry, regional, or national

Dynamic Negotiations: Teacher Labour Relations in Canadian Elementary and Secondary Education, ed. S. Slinn and A. Sweetman. Montreal and Kingston: Queen's Policy Studies Series, McGill-Queen's University Press.

level to that of the firm or enterprise (see also Bamber, Lansbury, and Wailes 2004; Katz 1993; Voos 1994).

The data and analysis presented in this chapter point to three general conclusions. First, since the provincial government assumed responsibility for funding public education in Ontario in 1998, successive administrations have driven centralization in order to assert greater control over bargaining practices and outcomes. These efforts to centralize education policy and funding have shifted key decision-making and budgetary powers from local school boards and toward the provincial Ministry of Education. Second, the process of centralization remains dynamic and unstable. Centralized bargaining has not been institutionalized to the same extent as funding and education policy development. While teacher and support worker unions are structured in a manner that allows them to operate at a provincial level, the Ontario Public School Boards' Association (OPSBA) and other parallel organizations lack the authority to serve as a provincial bargaining agent. For the government, centralization reflects a tool to control bargaining processes and mitigate politically and socially costly labour disruptions. Successive governments may employ other tools to control the process and constrain bargaining outcomes. Finally, the perspectives of unions and school boards toward centralization are decidedly mixed. On the one hand, centralization brings the key decision-maker (the provincial government) to the bargaining table. At the same time, centralization privileges provincial actors but leads to a loss of authority for local ones. Local actors are generally aware of the potential benefits of an increasingly centralized bargaining structure, but these changes require a new discussion and understanding of the role of local actors.

The chapter proceeds as follows. The first section introduces trends in Canadian public sector collective bargaining within the broader context of Anglo-American employment relations. The second section examines the evolution of collective bargaining in Ontario's education sector since the late 1990s. This section also outlines the key stakeholders involved in education sector employment relations and collective bargaining. The third section discusses the extent to which increasingly centralized bargaining in 2005 and 2008 met and balanced the needs of stakeholders. A conclusion follows.

CANADIAN PUBLIC SECTOR BARGAINING IN CONTEXT

The level at which collective bargaining occurs exists along a spectrum from complete centralization to complete decentralization. In a completely centralized system, all employers in a specific industry or sector in a defined region or state bargain jointly and simultaneously with the union or unions representing their employees. Centralized bargaining is designed to achieve consistency in key issues, such as wages and working conditions, thus taking them out of competition. Centralization also reduces the amount of resources each party directs toward bargaining. In Ontario, the 1995 *Ontario Labour Relations Act* permits the designation of centralized agents by employers and unions. These agents have the authority to negotiate terms binding upon their affiliated constituents. At the other end of the spectrum is a completely decentralized system, where agreements are bargained at the enterprise level between individual employers and union locals. Decentralized bargaining is designed to meet the specific contextual and operational needs of individual union locals and enterprises.

A number of other bargaining systems and strategies lie between complete centralization and decentralization. Many are designed to produce outcomes that mimic more formalized forms of centralization. Pattern bargaining occurs when one party in a certain industry or sector bargains an agreement with a union or employer counterpart that becomes the standard in the entire industry or sector; pattern bargaining is generally conceived of as relatively centralized (Marshall and Merlo 1996, 2). Whipsawing and leapfrogging occur when a union or employer attempts to bargain a series of agreements with individual bargaining units that contain provisions that are increasingly desirable to them; these strategies lie somewhere between pattern bargaining and complete decentralization. Two-tiered systems of collective bargaining are also common, where some key aspects of negotiations are conducted in a (relatively) centralized fashion (e.g., wages), while others are conducted locally (e.g., scheduling).

In the private sector, there is a notion that centralized bargaining, and systems or strategies designed to produce outcomes similar to those achieved by centralization (e.g., pattern bargaining), are more useful to unions seeking to increase wages than they are for employers seeking to control costs (Warrian 1996). There is therefore a tendency to equate centralized or coordinated bargaining structures or strategies with influential unions, who leverage their relative power to establish uniform wage rates and working conditions. In cases where centralization, pattern bargaining, or other coordinated attempts are made by the union, the remuneration and working conditions demanded in negotiations are generally established based on the most stable or successful employers (or at least those that the union believes are most willing to acquiesce). Other firms must then follow suit or risk being the target of job action. However, firms can also employ these systems or strategies in order to extract gains from unionized workers. The use of such systems or strategies generally reflects the state of the industry or economy, and the willingness of either party to invoke or accept their use can change over time. Centralized and coordinated bargaining systems and strategies also reduce the likelihood that certain firms can pass on their reduced labour costs to customers in order to undermine their competitors. However, since the 1980s, the need for firms to achieve cost efficiencies amid increased competition and the processes of trade liberalization have increased considerably. In turn, union density and bargaining power have decreased, and the ability of unions to convince employers to bargain centrally has waned appreciably.

Interestingly, public sector collective bargaining has become increasingly centralized in many instances, particularly since the 1990s. This occurred as governments—in their capacity as funders and/or employers—sought to control the processes and outcomes of collective bargaining. This is particularly the case in broader public (or para-public) sectors (e.g., education, health care, social services) where intermediary employers (e.g., school and hospital boards) exist and bargaining has traditionally been less centralized than in core public sector activities where the government, through various ministries or departments, is the direct employer. In order to maintain financial gains made by governments or public sector employers throughout the budget crises of the 1990s, the scope of bargaining has been limited, the ability of public sector workers to engage in strikes and other job action has been restricted, coercive bargaining tactics have become common, and the outcomes and processes of bargaining have been increasingly legislated (Hebdon and Warrian 1999; Rose 2002, 2004; Swimmer and Bartkiw 2003; Swimmer and Thompson 1995; Warrian 1996). The subject matter of this chapter—collective bargaining in Ontario's public education sector—should therefore be viewed within the context of efforts by the state to use centralization as a mechanism to influence processes and outcomes in order to maintain budgetary control while constraining or minimizing the political costs of public sector labour disputes.

EMPLOYMENT RELATIONS AND COLLECTIVE BARGAINING IN ONTARIO'S PUBLIC EDUCATION SECTOR

In the education sector, teachers, administrators, support workers, and other staff are not employed directly by provincial Ministries of Education (MoE) but rather by school boards that act as intermediaries. Yet funding for public education (and other broader public or para-public sector activities) comes primarily or exclusively from the government in most provinces. The provincial government has been the primary funder of public education in Ontario since the introduction of Bill 160 in 1998. Prior to this, school boards were funded by a combination of property taxes and provincial grants. The operational structure and funding of school boards is partly related to the provincial government's desire to exercise control over all facets of public education while simultaneously distancing itself from issues of political accountability that invariably accompany the administration and delivery of public schools (Swimmer and Bartkiw 2003). Through the system of wholly funded but regionally dispersed school boards, the provincial government is able to ensure relative equality in per student funding levels regardless of regional economic inequalities that constrain school boards' abilities to raise revenues through property taxes. It also increases the influence of the provincial government on the broader direction and philosophy of public education while leaving day-to-day accountability for delivery in the hands of individual boards and school administrators. However, this situation can prove problematic, as the further that government distances itself from its school boards, the more it risks losing control over them.

This leads to varied and highly politicized education sector employment relations across Canada. The governance and structure of collective bargaining is highly dependent on the policies of past and current governments and varies significantly between provinces (see Schucher and Slinn 2012). For example, collective bargaining in Alberta's education sector is governed by the province's general labour relations statute, while other provinces govern education sector bargaining through their general public sector labour relations statutes (e.g., New Brunswick), special teacher or education sector legislation (e.g., Nova Scotia, Newfoundland and Labrador, Saskatchewan, and Prince Edward Island), or a combination of general, public sector, and education-specific statutes (e.g., Ontario, British Columbia, Manitoba, and Quebec). This, not surprisingly, leads to different systems of education sector collective bargaining between provinces. Fully centralized bargaining takes place in three provinces: Newfoundland and Labrador, Prince Edward Island, and New Brunswick. Each has one collective agreement for all teachers throughout the province. Two-tiered bargaining occurs in British Columbia, Saskatchewan, Nova Scotia, and Quebec, and decentralized bargaining is practiced in Manitoba, Alberta, and Ontario. However, there has been a recent shift toward increased centralization in Alberta and Ontario, both of which have made changes to their education sector funding models since the mid-1990s. The case of the latter is discussed below.

The evolution of employment relations and collective bargaining in Ontario's education sector is covered in greater detail in this volume by both Shilton (2012) and Rose (2012). Therefore, this chapter focuses primarily on understanding the restructuring of employment relations since 1998, with a particular focus on the province-led centralization of collective bargaining in 2005 and 2008. The analysis begins with a brief description of the primary stakeholders in Ontario's public education sector.

There are 72 school boards in Ontario: 31 public English-language, 29 Catholic English-language, 4 public French-language, and 8 Catholic French-language.[3] The Ontario Public School Boards' Association (OPSBA) represents and advocates on behalf of all English- and French-language public school boards, the Ontario Catholic School Trustees' Association (OCSTA) does so on behalf of the province's English-language Catholic school boards, and the Association franco-ontarienne des conseils scolaires catholiques (AFOCSC) does so on behalf of French-language Catholic school boards. School board supervisory officers (directors and superintendents) are members of the Council of Directors of Education (CODE) and their professional associations, the Ontario Public Supervisory Officials' Association (OPSOA) and the Ontario Catholic Supervisory Officers' Association (OCSOA).

Ontario's public school teachers are represented by one of four unions. These bargaining units are defined by statute rather than certification. The Ontario Secondary School Teachers' Federation (OSSTF) represents teachers in public English-language secondary schools. The Elementary Teachers' Federation of Ontario (ETFO) represents teachers in public English-language elementary schools. The Ontario English Catholic Teachers Association (OECTA) represents teachers in Catholic English-language elementary and secondary schools. The Association des Enseignantes et des Enseignants Franco-Ontariens (AEFO) represents French-language elementary and secondary teachers, in both public and Catholic schools. Support workers, including administrative and clerical staff, professional student services personnel (e.g., social workers), plant staff (e.g., trades and custodians), educational assistants, early childhood educators, and information technology staff are represented by a mixture of teacher unions, other public sector unions such as the Canadian Union of Public Employees and the Ontario Public Service Employees Union, industrial unions such as the Canadian Auto Workers and United Steelworkers, and accredited trade and professional associations such as the Association of Professional Student Services Personnel and the United Brotherhood of Carpenters and Joiners.

Principals and vice-principals belonged to their respective teacher unions until 1998, when legislation enacted by Conservative premier Mike Harris's government removed them from bargaining units. This decision was and remains a major source of contention. This contention stems largely from the increasing managerial and administrative functions and responsibilities undertaken by principals and vice-principals—who are trained primarily as educators—which can create friction and conflict and jeopardize collegiality with teachers and support staff. Public school principals and vice-principals are currently members of the Ontario Principals' Council (OPC). Catholic school principals belong to the Catholic Principals' Council of Ontario (CPCO), and French-language principals and vice-principals belong to l'Association des Directions et Directions Adjointes des écoles Franco-Ontariennes (ADFO). These are voluntary professional associations and are not bargaining agents. However, there is a growing body of research that recognizes the importance of principals and vice-principals to the education system (Leithwood, Harris, and Hopkins 2008; Noonan, Walker, and Kutsyuruba 2008; Wallin 2010), and it is quite possible (and expected by many interview subjects) that the formal influence of the OPC, CPCO, and ADFO will increase in the near future.

While the formal signatories to collective agreements are school boards and individual union locals (although legislation gives provincial union officials the authority to bargain on behalf of locals), many of the associations and organizations listed above are increasingly influential in shaping the processes and outcomes of education sector collective bargaining. The influence of the provincial government and its MoE in collective bargaining and employment relations has also increased since the late 1990s; the province no longer merely constitutes what Warrian (1996, 44) described as the "ghost at the table" in public sector bargaining. This increased influence occurred initially amid the desire of the Harris Conservatives to control and institutionalize their recent initiatives, and was perpetuated by the efforts of McGuinty's Liberal government to achieve peace and stability in public education. Other stakeholders such as the Ontario College of Teachers, post-secondary teacher training institutions, and the parents of school-aged children also play an indirect role in establishing the context of education sector employment relations and collective bargaining.

Extrinsic rewards and working conditions persist as important bargaining issues, but the influence of this multitude of stakeholders often means that wages, benefits, and conditions are overshadowed in the public eye by complex and highly politicized issues more closely related to financing, teacher-pupil ratios, the deployment and training of teachers and support staff, and student achievement. Many of these issues were once negotiated and administered primarily by individual school boards and union locals, but are increasingly negotiated by or within the scope of the provincial government and its MoE, the provincial offices of teacher unions, and other provincial-level actors. The policies and structures developed at the provincial level tend to encourage (or discourage) local school boards and unions to adopt (or resist) bargaining processes and outcomes desired by provincial-level actors. Moreover, both provincial policy initiatives and the increased involvement of MoE personnel in employment relations represent opportunities for the provincial government to influence individual collective agreements and abet the process of centralization (Rotherham 2006).

The centralization of collective bargaining was initially discussed during the deliberations leading up to the 2001 *Stability and Excellence in Education Act*. This legislation required that all collective agreements in Ontario's education sector expire simultaneously, and all subsequent agreements extend for three years. In addition to minimizing inequality, a significant motivation for centralization was to increase provincial control over education financing and maintain the gains made by the government earlier in the decade (Rose 2004). Yet the provincial government remained reluctant to assume the political risks and accountability of centralization (Rose 2002). Localized bargaining therefore persisted relatively unchanged, and the provincial government focused on increasing its control over the education sector through other initiatives such as amalgamating school boards and centralizing school board funding.

The amalgamation and the centralization of funding that took place under the Harris government were both critical in determining the processes of bargaining that subsequently took place in 2005 and 2008. During negotiations between teacher unions and school boards in 2005, there was frustration on both sides concerning the ability to come to an agreement in light of new financing schemes put in place by the McGuinty government (Anderson and Ben Jaafar 2006). These frustrations led to the initial provincial framework discussions between the OPSBA, OSSTF, ETFO, and MoE facilitators in 2005. The discussions focused primarily on determining how best to carry out negotiations under new funding arrangements. Interestingly, representatives of individual school boards were absent despite the fact that collective bargaining remained their legal responsibility (Anderson and Ben Jaafar 2006). However, representatives of individual school boards eventually became involved through the efforts of the OPSBA.

A provincial framework emerged from these discussions. The framework agreements included proportionally uniform salary increases throughout the province, additional preparation and supervision time for ETFO teachers, and reductions in class sizes and instructional time for OSSTF teachers. The framework agreements also introduced a new teacher development initiative and included a one-time sum for professional development. These gains, when coupled with substantial per student funding increases, were designed to support struggling students and increase graduation while lowering dropout rates. The agreements also bode well for the Liberal mandate to maintain labour peace and stability in the highly politicized and publicized public education sector.

In a less formalized dialogue, the MoE and OSSTF tabled the idea of four-year collective agreements. When coupled with increased funding for teacher salaries and for educational initiatives, these agreements were commensurate with the notion that the McGuinty administration was willing to pay significantly to achieve and maintain peace and stability in public education. Also significant was the establishment of the Provincial Stability Commission, which was mandated to support boards and unions in resolving issues arising from the administration of collective agreements (with an emphasis on supervision time). Taken together, the Provincial Stability Commission and framework agreements signalled the intent of the government and teacher unions to centralize some aspects of negotiations.

An equally important result of these negotiations that proved contentious in later rounds of bargaining was the fact that salary increases were proportional rather than absolute. Given that discrepancies between teacher salaries were already common—particularly between secondary and elementary teachers—the percentage-based increases exacerbated existing salary gaps. Previous rounds of local bargaining also became highly significant, because increases were based upon salaries determined in those rounds. In short, the teachers who had made the most significant gains during negotiations prior to 2005 received the most significant increases in salary, and thus had the most to gain from the proportionally based raises outlined in the framework agreements.

The 2005 negotiations marked a significant departure from past practices and philosophies in education sector collective bargaining in Ontario. Although provincial frameworks were generally viewed favourably by OSSTF, ETFO, and OPSBA-affiliated school boards—all of which benefited from significant increases in funding—some concerns were raised by certain stakeholders. While provincial OSSTF and ETFO representatives—who had assumed lead roles in the discussions surrounding the provincial framework—generally viewed the process favourably, many district and local representatives felt that the gains made came at the expense of their agency and the more specific localized and contextual needs of their members. Similarly, OPSBA representatives generally viewed the 2005 framework agreements positively while the supervisory officers and human resource managers at individual school boards had mixed feelings concerning the process and outcomes. Many saw the value of an approach that emphasized mutual gains and cooperation, but felt that provincial-level discussions did not provide them with an official voice and undermined their authority and agency at local bargaining tables. Some school board personnel also noted that they felt tremendous pressure from the MoE to conclude agreements, and that the focus on avoiding labour unrest at all costs compromised other localized priorities (e.g., student health and safety). In summation, the primary concern was that the provincial frameworks prioritized broader issues related to funding, salaries, and working conditions at the expense of more diverse and localized issues critical to the operation and employment relations of individual bargaining units.

Efforts to centralize bargaining progressed in 2008. MoE-facilitated provincial discussion tables were expanded to all teacher and support staff unions in an effort to reach agreement on key issues before the simultaneous expiration of collective agreements on August 31. Discussion tables included OPSBA staff, provincial union representatives, and representatives of individual school boards. Both of the latter advised and liaised with their counterparts at local, school board, and district levels. In general, efforts to centralize bargaining were broader in scope and more formal in 2008 than in 2005.

The provincial government imposed additional incentives for boards and unions to negotiate centrally in 2008. These incentives were intensified with the threat of penalties for parties unwilling to comply with the provincial framework or unable to conclude an agreement by a specified date. For example, agreements ratified by November 30 would include funding for a 12 percent salary increase over four years. Failure to do so would result in funding for a 4 percent increase over two years. Agreements between support workers' unions, AEFO, OECTA, and their respective school boards were reached by the deadline, and signatories received all associated funding. However, OSSTF, ETFO, and their respective school boards did not meet the deadline. This is somewhat ironic considering that these parties were directly involved in the initial efforts to centralize bargaining in 2005.

OSSTF held that local bargaining served its members well despite centralized funding. Their initial bargaining efforts were primarily focused locally, but a provincial discussion table was established in mid-November with the approval of the membership. The OSSTF bargaining team intended to use the provincial discussion table to lobby the province for enough funding to ensure that parties could negotiate locally. There is also a notion that they agreed to participate out of fear that local negotiations would prove ineffective in the absence of a provincial framework agreement and that penalties for non-compliance would be imposed. A fully funded provincial agreement was negotiated by November 30, but the deadline for local ratification was extended to 31 January 2009. All but one board ratified a collective agreement by this date.

ETFO willingly took part in provincial discussions, partly with the intent to close the salary gap that existed between their members and those of the OSSTF. However, it soon became apparent that they would not receive terms exceeding those agreed to by AEFO and OECTA. ETFO withdrew from provincial discussions and entered bargaining with individual school boards, albeit through their provincial office. The November 30 deadline passed without an agreement, largely because ETFO was unwilling to accept anything less than wage parity with OSSTF. An extension until December 5 was granted, but ETFO failed to reach a provincial framework agreement with the OPSBA by the new deadline. Provincial representatives of ETFO then advised all boards to table full briefs by 15 February 2009. Briefs were to include all items deferred pending the outcome of provincial discussions concerning salary, benefits, preparation and supervision time, and staff meetings. Moreover, boards were warned that positions similar to OPSBA would result in strike votes. In an effort to find a resolution, the MoE presented a framework agreement to both OPSBA and ETFO on 10 February 2009. Both parties were given until February 12 to respond. Included in this agreement were salary increases of nearly 10.5 percent over four years. The terms were accepted by both parties.

The process and outcomes of ETFO's 2008 provincial framework agreement are significant for two reasons. First, the final proposal was disclosed to the media prior to the imposed deadline. This put significant public pressure on ETFO to come to an agreement during the recent economic downturn. Second, ETFO was penalized for not complying with the initial deadlines imposed in 2008. This increased the very wage gap between ETFO teachers and their OSSTF, OECTA, and AEFO counterparts that the former sought to eliminate. Complicating ETFO's agenda were the market pressures imposed by the onset of a recession. These were difficult to ignore, especially considering the highly publicized and politicized nature of education sector bargaining.

The 2008 round of bargaining was viewed by many as an improvement over the 2005 negotiations, but a number of issues persisted. School board representatives noted that while they were given license to address some issues locally, confusion remained regarding the extent to which they could do so. On the other hand, there was some sentiment that because the MoE-facilitated provincial discussion tables were more explicit in defining positions on key issues, school boards were better able to focus on addressing issues related to localized irritants. However, school board representatives noted that there was little provincial support to help address many of the most contentious localized issues. Confusion over the removal of agency to address local issues was often perceived to be a trade-off for increased funding under the province's highly formulaic, centralized system of financing.

Union representatives also had mixed feelings regarding the 2008 negotiations. Most OSSTF and AEFO representatives viewed the process as beneficial and felt that the majority of their members were satisfied with the outcomes (the primary exception being representatives in the one district that did not reach an agreement based on the provincial framework). ETFO representatives were (not surprisingly) much less satisfied than their OSSTF, OECTA, and AEFO counterparts. Many expressed concern that the punitive nature of the 2008–2009 negotiations between ETFO, OPSBA, and the MoE will negatively influence future negotiations. Moreover, and despite their opinions regarding the effectiveness of bargaining in 2008, there was a common belief that centralization was not negotiated, but achieved through a coercive process replete with ultimatums and threats of penalties. Concerns regarding discrepancies over the extent to which local needs were addressed amid the 2008 negotiations were also common, but many of these discrepancies may be attributable to the relationships between local parties themselves.

Relationships between school boards, unions at all levels, and the MoE were also significantly affected by the 2008 negotiations. While some interview subjects indicated that the negotiations had little impact on these relationships, many were quick to discuss the deterioration of the relationship between the MoE and ETFO. Others pointed out that the 2008 negotiations privileged and prioritized the roles and responsibilities of provincial-level actors over local ones. Interview subjects also agreed that a system of two-tiered bargaining is increasingly necessary and desirable given the centralization of education financing. This reflects a general trend to match the structure of bargaining to the level where power and resources are controlled (Zagelmeyer 2007). Subjects also agreed that local interests remain important, and that subsequent negotiations must include mechanisms that can adequately address these issues. Where subjects lacked consensus was in regard to the formalization of the bargaining process. Many saw a need for a legislative framework that clearly defined rules, roles, responsibilities, and timelines in place of what they perceived to be a more coercive means of centralization designed to avoid real accountability for the process and outcomes of bargaining. Others preferred a less formalized approach featuring general parameters within which parties must negotiate. The primary concern of the interviewees was that formal centralization may restrict the autonomy of local parties in addressing issues critical to their needs, and that more experience with a two-tiered process is required prior to codification and definitive and restrictive legislation.

DISCUSSION

Regardless of whether it manifests in fully centralized, two-tiered, or pattern bargaining, centralization can simplify negotiations, establish clear lines of accountability, and promote consistency across bargaining units. It also aligns bargaining with the locus of control, helping coordinate employment relations, education policy, and funding decisions (Wright 2004). Some form of centralization seems critical to achieve successful collective bargaining processes and outcomes. However, the unique needs of each board and union local may be overlooked if provincial agendas are overly prioritized. Given the complexity of education sector bargaining, it is seemingly impossible to balance the needs of all boards, provincial and district union offices, and individual schools in one common collective agreement. Doing so would invariably benefit some boards and union locals at the expense of others. For example, the majority of boards in Ontario face declining enrolment, and must address challenges not faced by those boards that have stable or rising enrolment. Similarly, larger boards can benefit from economies of scale in ways that smaller boards cannot. The systemic and operational needs of rural boards also differ from those of urban boards, and there is a fear that these needs will not be addressed by provincial framework agreements that might privilege administrators, teachers, and staff in large school boards and school boards with stable or increasing enrolment.

The shift from local to two-tiered bargaining also presents logistical challenges. Establishing an integrated framework across numerous collective agreements constitutes one such challenge. This process requires a time-consuming and complex blending and levelling of the provisions within multiple contracts (for the case of collective agreement integration in British Columbia's health-care sector, see Wright 2004). Moreover, the *Ontario Education Act* defines and establishes the composition of teacher bargaining units in a fashion that may impede further centralization. This notwithstanding, a strong impetus exists to avoid purely localized bargaining. Without financial autonomy, school boards lack the ability to negotiate many issues of monetary concern. They are also unable to negotiate non-monetary issues—such as staffing levels—as the authority to do so rests with provincial actors. Local bargaining also tends to create differentiation in outcomes and inequalities not only in the salaries and working conditions of teachers and support workers, but in the quality of students' educational experiences. Further, under a system of localized bargaining, there are few restrictions on whether school boards and union locals elect to bargain entirely on their own or with an OPSBA or a provincial-level representative present.

Education sector bargaining thus presents a paradox. The signatories to collective agreements are localized, but financing is centralized. This encourages union personnel to sidestep local boards and deal directly with the holder of the purse strings. Moreover, localized bargaining is itself subject to provincial influences related to political agendas, policy changes, or the active participation of trustees' associations, the Ministry of Education, and provincial-level union representatives. While there are many historical examples of provincial-level actors imposing their agendas on local bargaining teams, or even assuming total control of bargaining in the event of an impasse, this phenomenon has increased since 2005. This is particularly common in the case of teachers' unions, where provincial staff play an increasingly prominent role relative to the diminished role of local or district personnel.

All education sector stakeholders are interested in establishing a bargaining structure that fosters legitimacy while balancing power at provincial and local levels in a manner that helps address both systemic and localized needs. Despite legislation that permits localized bargaining, complete decentralization appears to be a decreasingly viable option so long as financing and governance are highly centralized. Similarly, completely centralized negotiations tend to neglect local needs and alienate or undermine the authority and agency of local union and school board negotiators. A two-tiered structure has thus emerged as the most realistic way to balance the needs of stakeholders. Two-tiered bargaining can capture the need for financial issues to be negotiated provincially while local parties can focus on the issues that are of particular concern to them. However, the sequencing of negotiations is critical, and it is recognized that local bargaining should follow provincial negotiations so that parties understand the scope of the issues to be negotiated locally.

Although support for two-tiered bargaining exists, concerns remain. The OPSBA's lack of formal authority concerns many teacher union representatives. In fact, the ETFO anticipates pressure from its membership to avoid bargaining with the OPSBA in 2012 so long as it lacks legitimate authority. The provincial government's rules of engagement are also concerning. For example, union and school board representatives alike believed the establishment and extension of deadlines during 2008–2009 bargaining was done arbitrarily. The extensions of deadlines created animosity between and within unions and school boards. This was especially the case for those who adhered to the original deadline, only to see modifications made for others. The lack of limitations and rules governing the issues tabled in provincial discussions also impeded bargaining efforts. More procedural and substantive clarity regarding the issues to be negotiated at the provincial and local levels was desired by many interview subjects.

What is clear is that the process of collective bargaining in Ontario's education sector is evolving. This is evident in the inclusion of local school board representatives and all teacher and support staff unions in the 2008 negotiations. The 2008 negotiations also featured lengthy pre-bargaining sessions that began in November 2007. Multiple stakeholder groups were included in these discussions, which were facilitated by the MoE. The process was marked by a clear agenda focused on peace, progress, student achievement, safe and healthy working and learning environments, and cooperative employment relations. Although critics remain, there is consensus that many aspects of the process leading up to the 2008 negotiations were more inclusive and successful than those of 2005.

There is also a sentiment that two-tiered bargaining could prove increasingly successful in 2012. That success, however, hinges on a number of yet-to-be-determined variables. First, the success of a two-tiered structure is ultimately determined by how the process unfolds at the "first" (or provincial) tier. Second, if the current economic situation persists, it is unlikely that significant wage and salary increases for teachers and support workers will be tabled. This is consistent with the general trend for public sector wages to make significant gains relative to the private sector during periods of prosperity or stability, only to have these gains dissipate over time (Gunderson 1995). Third, the potential for a political shift to the right looms large, as evidenced by the outcome of the 2010 municipal election in Toronto. Most stakeholders are concerned at least to some extent that if elected, a provincial Conservative government will not prioritize or finance an agenda of peace and stability in education sector employment relations to the same extent that McGuinty's Liberals have. Many subjects expressed skepticism regarding the success and efficacy of increasingly centralized bargaining without increases to funding.

CONCLUSION

Regardless of its form, the structure, strategies, and outcomes of collective bargaining reflect the relationships between and preferences of stakeholders. In the case of Ontario's public education sector, the relationships between teachers, support workers and their unions, school boards and their provincial organizations, the Ministry of Education, and the public interest are critical in shaping processes and outcomes. Whether or not these processes and outcomes adequately balance the needs and preferences of stakeholders at provincial and local levels remains in question. What emerges from this discussion is that while the increasingly formalized two-tiered bargaining structure is preferable to other bargaining structures, there is a risk of alienating or undermining the authority or autonomy of individual school boards and union locals: the eventual signatories to collective agreements. This is largely related to the risk that emerges when the parameters within which bargaining occurs are too narrow as a result of the provincial government's need to achieve budgetary control and manage political accountability. However, a carefully implemented two-tiered bargaining structure can create a process whereby overarching issues are addressed provincially, thus allowing individual school boards and union locals to focus their efforts on highly localized and contextual issues.

NOTES

1. The term *teachers' union* is, for our intents and purposes, synonymous with the term *teachers' federation*. The term *federation* reflects the professional origins of teachers' unions and is commonly used by those within the education sector and the broader Canadian labour movement.
2. The data collected by McWilliams include nine interviews conducted in 2008 with representatives of teachers' unions, the Ontario Public School Boards Association (OPSBA), the Ministry of Education, and school board superintendents and human resource managers. The data collected by Sweeney are drawn from 37 interviews conducted in 2010 with representatives of teachers' and support workers' unions, school board superintendents and human resource managers, and principals.
3. There are also 33 "School Authorities" that govern geographically isolated, institutional, and hospital schools.

REFERENCES

Anderson, S. and S. Ben Jaafar. 2006. "Policy Trends in Ontario Education: 1990–2006." ICEC Working Paper No. 1. Ontario Institute for Studies in Education, University of Toronto. http://fcis.oise.utoronto.ca/~icec/policytrends.pdf.

Bamber, G., R. Lansbury, and N. Wailes. 2004. *International and Comparative Employment Relations: Globalisation and Developed Market Economies*. 4th ed. Thousand Oaks: Sage.

Brunelle, A. 1990. "The Changing Structure of the Forest Industry in the Pacific Northwest." In *Community and Forestry: Continuities in the Sociology of Natural Resources*, edited by R. Lee, D. Field, and R. Burch, 107-24. Boulder and San Francisco: Westview Press.

Eaton, A. and J. Kriesky. 1998. "Decentralization of Bargaining Structure: Four Cases from the U.S. Paper Industry." *Industrial Relations* 53(3): 486-515.

Gunderson, M. 1995. "Public Sector Compensation." In *Public Sector Collective Bargaining in Canada*, edited by G. Swimmer and M. Thompson, 103-34. Kingston, ON: IRC Press.

Hebdon, B. and P. Warrian. 1999. "Coercive Bargaining: Public Sector Restructuring under the Ontario Social Contract, 1993–1996." *Industrial and Labor Relations Review* 52(2): 196-212.

Herod, A. 1997. "Labour's Spatial Praxis and the Geography of Contract Bargaining in the US East Coast Longshore Industry, 1953–1989." *Political Geography* 16(2): 145-69.

Holmes, J. 2004. "Rescaling Collective Bargaining: Union Responses to Restructuring in the North American Automotive Industry." *Geoforum* 35(1): 9-21.

Katz, H. 1993. "The Decentralization of Collective Bargaining: A Literature Review and Comparative Analysis." *Industrial and Labor Relations Review* 47(1): 3-24.

Leithwood, K., A. Harris, and D. Hopkins. 2008. "Seven Strong Claims about Successful School Leadership." *School Leadership and Management* 28(1): 27-42.

Marshall, R. and A. Merlo. 1996. "Pattern Bargaining." *International Economic Review* 45(1): 239-55.

Noonan, B., K. Walker, and B. Kutsyuruba. 2008. "Trust in the Contemporary Principalship." *Canadian Journal of Educational Administration and Policy* 85: 1-17.

Rose, J. 2002. "The Assault on School Teacher Bargaining in Ontario." *Industrial Relations* 57(1): 100-28.

—. 2004. "Public Sector Bargaining: From Retrenchment to Consolidation." *Industrial Relations* 59(2): 271-94.

—. 2012. "The Evolution of Teacher Bargaining in Ontario." In *Dynamic Negotiations: Teacher Labour Relations in Canadian Elementary and Secondary Education*, edited by S. Slinn and A. Sweetman, 199-220. Montreal and Kingston: Queen's Policy Studies Series, McGill-Queen's University Press.

Rotherham, A. 2006. *Collective Bargaining in Public Education*. Conference Report. Newport, Rhode Island.

Schucher, K. and S. Slinn. 2012. "Crosscurrents: Comparative Review of Elementary and Secondary Teacher Collective Bargaining Structures in Canada." In *Dynamic Negotiations: Teacher Labour Relations in Canadian Elementary and Secondary Education*, edited by S. Slinn and A. Sweetman, 13-49. Montreal and Kingston: Queen's Policy Studies Series, McGill-Queen's University Press.

Shilton, E. 2012. "Collective Bargaining for Teachers in Ontario: Central Power, Local Responsibility." In *Dynamic Negotiations: Teacher Labour Relations in Canadian Elementary and Secondary Education*, edited by S. Slinn and A. Sweetman, 221-246. Montreal and Kingston: Queen's Policy Studies Series, McGill-Queen's University Press.

Sweeney, B. and J. Holmes. Forthcoming. "Problematizing the Agency of Labour: The Case of Pulp and Paper Workers in Port Alice and Port Alberni, British Columbia." Submitted for publication.

Swimmer, G. and T. Bartkiw. 2003. "The Future of Public Sector Collective Bargaining in Canada." *Journal of Labor Research* 24(4): 579-95.

Swimmer, G. and M. Thompson. 1995. *Public Sector Collective Bargaining in Canada: Beginning of the End or End of the Beginning?* Kingston, ON: IRC Press.

Voos, P. 1994. "An Economic Perspective on Contemporary Trends in Collective Bargaining." In *Contemporary Collective Bargaining in the Private Sector*, edited by P. Voos, 1-23. Madison, IN: IRRA.

Wallin, D. 2010. "Wisdom for the Ages from the Sages: Manitoba Senior Administrators Offer Advice to Aspirants." *Canadian Journal of Educational Administration
and Policy* 103: 1-22.

Warrian, P. 1996. *Hard Bargain: Transforming Public Sector Labour-Management
Relations.* Toronto: McGilligan.

Widenor, M. 1995. "Diverging Patterns: Labor in the Pacific Northwest Wood
Products Industry." *Industrial Relations* 34(3): 441-63.

Wright, D. 2004. "Options for Teacher-Employer Collective Bargaining." Discussion Paper. British Columbia School Trustees Association, Victoria.

Zagelmeyer, S. 2007. "Determinants of Collective Bargaining Centralization:
Evidence from British Establishment Data." *Journal of Industrial Relations* 49(2):
227-45.

Chapter 10

LABOUR RELATIONS IN THE QUEBEC K–11 EDUCATION SECTOR: LABOUR REGULATION UNDER CENTRALIZATION

JEAN-NOËL GRENIER AND MUSTAPHA BETTACHE

The Quebec primary and secondary education sector is a product of the Quiet Revolution of the 1960s when the government established the Ministry of Education (now called the Ministry of Education, Leisure and Sports) to replace the Department of Public Instruction (Département de l'instruction publique).[1] This chapter aims to describe the current system of collective bargaining and labour relations in this sector. The underlying theme is that of progressive centralization of collective bargaining and labour management relations at the provincial level. The discussion is built around two questions of inquiry: (a) To what extent does the present regime of centralized bargaining promote cooperative labour relations? and (b) Is this model able to come to terms with the pressures induced by the current Reform agenda and provide the conditions for successful implementation at the local level? The chapter begins with a description of the basic features of the K–11 education system. We then move on to a discussion of the historical evolution of the collective bargaining regime. The final sections consider the outcomes of collective bargaining in terms of process, conflict, and working conditions.

Dynamic Negotiations: Teacher Labour Relations in Canadian Elementary and Secondary Education, ed. S. Slinn and A. Sweetman. Montreal and Kingston: Queen's Policy Studies Series, McGill-Queen's University Press.

THE QUEBEC K–11 EDUCATION SYSTEM:
BASIC FEATURES AND CURRENT CONTEXT

The Quebec K–11 education system is rather recent in historical terms.[2] Until the mid-1960s the public education system was a product of co-management between the government and religious congregations, and access was usually limited to primary schooling with a minority of pupils going on to secondary school (Fullan 1999, 27-28). Those men who moved on to further education attended Classical Colleges, which prepared them for liberal arts professions; while women were directed to Normal Schools (Écoles Normales), which prepared them for teaching or nursing careers (Desprès-Poirier 1999; see also Berthelot 2002 and Graveline 2003). Classical Colleges and Normal Schools were under the tight control of the Catholic Church and of religious congregations (Graveline 2007). This was especially true in the larger centres of Montreal and Quebec City, which had important contingents of religious personnel. Finally, in the years prior to the Quiet Revolution, the K–11 school system was strongly decentralized and it is estimated that there existed no less than 1,500 school boards in the province (Gagnon 2003).

Since then, the situation has greatly evolved and the Quebec K–11 education system has undergone rationalization and restructuring that have reduced considerably the number of school boards and removed religious control of schools. The latest reorganization of school structures was in 1997 when the provincial government amalgamated school boards and reorganized their affiliations along language lines rather than the historical Catholic-Protestant distinction. Today there are a total of 72 school boards across the province of which 60 are francophone, nine are anglophone, one has a mixed status (for both French and English on the North-Shore), and two are for aboriginals from the north (Commissions scolaires Crie and Kativik). School boards are managed by elected commissioners and hire their own school personnel. The boards vary in size, ranging from 700 to over 71,000 students for the largest boards in the Gatineau, Quebec City, and Montreal urban areas. The median size of a school board is 8,600 students. School boards draw 76 percent of their revenues directly from the provincial government while 15 percent is accounted for by local school taxes. Alongside the public school boards, a thriving private school system, subsidized at a level of 50 percent of operating costs, enrolled 6 percent and 18 percent of primary and secondary school pupils, respectively, in 2009. The text box presents some of the basic features of the K–11 system.

The total education budget in Quebec is the second-largest after health care and social services. Given the aging population, pressures for increased public spending in health care, and a policy of fiscal restraint, education saw its share of the provincial spending budget decline by an average of 1.5 percent per year over the 1996–2006 decade (Ministère de

Basic Features of the Quebec K–11 Education System

- The governing body is the Ministry of Education, Leisure and Sports (MELS).
- The total education budget is $14 billion, representing 24.6 percent of the provincial spending budget and 7.4 percent of Gross Domestic Product (GDP).
- Total spending at the school board level stood at $10.724 billion in current 2009 dollars and 3.6 percent of GDP.
- Spending per capita at the school board level is estimated at $1,393, and spending per student is estimated at $10,128.
- In 2007/08 student enrolment in public schools was 1,185,970: 925,688 in the youth sector and 260,282 in adult education; 18.1 percent of youth 19 years of age have not obtained a grade 12 diploma.
- A total of 822,294 youth attended French-speaking schools, 101,320 English-speaking schools, and 2,074 the Crie and Kativik schools.
- There are 2,362 public schools: 1,741 offer only preschool and primary school services; 427 offer only high school; 194 offer preschool, primary, and secondary education services; 193 offer vocational training for youth; and 189 are centres for adult education.
- Most schools have a daycare centre integrated within their facilities or under their authority.
- School boards employ 118,083 staff calculated in terms of full-time equivalents. Among non-managerial staff, 73,606 are teachers, 5,271 are non-teaching professionals, and 33,506 are support staff.

Source: Ministère de l'Éducation du Loisir et du Sport (2009).

l'Éducation du Loisir et du Sport 2009, 15). This trend has been somewhat reversed in recent years as a result of developments linked to the Reform package—Renouveau pédagogique or Pedegogical Renewal—and outcomes of collective bargaining, which will be discussed later on in this chapter. Declining student-teacher ratios, more hours of teaching for language skills, and the growth of adult education have contributed to an increase in the number of school personnel (full-time equivalents) even though the number of pupils in the public K–11 sector has declined by more than 100,000 over the past ten years (see Table 1).

As will be discussed later in this chapter, union-management relations are set within a three-tier system of labour regulation that involves union central bodies, labour federations, and employer associations at the provincial level; at the school board level, management and teachers' unions

TABLE 1
School Board Personnel, Full-Time Equivalents, 1999/00 to 2006/07

	1999/00	2000/01	2001/02	2002/03	2003/04	2004/05	2005/06	2006/07
Total	108,772	111,464	113,184	115,751	116,203	115,206	114,553	118,083
Teachers	71,288	71,918	71,984	72,820	72,606	71,596	71,136	73,606
Upper management	1,080	1,076	1,079	1,097	1,143	1,166	1,155	1,246
Principals	3,661	3,713	3,723	3,772	3,807	3,796	3,681	3,690
Mid-management	685	680	698	721	730	735	745	764
Non-teaching professionals	4,003	4,208	4,453	4,810	4,926	4,992	5,111	5,271
Support staff	28,055	29,869	31,247	32,531	32,991	32,921	32,725	33,506

Source: Fédération des commissions scolaires du Québec (2008).

are responsible for compliance with and enforcement of the provincial collective bargaining agreement. Local parties also negotiate local agreements on various issues permitted by law and for which the provincial parties delegate bargaining to the local level. As of 2010, provincial collective bargaining involves on the union side the Fédération des syndicats de l'enseignement, the Fédération autonome de l'enseignement, and the Quebec Provincial Association of Teachers. School boards are required to create bargaining committees composed of representatives of the school boards and the Ministry of Education. The employer associations are the Comité patronal de négociation pour les commissions scolaires francophones and the Comité patronal de négociation pour les commissions scolaires anglophones. Two other employee associations and management committees bargain agreements for the Crie and Kativik school boards.

The present day context of union-management relations is dominated by traditional issues such as wages and working conditions and debate over the direction and value of the Reform package. More than two decades of government restraint on public sector compensation have had adverse consequences to the point where, job security aside, public sector workers in Quebec no longer enjoy a sizeable compensation premium compared to their private sector counterparts (Grenier 2008, 2010). Other related issues are workloads, work-life balance, and access to regular employment for non-permanent teachers.

The Reform program, launched in 2000, aimed at increasing the ratio of people entering the workforce with at least a high school diploma by changing the curriculum, reducing class size, introducing competency-based teaching, and decentralizing decision-making on related issues to school boards and schools. Other important elements are the obligation for schools to develop special projects, the emergence of selective programs in public schools, and the integration of special-needs students into regular classrooms. Schools and school boards must develop success plans and are held accountable for increasing success rates.

The Fédération des syndicats de l'enseignement (FSE-CSQ; affiliated with the Centrale des syndicats du Québec), the Centrale des syndicats du Québec (CSQ), and the Fédération autonome de l'enseignement (FAE) have engaged the government in an intense public debate over the Reform program. Labour unions argue that Reform has delivered little in terms of teachers' individual autonomy and instead has resulted in increased workloads and confusion over their role. The unions also contend that greater accountability has come with little in terms of additional resources. From the union perspective, integration of special-needs children in regular classrooms has caused the teaching environment to deteriorate. Unions also oppose selective programs restricted to gifted children on the grounds that they stimulate competition among public schools and redirect resources away from regular and special-needs pupils. These issues, which were raised in the collective bargaining rounds in 2005 and 2010, and the looming battle over the role and funding of private schools may open the door for a new era of politicization of labour relations in public education.

This is not to say all elements of Reform are opposed by teachers and their representative organizations. The decline in student-teacher ratios in underprivileged areas is, for example, strongly supported, as are the increased funding for special projects and the different measures to encourage teacher involvement in school management and organization.

One of the goals of a labour regulation regime is to foster labour-management cooperation and contribute to resolving major issues facing workers and employers alike. It is with those principles in mind that we will first look at why the regime developed a centralized model of collective bargaining. We will then examine in detail the institutional requirements set forth by the current legislative framework.

THE COLLECTIVE BARGAINING AND LABOUR RELATIONS REGIME

The Path to Centralization

The current regime of labour relations and collective bargaining in the K–11 education sector is set by the requirements of Bill 37[3] and of the *Quebec Labour Code*.[4] Bill 37 sets out the structure and process of collective bargaining and identifies the issues that are bargained at the central bargaining table, at the sector level, and finally at the local level. Under the current regime, annual wage increases and other monetary issues are settled at the provincial cross-sector level, and normative and work organization issues are discussed at the sector level. Local bargaining, at the individual school board level, is residual and dependent on the dynamics of sector-level bargaining. Unions have the right to strike over issues discussed at either the sector or cross-sector levels, but strikes and lockouts are not permitted at the school board level.

The Quebec public sector and education labour relations regime can thus be conceived as a departure from the principles of the Wagner Model of worker representation and collective bargaining (Bolduc 1982; Bouchard 1982). That is to say, the legal employers are school boards, union recognition is also at the school board level, and unions enjoy a monopoly for worker representation—but most crucial issues are dealt with at the provincial bargaining table, and the provincial government has the final say on all strategic issues. Centralization was achieved through state intervention in response to labour troubles and conflicts that emerged at the school board level in the period prior to 1969. In that sense centralization was the culmination of different forms of government intervention in response to the development of unionization among teachers and conflicts at the school board level (Gaudreault 2005; Rouillard 2009). The text box "From Corporations to Unionization" offers an overview of the development of unionism among teachers and government intervention in labour relations.

The school year 1966/67 is considered to have had the greatest impact on the structure of collective bargaining and worker representation among public school teachers. From November 1966 to February 1967 more than 15,000 primary and secondary school teachers went on a legal strike over issues of wages and compensation and the right to bargain locally.[5] Under intense pressure by the population, the Union Nationale government enacted Bill 25, *Loi assurant le droit de l'enfant à l'éducation et instituant un nouveau régime de convention collective dans le secteur scolaire.* This Bill not only imposed back-to-work legislation, but also set one single date for the expiry of all collective agreements in the education sector and a provincial salary grid (Boivin 1972, 1993; Hébert 1982).

Centralization was pushed further in the 1970s with the result that collective bargaining and labour relations in the public sector became increasingly politicized as unions took a radical stand and governments responded through the use or threat of special legislation. This was the case in 1971 with Bill 46, *Loi sur le régime de négociation du secteur public et parapublic.* After a long period of struggle that was marked by occupations of public buildings, the imprisonment of labour leaders, and a ten-day general strike, the government enacted special legislation targeting teachers. In opposition to provincial spending cuts, major affiliated public sector and broader public sector unions formed an alliance called Common Fronts. There have been five Common Fronts since 1971, and they have differed in composition, size, and ability to maintain a unified

From Corporations to Unionization

- 1845–1936: Founding of Association des instituteurs laïcs de Québec, Association des instituteurs laïcs de Montréal, Provincial Association of Protestant Teachers, and Alliance catholique des professeurs de Montréal.
- 1936–1946: Thirteen newly created associations of Catholic rural women teachers join rank to form the Fédération catholique des institutrices rurales de la province de Québec (FCIR) while male teachers in rural areas create the Fédération provinciale des instituteurs ruraux (FPIR). More than 1,000 collective agreements are signed with local authorities.
- 1944/45: *Loi sur les relations ouvrières*. Right of association and collective bargaining but no right to strike in public services, compulsory arbitration. More than 200 school boards and local teachers' associations resort to compulsory arbitration. The three Catholic federations (FCIR, FPIR, and Fédération des instituteurs catholiques des villes) join ranks to form the Corporation générale des instituteurs et institutrices catholiques de la Province de Québec (CIC).
- 1946: *Loi pour assurer le progrès de l'éducation*. Minimum annual salary for rural teachers (women) is set at $600, but the right to compulsory arbitration for rural teachers is removed.
- 1950: *Code scolaire* is amended to allow school boards to fire all teachers at the end of the school year without any recourse. The unionization drive is stopped. In 1952 collective agreements are in force in only 23 school boards.
- 1959: Government makes membership to the CIC compulsory for all Catholic teachers in primary and secondary Catholic schools. Rand formula for union dues check-off. CIC membership grows from 16,000 to 28,000.
- 1964: The Ministry of Education and regional school boards are created. The 200 local unions affiliated with the CIC are regrouped into 60 unions. In 1965 clerical teachers join the CIC.
- 1965–1970: Bill 25, *Loi assurant le droit de l'enfant à l'éducation et instituant un nouveau regime de convention collective dans le secteur scolaire* (S.Q., C.-63, 1967), imposes back-to-work legislation, extends all collective bargaining agreements so they all come to term in 1968, and introduces provincial collective bargaining. The CIC, the Provincial Association of Catholic Teachers (PACT), and the Provincial Association of Protestant Teachers (PAPT) are obligated to form a single provincial-level bargaining committee. CIC becomes the Corporation des enseignants du Québec (CEQ), abandons its confessional and corporatist nature, and becomes increasingly radical and militant.
- 1970–1972: Bill 46, *Loi sur le régime de négociation du secteur public et para-public*, requires provincial collective bargaining for all public sector unions. First Common Front (an alliance of public sector unions) to oppose cuts in provincial spending budgets.
- 1975/76 and 1979/80: Second and third Common Fronts. Collective agreements are signed freely by the union peak councils but under the threat of legislative intervention.
- 1982/83: Fourth Common Front. The government-imposed settlement and repressive legislation targets teachers and other members of the CEQ. Wage freezes and concessions are legislated through Bills 70 and 111.
- 1998: CEQ becomes la Centrale des syndicats du Québec (CSQ).

Source: Centrale des syndicats du Québec (2000).

union agenda during the course of bargaining. Under the Common Fronts, the unions agree to a common set of demands and proposals over issues negotiated at the central bargaining table, namely, annual wage increases and the total compensation package.

In 1975/76, it was public pressure following a series of school board lockouts that prompted government intervention (Bill 95).[6] Successive legislation also built the institutional framework of centralization by giving structure to central employer committees and effectively removing meaningful bargaining from the school board level. This was the case of the third Common Front of 1979/80. In 1979, Bills 55[7] and 59[8] established provincial employer bargaining committees, created a Council on Essential Services (Conseil des services essentiels), reinforced the authority of the provincial Treasury Board over the mandates of the provincial employer committees, and imposed compulsory arbitration to settle local issues. The fourth round under the Common Front in 1982/83 was held in the midst of a severe recession to which the Parti Québécois government responded by introducing measures to reduce the public deficit. This time special legislation was not used to coerce compromise from unions but to impose concessions and take-backs in working conditions. In 1982, Bill 105[9] imposed severe cuts in most working conditions, including wages, pensions, and the partial loss of cost-of-living adjustments for a two-year period. With this legislation, the government bypassed the normal collective bargaining process and imposed working conditions and collective agreements on all bargaining parties in the public sector. Unlike other public sector workers, public school teachers walked off the job. In response, Bill 111[10] imposed severe fines, loss of seniority, and the possible dismissal for teachers unwilling to go back to work (Boivin 1993).

The present day regime of labour relations and collective bargaining in the Quebec K–11 sector is a product of the events presented above. Collective bargaining was progressively centralized through government intervention in response to pressure from the population and the inability of school boards to tip the balance of power in their favour. This culminated in the legislative interventions of the 1970s and the emergence of provincial employer bargaining committees and the Common Fronts. The life expectancy of these alliances, which independent unions such as the nurses' federation have joined on a sporadic basis, is limited to the duration of the bargaining process. After the bargaining round of 1982, public sector unions were unable to recreate this type of unity until the most recent round in 2010. There are many reasons for this, but one may point out union rivalry and the requirements of Bill 37 that bargaining be held mostly on a sector by sector basis.

Collective Bargaining under Bill 37

The Parti Québécois government, prior to its electoral defeat in 1985, introduced Bill 37, the central piece of legislation governing public sector collective bargaining today. We start our exposé with a discussion of the current structure of collective bargaining and the organization of the parties, and then move on to consider the issues that are discussed at each level of bargaining.

The current structure of collective bargaining. The stated goal of the government was to reduce the political tensions that accompanied public sector collective bargaining, but Bill 37 was also a response to criticism from public sector employers' organizations who felt they were being bypassed by provincewide collective bargaining (Leclerc and Quimper 2003). The government hoped that by establishing a clear process and structure for bargaining, it could depoliticize union-management relations and reduce conflicts that had accompanied each bargaining round since the late 1960s (Tardif 1993, 134-36). Bill 37 establishes the structure of collective bargaining, determines what issues are discussed at each level, requires employers to form provincial bargaining committees, and determines a timetable for the commencement of bargaining and the exercise of the right to strike. Table 2 details the main features of collective bargaining under Bill 37.

TABLE 2
The Structure of Collective Bargaining in the Quebec Education Sector

Level	Parties	Issues	Right to Strike
Provincial cross-sector	Main union central bodies CSN, CSQ, and FTQ Treasury Board and Ministerial Committee	Wages and compensation	Yes after mediation
Provincial education sector K–11	Union federations FSE-CSQ, FAE, and QPAT Four provincial employers' associations committees	Normative issues and ancillary from the central table	Yes after mediation
Local or regional school board	Local teachers' unions School boards	Items identified in Annexe A of Bill 37 and on which parties agree according to article 58 of Bill 37	No Voluntary mediation and voluntary arbitration Continuous bargaining

Note: CSN = Confédération des syndicats nationaux. CSQ = Centrale des syndicats du Québec. FTQ = Fédération des travailleurs et travailleuses du Québec. FSE-CSQ = Fédération des syndicats de l'enseignement–Centrale des syndicats du Québec. FAE = Fédération autonome de l'enseignement. QPAT = Quebec Provincial Association of Teachers.

Source: Bill 37, *Loi sur le régime de négociation des conventions collectives dans les secteurs public et parapublic*, L.R.Q., ch. R-8.2, art. 25, 44-48 and 52-58.

A provincial-level central bargaining table is established to discuss compensation (art. 52) and other issues after agreement of all parties concerned (e.g., parental leave, retirement plans, regional disparities, benefits). Formally, these are agreed to for the first year of the contract only, but in effect the parties usually settle wage and compensation for the duration of the collective agreement (Boivin and Grenier, forthcoming; Leclerc and Quimper 2003, 188-89). This level is responsible for co-ordination of the sector-level bargaining tables, to ensure that discussions and agreements fit within the parameters set at the central bargaining table. Given the emergence of non-affiliated unions representing key occupations such as civil servants, nurses, support staff, and health-care and social services professionals, the central table has been informally broadened to include these groups.

Issues and demands directly related to education are discussed at the sector-level bargaining tables. Primary and secondary education are grouped together and are separate from the colleges, which have their own bargaining agents and a separate collective agreement. Four man-agement committees are established by law: one for francophone school boards, another for anglophone school boards, and one each for the Crie and Kativik school boards.[11] These are constituted of representatives of the school board federations and the Ministry of Education, Leisure and Sports. The Treasury Board can send observers to each bargaining table. In addition, Bill 37 requires separate bargaining agents for each occupa-tional category. Teachers, non-teaching professionals, and support staff each have their own bargaining committees. The number of bargaining agents is then determined by the number of different unions or union federations representing workers from each occupational category. In the case of primary and secondary school teachers there are three bargaining agents: the Quebec Provincial Association of Teachers (QPAT), which bargains for the nine unions in the anglophone school board sector; the Fédération des syndicats de l'enseignement (FSE), which represents teach-ers at the Crie and Kativik school boards; and the FSE and the Fédération autonome de l'enseignement (FAE), which both represent teachers in the francophone school boards. Thus, unlike their anglophone counterparts, francophone teachers and their local unions face interunion rivalry. The FSE remains the largest union federation representing over 50 school board unions and their members, while the FAE represents nine school board unions from the Montreal and Gatineau regions.

These parties can discuss all normative issues with the exception of those which article 52 of the Bill deems to be bargained at the school board level. The parties can also agree to decentralize bargaining over other normative issues (but not those involving direct costs). However, in practice labour federations favour standardization of contract language and attempt to avoid delegation to the school board level. Typically, school board level negotiations cover issues such as union recognition and representation, discipline, union and employee participation, the organization of work, health and safety, grievance procedures and arbitration over local matters, teacher training, and the rules regarding internal mobility and displacements.[12]

The bargaining process is set out in Table 3. The legislation determines at what moment bargaining begins, the timetable for the presentation of union demands and management responses at the sector level, and the delays that must be respected prior to the exercise of the right to strike. In case of conflict, the parties must resort to mediation for a period of 60 days and then wait another period of 20 days between the mediator's report and the notice of an impending conflict. They then must wait another seven working days between the notification and the date of a legal strike. In short, the process imposes many delays between an impasse and the exercise of a strike.

TABLE 3
Bargaining Process under Bill 37

National, Cross-Sector	Sector Level	Local/Regional
November 30th : Report from the Institut de la recherche et d'information sur la rémunération (Bill 37, art. 19). Government and union proposals no later than 30 days following the report (art. 111.8, *Quebec Labour Code*). Right to strike and/or lockout: 20 days after the Treasury Board receives a notice of pending conflict (Bill 37, art. 50; and *Quebec Labour Code*, art. 111.11).	Process starts 180 days prior to the expiry of the current collective bargaining agreement (CBA) or Decree (*Quebec Labour Code*, art. 111.7). Union initial demands must be presented no less than 150 days prior to the expiry of the CBA or Decree (art. 111.8, *Quebec Labour Code*). Management offers and demands must be presented no later than 30 days after the union proposals (art. 111.8, *Quebec Labour Code*). Right to strike: Nomination of a mediator following a demand from one or other party (art. 46, Bill 37). The right to strike is acquired 20 days after the mediator's report.	Following an agreement at the sector level on the items for which bargaining at the individual school board is determined best suited (art. 57, Bill 37). At any time for the items determined in Appendix A of Bill 37. No requirements concerning the presentation of union and management demands and offers. Strike or lockout is not allowed (art. 111.14, *Quebec Labour Code*), but possibility of mediation and voluntary arbitration at the request of one of the local bargaining agents (art. 62-65, Bill 37).

Source: *Loi sur régime de négociation des conventions collectives dans les secteurs public et parapublic*, L.R.Q., ch. R-8.2.

Local bargaining is residual from the sector-level agreement to the extent that the timetable for local bargaining depends on agreement at the sector level. While bargaining over issues clearly identified as local matters can start at any time in the process, this occurs rarely since the labour federations and their local unions prefer settling sector-level issues first.

Does this mean that local unions and school boards are bystanders observing, like the general public, the political Grand Ballet of collective bargaining and political jousting between the peak labour councils and government representatives?

The answer to this question is often a resounding yes. Many observers have criticized the Quebec approach on the basis that the centralized and political nature of collective bargaining is unable to deliver solutions for local problems and that standardization of contract language is unsuited to the decentralized nature of the public education system (Hébert 1995; Morin 1985). Others have criticized the model on the basis that the role of local parties is limited to applying and enforcing rules and regulations determined above their heads and with which they do not necessarily agree (Bolduc 1982; Bouchard 1982; Hébert 1995).

Local parties do, however, play a key role in issues related to work organization and how agreements over specific issues at the sector level are translated in actual practice. Issues such as teacher involvement in decision-making and assignment, unpaid leave, bumping rights and internal mobility, the annual teaching calendar, and work-life balance are left to the dynamics of local bargaining. Needless to say, under the current regime of voluntary binding arbitration, the content and process leading to local agreements depends greatly on the quality of labour relations between the school board and the local union. The main theme is variability with some form of isomorphism through the influence of the teachers' and the school boards' federations who promote best practices and provide information and technical support for local bargaining agents.

In summary, the emergence and consolidation of the current centralized labour relations regime is the result of government response to the militancy and mobilization of public sector workers and the political consequences of strikes. Teachers in public education were among the most militant workers; they often challenged special legislation and opposed the progressive centralization of union-management relations at the sector level. If centralization facilitates government intervention to end conflicts or prevent the exercise of an impending strike, it increases the political nature of public sector collective bargaining as demonstrated by the Common Fronts of the 1970s. This was a time of political turbulence in the province, and central labour organizations sought to use public sector collective bargaining to challenge overall government economic and social policies. Government responses were quite predictable: clear refusal to bargain political issues and the recourse to special ad hoc legislation.

COLLECTIVE BARGAINING OUTCOMES IN A TIME OF RESTRAINT

Hébert's (1995) analysis of the outcomes of the collective bargaining regime identifies three distinct periods: the Emergence or Introductory Period (1960–1971); the Period of Turbulence, which is linked to institutionalization of the centralized system and the emergence of Common Fronts (1972–1982); and, finally, what he calls Marking Time (1982–1994). These correspond roughly to three distinct periods of Canadian public sector development identified by Rose (2004): expansion (1962–1970s), restraint (1980s), and retrenchment (1990s). Rose adds that since the late 1990s, public sector labour relations have entered a period of consolidation in which governments have protected the gains made during the period of retrenchment and labour unions have sought to recover the concessions from the 1980s and 1990s.

Our historical account ties into these two lines of analysis (see also Déom and Grenier 2009). Indeed, during the 1960s, teachers in Quebec acquired the right to strike and union representation spread rapidly in public education. The most important result of this period was organizational in that unions developed complex structures of representation that tied together local and sector-level representation and acquired expertise in collective bargaining. From a government point of view, the most important result was the gradual transfer of bargaining authority away from school boards to the provincial government and the development of an institutional framework to support centralization. If centralization was a strategic option pursued by other public sector workers, it was imposed on public school teachers who had always favoured area-wide or regional collective bargaining (Hébert 1995, 210-11). The 1970s were a rather turbulent period with large Common Fronts resorting to strikes and the government resorting to special legislation suspending the right to strike and ordering workers back to work. Substantive outcomes were, however, positive for public sector workers and those in education. Most government decrees, except the one in 1982, met the demand of public sector workers in terms of base wage increases, cost-of-living adjustments, employment security provisions, and maternity leave (Beaucage 1989; Déom 1982; Hébert 1995, 218-20). Thus, during the expansionary years as labelled by Rose (2004), teachers, like other public sector workers in Quebec, benefited from important improvements in working conditions.

The eras of restraint and consolidation overlap collective bargaining under the current regime as set out by Bill 37 (Déom and Grenier 2009). Union-management relations have, for the most part, been conducted in the context of severe recessions and, in Quebec especially, mounting deficits and public debt. Table 4 summarizes the major outcomes in terms of process and substantive results for the period since 1985.

TABLE 4
Collective Bargaining Outcomes under Bill 37

Round	Context	Agreement/Decree	Outcomes
1985–1987	No Common Front Bill 37	Agreement No strike	Salary increases, parental leave
1988–1990	No Common Front	Strike in education (5 days) Agreement	Salary increases, additional increases for substitute teachers, part-time contracts for non-permanent teachers
1991–1992	No Common Front Recession	Agreement No strike	Salary increases and pay relativity List for hiring priority in education (based on seniority)
1994	No bargaining Recession	Bill 102 extending previous CBA until 1995	Wage freeze, mandatory 2 days of unpaid leave
1995	No Common Front Referendum	Agreement to extend CBA until 1998	Three annual salary increases, access to full retirement at age 55 if 35 years of service or age 60 if 20 years of service
1997	Balanced budget legislation 6% cut in wage bill	Agreement No strike	Wage freeze, reduction in salary insurance benefits, voluntary early retirement program
1998–2002	No Common Front	Agreement No strike	Wage increase of 9% over 4 years, partial cost-of-living adjustment for pensions
2004	New Liberal government No Common Front	Decree (Bill 142) No strike	6-year-term CBA Wage freezes for 2004 and 2005 2% annual increases (2006–2009)
2010	Liberal government Common Front	Agreement in principle	5-year-term CBA 7.5% base wage increase over the life of the agreement Productivity agreement with possible additional 3% increase in base wages Easier access to contracts for non-permanent teachers Issues related to Reform

Note: CBA = collective bargaining agreement.
Source: Centrale des syndicats du Québec (2010).

Since 1985 strike activity has all but come to a grinding halt; teachers have walked off the job only once, in 1988, for a period of ten days. Unlike the previous years, the government has resorted to special legislation only once, in 2005, and even then there was no threat of an impending general strike in the public sector including public education. What is also remarkable of the period since 1985 is the difficulty public sector unions have had in forming a Common Front. There are many reasons for this. Union rivalries in education, health, and social services are often cited, but a review of union demands since 1987 reveals that sector-specific and occupation-specific issues have climbed to the top of the bargaining agenda, making overarching union coalitions difficult to generate or sustain (Déom and Grenier 2009; Grenier and Malo 2008).

In the period since 1985, the parties have come to negotiated settlements in seven out of nine bargaining rounds, a sharp contrast to the prevailing tensions of the 1960s and 1970s. The nine bargaining rounds have been held in a context of either an economic or a public financial crisis (rounds of 1991/92, 1994, and 1997) or when the government of the day had other political imperatives such as a referendum on sovereignty or an upcoming provincial election (1995 and 2002). The contract extensions of 1994 and 1995 are examples of the political sensitivity of public sector labour relations. The close political ties between the Quebec labour movement and the Parti Québécois, and the government's more active labour market agenda, explain the willingness of the public sector unions to agree to such extensions. One interesting outcome has been the length of the agreements or, in 2005, of the decrees.[13] Under the *Quebec Labour Code* (art. 111.1), public sector collective agreements are limited to a maximum length of three years, but recent agreements or decrees have longer terms. The main reasons for this phenomenon could be attributed to the recent trend toward longer-term collective agreements in major industries in Quebec; the declining willingness of governments to negotiate with the representatives of their employees on a recurring basis; the length of the bargaining process; the decline in union militancy, which may motivate union leadership to seek extended periods of labour peace; the determination of governing parties to avoid entering into collective bargaining at the same time as they prepare for elections; and the desire of the union leaderships to stabilize gains made over compensation issues as a consequence of past experiences with compensation take-backs during periods of fiscal crisis. It is difficult to identify the long-term consequences of these settlements, but one may point out the decline in union-management conflicts, a certain depoliticization of public sector labour relations, and a decline in unions' capacity to mobilize their members.

In terms of substantive outcomes, the picture is much bleaker in the years since 1985 than in the previous period (Grenier 2010). Following the 1988 strike, teachers saw improvement in working conditions for non-permanent staff, and in 1992 and 1995 they were able to bargain lower criteria for qualifying for full retirement benefits. They did, however, accept concessions in 1994, 1997, and 2004. The concessions made in 1997 were in the context of the government balanced-budget policy, which demanded a 6 percent reduction in the total wage bill. The teachers represented by the Centrale des syndicats du Québec federation of teachers were faced with a choice: either find a way to reduce compensation or the government will eliminate 3,000 full-time teaching jobs across the province. The federation's response was to agree to a wage freeze for non-permanent teachers in what came to be known as the saga of the *clauses orphelins*, which would lead younger non-permanent teachers to launch a successful complaint to the Quebec Human Rights Tribunal. In fact since 1997, teachers, like other public sector workers, have had to accept either wage freezes or annual increases below the rise in the cost of living.

The Centrale des syndicats du Québec (CSQ) and its federations adopted a policy of favouring employment over wage increases in the bargaining rounds of 1998, 2000, and 2003 (Piotte 1998, 200-201; Rouillard 2009). This strategic choice has, however, contributed to a deterioration of real wages by a total of 10 percent over the last decade, and public sector workers' average salaries have gone from a 3.7 percent advantage compared to their private sector counterparts in 1996 to a 3.5 percent disadvantage in 2008 (Grenier 2008, 2010). Public school teachers in Quebec have also seen a growing gap between their average salaries and those of educators in other Canadian provinces and the United States (Ministère de l'Éducation du Loisir et du Sport 2009). While it may be argued that cost-of-living differentials justify lower average annual salaries than in Ontario, this can hardly be the case for other comparator provinces such as New Brunswick. We would argue that the growing differential is a combined result of government restraint policies and the strategic choices of teachers' unions to favour non-monetary gains.

Improvement in compensation and wages since 1985 has come about through the pay equity process rather than traditional collective bargaining. After nearly ten years of bargaining and political activity, an agreement was finally concluded in 2006 in which teachers saw their annual salary increase by an average of 5.67 percent (CSQ 2007). This followed gains made under the previous pay-relativity exercise when the teachers' salary grid was collapsed into two different scales (one for those with doctoral degrees[14] and another for all other teachers) with teachers being granted a progression of at least two years in the scale. According to union documents, these measures amounted to salary increases of approximately 8 percent during the 1990s and early 2000s (Gagnon 2003). It needs to be said, however, that the unions and especially teachers were disappointed by the government's decision in 2006, approved by the Pay Equity Commission in 2007, to spread the salary adjustments over a period of six years, rather than four years as is the usual process.

One important outcome addressing the issue of workloads has been agreements to reduce the student-teacher ratios, first at the primary school and in lower-income areas, and recently at the secondary school level. The student-teacher ratio was lowered from an average of 16.5 pupils in 1997/98 to 14.6 in 2007/08. This compares favourably with the United States, which has a ratio of 15.1 pupils per teacher (Ministère de l'Éducation du Loisir et du Sport 2009, 75). Government data show that the student-educator ratio declined from 15.2 in 1997/98 to 13.6 in 2006/07,[15] a trend similar to what can be observed elsewhere in Canada (a 14.6 ratio). Reform has also made available preschool for four-year-old children in low-income areas, while parents can now send their five year olds to kindergarten full time on a voluntary basis.

At the outset of this chapter we mentioned that the current collective bargaining agenda was partially set by issues related to the Reform program. The recent round of negotiations clearly illustrates that point. Following an intense and sustained public campaign, teachers were able to make significant inroads on issues that they believed were contributing to a degraded teaching environment. The collective agreement promises additional resources to support special-needs pupils, a formula to take into account their impact on the teaching load, and further reductions in class size. The tentative agreement also holds the promise of improved working conditions and more resources dedicated to student services. Teachers unions have been unable, however, to end the wave of selective programs being developed in public schools and to impose limits on competition for pupils among public schools. The outcome of the recent bargaining round has made it clear that bargaining over wages and compensation has become more of a façade, as once again the government was able to impose a settlement on its own terms and conditions. In terms of compensation, teachers like other public sector workers will continue to fall behind private sector counterparts and education personnel elsewhere in Canada.

Any appraisal of the advantages and disadvantages of the current regime of centralized bargaining depends on the perspective from which the evaluation is made. From the point of view of the government and the population, the regime can be considered a success to the extent that strikes have become an oddity since 1985. The regime has also been able to foster agreements on sector-level issues even though the parties have rarely come to agreement on compensation issues. That is not to say that conflict has given way to cooperation in labour-management relations. In any event, successive governments have made clear that strikes will be dealt with swiftly through special legislation. This serves as a reminder that centralization is a double-edged sword in the public sector. If in theory it increases the bargaining power of unions who can disrupt an entire sector, centralization makes it easier for governments to intervene to end conflicts and impose settlements under the justification that disruptions to public services threaten the well-being of the entire population. Another line of argument that runs against centralization is that the bargaining process has its own dynamics, separate from those at the level of the workplace, and that bargaining agents develop their own agenda sometimes at the expense of local priorities. While this may partly be true, as the Common Fronts seem to suggest, such an observation may ignore the particular features of public sector collective bargaining. Collective bargaining issues in the public sector are eventually political since they are closely linked to the choices made by the governing party in terms of policy orientation and the role of the state in a modern economy. Thus, while it may be true that workplace issues get lost in the shuffle over sector-level questions such as educational policy and resources, it must be considered that by intervening at the level of the sector, unions and their federations in the education sector are able to intervene in the decision-making process and have some influence over education policies and resources. The most recent round of collective bargaining illustrates this point. The two teachers' federations pushed forward an agenda that made a direct link between education resources, working conditions, and the successful implementation of the Reform agenda. While we can only speculate, it is rather unlikely that local or area-wide bargaining would have allowed for such a broad agenda that went beyond traditional bargaining issues to set conditions for the successful implementation of a central piece of public policy.

As the experience of Quebec education unions reveals, however, centralization does make it easier for government representatives to push trade-offs between union demands. Since the early 1990s, the retrenchment years according to Rose (2004), unions in public education have been faced with a choice between increased compensation for their members and increased funding for the public education system (Boivin and Grenier, forthcoming; Déom and Grenier 2009). As the account presented above suggests, under the centralized regime, unions have come to accept that in the absence of a strong wave of worker mobilization, the government will eventually impose a settlement on its own terms. The CSQ option to prefer employment and funding of services over increases in compensation illustrates the inability of the public sector labour movement to recreate the mobilization of 1970s.

That is not to say that the public teachers' union movement does not face significant challenges in the future. On the Reform front one of the most important of these challenges is to build better organizational capabilities and reinforce the quality of worker representation at the workplace level. As was said previously, centralized collective bargaining has fostered the development of capabilities and union expertise on sector-level issues, while local unions act mostly as enforcers of the collective bargaining agreements at the level of the school board. One of the innovations of Reform and subsequent policy initiatives has been the emergence of a number of workplace committees on issues related to the organization of teaching and school policies. While such initiatives are to be encouraged in that they give school personnel some input over matters that directly impact the quality of working life, they can also serve to circumvent the local union and worker representation. Discussions with local union officials reveal that this is a central concern given the relative weakness of union representation at the workplace level. Typically, union representatives have very limited release time and resources to accomplish their role and in many schools, especially primary schools, there is often no union representative. This weakness could be ignored in the years prior to the introduction of Reform, but the decentralization of decision-making to individual schools has put pressure for a corresponding devolution of union resources to schools in order to better support union representatives.

The stance taken by the main teachers' federation, the FSE, toward Reform and decentralization has caused a major rift in the teachers' union movement. Indeed, in 2004, a large and more militant faction of the teachers' labour movement split from the FSE and CSQ on the grounds that they were too accommodating toward the government and not forceful enough in pushing forward an autonomous agenda that would reject Reform. Nine more militant unions from the Montreal, Laval, and Gatineau regions left the FSE and the CSQ to form the Fédération autonome de l'enseignement (FAE). While this split is not a direct consequence of the centralized regime of collective bargaining under Bill 37, it does speak to the challenges of union representation on a provincewide basis. Indeed, one of the major grievances of the nine unions was that the positions adopted by the FSE regarding education policies did not reflect the context and needs of schools in the major urban areas. They also believed that the FSE had become too complacent in collective bargaining and was willing to accept unfavourable terms of agreement to avoid mobilization and strikes. In our view, this split speaks to the difficult trade-offs that are made under a provincewide system and to the difficulties of taking into account specific situations or conditions.

In short, the centralization versus decentralization debate will remain unresolved for some time. Our view is that the balance of advantages and disadvantages depends on the specific context and how it evolves over time. In the 1970s, centralization was very favourable to workers and unions in the Quebec public sector. The overall context was, however, one of economic expansion and a strongly mobilized membership behind a set of demands that were deemed reasonable in economic and political terms. Today, the context is much less favourable to major improvements in working conditions, and governments no longer feel compelled to respond favourably to the demands of their employees (Swimmer 2001; Swimmer and Bartkiw 2003; Swimmer and Thompson 1995). Even in the recent period of economic prosperity, the provincial government has not been compelled to offer major improvements in working conditions for the majority of public sector workers (Grenier 2010). One reason is certainly that public sector workers can no longer count on public support for their demands. Another is that the regime established under Bill 37 has been favourable to sector-level bargaining and retrenchment of unions on issues that are specific to their constituents rather than to the overall public sector (Grenier 2010).

It is our view, then, that the current regime does foster less conflict in labour relations. This outcome, however, has been achieved mainly through weakening of unions rather than by creating a common purpose between government and union representatives. The decline in strike activity is the result of past legislative interventions of the state that have made public sector unions, including those in education, lukewarm toward any form of strike activity. Is this regime capable of coping with the pressures induced by Reform? We believe so. On the balance, the sector-level bargaining over education policy implementation has allowed teachers' voices to be heard, and the government has responded with a series of measures that meet union priorities. Thus, under the current regime, sector-level representation has been partially successful in linking improved performance and success rates to better working conditions. It is unlikely that a decentralized regime would have delivered such results other than through political lobbying from teachers' representatives.

CONCLUSION: A NEW ERA OF POLITICIZATION?

The previous account is one of progressive centralization of union-management relations that culminated in the radicalization of public sector unions in the 1970s and the emergence of Common Fronts that challenged government policy orientations. Teachers were at the heart of many of the public sector labour conflicts, and the government responded by erecting an impressive legislative framework that leads to the current regime (Bill 37). One consequence of Bill 37 is that collective bargaining and labour-management relations are conducted in a structured framework where the behaviour of the parties is more predictable than in the previous decades. Another has been to remove any possibilities of local union-management conflicts affecting the public's access to services since strikes are no longer permitted at the school board level. In terms of traditional collective bargaining issues, Quebec public sector unions, including public school teachers, have been unable to replicate the gains made in the 1970s. Collective bargaining, even in times of economic prosperity, has not delivered positive results in terms of compensation and other monetary issues. In the specific case of education and public school teachers, inroads have been made on normative issues, albeit at a snail's pace, and mostly following public relations campaigns from the main education union peak council. Today, however, the education sector union movement is experiencing a difficult period as the split among teachers' unions demonstrates.

The CSQ and its federations have expressed increasing dissatisfaction with the current regime of public sector collective bargaining. One crucial issue has been the inability to engage the government of the day in any meaningful bargaining over compensation issues. As the previous account has made clear, the government is able to impose a settlement on its own terms through special ad hoc legislation. This is to be expected given that compensation represents more than 50 percent of the provincial government's total expenditures budget. Any agreement is thus dependent on increases in government revenue that would not be absorbed by demands from other sectors, most notably health care. The current model also places unions at a strategic disadvantage to the extent that improvements in government offers at the central table are always conditional on concessions over normative issues at the sector-level bargaining tables (Grenier 2010). This zero-sum context is reinforced by cross-sector negotiations: improvements in government compensation offers must be made to all public sector workers while the trade-offs to satisfy the demands of one group may be felt at the sector level by all groups. It is our view that this regime is reaching a point where the parties must find a new method for determining annual increases in compensation. However, as Swimmer (2001) noted, it is very unlikely that government will thrust its wage policies in the hands of independent arbitrators and run the risk that awards exceed the government's willingness or ability to pay. This is especially true in Quebec where the ability of successive governments to manage the public deficit and debt is increasingly important in political debates. For such a reason we believe that bargaining over annual wage increases will remain unchanged for the foreseeable future with government resorting to legislation to impose settlements on disgruntled unions. We believe, though, that unions will have more success in bargaining compensation adjustments outside the formal process, as was the case of the pay equity settlements, for teachers and for other groups such as nurses, doctors, pharmacists, and police officers.

Under such a scenario we expect public sector unions, and especially the teachers, to turn to politics in a more sustained and systematic way than in the last two decades. Rather than the politics of sovereignty versus federalism that have dominated discussions over the last 20 years, we expect unions to attempt to bring about political debates on the future of public services and public policies in the province of Quebec and to continue the present drive to build alliances with other progressive movements in the province and internationally. The CSQ has undertaken many initiatives to that end such as the new Secretariat de Défense des Services Publics (SISP) and the organization of regional public forums on the future of public education in 2008–2010. These are only two of many initiatives since 2000 when the leadership of the CSQ concluded that political influence was a precondition for gains at the bargaining table. All federations and labour unions involved in education have taken initiatives to oppose marketization and privatization in education (Déniger, Berthelot, and Roy 2005). The FAE has organized its own forums on public education in the Montreal region while the CSQ has been the main driver of a campaign to oppose public funding of private schools. This campaign is based on wide-ranging alliances with other unions and stakeholders in local communities. Thus, our general conclusion is that we are likely to see an increase in political activity that seeks to broaden the debate beyond labour relations to the future of public education in particular and public services in general.

In short, if the current regime has succeeded in regulating conflict in the education sector, contemporary issues have more to do with policies and politics and will push the union leadership in that direction. This is most likely the case given the difficulties in making progress over traditional issues of collective bargaining.

NOTES

The authors extend their gratitude to the staff of the Fédération des syndicats de l'enseignement (FSE-CSQ) and to M. Guillaume Caron who acted as research assistant.

1. The Département de l'instruction publique was a type of co-management of public education with two committees, one Catholic and the other Protestant, composed of clerics and representatives of the government. These committees established education policies and curricula for public schools.
2. The Quebec public education system differs from that of other Canadian provinces in terms of its structure. Kindergarten is voluntary while grade school extends from grades 1 through 6 and high school covers grades 8 to 12, for a total of 11 years of schooling. Upon successful completion of high school requirements, students can move on to public colleges (Cégeps), which serve as the entry level of post-secondary education and as vocational-technical schools. Pre-university college programs last two years while vocational-technical programs usually take three years. It is to be noted, however, that even those who complete vocational-technical programs can move on to university programs.
3. *Loi sur le régime de négociation des conventions collectives dans les secteurs public et parapublic*, L.R.Q., R-8.2.
4. *Code du travail du Québec*, L.R.Q., c.C-27.
5. Prior to 1966, collective bargaining was decentralized at the local school board level for all issues including wages and compensation. In 1966 the provincial government intervened in local bargaining and developed a single provincewide salary and wage grid. This resulted in progressive centralization of collective bargaining, which the different teachers' unions opposed strongly. See Lemelin (1984).
6. *Loi sur les négociations collectives dans les secteurs de l'Éducation, des Affaires sociales et les organismes gouvernementaux*, L.Q., 1974, c. 8. This Bill identified the provincial-level bargaining parties and established the rules and processes for provincewide collective bargaining. See Déom (1982).
7. *Loi sur l'organisation des parties patronale et syndicale aux fins des négociations collectives dans les secteurs de l'éducation, des affaires sociales et des organismes gouvernementaux* (P.L. 55) L.Q., 1978, c. 14.

8. *Loi modifiant le Code du travail* (P.L. 59), L.Q., 1979, c.-15.
9. *Loi concernant la rémunération dans le secteur public* (P.L. 105), L.Q., 1982, c. 35.
10. *Loi assurant la reprise des services dans les collèges et les écoles du secteur public* (P.L., 111), L.Q., c. 23.
11. These are respectively the Comité national de négociations pour les commissions scolaires francophones, Comité national de négociation pour les commissions scolaires anglophones, Comité national de négociation pour la commission scolaire Crie, and the Comité national de négociation pour la commission scolaire Kativik.
12. Local unions and school boards bargain over 28 issues identified in Annexe A-II of the *Loi sur le regime de négociation des conventions collectives dans les secteurs public et parapublic* (L.R.Q., c. R-8.2). Local parties can also come to agreement on other issues that either are delegated from the sector-level bargaining table or are not covered by agreement.
13. We use the term *decree* to refer to a government-imposed settlement through special legislation.
14. At the time of writing the authors did not have data on the number of teachers holding a doctorate degree, but information from officials indicates that there are few. The inclusion of a scale for doctorates seems to be the result of an effort to harmonize the salary grids for school board teachers with those of teachers at the collegiate level.
15. This indicator is broader than the student-teacher ratio since it includes not only teachers but all school personnel who intervene, directly or indirectly, in the education of pupils including non-teaching staff, professionals, and school principals.

REFERENCES

Beaucage, A. 1989. *Syndicats, salaires et conjoncture économique. L'expérience des fronts communs du secteur public québécois de 1971 à 1983*. Montreal: Presses de l'Université du Québec.

Berthelot, J. 2002. "Du clergé au marché." *Options CSQ* 22: 15-31.

Boivin, J. 1972. "La négociation collective dans le secteur public québécois. Une évaluation des trois premières rondes (1964–1972)." *Relations Industrielles/Industrial Relations* 27(4): 679-708.

—. 1993. "Bilan de la négociation collective dans les secteurs public et parapublic." In *La négociation collective du travail : adaptation ou disparition*, edited by C. Bernier, R. Laflamme, F. Morin, G. Murray, and C. Rondeau, 171-94. Quebec City: Les Presses de l'Université Laval.

Boivin, J. and J.-N. Grenier. Forthcoming. "La négociation collective dans les secteurs public et parapublic au Québec." In *La négociation collective*, edited by J.-G. Bergeron and R. Paquet. Montreal: Gaetan Morin Editeur.

Bolduc, R. 1982. "Le régime québécois de négociation des secteurs public et parapublic. Bilan et perspectives." *Relations Industrielles/Industrial Relations* 37(2): 403-11.

Bouchard, L. 1982. "À quand la maturité ?" *Relations Industrielles/Industrial Relations* 37(2): 411-20.

Centrale des syndicats du Québec (CSQ). 2000. *Origine et développement de la CSQ. Origine de la CIC-CEQ (1936–1969) et de la CEQ de 1970 à 1984*. www.csq.qc.net/histoire.

—. 2007. *Les résultats des négociations...de 1985 à 2005*. www.csq.qc.net/documents/négociations.

—. 2010. *Les résultats des rondes de négociations 1967–2005*. www.ceq.qc.net/documents/négociations.

Déniger, M.A, J. Berthelot, and G. Roy. 2005. "Décentralisation et nouvelle gouverne scolaire au Québec. Le point de vue du personnel enseignant sur les conseils d'établissement." *Recherche et Formation*, no. 49: 118-36.

Déom, E. 1982. "La négociation collective chez les fonctionnaires et les enseignants québécois : 1975–1976." *Relations Industrielles/Industrial Relations* 37(1): 141-63.

Déom, E. and J.-N. Grenier. 2009. "Union-Management Relations in Québec." In *Union-Management Relations in Canada*. 6th ed. Edited by M. Gunderson and D. Taras. Toronto: Addison Wesley Longman.

Després-Poirier, M. 1999. *Le système d'éducation du Québec*. 3rd ed. Boucherville, QC: Gaëtan Morin.

Fédération des commissions scolaires du Québec. 2008. *Personnel des commissions scolaires*. Montreal: PERCOS.

Fullan, M. 1999. "Quatre décennies de réformes de l'éducation." In *La réforme de l'éducation : des résultats encore incertains*, edited by L. Allaire. *Options CEQ*, no. 18: 27-40.

Gagnon, M. 2003. *De mémoire vive : la CSQ depuis la révolution tranquille*. Outremont, QC: Lanctôt Éditeur.

Gaudreault, L. 2005. *La syndicaliste de Charlevoix*. Montreal: XYZ Éditeur.

Graveline, P. 2003. *Une histoire de l'éducation et du syndicalisme enseignant au Québec/Essai*. Montreal: Typo.

—. 2007. *Une histoire de l'éducation au Québec*. Montreal: Éditions BQ.

Grenier, J.-N. 2008. "Public Sector Reform and Neoliberalism: The Case of Québec." *XLIV Congrès de l'Association canadienne des relations industrielles*, Université de la Colombie-Britannique, Vancouver, 4–7 juin.

—. 2010. "La restructuration du secteur public: la fin de l'employeur-modèle?" Actes du 64e Congrès des relations industrielles, *Main-d'œuvre et conditions de travail*, 99-111. Quebec City: Presses de l'Université Laval.

Grenier, J-N. and F.-B. Malo. 2008. "La restructuration des services publics et les relations du travail dans l'administration publique québécoise." Numéro spécial sur les restructurations d'entreprise, *Management International/International Management* 12: 31-39.

Hébert, G. 1982. "Réflexions." *Relations Industrielles/Industrial Relations* 37(2): 420-30.

—. 1995. "Public Sector Bargaining in Québec: The Rise and Fall of Centralization." In *Public Sector Collective Bargaining in Canada*, edited by G. Swimmer and M. Thompson, 201-35. Kingston, ON: IRC Press.

Leclerc, M. and M. Quimper. 2003. *Les relations du travail au Québec : une analyse de la situation dans le secteur public*. 2nd ed. Sainte-Foy: Les Presses de l'Université du Québec.

Lemelin, M. 1984. *Les négociations collectives dans les secteurs public et parapublic. Expérience québécoise et regard sur l'extérieur*. Montreal: Éditions Agence d'ARC.

Ministère de l'Éducation du Loisir et du Sport (MELS). 2009. *Les indicateurs de l'éducation-Édition 2009*. www.mels.gouv.qc.ca/indicateurs.

Morin, F. 1985. "Rapports collectifs du travail dans les secteurs publics québécois ou le nouvel équilibre selon la Loi du 19 Juin 1985." *Relations Industrielles/Industrial Relations* 40(3): 629-45.

Piotte, J.-M. 1998. *Du combat au partenariat. Interventions critiques sur le syndicalisme québécois*. Montreal: Éditions Nota Bene.

Rose, J.B. 2004. "Public Sector Bargaining: From Retrenchment to Consolidation." *Relations Industrielles/Industrial Relations* 59(2): 271-94.

Rouillard, J. 2009. *L'expérience syndicale au Québec : ses rapports avec l'État, la nation et l'opinion publique*. Montreal: VLB Éditeur.

Swimmer, G. 2001. "Public-Sector Labour Relations in an Era of Restraint and Restructuring: An Overview." In *Public-Sector Labour Relations in an Era of Restraint and Restructuring*, edited by G. Swimmer, 1-35. Don Mills, ON: Oxford University Press.

Swimmer, G. and T. Bartkiw. 2003. "The Future of Public Sector Collective Bargaining in Canada." *Journal of Labor Research* 24(4): 579-95.

Swimmer, G. and M. Thompson. 1995. *Public Sector Collective Bargaining in Canada: Beginning of the End or End of the Beginning?* Kingston, ON: IRC Press.

Tardif, J.-C. 1993. *Le mouvement syndical et l'État. Entre l'intégration et l'opposition. Le cas de la C.E.Q. de 1960–1992*. Thèse de Doctorat, École des Gradués, Université Laval.

Chapter 11

K–12 TEACHER COLLECTIVE BARGAINING IN NEWFOUNDLAND AND LABRADOR

TRAVOR C. BROWN

A SYSTEMS APPROACH

This chapter examines the collective bargaining system for teachers employed in the kindergarten to grade 12 (K–12) public school system in the province of Newfoundland and Labrador. To ground this work, the industrial relations (IR) system model will be used as that model has often been the analytical, if not theoretical, framework for the IR discipline (Meltz 1993, 164). While American scholar John Dunlop (1958, 1993) examined what is perhaps the seminal IR system, a modified version developed by Alton Craig (1988, 10) has frequently been used as the foundation for Canadian teaching and research (Taras, Ponak, and Gunderson 2001, 6). In this chapter, Hebdon and Brown's model (2008, 9), an expanded version of Craig's system, will be used to structure the analysis. A brief summary of that model is now presented.

According to the systems model, the main actors of the system (e.g., employer, employees/unions, and governments/governmental agencies) are influenced by both external inputs (e.g., legal, economic, ecological, political, and sociocultural) from the environment in which they operate as well as internal inputs (e.g., the actors' power, goals, and values). Through a series of conversion mechanisms (e.g., collective bargaining, grievances, joint committees, and strikes), the actors convert these inputs into outputs (e.g., terms and conditions of employment, affect toward the employer or union, and conflict).

Dynamic Negotiations: Teacher Labour Relations in Canadian Elementary and Secondary Education, ed. S. Slinn and A. Sweetman. Montreal and Kingston: Queen's Policy Studies Series, McGill-Queen's University Press.

Using this framework as a foundation, the chapter will first briefly overview the actors of the system and then present key environmental elements germane to the context of Newfoundland and Labrador teachers, with special emphasis on the sociocultural, political, economic, and legal factors. Given that the legislation that covers collective bargaining in this sector, namely, the *Teachers' Collective Bargaining Act* (1990), contains language related to numerous conversion mechanisms (e.g., strikes, conciliation), this section will also discuss conversion mechanisms related to third-party interventions and strikes. This is followed by a discussion of outputs. The chapter concludes with an assessment of strengths and weaknesses of the system.

However, prior to starting the analysis, it is necessary to discuss the research methods used to develop this chapter. The present study used both secondary and primary data sources. Secondary data sources included reviews of relevant legislation and scholarly sources, archival union and government publications, organizational websites, as well as media sources germane to the collective bargaining system for K–12 teachers in Newfoundland and Labrador. Of note, perhaps due to the province having the highest union density in Canada (Statistics Canada 2007, 1), there was considerable media coverage regarding this topic and in some cases these media sources were the sole data sources available. As such, this chapter may reference media sources more extensively than other chapters in this collection.

The primary data sources used in this study consisted of interviews conducted by the author with three stakeholders, one interviewee each from the Eastern School Board (ESB), the Newfoundland and Labrador Teachers' Association (NLTA), and the Newfoundland and Labrador School Boards Association (NLSBA). The purpose of these interviews was to seek clarification concerning some information uncovered in secondary sources as well as gain the interviewees' perspectives regarding the strengths and weaknesses of the current collective bargaining system. These interviews lasted approximately one hour and were semi-structured in nature (i.e., several specific questions related to the interviewee's experience in the K–12 IR system followed by probing questions based on the interviewee's response). The interview protocol was approved by an ethics committee at Memorial University, and all interviewees were assured that they would not be named in this chapter. For this reason, these interviewees are identified only as a representative of their organization.

THE ACTORS

The three key actors of the current K–12 system in the province are the provincial school boards, the provincial government, and the Newfoundland and Labrador Teachers' Association.[1] This section provides a brief overview of the NLTA, the actor that represents employees.

The association was formed well over a century ago, in the fall of 1890, when it "was struck," as the *Harbour Grace Standard* put it, "to secure the formation of a Teachers' Association for the Island" (quoted in Pitt 1990, 10). While the association was officially formed to examine issues of mutual interest, a review of the historical data suggests that, like most North American unions, the focus of the NLTA was pure and simple "bread and butter" unionism in terms of seeking to improve the wages, benefits, and working conditions of employees (Hebdon and Brown 2008, 9). For example, at its inaugural meeting the association discussed increasing pay and the provision of life insurance and pension benefits (Cuff 1985, 5).

From these very early days, the NLTA made two decisions that still ground the association today. First, in its inception, the NLTA was designed to be an interdenominational association representing all teachers throughout the province (Cuff 1985, 5). That decision was interesting given the long history of religious-based schools in the province. Second, the NLTA was very politically astute, understanding the need for government support. In fact, the association invited a member of the House of Assembly to the first meeting in 1890 (ibid., 4). As will be shown throughout this chapter, the provincewide, non-sectarian focus and provincial bargaining scope remains today and the union continues to understand the importance of the political arena.

As will be discussed in more detail later in this chapter, the sole piece of legislation concerning K–12 labour relations, the *Teachers' Collective Bargaining Act*, entrenches many of the details concerning who represents each of these actors in the collective bargaining process. The next section provides an environmental overview of the political history of the government and the role of the churches, who were traditionally the employers of teachers in the province.

THE EXTERNAL ENVIRONMENT: POLITICAL, SOCIOCULTURAL,
AND ECONOMIC CONTEXTS

Political and Sociocultural Context

Following the amendment to the *British North America Act* in 1949, Newfoundland became the last province to join Canada. Hence, relative to other provinces, the actors of this IR system operated in a unique political, sociocultural context that plays an important role in the K–12 educational system. In particular, the churches played a key role in early Newfoundland society, and thus in the province's educational system.

The role of the churches. While statistics suggest that over 95 percent of the 1940s population of Newfoundland had ethnic ties to the British Isles (Government of Newfoundland and Labrador 1971, Appendix A11), this statistic hides a significant issue that has often divided the province, namely, religion. Religion is such a pervasive element of the province's culture that it is difficult to examine almost any public issue without considering the role of the churches. For example, during the restructuring of the House of Assembly from its pre-Confederation British roots to its post-Confederation status as a Canadian province, "representation by religious denomination [was seen] as an important factor in the redistribution" of seats (Rothney 1962, 557).

Note that the word churches, versus church, is used here as the province's population largely traces its ancestry both to Ireland, where most immigrants to the province were Catholic, and to England, where most immigrants were Protestant (Keough 2005, 18). Analysis suggests that between 1790 and 1830 over 45 percent of Newfoundlanders were Catholic (Handcock 1977, 33), resulting in a population that "was divided equally between English Protestants and Irish Catholics" (McCann 1989, 181-82). Throughout the 1800s and early 1900s, there was ongoing tension between these two religious groups. This unrest included religious marches, protests, and even acts of violence that required intervention by law enforcement (Keough 2005, 24). The divide between the two groups was sufficiently entrenched that many communities of the province were historically divided into Catholic versus Protestant sections (ibid., 19).

Given the importance of religion in Newfoundland society, the churches were key players in the early educational system, founding and operating local public schools as well as employing the teaching staff (Pitt 1990, 3-6). Indeed, the churches were so prevalent in the education system that some scholars have concluded that the clergy "controlled the educational system" (Brym and Neis 1978, 401). This church control was facilitated, legislatively, as far back as 1836, when Newfoundland was still a British colony. That year *An Act for the Encouragement of Education in This Country* was passed, which provided "£300 for Church of England schools and £300 for Roman Catholic schools" (Fitzgerald 1999, 29-30). In fact, it was Canon William Pilot, who was both a minister and the Church of England superintendent of education, who encouraged the formation of a Teachers Institute in 1888 that would focus on issues of mutual interest (Pitt 1990, 9), perhaps leading the way to the association being formed one year later.

This religious-grounded education system, known as the denominational school system because different Christian denominations operated different schools, was a key feature of the province's public education system until the late 1990s. In fact, Term 17 of Newfoundland's Union with Canada replaced section 93 of the *British North America Act* of 1867 in order to preserve the role of the churches in the public education system. More specifically, Term 17 of the memorandum of agreement between Canada and Newfoundland stated:

> In lieu of section ninety-three of the British North America Act, 1867, the Province shall have exclusive authority to make laws in relation to education,

but the Legislature will not have authority to make laws prejudicially affecting any right or privilege with respect to denominational schools, common
(amalgamated) schools....

The legislation even entrenched the public funding of the denominational system stating, in section 17(a), that "all such schools shall receive
their share of such funds in accordance with scales determined on a
non-discriminatory basis." In so doing, Term 17 was seen to guarantee
"religious denominations the right to state funding for their schools, and
rights to control school administration, the religious studies curriculum,
and the hiring and firing of teachers" (Fitzgerald 1999, 28). As a result,
public education in the province was divided along religious lines until
almost the end of the millennium. It was not until a public referendum in
the fall of 1997 that the population agreed to amend the Constitution to
create a single public school system, free from direct involvement of the
church (Government of Newfoundland and Labrador 1997). As a result of
that vote, on 8 January 1998 the Canadian Governor General proclaimed
that Term 17 had been amended to end the public denominational school
system.[2]

The influence of religion on the NLTA. The Newfoundland and Labrador
Teachers' Association was formed with the explicit understanding that it
be free of religious affiliations (Pitt 1990, 11). One author suggests that this
decision may have been made out of fear that the NLTA "might be used
for political purposes" (Cuff 1985, 7) given that the first NLTA president
was a supporter of Premier Whiteway, who in turn was supported by
the Protestant-based Orange Society. Nevertheless, it is interesting to
note that from the very beginning the association ensured that its senior
leadership was religiously diverse and representative of Catholic and
Protestant faiths (ibid., 8).

Despite the absence of religious affiliation during its formation,
religious divides have taken place in the NLTA. Historical records show
that there have been at least two serious attempts to break ranks based
on religion. In the 1980s, following the 1983 strike when the Pentecostal
teachers continued to teach and rejected strike action on religious grounds,
there was a movement among Pentecostal teachers to split from the NLTA
(NLTA representative, 26 May 2010; School Boards Association representative, 20 May 2010). In fact, 80 percent of these teachers voted to form a
separate bargaining unit in the mid-1980s ("Pentecostal Teachers May
Split with Union" 1984). The issue was finally ironed out by an agreement that allowed Pentecostal teachers to continue teaching in the event
of a strike; they would be paid the same strike pay as other "striking"
teachers and their salaries would go into a special fund (Cleary 1991, 3).
Interestingly, when put to the NLTA membership, the vote to support this
special agreement for Pentecostal teachers passed by a slim majority of

50.3 percent (ibid., 3). The agreement was carried out during the strike of 1994, when "Pentecostal teachers received the equivalent of strike pay while their salaries went into a special Professional Development Fund" (NLTA representative, 26 May 2010).

The second religious split that almost divided the union was the call for a "special interest council for Roman Catholic teachers" to be established within the NLTA ("No Special NTA Council" 1992, 6). This group, which came to be known as the Community of Catholic Teachers, was perceived as a movement to remove Catholic teachers, who then represented 42 percent of the NLTA membership, from the association (Swain 1992, 3). While the group never gained sufficient support, perhaps due to the movement toward a single school system in the mid-to-late 1990s, it is noteworthy that the two private Catholic schools in the province are not currently represented by the NLTA nor are they members of the School Boards Association (NLTA representative, 26 May 2010; School Boards Association representative, 20 May 2010; School District representative, 27 May 2010).

Perhaps due to these internal religious tensions in the 1980s and 1990s, documents reveal several reasons why the NLTA was supportive of ending the denomination system through a change of Term 17. First, the former religious system had resulted in religious discrimination as teachers could be hired, denied positions, and fired on the basis of religion (Bennett 1997, 4; Newfoundland and Labrador Teachers' Association 1997, 6; "Teachers' Union Also with Yes Forces" 1997; School Boards Association representative, 20 May 2010). Second, the association felt that the movement to a single system would bolster educational quality ("Teachers' Union Also with Yes Forces" 1997, 4). In the former religious-based system, many small communities in the province had two religious-based schools (a Catholic and a Protestant school), each fighting for its share of resources. As one interviewee noted, the movement to a single, non-religious-based school system would mean a more efficient system as different religious-based schools, or school boards, would not be competing over a small pot of money and the budget could be better allocated to improve resources and educational experiences at single schools (School Boards Association representative, 20 May 2010).

Interestingly, the NLTA leadership did not actively campaign on the Term 17 issue at first, rather seeking to ensure that "religious education and observances will be guaranteed ... [and focusing its efforts on] ... communicating information to all members" concerning the proposed changes to the system ("Teachers' Union Also with Yes Forces" 1997, 4). However, the NLTA leadership later urged members to vote in favour of the referendum to end the denominational system as it would ensure "hiring, reassignment and transfer of teachers based upon qualification" only and not religion (Bennett 1997, 4). The association even submitted a brief to the Special Joint Committee struck on Term 17, seeking "to impress upon … [the] Committee, in the strongest possible way, why it is imperative to change Term 17 and do so in the shortest time possible" (Newfoundland and Labrador Teachers' Association 1997, 1).

The Ecological, Political, and Economic Contexts

The actors of the system currently operate in a province with a relatively small population of approximately 500,000 citizens (Government of Newfoundland and Labrador 2010a). This small population is spread across a large land mass of over 400,000 square kilometres, of which about 111,000 square kilometres represents the island of Newfoundland and another 294,000 square kilometres represents the Labrador region that borders Quebec (Government of Newfoundland and Labrador 2010e). The economy of the province has often been grounded in natural resources. As shown by a provincial analysis of census data, in 1951, near the date of Confederation, over one-third of workers (36,181 out of a total of 105,179) were employed in the primary resources sector, where (a) fishing and trapping, and (b) logging and forestry represented the lion's share of employment opportunities (i.e., employing over 28,000 workers; see Government of Newfoundland and Labrador 2010d). Given this natural resource–based economy, many teachers historically worked in small rural communities, often located along the coastline of the province. This rural population often placed special privileges and responsibilities on the school teacher, calling upon teachers to be leaders of the community in non-teaching roles such as serving as religious lay leaders when an ordained minister was not available or addressing community issues.[3]

Perhaps due to the special position of teachers in the community, it is interesting to note that three of the nine premiers of the province were teachers by training: Brian Peckford (Beltrame 1989), Beaton Tulk (Government of Newfoundland and Labrador 2000a), and Roger Grimes ("Roger Grimes Made Honorary Member of the NLTA" 2009). Moreover, Roger Grimes had been elected president of the NLTA in 1985 ("Grimes New NTA President" 1985) and was named an honorary member after leaving politics in 2009 ("Roger Grimes Made Honorary Member" 2009; NLTA representative, 26 May 2010).

Building on the smallness of the population, it is evident that the key players know each other on a personal level; indeed, we see circumstances where people have moved from representing one actor of the IR system to another. Historically, we have seen members, and leaders, of the NLTA or the NLSBA take on key government roles such as premier or minister of education (NLTA representative, 26 May 2010; School Boards Association representative, 20 May 2010). For example, Darin King, the minister of education from April 2009 to January 2011, was previously positioned on the employer side as the CEO of the Eastern School District (Government of Newfoundland and Labrador 2010f). There are even examples of leaders moving from the employee to the employer representative as in the case of Wayne Noseworthy, the current director of labour relations with the Newfoundland and Labrador School Boards Association (Newfoundland and Labrador School Boards Association 2010b). Interestingly, Noseworthy was a former executive director of the NLTA, was elected by the membership to the position of president of the NLTA, and worked as the executive director of the Nova Scotia Teachers Union (Nova Scotia Teachers Union 2010b). We also see evidence of mutual support between the union and the employer including joint press releases that critique the provincial government's educational policy and decisions (Newfoundland and Labrador Schools Trustees Association and Newfoundland Teachers' Association 1988).

Not only have we seen key politicians from the teacher ranks, we have seen a keen interest in education in the political arena. For example, from its conception the NLTA involved politicians in its early meetings (Cuff 1985, 4), and soon after joining Canada in 1949 there is media evidence of the association meeting with government leaders concerning pay issues (Meaney 1949, 19). Since the formalized right of collective bargaining was established in 1973, there has been extensive media coverage of requests for meetings between the NLTA and premiers ("Premier Considering Meeting with NTA" 1984), concerns voiced by the NLTA on educational issues and policies (Sullivan 1999), and evidence of the NLTA being singled out by certain premiers for its actions (Jackson 1994). In fact, when Premier Clyde Wells called the 1993 election, he challenged: "Who's going to run this province? The teachers or me as premier?" (School Boards Association representative, 20 May 2010). As one newspaper article stated, "Wells singled out teachers ... when he called the election, saying they're risking the province's financial stability" ("Nfld. Unions Hit Back" 1993, 13).

Finally, we see the importance of the NLTA, and the teaching profession, in the post-secondary education system of the province. From the very early days of its founding by the government, Memorial College, the predecessor of Memorial University, was a "two-year liberal arts and teacher-training institution" (Downey 1988, 14). We also see the close link between the university and the NLTA with the association holding meetings on campus and even having a branch devoted to the campus for teachers and student teachers (Newfoundland Teachers' Association 1964). Arguably, given that Memorial is the only provider of post-secondary education degrees in the province, the NLTA could form ties with future teachers earlier and more effectively than associations in other provinces.

Leaving the historical economic and social context, we do see important changes taking place in both the economy and the population. While the province has colloquially been described as a "have-not" province

since joining Canada, the current economic outlook is much more positive. An analysis of the 2006 census data shows a more diverse economy
taking shape in the province. For example, of the 214,880 experienced
workers in the province, only 14,300, or less than 6 percent, were employed
in the traditional stronghold industries of agriculture, forestry, fishing,
and hunting. More than 30,000 (12 percent) were employed in the retail
trade or health care / social assistance sectors, and almost 8,000 (3 percent)
worked in the mining and oil and gas extraction sector (Government
of Newfoundland and Labrador 2010c). While the oil sector represents
only a small percentage of direct employment, it is a key industry in the
province; the government's economic outlook states that in 2008 "the
industry accounted for almost 40 percent of the total value of all goods
and services produced in the province" (i.e., nominal GDP; Government
of Newfoundland and Labrador 2010b, 16). That same report indicated
that the province's economy was strong relative to its provincial peers,
ranking first in retail sales and second in both labour income and housing
starts in 2009 (ibid., 12). Clearly, this is a different view of the province
relative to its "have-not" historical status and can explain why we see
current provincial collective agreements with four-year increases of 8
percent in the first year and 4 percent in each of the three subsequent
years. By contrast, in other provinces (e.g., Ontario) we see union concerns
regarding wage freezes (Thomas 2010) as well as wage restraint legislation
(*Public Sector Compensation Restraint to Protect Public Services Act* 2010).

A final element of the environmental context that has impacted the
parties over the past two decades relates to demographic changes. The
total population of the province has dropped from about 580,000 in 1992
to 508,000 in 2009 (Government of Newfoundland and Labrador 2010a),
a drop of over 12 percent. Much of this has been due to out-migration
where people, many of whom are young adults, have left the province
to pursue higher education or employment opportunities (Government
of Newfoundland and Labrador 2006, 4). This loss of youth has led to
an aging population: the median age in 2006 was 2.5 years higher than
the Canadian median, when it was five years lower than the Canadian
median in 1971 (ibid., 6).

Perhaps more important for the education sector is the rapid decline in
the number of school-aged children (between the ages of 5 and 19), drop-
ping almost 50 percent from 1986 to 2008 (Government of Newfoundland
and Labrador 2010a, 2011). Thus, the parties have expressed considerable
concern since the 1980s about the reduction in student numbers and the
associated impacts on teaching positions in the province ("Teachers Plan
Massive Action" 1980). Arguably, these demographic trends can explain
the political rationale for the collapse of the religious-based school system; communities, and school boards, could no longer afford to support
multiple schools in single regions.

THE LEGAL ENVIRONMENT: STRUCTURE AND FEATURES
GOVERNING K–12 COLLECTIVE BARGAINING

This section of the chapter reviews the legal structure and features that govern the K–12 collective bargaining process in the Newfoundland and Labrador public school system. This includes an examination of the statute that both regulates teacher collective bargaining and defines the bargaining agent. The section will conclude with a discussion of conversion mechanisms (e.g., collective bargaining and the scope of issues that can be negotiated, the dispute resolution procedures available, and any restrictions on strikes or lockouts).

The *Teachers' Collective Bargaining Act*

Unlike some other provinces discussed in this book, in Newfoundland and Labrador a sole statute regulates the collective bargaining process for all K–12 teachers in the provincial public school system. This statute is the *Teachers' Collective Bargaining Act*.[4] The first version of this Act was passed in 1973, and the first "official" collective agreement was passed that same year (Newfoundland Teachers' Association 1973, 1). However, as previously discussed, the history of collective representation in the school system dates back to the 1890s (Cuff 1985, 3). From that period on, collective representation and negotiations have focused on the provincial level. Today the NLTA is formally named in the statute as the exclusive bargaining agent. As article 9 states:

> Unless it is replaced by a certified bargaining agent, the *Newfoundland Teachers' Association* referred to in the Teachers' Association Act *shall be the bargaining agent for all teachers* and shall be so recognized for all of the purposes of this Act, as if it had been certified by a valid and existing certification. (emphasis added)

Moreover, the Act explicitly states in section 4.(2) that "all teachers shall, notwithstanding that they are employed by different school boards, be grouped in the same unit." The only exception, stated in section 4.(4), is for "schools operated or supported by companies in Labrador," in which case the teachers "may be included in a unit separate from the unit." However, the number of teachers who meet those conditions is rather small. Less than 100 of the current almost 6,000 members of the NLTA are in a separate bargaining unit, which has a separate agreement known as the Labrador West Collective Agreement (2009) due to its historical and now-defunct funding by mining companies (NLTA representative, 26 May 2010). Perhaps the only school to truly fall into this category today would be located in Churchill Falls, a company town created in the 1960s to house one of the world's largest hydroelectric generators ("Construction Starts"

1967; Nalcor Energy 2010). The school in that town is operated by Nalcor Energy and employs about 20 teachers (Eric G. Lambert School 2010).

Interview data further demonstrate the exclusive jurisdiction of the NLTA (NLTA representative, 26 May 2010; School Boards Association representative, 20 May 2010). The vast majority of teachers are members of the provincial bargaining unit, represented by the NLTA, where their contract is referred to as the Provincial Collective Agreement, 2009. The 100 or so teachers working in schools in the Western Labrador bargaining unit are also represented by the NLTA, and their agreement is very similar to that of the provincial agreement. The Churchill Falls teachers are represented by the NLTA for professional development but not collective bargaining issues.

In short, the only teachers not represented by the NLTA in either a professional or a collective bargaining capacity are those working in private schools (i.e., the single non-denominational private school or the two private Catholic schools) or in aboriginal schools operated by the aboriginal communities and governments (NLTA representative, 26 May 2010).

Centralized Bargaining Structure

Given the exclusive jurisdiction granted to the NLTA through legislation, the bargaining structure is very centralized. While the province currently comprises five school boards—four based on geographic region (Eastern, Nova Central, Western, and Labrador) and one based on language (Conseil Scolaire Francophone)—these school boards are all members of the Newfoundland and Labrador School Boards Association (2010c), or NLSBA. Of particular note is that the NLSBA, which was formed in 1971 just prior to the 1973 *Teachers' Collective Bargaining Act*, "exists to promote the role and common interest of the five publicly elected School Boards within the province ... [including] to facilitate the discharge of the statutory mandates of School Boards in the conduct of labor relations respecting unionized school board employees" (Newfoundland and Labrador School Boards Association 2010a). Thus, the NLSBA represents the employer in this IR system.

The role of the NLSBA, and the degree of centralization in the system, becomes more evident upon examining the Act as it mandates the structure of the bargaining committee representing the employer. The Act, in section 10.(1), discusses a seven-member School Board Committee that is appointed by the Lieutenant-Governor in Council. The rest of section 10 specifies procedures for the nomination of these committee members. Four members are to be nominated from the NLSBA and must be supported by "not less than 75 percent of the total number of school boards in the province" (see section 10.(4)). The three remaining members—the chief negotiator and two non-specified nominees—are selected by the president of the provincial government's Treasury Board.

Not only does the Act specify the structure of the School Board Committee negotiations team that represents the employer, it further provides this group with the exclusive right to bargain on behalf of *all* public school boards in the province. Section 28 specifically states:

> Provisions of a collective agreement or of a decision or award of a board of arbitrators made under this Act which relate either directly or indirectly to the expenditure of public funds of the province provided for education are *binding on every school board in the province, whether or not the school board was represented on the school board committee* or is a party to the collective agreement or the appropriate arbitration. (emphasis added)

It is also interesting to note that while the chief negotiator is expected to act in consultation with members of the School Board Committee, all decision-making power rests with him or her. Sections 11.(2) and 11.(3) of the Act state:

> (2) The chief negotiator for the school board committee shall *have charge of all negotiations* entered into in collective bargaining conducted under this Act by the school board committee but he or she shall act at all times in consultation with the other members of the school board committee.

> (3) The chief negotiator shall make the *sole and final decision* on the tentative approval or rejection of a proposal considered at negotiations referred to in subsection (2) where the proposal involves the expenditure, directly or indirectly, of public money. (emphasis added)

Thus the legislation and history of the public school system have resulted in a centralized approach to labour relations at the provincial level.

Bargaining Scope

There are no statutory restrictions concerning bargaining scope in this IR system. As one interviewee highlighted, the only restrictions pertain to "what the other party will accept" and what the Treasury Board will agree to given that the chief negotiator representing the employer is appointed by the Treasury Board (School Boards Association representative, 20 May 2010). In addition to this primary data, secondary data confirm the broad bargaining scope. An examination of the Act shows an absence of any excluded area for negotiation. Reviews of the bargaining history in recent decades further reveal an unrestricted bargaining scope. For example, the NLTA has bargained on issues related to wages and wage freezes, class size, hours of work, job security/reductions of teaching positions, as well as issues related to usage, budgets for, and pay of substitute teachers (Callahan 1991; Government of Newfoundland and Labrador 1999; Taggart 1983). In essence, the NLTA has had no restrictions on what it can attempt to bargain into its collective agreement.

Dispute Resolution Procedures

A review of the Act and past history shows that a number of dispute resolution procedures exist in this relationship. In fact, sections 13–33 deal almost exclusively with dispute resolution procedures, with particular focus on conciliation and arbitration. Given that conciliation and arbitration procedures are fairly common across all the jurisdictions included in this book, they will be briefly overviewed here.

In terms of conciliation, the Act explicitly defines the role, membership, and financial obligations of the parties, and time frames. For example, the conciliation board is composed of three members: one member appointed by each of the union and employer representatives, and a third member who serves as the chair, whose appointment the other two members must mutually agree upon (see 14.(3) and 14.(4)). The board has 14 days to report its findings (see section 14.(16)).

While the Act is clear on the board's role "to try to bring about a collective agreement," it is mute on the procedure to be used to bring about an agreement, as indicated in section 14.(10) and (11):

> (10) A conciliation board shall, immediately after the appointment of the chairperson, try to bring about a collective agreement between the parties.

> (11) Except as otherwise provided in this Act, a conciliation board *may determine its own procedure* but shall give full opportunity to all parties to present evidence and make representations. (emphasis added)

The Act is also explicit on the power of the conciliation board, stating in section 14.(15) that the "board is considered to be an 'investigating body.'" However, it is expected to make recommendations toward a settlement (see section 14.(16)). Once the conciliation report is filed, each of the parties must file a report with the Minister stating "(a) whether the recommendations contained in the report have been accepted or rejected wholly or partly; and (b) which recommendations have been rejected" (section 17). The practice has been that the parties must also indicate the reason(s) they reject any of the recommendations (NLTA representative, 26 May 2010).

Arbitration and Right to Strike

A review of the Act reveals that both grievance and interest arbitration are contained in the statute. Section 17 explicitly references grievance arbitration as "a provision for final settlement, without stoppage of work, by arbitration ... where those differences arise out of the *interpretation, application, administration or alleged violation of the agreement*" (emphasis added). As with the conciliation board, the Act discusses the make-up of the panel and time frames.

The agreement also provides for interest arbitration as a strike replacement. However, section 22 of the Act is clear that this is a mutual choice:

> Where the procedure prescribed by sections 12, 13, and 14 is followed and a collective agreement is not reached, the parties to the collective agreement *may, where they mutually agree* in writing, refer all matters on dispute to a board of arbitrators. (emphasis added)

Thus, while the Act references the option of interest arbitration, there is no requirement for arbitration that would place formal restrictions on the use of strikes or lockouts. To date, this form of arbitration has never been used, even though there have been two strikes since the Act was passed, one in 1983 (Collins 1983, 22-23) and a second in 1994 (Government of Newfoundland and Labrador 1994). Both were settled by the parties and did not involve arbitration or back-to-work legislation (NLTA representative, 26 May 2010). Moreover, as far back as 1949, prior to being given union status through the Act in the 1970s, the NLTA discussed the option of a strike (Meaney 1949). Thus, as is common in Canadian labour relations laws, the Act does not prohibit strikes; rather, it requires that the parties submit to conciliation prior to a strike or lockout. Specifically, the Act states that prior to a strike, the parties must submit to conciliation, the conciliators' report must be filed, both parties must accept/reject the report, and a period of seven days must have elapsed since both parties accepted or rejected the report (see section 31.(1).(a)). It is interesting to note, however, that in 1980 Jerry Dinn, then Minister of Labour, publicly alluded to the potential of removing the right to strike for all public sector employees in the province (Woolridge 1980). To date, there has been no movement toward such strike restrictions.

In addition to the "formal" dispute resolution mechanisms provided in the Act, history has shown that the parties have used other, informal, dispute resolution mechanisms. First, we see evidence of public relations and media campaigns. For example, in 1980 the union planned an extensive public awareness campaign focusing on issues of education quality at a time when the government was reducing teaching positions and restructuring the education system ("Teachers Plan Massive Action" 1980). Similarly, in 1997 the union encouraged parents to take actions concerning proposed cuts to the education system that would have resulted in reductions in teachers (Sullivan 1997). In fact, public relations has even been highlighted as an association priority in some years (Newfoundland and Labrador Teachers' Association 2003).

Second, there is media evidence of work to rule. For example, in 1991, teachers refused to perform non-teaching duties related to sports coaching, after-school activities, and so on that were considered voluntary and outside of their job scope (Callahan 1991).

Finally, the use of special committees and task forces outside of the normal collective bargaining process is also evident. For example, in 1983, as part of the settlement that ended the strike, the parties agreed to a task force, comprised equally of association and employer representatives as well as an independent chair, that would examine issues related to workload, class size, and pay for substitute teachers (Collins 1983, 23-24). Similarly, a workload committee was established in a round of bargaining in the late 1990s (Newfoundland and Labrador Teachers' Association 2000, 2). As suggested by interviewees, such committees have been used to address issues that could not be easily resolved at the bargaining table, may have fallen outside of a desired pattern set by the government of the day, or just needed additional focus (School Boards Association representative, 20 May 2010; NLTA representative, 26 May 2010). However, in all instances where these committees came up with resolutions that required public expenditures, they still, in essence, required government (i.e., Treasury Board) approval (NLTA representative, 26 May 2010).

STRENGTHS AND WEAKNESSES OF THE SYSTEM

Criteria

Any discussion of strengths and weaknesses of the Newfoundland system needs to be grounded in a set of criteria. For example, one can examine outcomes of the IR system in terms of employer outcomes (e.g., management rights), union/labour outcomes (e.g., terms and conditions of employment), conflict/conflict resolution (e.g., strikes and lockouts), as well as affect measures (e.g., attitudinal measures related to satisfaction and commitment). While the employer and union/labour outcomes are important elements, any analysis of such outcomes would be best served by a cross-jurisdictional comparison given that a sole collective bargaining relationship exists for the whole province. Because the opening chapter of this book includes cross-jurisdictional comparisons, the focus here will be on criteria related to conflict/conflict resolution and affect measures.

Examinations of labour relations in the Canadian public sector (Hebdon and Stern 1998, 204; Rose 2008, 545-48) often discuss issues related to various conflict (e.g., strikes/lockouts) and conflict resolution (e.g., settlement, arbitration, conciliation, back-to-work legislation) mechanisms. These sources currently highlight the movement away from true collective bargaining toward a process whereby legislation, in particular back-to-work legislation, replaces collective bargaining (e.g., the government passes legislation requiring workers to return to work and, at times, even legislates the terms and conditions of the collective agreement).

Like many provinces in Canada, the Government of Newfoundland and Labrador has used back-to-work legislation to address public sector collective agreement impasses or strikes (Rose 2008, 557). As recently as 2004, the Progressive Conservative government headed by then premier Danny Williams announced the tabling of legislation to end a three-week public sector–wide strike that included legislating the terms and conditions of the settlement (e.g., wage rate and reductions in benefits; CBC News 2004). The legislation came into effect shortly thereafter (*Public Services Resumption and Continuation Act* 2004). Similarly, in 1999, the Liberal government, led by former premier Brian Tobin, tabled similar legislation to end a nurses' strike (*Health and Community Services Resumption and Continuation Act* 1999).

When one considers the Newfoundland K–12 public education context, we see that from a conflict resolution perspective, there have been few strikes (only two since 1973, when the first collective agreement was signed) and no legislated agreements in the education sector. In both strikes, the parties returned to the table and negotiated their own agreements (School Boards Association representative, 20 May 2010; School District representative, 27 May 2010). An analysis of secondary data concerning these strikes reveals that the first, in 1983, was related primarily to economic issues such as the acceptance of a government wage restraint, and constraints on the pay rate for substitutes (Collins 1983, 22-23). The second strike, in 1994, related to workforce reductions and the NLTA's desire to limit the number of reductions in teaching positions in any single school district to a maximum of 2 percent of teachers in any one year (Rumbolt 1994).

Turning to the elements related to affect, it is important to note that all representatives interviewed expressed general satisfaction with, and commitment to, the system and the relationship between the parties. The fact that the legislation has remained largely unchanged since its original passing almost 40 years ago further suggests that it is meeting the needs of the parties.

Taking account of these outcomes, one can conclude that the overall system is working effectively. However, this does not mean that the system is without areas for improvement. In the following sections, both the strengths and weaknesses of the provincial system are presented.

Strengths

In terms of specific strengths of the system, five elements are evident that could be considered as potential "best practices" by other jurisdictions. First, the high level of centralization of the system appears to be a strong advantage. Given the Act and historical practices, there has always been, in essence, one bargaining unit and one bargaining agent for the entire K–12 public education system in the province. As discussed earlier, more than 95 percent of all teachers in the province are covered by the provincial agreement (NLTA representative, 26 May 2010). Interviewees commented on how this centralized system made it easier to negotiate agreements relative to places where multiple bargaining units exist. For example, one interviewee observed that Nova Scotia has "two-tier bargaining, so each school board … has its own local collective agreement and they deal with certain [local] elements and then you have a provincial collective agreement that covers everybody" (School Boards Association representative, 20 May 2010). If one takes the institutional perspective on labour relations that sees unions as a way to counterbalance the power of workers relative to their employer (Kaufman 2003, 4), this centralization of the system can help balance the power of the union relative to the key decision-maker on the school board committee side (namely, the government's Treasury Board that operates on a provincial scale).

A second strength is the clarity of the Act as it relates to the bargaining agent, namely the NLTA, and the bargaining unit, namely all teachers. The simplicity of this approach minimizes the challenges associated with multiple certification applications, where multiple unions could attempt to represent teachers, and the employer could try to restrict membership in the bargaining unit. Moreover, as pointed out in the preceding paragraph, a single union ensures a certain levelling of the power between the bargaining parties. As one interviewee pointed out based on his/her knowledge of the system in Nova Scotia where the teachers' union represents several occupational groups,[5] the NLTA represents only teachers (School Boards Association representative, 20 May 2010). Given the duty of fair representation, the decision to include only teachers in the Act potentially limits conflicts related to the union trying to represent the needs of public school teachers versus other occupations (e.g., university professors, clerical staff).

A third strength is the dispute resolution mechanisms. As one party pointed out, not only must the parties accept or reject the conciliation report, they must also state the reasons why they reject the report. In so doing, the current system helps ensure that the "parties truly understood the key areas of disagreement"; it also results in a system where "cool heads prevail" given the requirement of having to wait prior to a strike/lockout (NLTA representative, 26 May 2010). Another advantage of the process is the internal NLTA procedure, which requires that conciliator reports be sent to the general membership for approval/rejection (NLTA representative, 26 May 2010). Thus, we see that these processes ensure that the parties enter into strike/lockout positions only when there is truly a significant disagreement between them and, when this occurs, the parties are aware of the grounds for the disagreement.

Fourth, less attached to the Act, there are sociocultural strengths of the system. These strengths play out in two ways. First, the province is the most heavily unionized in the country (Statistics Canada 2007).

Unionization is so prevalent that even offshore oil workers have collective agreements in an industry that is largely union-free. These strong
union roots may place less pressure on the parties to change or move to a
union-free status. Additionally, most of the key players in this IR system
have relevant teaching experience that helps them understand the issues
at hand. Building on this theme is the smallness of the community where
people know each other, and key players have moved from representing
one actor (e.g., NLTA) to another (e.g., government, the employer). In essence, there is a familiarity between the players that has resulted in solid
relationships. Interviewees all commented that while the parties may
have different goals, they have the ability to work out these differences
in a respectful manner. This perspective would seem representative of
integrative, or win-win, bargaining where the parties use problem-solving
approaches to develop collective agreement solutions that are beneficial
to all parties involved (Walton and McKersie 1991, 144-59). A key element of integrative bargaining is a strong desire to maintain a positive
relationship between the parties. This, too, seems to be strength of the
provincial system.

Fifth, again not directly related to the Act, is the fact that the parties have engaged in a form of continuous bargaining. As previously
discussed, the parties have used task forces and committees to examine
issues between rounds of bargaining. This can be an advantage as it keeps
the lines of communication open between the parties as well as helps get
some issues settled prior to formal negotiations.

Weaknesses and Challenges of the Current System

An examination of the Act, coupled with insights from the interviewees,
failed to identify a large number of critical weaknesses or challenges
with the current system. One of the few concerns raised related to
what can be seen as a downside of the very centralized system. While
centralization is an overall advantage, it does mean that issues that are
important to a certain group of teachers may "never see the light of
day" (NLTA representative, 26 May 2010). In essence, while the union
conducts an extensive consultation process across the membership,
any issue that is pertinent for only a small number of teachers is less
likely to be a key bargaining issue, unless the broader membership is
willing to support the importance of the issue for that smaller group
(School District representative, 27 May 2010). For example, one could
imagine a scenario where issues pertinent to a 100 or so teachers in
Western Labrador (e.g., northern allowances, cost of travel) would not
be sufficiently important to the remaining 5,000 members to become
key bargaining priorities. Thus, such issues may remain unresolved,
potentially increasing the dissatisfaction and frustration of the teachers

and administrators affected (NLTA representative, 26 May 2010; School District representative, 27 May 2010).

Another potential weakness of the system is the absolute power that the Act bestows on the Treasury Board. The author's own experience, coupled with comments from all interviewees, highlighted the movement to a form of pattern bargaining over the past two decades—a movement to a common wage settlement pattern for all public sector employees in the province. As discussed earlier, the current pattern is a four-year agreement. Given the great power provided by the Act to the chief negotiator of the School Board Committee, who is the Treasury Board representative, important non-monetary issues, or monetary issues outside of the "pattern," may never be addressed or even examined. For example, non-monetary issues pertinent to the administration of the collective agreement often do not make it to the table (NLTA representative, 26 May 2010; School District representative, 27 May 2010). While there is no immediate solution to this challenge, it is the opinion of the author that should the parties not start to enable a focused discussion of the various issues that affect the parties beyond the pattern, the current effectiveness of the system could be jeopardized as dissatisfaction levels will probably increase. A potential method to start such focused discussions would be to build upon the continuous bargaining mechanisms that have been used by the parties in the past.

A potential third limitation, while not yet materialized, relates to the movement toward legislated settlements in the province. As noted earlier, there has been an increased usage of legislated settlements throughout the Canadian public sector, and these can be seen as a movement away from true collective bargaining. Should this occur in the public education system in the province, especially when combined with a strong governmental push for a pattern settlement, it is the opinion of the author that the system will become less effective and more turbulent. Take, for example, the Newfoundland and Labrador Nurses Union, a similar provincial occupation-based association. The nurses have been legislated back to work with the settlement included in such legislation (*Health and Community Services Resumption and Continuation Act* 1999). The backlash from this legislation included widespread adoption of vehicle license plates stating "Mr. Tobin, Nurses Will Remember,"[6] and nurses referring to their agreement as the "non-collective agreement." Even their most recent settlement came within mere hours of a strike, after a heavy round of bargaining, extensive media campaigns, and third-party interventions (CBC News 2009). The increased use of strikes, near strikes, and legislation suggests that the relationship between that association and the government is becoming more strained. This is not a road that would seem desirable for either party in the K–12 educational labour relations system at present.

CONCLUSION

As shown in this chapter, collective representation in the public school system of Newfoundland and Labrador dates back to the 1890s. This long tradition of centralized labour relations, reinforced by legislation that preserves this centralized system, appears to serve the parties well. This conclusion is based on the fact that from a legislative perspective the Act has largely remained unchanged since 1973, the finding that the employer and union representatives express satisfaction with the current Act and system, as well as the evidence that this sector has had limited strikes and no back-to work legislation. These factors all suggest that the system functions well. In conclusion, it appears that while some fine-tuning may be needed, there is no need for significant changes in the Act or the system moving forward.

NOTES

The author thanks research assistants Andreia Santos and Vipul Khattar for their assistance on this paper as well as the anonymous reviewers and editorial team for their helpful suggestions and feedback. A special thank you to the anonymous interviewees who agreed to participate in this study.

1. Note that at its formation the association was named the Newfoundland Teachers' Association (NTA). The organization is now known as the Newfoundland and Labrador Teachers' Association, or NLTA. For reader clarity, it is called the Newfoundland and Labrador Teachers' Association, or NLTA, throughout the chapter. For a comprehensive history of the NLTA, please refer to Cuff (1985).
2. For an excellent review of the legislative history related to Term 17 and the public referendum please see *Hogan v. Newfoundland* (Attorney General), 2000 NFCA 12 (Newfoundland 2000).
3. This information is based on the author's experience in the province given that his family heralds from rural areas of the province.
4. Unless otherwise noted, all legislative references in this section refer to the *Teachers' Collective Bargaining Act* of Newfoundland and Labrador.
5. The Nova Scotia Teachers Union represents public school teachers, community college faculty, and support staff (Nova Scotia Teachers Union 2010a).
6. "Mr. Tobin" referred to then premier Brian Tobin whose government tabled the back-to-work legislation.

REFERENCES

An Act for the Encouragement of Education in This Country, 1836. St. John's, Newfoundland.

Beltrame, J. 1989. "Premier Brian Peckford Appears Ready to Retire." *CanWest News*, 19 January, p. 1.

Bennett, B. 1997. "Union Urges Teachers to Vote Yes." *Evening Telegram*, 26 August, p. 4.

British North America Act, 1949, 12-13 Geo. VI, c. 22 (U.K.).

Brym, R.J. and B. Neis. 1978. "Regional Factors in the Formation of the Fishermen's Protective Union of Newfoundland." *The Canadian Journal of Sociology / Cahiers canadiens de sociologie* 3(4): 391-407.

Callahan, B. 1991. "Teachers and Government Reach Tentative Agreement." *Evening Telegram*, 25 March, p. 2.

CBC News. 2004. "Nfld. to Order Strikers Back to Work," 23 April. Accessed 27 May 2010. http://www.cbc.ca/canada/story/2004/04/22/newfoundland-strike2_040422.html.

—. 2009. "Full Text of Debbie Forward Memo to NLNU Members," 28 January. Accessed 26 May 2010. http://www.cbc.ca/canada/newfoundland-labrador/story/2009/01/28/nlnu-memo.html#ixzz0p5M8cHxM.

Cleary, R. 1991. "Split with Pentecostal Members Could Kill NTA, Says President." *Evening Telegram*, 4 April, p. 3.

Collins, J.F. 1983. Statement by Hon. John F. Collins on 3 May. Government of Newfoundland and Labrador Executive Council, St. John's.

"Construction Starts on Churchill Falls Development." 1967. *Montreal Gazette*, 19 July, p. 27.

Craig, A.W.J. 1988. "Mainstream Industrial Relations." In *The State of the Art in Industrial Relations*, edited by G. Hebert, H.C. Jain, and N.M. Meltz. Toronto and Kingston, ON: Canadian Industrial Relations Association.

Cuff, H.A. 1985. *A History of the Newfoundland Teachers' Association 1890–1930*. St. John's, NL: Creative Publishers.

Downey, J. 1988. "A Scun from the Barrel: A Presidential Sitting on University Continuing Education." *Canadian Journal of University Continuing Education* 14(1): 13-23.

Dunlop, J.T. 1958. *Industrial Relations System*. New York, NY: Henry Holt and Company.

—. 1993. *Industrial Relations System*. Rev. ed. Boston, MA: Harvard Business School Press. First published 1958 by Henry Holt and Company.

Eric G. Lambert School. 2010. "Eric G. Lambert School Staff 2009–2010." Accessed 27 May 2010. http://www.k12.nf.ca/eglambert/EGLS%20Staff/staff.html.

Fitzgerald, J.E. 1999. "Archbishop E.P. Roche, J.R. Smallwood, and Denominational Rights in Newfoundland Education, 1948." *CCHA, Historical Studies* 65: 28-49.

Government of Newfoundland and Labrador. 1971. *Historical Statistics of Newfoundland and Labrador*. Prepared by the Economics and Statistics Division, Department of Finance. St. John's: Creative Printers and Publishers.

—. 1994. "Oral Questions: May 16, 1994." Government of Newfoundland and Labrador, St. John's.

—. 1997. Premier Tobin's address on referendum night, 2 September. Government of Newfoundland and Labrador, St. John's.

—. 1999. "Minister Disappointed in Comments from NLTA President." News release, 6 January. Ministry of Education, St. John's.

—. 2000a. "Acting Minister Salutes Province's Teachers." News release, 4 October. Ministry of Education, St. John's.

—. 2000b. "Statement by the Premier." News release, 16 October. Executive Council, St. John's.

—. 2006. *Demographic Change: Issues and Implications*. Prepared by the Economic Research and Analysis Division, Department of Finance. St. John's: Government of Newfoundland and Labrador.

—. 2010a. "Annual Estimates of Population for Canada, Provinces and Territories, from July 1, 1971 to July 1, 2009." Prepared by the Economics and Statistics Branch (Newfoundland and Labrador Statistics Agency), St. John's.

—. 2010b. *Budget 2010: The Right Investments for Our Children and Our Future.* Prepared by the Economic Research and Analysis Division, Department of Finance. St. John's, NL: Queen's Printer.

—. 2010c. "Experienced Labour Force by Detailed Industry: Newfoundland and Labrador, 2001." *2006 Census.* Prepared by the Economic Research and Analysis Division, Department of Finance, St. John's.

—. 2010d. "Experienced Labour Force by Industry, Newfoundland and Labrador, 1951–1996 Census." Prepared by the Economic Research and Analysis Division, Department of Finance, St. John's.

—. 2010e. "Land Area." Accessed 20 May 2010. http://www.gov.nl.ca/aboutnl/area.htm.

—. 2010f. "Minister Hon. Darin King." Accessed 4 October 2010. http://www.ed.gov.nl.ca/edu/department/minister.html.

—. 2011. "Population Projections Newfoundland and Labrador: Medium Scenario, Population by Five Year Age Groups 1986 to 2025." Table prepared by the Economics and Statistics Branch, Department of Finance. http://www.economics.gov.nl.ca/pdf/Popbyagemedium-web.pdf.

"Grimes New NTA President." 1985. *The Evening Telegram,* 11 April, p. 3.

Handcock, W.G. 1977. "English Migration to Newfoundland." In *The Peopling of Newfoundland: Essays in Historical Geography,* edited by J. Mannion, 15-48. St. John's: Institute of Social and Economic Research, Memorial University of Newfoundland.

Health and Community Services Resumption and Continuation Act, S.N.L. 1999, c. H-37.2.

Hebdon, R. and T.C. Brown. 2008. *Industrial Relations in Canada,* edited by M. Belcourt. Nelson Series in Human Resources Management. Toronto, ON: Nelson.

Hebdon, R.P. and R.P. Stern. 1998. "Tradeoffs among Expressions of Industrial Conflict: Public Sector Strike Bans and Grievance Arbitrations." *Industrial and Labor Relations Review* 51(2): 204-21.

Hogan v. Newfoundland (Attorney General), 2000 NFCA 12 (Newfoundland 2000).

Jackson, C. 1994. "Teachers' Stand Angers Premier." *Evening Telegram,* 27 April, p. 1.

Kaufman, B.E. 2003. "John R. Commons and the Wisconsin School on Industrial Relations Strategy and Policy." *Industrial and Labor Relations Review* 57: 3-30.

Keough, W. 2005. "Ethnicity as Intercultural Dialogue: Eighteenth- and Nineteenth-Century Newfoundland." *The Canadian Journal of Irish Studies* 31(1): 18-28.

McCann, P. 1989. "Class, Gender and Religion in Newfoundland Education, 1836–1901." *Historical Studies Education/Revue d'histoire de l'éducation* 1.

Meaney, R. 1949. "Newfoundland Teachers Resent Cutting Suggested Wage Allotment: N.T.A. Executive Given Power to Call Strike If Necessary." *Evening Telegram,* 9 July, p. 19.

Meltz, N.M. 1993. "Industrial Relations System as a Framework for Organizing Contributions to Industrial Relations." In *Industrial Relations Theory: Its Nature, Scope, and Pedagogy,* edited by R.J. Adams and N.M. Meltz, 161-82. Metuchen, NJ: Scarecrow Press.

Nalcor Energy. 2010. "Churchill Falls." Accessed 19 May 2010. http://www.nalcorenergy.com/churchfalls.asp.

Newfoundland and Labrador School Boards Association. 2010a. "About NLSBA." Accessed 10 May 2010. http://www.schoolboardsnl.ca/aboutnlsba.jsp.

—. 2010b. "Contact Information." Accessed 19 May 2010. https://www.schoolboardsnl.ca/contacts.jsp.

—. 2010c. "Our Districts." Accessed 19 May 2010. http://www.schoolboardsnl.ca/ourdistricts.jsp.

Newfoundland and Labrador Schools Trustees Association, and Newfoundland Teachers' Association. 1988. "Government Statements on Educational Funding Misrepresent Position of School Trustees and NTA." News release, St. John's.

Newfoundland and Labrador Teachers' Association. 1997. "Education Reform in Newfoundland and Labrador." A brief submitted to the Special Joint Committee to Amend Term 17. St. John's.

—. 2000. "Workload Committee." 6-7 April, 2.

—. 2003. "Association Priorities for 2002–03." *Executive Notes*, 20-22 February, p. 1.

—. 2011. "Honorary Members and Award Winners." https://www.nlta.nl.ca/hon_mbrs_awrd_winners.

Newfoundland Teachers' Association. 1964. "The Memorial Branch of the Newfoundland Teachers' Association Is Pleased to Greet Teachers and Student Teachers for the 1964–1965 Academic Year." St. John's.

—. 1973. "NTA Has Own Collective Agreement Legislation." *NTA Bulletin*, p. 1.

"Nfld. Unions Hit Back at Wells." 1993. *Daily News*, 7 April, p. 13.

"No Special NTA Council for Catholic Teachers." 1992. *Evening Telegram*, 28 March, p. 6.

Nova Scotia Teachers Union. 2010a. Home page. Accessed 9 September 2010. http://www.nstu.ca/.

—. 2010b. "NSTU Appoints Executive Director." Accessed 19 May 2010. http://www.nstu.ca/teacher/2001/nov/execdir.html.

"Pentecostal Teachers May Split with Union over Strike Action." 1984. *Evening Telegram*, 3 March, p. 1.

Pitt, R.D. 1990. *A Legacy of Leadership*. St. John's: Newfoundland Teachers' Association.

"Premier Considering Meeting with NTA." 1984. *Evening Telegram*, 14 March, p. 3.

Public Sector Compensation Restraint to Protect Public Services Act, 2010, S.O. 2010, c. 1, Sch. 24.

Public Services Resumption and Continuation Act, S.N.L. 2004, c. P-44.1.

"Roger Grimes Made Honorary Member of the NLTA." 2009. *The Telegram*, 16 April, p. 5.

Rose, J. 2008. "Regulating and Resolving Public Sector Disputes in Canada." *Journal of Industrial Relations* 50(4): 545-59.

Rothney, G.O. 1962. "The Denominational Basis of Representation in the Newfoundland Assembly, 1919–1962." *Canadian Journal of Economics and Political Science / Revue Canadienne d'Economique et de Science Politique* 28(4): 557-70.

Rumbolt, C. 1994. "Teachers, Government Reach Tentative Deal." *The Express*, 1 June, p. A3.

Statistics Canada. 2007. "Unionization." *Perspectives on Labour and Income* 8(8): 8.

Sullivan, D.S. 1997. "NLTA Urges Parents to Have Budget Say." *Evening Telegram*, 7 April, p. 3.

—. 1999. "NLTA Meeting: Special Needs Services High on Teachers' List of Priorities." *Evening Telegram*, 7 April, p. 3.

Swain, E. 1992. "NTA President Cautioning Membership against Joining Catholic Teachers' Group." *Evening Telegram*, 30 January, p. 3.

Taggart, J. 1983. "NTA Got Victory, Stopped Contract Stripping: Noseworthy." *Evening Telegram*, 5 May, p. 1.

Taras, D.G., A. Ponak, and M. Gunderson. 2001. "Introduction to Canadian Industrial Relations." *In Union-Management Relations in Canada*, edited by M. Gunderson, A. Ponak, and D.G. Taras. Toronto: Addison Wesley Longman.

Teachers' Collective Bargaining Act, R.S.N.L. 1990, c. T-3.

"Teachers Plan Massive Action to Reverse Education Policies." 1980. *Evening Telegram*, 11 April, p. 1.

"Teachers' Union Also with Yes Forces ... But NLTA Has Concerns about Term 17." 1997. *Evening Telegram*, 6 August, p. 4.

Thomas, W. 2010. "President's Message: The Wage Freeze: A Labour Day Response," 7 September. http://www.opseu.org/presidentsmessage/sep-02-2010.htm.

Walton, R.E. and R.B. McKersie. 1991. *A Behavioral Theory of Labor Negotiation: An Analysis of a Social Interaction System*. 2nd ed. Ithaca, NY: ILR Press.

Woolridge, B. 1980. "High Priority on Education: Government Commitment Questioned by NTA Head." *Evening Telegram*, 9 April, p. 4.

Interviews

Eastern School District representative, 27 May 2010, St. John's.

Newfoundland and Labrador School Boards Association (NLSBA) representative, 20 May 2010, St. John's.

Newfoundland and Labrador Teachers' Association (NLTA) representative, 26 May 2010, St. John's.

ABOUT THE AUTHORS

MUSTAPHA BETTACHE is an associate professor in the Industrial Relations Department at Laval University, and director of the Master's Studies program. He holds a PhD in Industrial Relations from the University of Montreal and is a researcher in the Alliance of Research Universities-Communities (ARUC) and in the Research Centre on Social Innovations (CRISES), and a visiting professor at ESCP-EAP Paris.

TRAVOR C. BROWN is a professor of Industrial Relations and Human Resources in the Faculty of Business Administration at Memorial University and is director of the Master of Employment Relations program. Dr. Brown's research interests include a broad range of human resources and industrial relations topics. He is co-author with Robert Hebdon of a leading industrial relations textbook, *Industrial Relations in Canada*, 2nd edition, 2012.

THOMAS FLEMING is a professor emeritus at the University of Victoria. He is known for his work on school and administrative history, including *A History of Thought and Practice in Educational Administration; School Leadership: Essays on the British Columbia School Experience, 1872–1995; The Principal's Office and Beyond: Public School Leadership in British Columbia, 1849-2005, Volumes 1 and 2;* and *Schooling in British Columbia: Voices from the Educational Past, 1849–2005.*

JEAN-NOËL GRENIER is an associate professor in the Department of Industrial Relations, Laval University. Dr. Grenier has focused on work organization and is currently involved in research on the restructuring of the state, the implications for labour relations, and worker representation in comparative perspective. He has written and published on the Quebec experience. Dr. Grenier teaches public sector labour relations and collective bargaining courses.

ROBERT HICKEY is an assistant professor of industrial relations in the School of Policy Studies at Queen's University. Dr. Hickey's research focuses on the impact of industrial restructuring and public policy reforms on labour relations and human resource practices. He teaches courses on unions, negotiations, and dispute resolution in the Master of Industrial Relations program at Queen's University.

VALERIE J. MATTHEWS LEMIEUX holds a law degree from the University of Manitoba and a Master's in Law from Osgoode Hall Law School. She was involved in modernizing Manitoba's labour relations and employment standards legislation, has served as counsel to the Departments of Labour and Workplace Safety and Health in Manitoba, and is currently in private legal practice, acting on behalf of unions and First Nations. She has appeared in all levels of courts and tribunals on a variety of constitutional, labour, and human rights matters and has published several articles on labour law.

SUSAN MCWILLIAMS is the human resources manager at the Limestone District School Board in Kingston, Ontario. In addition to extensive experience in public sector labour relations, she holds a Certified Human Resources Professional designation and a Master's of Industrial Relations degree from Queen's University.

JOSEPH B. ROSE is a professor in the DeGroote School of Business at McMaster University. Dr. Rose specializes in collective bargaining and dispute resolution. His research interests include construction labour relations, trade unions, public sector collective bargaining, and dispute settlement procedures. He has published widely addressing public sector restructuring and collective bargaining, and has written a key article on Ontario teacher labour relations, "The Assault on School Teacher Bargaining in Ontario," published in the journal *Relations Industrielles*.

KAREN SCHUCHER is a doctoral candidate at Osgoode Hall Law School, York University, and a faculty member in the paralegal and law clerk programs at the Humber Institute of Technology and Advanced Learning. Before returning to academics, Karen practiced labour, human rights, and administrative law for many years as a partner with Cavalluzzo Hayes Shilton McIntyre & Cornish law firm. She is also an original co-author of *Education Labour and Employment Law in Ontario* (2nd edition, Canada Law Book).

ELIZABETH SHILTON is a senior fellow with the Centre for Law in the Contemporary Workplace, Faculty of Law, Queen's University, where she is currently pursuing research on employment pension and labour law issues. For many years, she practiced labour and employment law with the firm of Cavalluzzo Hayes Shilton McIntyre & Cornish, where she represented teachers' unions and co-authored two editions of *Education*

Labour and Employment Law in Ontario (Canada Law Book). She also holds an SJD in law from the University of Toronto.

Sara Slinn is an associate professor at Osgoode Hall Law School, York University. Her research focuses on public and private sector labour relations, and on labour, employment, and constitutional law.

Brendan Sweeney is a post-doctoral fellow in the Industrial Relations Centre/School of Policy Studies at Queen's University. His research focuses on employment relations and collective bargaining in Ontario's education sector and British Columbia's forest industry.

Arthur Sweetman is a professor in the Department of Economics at McMaster University where he holds the Ontario Research Chair in Health Human Resources. Most of his research focuses on empirical issues regarding labour markets, social policy, and health economics.

Kelly Williams-Whitt is an associate professor in the Faculty of Management, University of Lethbridge, Calgary campus. She also acts as a labour arbitrator and holds an appointment with Human Resources and Skills Development Canada, adjudicating disputes under Part III of the Canada Labour Code. She teaches labour relations, employment law, and collective bargaining. Dr. Williams-Whitt conducts the majority of her research in the area of disability accommodation. She is co-author of *Employment Law for Business and Human Resource Managers in British Columbia and Alberta* (Emond Montgomery).

Queen's Policy Studies
Recent Publications

The Queen's Policy Studies Series is dedicated to the exploration of major public policy issues that confront governments and society in Canada and other nations.

Manuscript submission. We are pleased to consider new book proposals and manuscripts. Preliminary enquiries are welcome. A subvention is normally required for the publication of an academic book. Please direct questions or proposals to the Publications Unit by email at spspress@queensu.ca, or visit our website at: www.queensu.ca/sps/books, or contact us by phone at (613) 533-2192.

Our books are available from good bookstores everywhere, including the Queen's University bookstore (http://www.campusbookstore.com/). McGill-Queen's University Press is the exclusive world representative and distributor of books in the series. A full catalogue and ordering information may be found on their web site (http://mqup.mcgill.ca/).

School of Policy Studies

Where to from Here? Keeping Medicare Sustainable, Stephen Duckett 2012. ISBN 978-1-55339-318-4

International Migration in Uncertain Times, John Nieuwenhuysen, Howard Duncan, and Stine Neerup (eds.) 2012. ISBN 978-1-55339-308-5

Life After Forty: Official Languages Policy in Canada/Après quarante ans, les politiques de langue officielle au Canada, Jack Jedwab and Rodrigue Landry (eds.) 2011. ISBN 978-1-55339-279-8

From Innovation to Transformation: Moving up the Curve in Ontario Healthcare, Hon. Elinor Caplan, Dr. Tom Bigda-Peyton, Maia MacNiven, and Sandy Sheahan 2011. ISBN 978-1-55339-315-3

Academic Reform: Policy Options for Improving the Quality and Cost-Effectiveness of Undergraduate Education in Ontario, Ian D. Clark, David Trick, and Richard Van Loon 2011. ISBN 978-1-55339-310-8

Integration and Inclusion of Newcomers and Minorities across Canada, John Biles, Meyer Burstein, James Frideres, Erin Tolley, and Robert Vineberg (eds.) 2011. ISBN 978-1-55339-290-3

A New Synthesis of Public Administration: Serving in the 21st Century, Jocelyne Bourgon, 2011. Paper ISBN 978-1-55339-312-2 Cloth ISBN 978-1-55339-313-9

Recreating Canada: Essays in Honour of Paul Weiler, Randall Morck (ed.), 2011. ISBN 978-1-55339-273-6

Data Data Everywhere: Access and Accountability? Colleen M. Flood (ed.), 2011. ISBN 978-1-55339-236-1

Making the Case: Using Case Studies for Teaching and Knowledge Management in Public Administration, Andrew Graham, 2011. ISBN 978-1-55339-302-3

Canada's Isotope Crisis: What Next? Jatin Nathwani and Donald Wallace (eds.), 2010. Paper ISBN 978-1-55339-283-5 Cloth ISBN 978-1-55339-284-2

Pursuing Higher Education in Canada: Economic, Social, and Policy Dimensions, Ross Finnie, Marc Frenette, Richard E. Mueller, and Arthur Sweetman (eds.), 2010. Paper ISBN 978-1-55339-277-4 Cloth ISBN 978-1-55339-278-1

Canadian Immigration: Economic Evidence for a Dynamic Policy Environment,
Ted McDonald, Elizabeth Ruddick, Arthur Sweetman, and Christopher Worswick
(eds.), 2010. Paper ISBN 978-1-55339-281-1 Cloth ISBN 978-1-55339-282-8

Taking Stock: Research on Teaching and Learning in Higher Education, Julia Christensen
Hughes and Joy Mighty (eds.), 2010. Paper ISBN 978-1-55339-271-2
Cloth ISBN 978-1-55339-272-9

Centre for the Study of Democracy

Jimmy and Rosalynn Carter: A Canadian Tribute, Arthur Milnes (ed.), 2011.
Paper ISBN 978-1-55339-300-9 Cloth ISBN 978-1-55339-301-6

*Unrevised and Unrepented II: Debating Speeches and Others By the Right Honourable Arthur
Meighen,* Arthur Milnes (ed.), 2011. Paper ISBN 978-1-55339-296-5
Cloth ISBN 978-1-55339-297-2

Centre for International and Defence Policy

*Security Operations in the 21st Century: Canadian Perspectives on the Comprehensive
Approach,* Michael Rostek and Peter Gizewski (eds.), 2011. ISBN 978-1-55339-351-1

Europe Without Soldiers? Recruitment and Retention across the Armed Forces of Europe,
Tibor Szvircsev Tresch and Christian Leuprecht (eds.), 2010.
Paper ISBN 978-1-55339-246-0 Cloth ISBN 978-1-55339-247-7

Mission Critical: Smaller Democracies' Role in Global Stability Operations,
Christian Leuprecht, Jodok Troy, and David Last (eds.), 2010. ISBN 978-1-55339-244-6

John Deutsch Institute for the Study of Economic Policy

The 2009 Federal Budget: Challenge, Response and Retrospect, Charles M. Beach,
Bev Dahlby and Paul A.R. Hobson (eds.), 2010. Paper ISBN 978-1-55339-165-4
Cloth ISBN 978-1-55339-166-1

Discount Rates for the Evaluation of Public Private Partnerships, David F. Burgess and
Glenn P. Jenkins (eds.), 2010. Paper ISBN 978-1-55339-163-0 Cloth ISBN 978-1-55339-164-7

Institute of Intergovernmental Relations

The Evolving Canadian Crown, Jennifer Smith and D. Michael Jackson (eds.), 2011.
ISBN 978-1-55339-202-6

The Federal Idea: Essays in Honour of Ronald L. Watts, Thomas J. Courchene, John R. Allan,
Christian Leuprecht, and Nadia Verrelli (eds.), 2011. Paper ISBN 978-1-55339-198-2
Cloth ISBN 978-1-55339-199-9

Canada: The State of the Federation 2009, vol. 22, *Carbon Pricing and Environmental
Federalism,* Thomas J. Courchene and John R. Allan (eds.), 2010.
Paper ISBN 978-1-55339-196-8 Cloth ISBN 978-1-55339-197-5
